The international politics of East Central Europe

The countries of East Central Europe – Hungary, Poland and what was then Czechoslovakia – played a pivotal role in the central political drama of the late twentieth century, the 1989 revolutions. This textbook analyses the changing nature of international politics in the region since 1989, and the influence upon it of history, national identity and geopolitics.

Developments in East Central Europe today are acting as a catalyst for the reshaping of international politics throughout Europe. This book considers the changing bilateral relationships in the region; the prospects for multilateral conflict and cooperation; relations with the new states to the East; relations with the West; and regional security issues. The author argues that the 'return to Europe' of Poland, Hungary, the Czech Republic and Slovakia not only has profound implications for domestic politics and national identity in the region; it will also significantly alter the dynamics of the European integration process, and consequently the shape of the international system into the next century. The book concludes by assessing the impact of political democratisation, institutional integration and globalisation on international politics in contemporary East Central Europe.

The international politics of East Central Europe will be a valuable book for students of international relations, European politics and international history.

The international politics of East Central Europe

Adrian Hyde-Price

Manchester University Press

Manchester and New York

Distributed exclusively in the USA and Canada by St Martin's Press

Copyright © Adrian Hyde-Price 1996

Published by Manchester University Press
Oxford Road, Manchester M13 9NR, UK
and Room 400, 175 Fifth Avenue, New York, NY 10010, USA

Distributed exclusively in the USA and Canada
by St Martin's Press, Inc., 175 Fifth Avenue, New York,
NY 10010, USA

British Library Cataloguing-in-Publication Data
A catalogue record for this book is available from the British Library

Library of Congress Cataloging-in-Publication Data applied for

ISBN   0 7190 4096 5   *hardback*
          0 7190 4097 3   *paperback*

First published 1996

00 99 98 97 96   10 9 8 7 6 5 4 3 2 1

Printed in Great Britain by Bell & Bain Ltd, Glasgow

*This book is dedicated
with love
to my two sisters,
Caroline and Julia*

Contents

Preface

This book is not primarily a book by a regional specialist. Rather, it is written by a student of European international relations who has long been interested in the politics and international relations of East Central Europe.

My fascination with the region stems from my doctoral research. My thesis, which was primarily a study in political ideas and concepts, was entitled *Lenin's Theory of the State and Democracy: From Parliamentarism to Soviet Power* (University of Kent at Canterbury, 1983). This research kindled an interest in Soviet history and comparative communist politics. In 1984, and again in 1986, I spent two months in the German Democratic Republic undertaking post-doctoral research with the generous support of the British Council. In 1987 I became a Research Fellow at the Royal Institute of International Affairs (Chatham House) in London, where I worked on the International Security Programme studying the East–West conflict in Europe.

This gave me the opportunity to meet a wide variety of colleagues from Central and Eastern Europe, and made it possible for me to travel to the region on conferences and research trips. During this time, I made many good friends in Hungary, Czechoslovakia, Poland, Romania, Bulgaria and the Soviet Union. It was thus during my sojourn at Chatham House that my interest in the peoples, cultures and history of Central and Eastern Europe really blossomed.

Whilst I was still at Chatham House, the East–West conflict came to an end. I not only had to begin rewriting my book on the European security system, but I also lost my academic specialism – the GDR. Nonetheless, those heady times opened up much better opportunities for travel, study and research in Central and Eastern Europe.

Having taken up a lectureship at the University of Southampton in 1990, and having completed my book on *European Security Beyond the Cold War: Four Scenarios for the Year 2010* (London, Sage, 1991), I increasingly began to feel that the most dynamic and changing part of post-Cold War Europe was East Central Europe. Indeed, this region, it seemed to me, constituted the fulcrum around which European international relations were being recast. Given my long interest in East Central Europe, I therefore decided to begin work on a book analysing how, and with what implications, international relations in the Visegrad countries have been evolving since 1989. My research for this book has confirmed in my mind two things above all: first, that the changes in international politics in East Central Europe are without doubt amongst the most fascinating and absorbing in the global system; and second, that the economic, political and institutional developments currently under way in the region will have far-reaching consequences for the future of European international relations in the twenty-first century.

Adrian Hyde-Price
Southampton
31 March 1995

Acknowledgements

Many people have contributed to this book in a variety of ways. First and foremost amongst them is Lisbeth Aggestam, of the University of Stockholm. She has read nearly all of the manuscript, and has been an unstinting source of encouragement, criticism and support. My parents and my two sisters have also encouraged me with their love and support. Julia was a particular help: having spent a year working in Budapest, she was able to furnish me with her insights into the region, and to help me with contacts.

My colleagues in the Department of Politics at the University of Southampton have been another invaluable source of help and advice. Since joining the Department in 1990, I have benefited from its challenging intellectual atmosphere. The existence of the University's interdisciplinary Mountbatten Centre for International Studies (MCIS) has also been a great boon for my own research. The quality of the intellectual life of the Department has been even further enhanced by the recent appointment of two new professors, Chris Brown and Joni Lowenduski, who join our existing professoriate, Peter Calvert and John Simpson. A number of my colleagues have read and commented on parts of this book. I would like to thank in particular Tony Evans, Darryl Howlett, Frank Gregory, Peter Calvert, and Chris Brown. Our vibrant postgraduate community has also been a great source of inspiration, not least by comments on my MCIS presentation in December 1994. As importantly, the clerical and administrative staff have provided me with considerable practical help, along with much appreciated cups of coffee and chocolate biscuits (and even the occasional glass of wine!).

A number of friends and colleagues have been kind enough to give me detailed comments on earlier versions of individual chapters. They include Vladimír Handl (Institute for International Relations,

Prague); Pál Dunay (Eötvös Loránd University, Budapest); William Wallace (St Anthony's College, Oxford); Alice Landau (University of Geneva); Bill Parks (Royal Naval College, Greenwich); and Virgil George Baleanu (University of Southampton and Conflict Studies Research Centre, RMA Sandhurst). Their comments helped me clarify my own thoughts and correct a number of factual errors. I am of course responsible for any remaining mistakes and misunderstandings.

I would also like to thank my friends and colleagues in Central Europe, many of whom have been extraordinarily generous with their time and advice over the years. They include Gabor Horvath, József Baráth, Pavel Wodecki, Pavil Zívalík, Lubomír Molnár, Peter Mooz, Jirí Kalašhnikov, Jirí Stepanovsky, Przemyslaw Grudzinski, Libor Roucek, Fritz Tech, Heinz Gärtner, and Hans-Joachim Giessmann.

Finally, I would like to thank Richard Purslow for his unwavering encouragement and support over the past three years, and all at Manchester University Press who have helped transform my primordial text into book form.

Abbreviations

AHG	Ad Hoc Group on Cooperation in Peacekeeping (NACC)
BRD	Federal Republic of Germany
CAP	Common Agricultural Policy
CEFTA	Central European Free Trade Area
CEI	Central European Initiative
CFE	Conventional Forces in Europe (Treaty)
CFSP	Common Foreign and Security Policy
CoCom	Coordinating Committee
CIS	Commonwealth of Independent States
CMEA/COMECON	Council of Mutual Economic Assistance
CPSU	Communist Party of the Soviet Union
CSCE	Conference on Security and Cooperation in Europe
CSFR	Czech and Slovak Federal Republic
EBRD	European Bank for Reconstruction and Development
EC	European Community
ECB	European Central Bank
ECE	Economic Commission for Europe (UN)
ECHR	European Court of Human Rights (Strasbourg)
ECU	European Currency Unit
EEC	European Economic Community
EIB	European Investment Bank
EPC	European Political Cooperation
ERDF	European Regional Development Fund
EU	European Union
FIDESZ	Alliance of Young Democrats (Hungary)
GATT	General Agreement on Tariffs and Trade
GDM	Group on Defence Matters (NACC)

GDR	German Democratic Republic
HCNM	High Commissioner for National Minorities (CSCE)
HLWG	High Level Working Group (NACC)
HZDS	Movement for a Democratic Slovakia
ICJ	International Court of Justice (Hague)
IEO	International Economic Organisation
IISS	International Institute for Strategic Studies (London)
IMF	International Monetary Fund
KDU-CSL	Christian Democratic Union–Czech Peoples' Party
KGB	Committee of State Security
KOR	Workers' Defence Committee (Poland)
MDF	Hungarian Democratic Forum
MSP	Hungarian Socialist Party
MSzMP	Hungarian Socialist Workers Party
NAC	North Atlantic Council
NACC	North Atlantic Cooperation Council
NATO	North Atlantic Treaty Organization
NKVD	People's Commissariat of the Interior (forerunner of the KGB)
OECD	Organization for Economic Cooperation and Development
OSCE	Organization for Security and Cooperation in Europe
PCC	Political Consultative Committee (Warsaw Pact)
PFP	Partnership for Peace (NATO)
PHARE	Poland/Hungary Aid for Restructuring Economies
PZPR	Polish United Workers' Party
RIIA	Royal Institute of International Affairs (Chatham House, London)
RSFSR	Russian Soviet Federated Socialist Republic
SACEUR	Supreme Allied Commander Europe (NATO)
SDL	Party of the Democratic Left (Slovakia)
SIPRI	Stockholm International Peace Research Institute
UN	United Nations
USSR	Union of Soviet Socialist Republics
WEU	Western European Union
WTO	Warsaw Treaty Organization

Maps

Map 1. East Central Europe

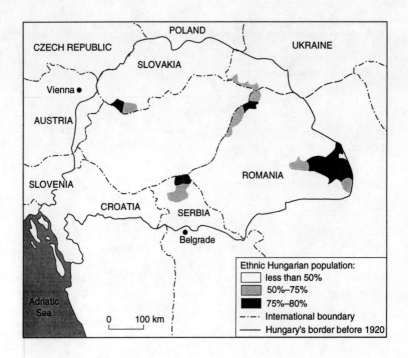

Map 2. Ethnic composition

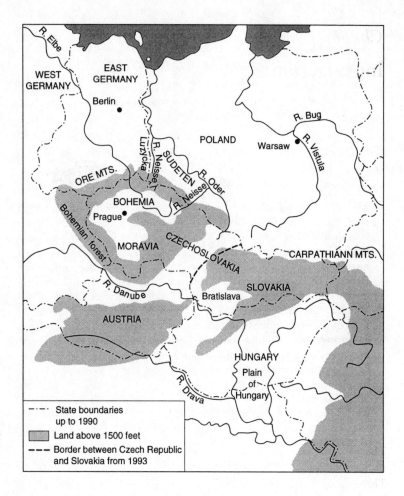

Map 3. Topological features of East Central Europe

Chapter One
Introduction

East Central Europe is a much neglected region. Except from specialists it attracts little general interest. Its history seems complicated and confused; it is seen as a medley of troublesome nationalities with unpronounceable names. East Central European history is neither exotic enough to arouse curiosity nor sufficiently familiar to facilitate understanding. And yet its importance is undeniable. Two world wars began in this region, as did the Cold War. The phrase of the British geographer H. MacKinder, 'Who rules Eastern Europe commands the heartland, who rules the heartland commands the world', sounded ominous in the days of Soviet ascendancy. The Polish Solidarity, which flashed suddenly over the horizon, was to many observers one of those events that shape world history. The collapse of communism in East Central Europe and its unprecedented transition to political and economic freedom carries with it hopes and dangers of great magnitude. (Piotr S. Wandycz[1])

This book seeks to describe, analyse and explain the evolving pattern of international politics in post-communist East Central Europe. Throughout the post-communist world – from the borders of Germany to the heartlands of Russia – a profound process of change is under way, as new economic and political systems are constructed from the ashes of communism. The collapse of the Soviet bloc has led to the emergence of distinctive regional groupings of post-communist states, formed by 'countries which share historical experience and comparable levels of development'.[2] One such regional grouping is East Central Europe. This region – consisting of Poland, Hungary, the Czech Republic and Slovakia – has long enjoyed a distinctive sense of its own identity. Although its regional identity was partly submerged during the Cold War, it never disappeared. With the collapse of the Soviet bloc, these countries have regained 'their former, pre-war status – nations with a distinctive identity and close relations with the west of Europe, but separate from neighbouring states like the Baltic republics, Finland, Belorussia, the Ukraine and the western portion of a still extensive Russia, which could reasonably be called Eastern Europe'.[3]

The choice of East Central Europe as the focus of this study has been guided by five considerations. First, the history of this region has been as exciting, tragic and eventful as any in the world, and this history continues to influence contemporary political attitudes and behaviour. Second, these four states are the most advanced along the road to market economies and stable liberal democracies. Consequently they constitute a distinct grouping amongst the post-communist regimes of Central and Eastern Europe. Third, these states already enjoy a privileged relationship with many Western countries and international organisations, and may well be members of the European Union and NATO by the end of the century. Fourth, they occupy a fascinating geopolitical position between Germany in the West and the Soviet successor states in the East. Because of their pivotal location, they are bound to play a key role in determining the geopolitical topology of post-Cold War Europe. Finally, all four states straddle the national, ethnic and religious fault lines which bedevil the politics of Central and Eastern Europe: consequently, all four are sensitive to the shock waves emanating from the break-up of the USSR, the civil war in former Yugoslavia, and the re-emergence of ethnic conflict in Europe.

East Central Europe has long played a crucial role in modern European history, and is destined to be the focus of some of the most far-reaching changes in global politics in the *fin de siècle* years of the twentieth century. Its importance is undeniable. East Central Europe, Charles Gati has noted, 'has been the enfant terrible of the international politics of this century. It has probably caused, contributed to, or been victimized by more wars and international conflict than any other region in the world, even the always volatile Middle East'.[4] World War Two erupted because of German territorial ambitions in the region. The Cold War developed as a result of conflicts over Eastern Europe (particularly communist policy in Poland and the Prague coup of 1948). More recently, it was events in Poland and Hungary which precipitated the collapse of communist autocracy in Eastern Europe and heralded the demise of the East–West conflict.[5] Today, it is developments in East Central Europe which are acting as a catalyst for the reshaping of international politics across the continent.

During the Cold War, East Central Europe's importance was primarily military and strategic: it provided the staging post for the Soviet Union's forward-deployed armoured divisions, and acted as a glacis for the 'socialist community'. With the end of the Cold War, the reasons for the region's continuing importance have changed. East Central Europe is no longer the front line for an authoritarian superpower harbouring hostile intentions towards the West. Instead, it finds itself acting as a 'grey zone' or 'buffer region' between the EU and the instability of Eastern Europe and the Balkans. However, this is not a role the East Central Europeans relish. They have therefore announced their determination to 'return to Europe', by which they mean full integration into the economic, political and security structures of the West.[6] This may well mean that by early next century, the 'Visegrad' countries (as they have become known – see pp. 122–131) will be members of the EU, the WEU and NATO. If – as is now expected – this does indeed occur, it will have far-reaching implications for the nature and functioning of these key Western organisations.

As the Visegrad countries engage in a process of radical domestic change (replacing centralised planning with market economies, and communist autocracies with pluralist liberal democracies), they are also implementing a profound reorientation of their international relations. This is apparent not only from the dramatic reorientation of their foreign trade from East to West, but also from their changing political allegiances, their new diplomatic alliances and their evolving security relationships. It is therefore evident that the most profound, far-reaching and dramatic changes in the global system today – both domestic and international – are taking place in East Central Europe.

East Central Europe's 'vale of tears'

As once-feared communist regimes crumbled in the face of peaceful mass demonstrations, a mood of euphoria engulfed the continent. People began looking forward optimistically to a Europe 'whole and free'. At the CSCE summit in November 1990, a *Charter of Paris for a New Europe* was unanimously adopted which outlined a vision of a Europe without artificial divisions, in which democratic government, market economies and respect for human rights would be complemented by the peaceful settlement of international disputes.[7] Sadly, this euphoria quickly evaporated as new and unexpected problems emerged. The costs of German unification exacerbated the problems of recession elsewhere in Western Europe; bloody fighting broke out in the Balkans and around the fringes of the former Soviet Union; ancient animosities were rekindled throughout much of Central and Eastern Europe; and the EU entered a phase of introspection and self-doubt.

In East Central Europe, the sense of disillusionment was even sharper. 'Shock therapy' plunged much of East Central Europe into severe economic depression; social inequalities widened; racism and aggressive nationalism resurfaced; Czechoslovakia's 'velvet revolution' was followed by a not so velvet divorce; relations between Hungary and Slovakia deteriorated; NATO prevaricated when asked to give either firm security guarantees or the promise of future membership of the alliance to its suitors from the East; and the EU proved shamefully reticent in opening up its markets to exports from Eastern Europe. Within the space of just a few short years, therefore, the initial mood of optimism in East Central Europe was replaced by a more sombre awareness that the end of communism still left the region facing its historic problems of nationalist rivalries, economic backwardness and political instability. Moreover, it was also depressingly clear that neither the EU, still less the USA, was going to act as a *deus ex machina* and solve the problems of East Central Europe.

Thus for the Visegrad countries, the end of the Cold War has meant not the end of history as Francis Fukuyama suggested, but rather the rebirth of history.[8] The icy grip of Moscow simply froze ancient animosities; it did not resolve them. Neither did communism fulfil its emancipatory promise of providing an alternative path to economic prosperity, social justice and legitimate government. The East Central Europeans are thus facing once again many of their traditional problems: completing the process of state building, escaping from their economic marginalisation, and integrating into the mainstream of European affairs.[9]

Yet this does not mean that we can understand the contemporary politics and international relations of East Central Europe simply by re-reading our history books. The past is not, and never has been, a reliable guide to the future. In East Central Europe today, elements of historical continuity are interacting with new factors in a complex, dialectical relationship. Regional politics are not simply reverting to past patterns of cooperation and conflict as some have implied.[10] Instead, traditional political and economic concerns are resurfacing in the context of a domestic and international environment which has been profoundly and irrevocably altered by the forces of twentieth century modernisation. The societies of East Central Europe today are very different from those of the 1930s, let alone those of the nineteenth century. They have been transformed by urbanisation, rising living standards, the irradication of illiteracy, the spread of democratic values, accelerating technological innovation and a more developed political culture. Similarly, international relations in the region have been transformed by globalisation, complex inter-dependence and multilateral institutions. Ethno-national conflicts, along with traditional issues of economic and political modern-isation, are therefore emerging in a markedly different environment from that of the inter-war years. Thus although the past may provide some clues to the changing patterns of domestic and international politics in the region, the processes of late twentieth century modernisation have created a unique historical conjucture in East Central Europe – significantly different from anything that has existed before.

Indeed, it is this which makes the study of international politics in East Central Europe so rewarding. The region provides an ideal case study to examine the changing nature of international relations on the eve of the twenty-first century. A 'most fundamental paradox of our era', K. J. Holsti has argued, is the 'intense trend toward political fragmentation within the context of globalizing economy'.[11] This trend is clearly evident in East Central Europe. A resurgence of nationalism and ethnic identity has occurred throughout the region – as Michael Walzer has observed, 'the tribes have returned'.[12] Yet at the same time, the region has been increasingly exposed to the chill winds of global economic competition and informal integration. This raises some of the most interesting issues in contemporary inter-national relations theory: namely, the extent to which globalisation and transnational interactions are eroding the sovereignty and autonomy of the state, the organisation which has traditionally been seen as the primary actor in the global system.[13] Some suggest that the international system is no longer a 'state-centric' system. Others, however, maintain that the state continues to be the 'supreme normative principle of the political organisation of mankind', and the 'fundamental or constitutive principle of world politics in the present era'.[14] An underlying concern of this book, therefore, will be to explore the extent to which changes in the wider global system have affected international politics in East Central Europe. In particular, we will consider the impact on the region of economic globalisation, political democratisation and multilateral institutions.

Defining 'East Central Europe'

Definitions in political science are never straightforward. Political analysis by its very nature involves categorisation and delineation. This is the only way to make sense of an infinite mass of empirical data. Yet deciding the criteria upon which one categorises one's empirical data often entails controversial judgements. This is certainly the case when one attempts to define discrete groupings of states and peoples.

In the case of Europe, definitions of where the continent's boundaries lie have long generated intense and heated debates. Prince Metternich once declared that immediately across the Rennweg, the street which runs right through Vienna, one is already in the Balkans, and in Asia.[15] Others, more generously, have located the boundaries of Europe at the Ural Mountains or on the Bosphorus. In the 1980s, at time of the 'Second Cold War', a highly emotional and politically charged debate raged over what constituted 'Europe'.[16] There was also a very lively exchange amongst Central European intellectuals on the meaning and implications of *Mitteleuropa*. These disputes were not simply about geography. They were much more about *identity*, an issue which almost always arouses primordial passions.[17] It is therefore necessary to begin this study of international politics of East Central Europe by addressing the problems of defining this region.

The term 'East Central Europe' is neither geographically precise nor politically self-evident. Throughout most of the post-war period, the region was lumped together with the other Warsaw Pact states under the rubric of 'Eastern Europe' – a political definition which did not correspond to geographical realities. Before the war it was frequently described simply as 'Central Europe'. Since the end of the Cold War, some writers have used the term 'East Central Europe' to cover all the countries between Germany and Russia, and all the lands situated between the Baltic, Black Sea, Adriatic and Aegean.[18] This definition, however, is so broad that it obscures the complex processes of change and differentiation at work in the former Soviet bloc. It is for this reason that East Central Europe is more usually defined as the four countries of Poland, Hungary, the Czech Republic and Slovakia. This term denotes a common regional identity which distinguishes them from their many neighbours: from West Central European states such as Germany and Austria; from the Soviet successor states to their east such as Russia, Ukraine, Belarus and the Baltic republics; and from the states of south-east Europe and the Balkans, such as Romania, Bulgaria, Slovenia, Serbia, Croatia, Albania and Greece. The new democracies of East Central Europe undoubtedly share many characteristics and problems with other post-communist states. Nonetheless, they form a distinct group by virtue of their unique culture and history; their relatively advanced economic and political reforms; their particularly close relations with the West; and the degree of regional cooperation they have forged within the Visegrad framework.

Although East Central Europe can be defined politically in terms of the four Visegrad states, this should not obscure the fact that geographically, culturally and historically, the borders of this region are less easy to delineate. The essential problem here is that the political borders of East Central European states have changed extensively over the centuries, making a precise geographical definition of the region impossible. At times their borders have extended into what are today Lithuania, Belarus, Ukraine, former Yugoslavia and Romania. This is reflected in the different names given to the same place. For example, Pozsony (Hungarian), Pressburg (German) and Bratislava (Slovak) are all one and the same. Vilnius, the Lithuanian capital, is called Wilno by the Poles and Vilna by the Russians. Timisoara in present-day Romania has also been known as Temesvár in Hungarian and Temeschburg in German. Most striking is the example of an individual born in Ungvár in 1900, then part of the Habsburg Empire. In 1918 he or she would have been a citizen of Czechoslovakia, living in a place renamed Uzhorod. In 1939 this town briefly became part of a Carpatho-Ukrainian state before joining Hungary. After World War Two, he or she would have been a citizen of the USSR. Since 1991, they would have found themselves living in a new state – Ukraine.[19]

Today, the region to which we will refer as 'East Central Europe' comprises an area of 533,606 square kilometres situated between the Teutonic peoples of Germany and Austria in the West, and the Slavic peoples of Eastern Europe. This region – described by Timothy Garton Ash[20] as the 'heartlands' of Central and Eastern Europe – is occupied by 64.26 million inhabitants. The majority are either western Slavs or Magyars, although with a livening of Germans, Jews and Roma (Gypsies). Their history has been exciting, dramatic and turbulent: it has also all too often been violent, tragic and traumatic. For this reason, it is impossible to understand contemporary international politics in the region without knowing something of their history. It is therefore to the history of East Central Europe that we now turn.

Endnotes

1   Piotr S. Wandycz, *The Price of Freedom: A History of East Central Europe From the Middle Ages to the Present*, London, Routledge, 1992, p. 1.
2   Jeffrey Laurenti, 'Introduction. Whither East Central Europe in the international system?', in Jeffrey Laurenti, ed., *Searching for Moorings. East Central Europe in the International System*, New York, UN Association of the USA, 1994, pp. 1–7 (p. 2).
3   Paul Lewis, *Central Europe Since 1945*, London, Longman, 1994, p. 8.
4   Charles Gati, 'From Cold War origins to detente: introduction to the international politics of Eastern Europe', in Charles Gati, ed., *The International Politics of Eastern Europe*, New York, Praeger, 1976, pp. 3–14 (p. 3).
5   Geoffrey Swain and Nigel Swain, *Eastern Europe Since 1945*, London, Macmillan, 1993.
6   The notion of a 'return to Europe' (*powrót z Europy*) was explicitly articulated by the Polish Prime Minister Tadeusz Mazowiecki when he addressed the Council of Europe on 30 January 1990. His speech, 'Belonging to Europe', is reprinted in Adam Daniel Rotfeld and Walther Stützle, eds, *Germany and Europe in Transition*, Oxford, OUP for SIPRI, 1991, pp. 131–4.
7   'The Charter of Paris for a New Europe', Paris, 21 November 1990. Reprinted in Adam Daniel Rotfeld and Walter Stützler, eds, *Germany and Europe in Transition*, Oxford, OUP for SIPRI, 1991, pp. 219–30.
8   Francis Fukuyama, 'The end of history', *The National Interest*, 16, summer, 1989, pp. 3–18. See also his book *The End of History and the Last Man*, London, Hamish Hamilton, 1992. For a sustained critique of Fukuyama's 'end of history' optimism see Samuel Huntington, 'No exit: the errors of endism', *The National Interest*, 17, autumn, 1989, pp. 3–11.

9   In his book *Intimations of Postmodernity*, London, Routledge, 1992,
    Zygmunt Bauman has argued that the 1989–90 crisis of socialism represented
    the final stage of the crisis of modernity. However, the evidence for this is not
    very convincing. As Les Holmes argues in *The End of Communist Power:
    Anti-Corruption Campaigns and Legitimation Crisis*, Cambridge, Polity,
    1993, the notion that post-communist states should be seen as being 'in
    transition to a post-modern political condition would appear to be quite
    inappropriate'. On the contrary, he suggests, they 'display rather more
    features of what can in the absence of any better term, be called early
    modernity than of late modernity or of post-modernity – even though
    elements of both of the latter can be found' (pp. 326–7).
10 Gregory F. Treverton, 'Finding an analogy for tomorrow', *Orbis*, winter,
    1993, pp. 1–19.
11 K. J. Holsti, 'International relations at the end of the millenium', *Review of
    International Studies*, 19, no. 4, October, 1993, pp. 401–8 (p. 407).
12 Michael Walzer, 'Notes on the new tribalism', in Chris Brown, ed., *Political
    Restructuring in Europe. Ethical Perspectives*, London, Routledge, 1994, pp.
    187–200 (p. 187).
13 Steve Smith in his recent survey of the key disputes and positions within
    international relations theory lists 'State-Centrism versus Transnationalism'
    and 'Neo-realism and Neo-liberalism' among his 'top ten'. However, he
    regards them as less important and less exciting than the debates on
    'Constitutive versus Explanatory Theory' and 'Foundationalism and Anti-
    Foundationalist International Theory'. Yet to privilege this intellectual navel-
    gazing seems perverse in a world of war, ethnic cleansing and genocide. This
    is particularly so given that he begins his chapter by referring to the evil of
    the Holocaust and yet later offers an implicit defence of post-positivism by
    arguing that to ask 'a postmodernist to list his or her policies for the Bosnian
    crisis is to allocate disciplinary power in a most effective way'! S. Smith, 'The
    self-images of a discipline: a genealogy of international relations theory', in
    Ken Booth and Steve Smith, eds, *International Relations Theory Today*,
    Cambridge, Polity, 1995, pp. 1–38 (p. 26). This seems to illustrate the point
    made by K. J. Holsti in his review of the state of contemporary international
    relations: 'Rather than creating understanding of "what is going on", as
    students often put it, the field may be verging towards scholasticism and
    making itself inaccessible to those to whom it should be addressed, namely
    students and policy-makers'. Holsti, *op. cit.*, p. 408.
14 Hedly Bull, *The Anarchical Society*, London, Macmillan, 1977, p. 140.
15 Claudio Magris, *Danube*, London, Collins Harvill, 1990, p. 241.
16 See Adrian Hyde-Price, *European Security Beyond the Cold War*, London,
    Sage, 1991, pp. 8–10; and Barry Buzan, Morten Kelstrup, Pierre Lemaitre,
    Elzbieta Tromer and Ole Waever, *The European Security Order Recast*,
    London, Pinter, 1990, pp. 47–9.
17 The issue of identity is an important one to which we will return in chapter
    three, when we consider the implications of nationalism for the region. There
    is a burgeoning literature on this topic. See for example W. Bloom, *Personal
    Identity, National Interest and International Relations*, Cambridge, CUP,
    1990; S. Garcia, ed., *European Identity and the Search for Legitimacy*,

London, Pinter, 1990; R. Robertson and B. Holzner, *Identity and Authority. Explorations in the Theory of Society*, Oxford, OUP, 1980; and O. Waever, B. Buzan, M. Kelstrup and P. Lemaitre, *Identity, Migration and the New Security Agenda in Europe*, London, Pinter, 1993.

18   Richard F. Staar, ed., *East-Central Europe and the USSR*, London, Macmillan, 1991.
19   See Wandycz, *op. cit.*, p. 8.
20   Timothy Garton Ash, *The Uses of Adversity*, Cambridge, Granta Books, 1989, p. 271.

Chapter Two

East Central Europe: a brief history

The year 1989 saw the crumbling of the Soviet bloc and the reemergence of an independent East Central Europe. Yet freedom had a bitter taste and the price that needed to be paid seemed exorbitant.... Problems of transition in a post-communist era, whether economic, social or political proved immense, and Poles, Hungarians, Czechs, and Slovaks have been put to what may be the hardest test in their history. Will they succeed? Will they try to go it alone or give some meaning to the term East Central Europe by practicing regional cooperation? Will they resume their old place or gain a new place in Europe, possibly a united Europe? The future alone will provide some answers, but the past may provide some guidance. (Piotr S. Wandycz[1])

Milan Kundera has argued that the people of East Central Europe have had 'the experience of an extremely concentrated history'.[2] By this he meant that their history has been all too full of wars and revolutions, foreign invasions and domestic upheavals; of endless struggles against backwardness, misery and oppression, punctuated by moments of great glory and triumph. For many in East Central Europe today, the past lives on in the present in a very tangible way: myths and legends continue to exert a powerful sway on political behaviour, and many people continue to identify with their historical forbears. Attempting to understand current political debates without knowing something of the history of East Central Europe is therefore extremely difficult. Although the past does not – and never can – provide a guide to the future, it does help us understand the cultural perspectives and political assumptions of policy-relevant actors in the region. The concern of this chapter is thus to provide an historical overview of the history of East Central Europe, focusing primarily on the international dimension.

Poland

Of the four countries, Poland is by far the largest. Given its size and location, this country – 'God's playground', as Norman Davies dubbed it[3] – is destined to play a pivotal role in the economic, political and strategic affairs of the region. The character of Poland today has been shaped by the country's sometimes glorious but all too often tragic history. Since its earliest days, the Polish state has had to battle for its very survival. Being situated on the lowlands of the North European Plain, Poland lacks natural borders. It has therefore been vulnerable to invasion from both east and west. In the twelfth century, Poland faced a military threat from the Teutonic knights. In the thirteenth century, the threat came from the east, from the Mongol horde who brought death and destruction to the exposed Polish kingdom.[4] From the start, therefore, the Polish state has had to fight to preserve its existence and identity against its neighbours, be they Swedes, Russians, Germans, Turks or Tartars.[5]

Throughout the medieval era, the Poles proved themselves formidable warriors, building up a large dynastic state through a series of impressive military victories. Poland's military reputation was based primarily on its powerful feudal cavalry, above all the famous 'winged hussars', who formed the core of the Polish military machine. These magnificently attired knights rode into battle decked out in chain mail and animal furs, with eagles' feathers flapping from wooden 'wings' fastened to their backs.[6] The military potency of this cavalry horde meant that, following the union of Kingdom of Poland and the Grand Duchy of Lithuania in 1386 under the Jagiellonian dynasty, the Polish–Lithuanian Commonwealth (*'Rzeczpospolita Obojga Narodow'*) grew to be the largest state in Europe. By the mid-seventeenth century it stretched from the Baltic coast to the Black Sea, and occupied large swathes of what today are Ukraine, Russia, Romania and Germany. At this formative moment in the history of the European states system, the Polish–Lithuanian *Rzeczpospolita* had a population of between seven and nine million, and controlled a fertile agricultural region of 375,000 square miles from the Baltic to the Black Sea.[7] It thus ranked as one of Europe's great powers.

Yet in the late eighteenth century, weakened by internal divisions and with an antiquated military capability, the Polish state finally succumbed to unremitting external pressure and was partitioned by its more powerful neighbours. Between 1795 and 1918 the once mighty Polish state ceased to exist.[8]

The reasons for the dismemberment of the Polish state have long been debated. Poland was unfortunate to find itself in the unenviable geopolitical situation of being surrounded by three expansionist empires. Poland also lacked any natural boundaries to facilitate defence against invaders (unlike the Swiss with their mountains, or the English with 'their' channel). However, as Brian Downing has argued,[9] such 'geographic-determinist' arguments tend to overlook the fact that both Brandenburg-Prussia and Austria occupied equally exposed geopolitical locations, and – in the case of Prussia – lacked the agricultural and human resources of Poland. Downing concludes that the underlying reason for Poland's partition must therefore be sought not in geography but rather in the domestic weaknesses of the Polish state, which in turn derived from its social structure: Poland, he argues, failed 'to build state structures capable of developing and fielding large modern armies'.[10]

The reason for this crippling military/bureaucratic failure is to be found in the structure of medieval Polish society. The character of the early Polish state and its military machine directly reflected the unique structure of Polish society of the pre-modern era. The military prowess of the Polish state was based on the levy of gentry knights, augmented by occasional mercenary forces and a levy of poorly trained and equipped peasant infantry. The knights came from the large and politically influential gentry and lesser nobility, who were organised on the basis not of individual families, but of clans.[11] This class, the *szlachta*, became so powerful that they succeeded in constructing a cumbersome constitutional order with a diet-centred government which left the elected monarch as a largely ineffectual figure.[12] With the demise of the Jagiellonian dynasty in 1572, the *szlachta* were able to strengthen their position further, at the expense of the monarchy.

The consequences for Poland were tragic: in the seventeenth and eighteenth centuries, the *szlachta* blocked any substantial military or administrative reform. This was at a time when Poland's neighbours – Prussia, Austria and Russia under Peter the Great – were all building modern armies, with large and well trained infantry formations, rational supply and logistical systems and substantial artillery trains. Moreover, numerous factions within the *szlachta* 'ignored national interests in favour of conspiring with foreign powers to prevent a strong state and to place sympathetic monarchs on the throne'.[13]

Thus at the time when the formation of the modern European states system was taking place (a development codified by the 1648 Treaty of Westphalia[14]), Poland's international standing was already compromised by the short-sightedness and selfishness of the *szlachta*, a class described as 'perhaps the most irresponsible elite in all European history'.[15] The seventeenth century was a period of rapid and profound change in both military technology and organisation, and in the administrative structures of European states. Large, professional, infantry-based standing armies were created, organised and supplied by the centralising, absolutist monarchies in Western and Central Europe.[16] Poland's lesser nobility and gentry, however, prevented the Polish state from embracing this 'military revolution'. The motivations were mixed: in part they did not want to pay the additional taxation such a development would entail; they also wanted to preserve a feudal military structure which gave them status, rights and privileges, rather than creating an infantry-based army drawn primarily from those of lower social class.

Whatever the reason, whether from meanness or social prejudice, 'Poland entered the post-Westphalian world with a military structure ably suited for frontier skirmishes, but hopelessly incapable of ensuring territorial sovereignty in a time of continuous military growth. Though it was hardly favoured by natural barriers, Poland's demise must be attributed to failure to modernize, as did surrounding powers'. Poland's failure to modernise meant that by the late eighteenth century the country was 'only a weak and tempting target for surrounding states, a source of regional instability and tension that the major powers only too willingly removed'.[17] In the striking words of Frederick the Great, Poland was like 'an artichoke ready to be consumed leaf by leaf'.[18] In a last desperate attempt to prevent the first partition in 1772, an undersized army led by the feudal cavalry was sent out to do battle with the large professional armies of infantry, cavalry and artillery fielded by the great powers – 'a mismatch almost as great as one pitting cavalry against panzers'.[19] In the end, Poland was divided up between Russia, Prussia and Austria, and finally ceased to exist as a sovereign state in 1795.

For the next hundred years or so, Polish history was marked by a series of heroic but doomed nationalist uprisings. 'Between 1794 and 1905', Piotr Wandycz has commented, 'the Poles engaged in six uprisings and in one revolution, paying in blood, devastated country, cultural losses, and exile. Their battle cry "For your freedom and ours" invoked the solidarity of the oppressed, and the Poles seemed to epitomize the freedom fighters throughout Europe'.[20] Yet, in the end, Poland's national independence came about not as a result of a glorious popular uprising, but as a consequence of the cataclysm of World War One. This cataclysm precipitated the subsequent collapse of Europe's four once mighty multinational empires – the Habsburg, Russian, German and Ottoman – and allowed Poland to re-emerge as a sovereign state. Almost from the very moment of its rebirth, however, this new and aggressively assertive Polish state found itself embroiled in brief but bloody wars with Lithuania (its former Commonwealth partner) and Russia (one of its historic enemies). It also had border disputes with the new Czechoslovakian state to its south (over Teschen – known as Těšín to the Czechs and Cieszyn to the Poles – which contained 140,000 Poles), and with Germany.[21] Moreover, over a third of the inhabitants of this new Polish state were national minorities, some of whom constituted majorities in certain regions.[22]

Given its lack of domestic cohesion and the harsh environment into which it was born, it is perhaps not surprising that Poland's fragile democracy quickly collapsed into anarchy, and that from 1926, the country was ruled by a military man, Marshal Pilsudski. The country's domestic travails were compounded by its adverse geopolitical situation: in the inter-war years, Poland found itself sandwiched between Europe's two 'rogue' states, Nazi Germany and Soviet Russia. The result was another partitioning of the country. The Hitler–Stalin pact of 1939 led to invasion and the destruction of the Polish state.[23] This national disaster was the prelude to a period of unbearable suffering for the Polish people, for in World War Two,

No country in Europe witnessed such a sustained programme of barbarism during the war as Poland. After the bulk of its territory was ravaged by the *Wehrmacht* what remained in the East was swallowed up by the Red Army. The Polish population was decimated: an average of 3,000 citizens lost their lives every day of the war. Six million Poles, roughly half of them Jewish, were slaughtered during the occupation, while Hitler chose Polish territory on which to erect the instruments for his 'final solution of the Jewish question' – the death camps of Oświeçim (Auschwitz), Majdanek and Treblinka.[24]

After the trauma of the war, Poland found itself occupied by the victorious Red Army – dubious liberators who quickly installed a pro-Soviet regime in power. Despite Stalin's promise of free elections, by 1947 Polish communists had succeeded in marginalising the opposition and seizing control of the state apparatus.[25] But Polish communism was from the very start built on shaky foundations. Communism could put down few indigenous roots in this Catholic, largely rural and fiercely nationalist country. It is therefore no surprise that, within the Soviet bloc, it was Poland that experienced the greatest number of popular uprisings against what was widely perceived as a foreign, atheistic imposition. In 1956, 1968, 1970, 1976, 1980–81 and finally in 1988–89, Polish people demonstrated en masse their opposition to the illegitimate and increasingly ineffectual role of the Polish United Workers' Party (PZPR).

Polish communism finally imploded at the end of the 1980s. The catalyst for its demise was *Solidarnosc* ('Solidarity'), the free trade union movement born from the strike movement of 1980.[26] The most charismatic leader of *Solidarnosc* was Lech Walesa, the Gdansk shipyard electrician who later became president of post-communist Poland. Since the transfer of power from the PZPR to the first *Solidarnosc* government of Prime Minister Mazowiecki, Polish foreign policy has demonstrated a remarkable degree of continuity. Indeed, it often appears to be the sole element of stability in an otherwise turbulent domestic political scene. This is all the more surprising given the dramatic upheavals in Poland's external environment: in 1990, Poland had only three immediate neighbours: the GDR, the USSR and Czechoslovakia. Since then, all three of these states have ceased to exist, and Poland now finds itself with seven new neighbours; the BRD, Lithuania, Russia, Ukraine, Belarus, Slovakia and the Czech Republic.

Much credit for this foreign policy stability lies with Krzysztof Skubiszewski, Poland's Foreign Minister from 1989 to 1993. He helped build a broad consensus on the main lines of Polish foreign and security policy involving three key elements: developing and broadening cooperation with the country's neighbours east and west; integrating Poland in Western economic, political and security systems (particularly the EU and NATO); and building wider regional and pan-European frameworks for institutionalised multilateral cooperation. The broad thrust of this foreign policy strategy remains in place despite the change of government in

October 1993 (when a left-wing coalition led initially by Prime Minister Pawlak came into office), in part because the direction of external relations remains firmly in the hands of the President,[27] but also because Warsaw's foreign policy has been 'determined by Poland's basic national interests, the country's *raison d'etat* that was accepted in 1989, and not by some party preferences of occasional electoral winners'.[28]

Poland today contains 38 million inhabitants, in an area approximately the size of the UK and Eire (312,685 square kilometres). It is unusual in being both Slavic and Roman Catholic. In contrast to the inter-war years, Poland is now a fairly homogenous state. Nonetheless, there is a small but politically influential German minority of 200,000 in Silesia and Pomerania (approximately 0.5% of the total population), along with 200,000 Belarussians in eastern Poland (0.8%) and small numbers of Lithuanians and Jews. On the other hand, there are comparatively larger Polish communities in neighbouring states, including 418,000 in Belarus, 300,000 in Ukraine and 258,000 in Lithuania. As we shall see, these trans-national ethnic and religious bonds have important consequences for Poland's external relations.

Poland's foreign and security policy continues to be much affected by its geography. Poland today occupies approximately the same territory as it did under its first ruler, Mieszko I, leader of a Slavonic tribe called the Polanie. But post-war Poland actually lost nearly 50% of the territory it had occupied after World War One. Poland lost territory in the east to the Soviet Union, whilst gaining the German provinces of Silesia and Pomerania in the west. In effect, the country's borders were shifted about 200 kilometres westwards. The effect of this was to leave post-war Poland fearful of German revanchism and largely dependent on the USSR for security guarantees. This became important during the 'two-plus-four' negotiations leading up to German unification, whilst lingering uncertainty over the status of Poland's eastern borders introduced an element of tension into Warsaw's relations with the newly independent Soviet successor states of Belarus and Ukraine.

Poland today therefore continues to face geopolitical dilemmas similar to those with which it had to grapple in the inter-war years: namely, how to preserve its sovereignty whilst being sandwiched between two of Europe's great powers – Germany and Russia.[29] The options include aligning with one or the other; keeping an equal distance from both (the policy pursued by Pilsudski's government in the inter-war years); or developing close relations with both. It is this third option – pursuing a policy of equal closeness to Germany and Russia – that has been endorsed by Poland's post-communist governments since 1989. At the same time, the break-up of the Soviet Union has eased some of Warsaw's immediate security concerns (given that it now shares a only small border with Russia), but has also complicated the country's *Ostpolitik*. In particular, Poland must avoid becoming entangled in intra-CIS disputes between Russia and its neighbours, such as Ukraine.[30]

Thus, as we shall see, Poland's geostrategic location between Western Europe and the Soviet successor states gives it a pivotal role to play in Europe's post-Cold War system of international relations. How Polish foreign and security policies evolve over the next few years will therefore be of crucial importance for the wider pattern of international relations in Europe as a whole in the twenty-first century.

The Czech lands: Bohemia and Moravia

To the south-west of Poland lies the Czech Republic. It has a population of 10.3 million inhabiting an area of 30,450 square kilometres. The Czech Republic consists of two ancient lands, Bohemia and Moravia. Of the two, Bohemia has been the most important, largely subsuming Moravia within it for most of its history. The Czechs belong to the same western Slavic ethno-linguistic group as the Poles, and, like the Poles, they converted to Christianity around the end of the first millennium. Although missionaries from the Eastern Orthodox Church had been active in Bohemia and Moravia in the tenth century, the Czechs – again like the Poles – converted to Christianity under the tutelage of the Roman Catholic Church. They did so in no small measure because of the pressure they were under from aggressive German princes intent on subduing 'pagans' on their borders.

Following their entry into medieval Christendom, the principal issue of foreign policy for Bohemia and Moravia, as for Poland and Hungary, was their relations with the papacy and with the Holy Roman Empire. These were the two key institutions of medieval Europe.[31] In the Polish case, a major reason for adopting the Roman Catholic faith was political: the Polish king Mieszko hoped to be able to play the papacy off against the Empire, which at this time was busy expanding westwards through a process of conquest and forced conversion of the pagans on its borders. Indeed, at one stage Mieszko even placed his kingdom under the protection of Rome.[32]

Bohemia's relationship with the Holy Roman Empire was very different. From the very start, Bohemia came under direct and pervasive German pressure. The Premyslid dukes were quick to recognise the feudal overlordship of the Emperor during the early period of state building in Bohemia, and Bohemia was to become an integral element of the Empire. German influence on the Czech lands was to grow throughout the Middle Ages, not least because of a steady influx of German settlers. This process of German colonisation was also experienced by Poland and Hungary. It was officially encouraged in order to repopulate areas devastated by the Mongol invasions of the thirteenth century, and to stimulate economic development. By the early fifteenth century, German had become the lingua franca of most large towns and cities throughout East Central Europe, and was used along with Latin in the courts of Prague and Visegrad.

The close relationship between Germany and the Czech lands which developed in the Middle Ages became a central leitmotiv of Czech history. Bohemia and Moravia have been described as 'a small Slav promontory in the German sea'.[33] František Palacký, the noted nineteenth century Czech historian, argued that most of Czech history has revolved around the issue of confrontation and cooperation between Teutons and Czechs.[34] German cultural, economic and political influence on Bohemia and Moravia has been pervasive, and much of Czech history revolves around this intimate yet often tense relationship between Czechs and Teutons.

At times, the Czechs have felt oppressed by their powerful German neighbours. In 1469 this gave rise to the rallying cry, 'Out of Bohemia, evil German soul'.[35] But their proximity to Germany has also provided many and varied benefits for the Czechs. Bohemia's close involvement in the predominantly German Holy Roman Empire meant that it was the first Slav state to be drawn directly into the affairs of western Catholic Europe. By the fourteenth century the King of Bohemia had become the most important political figure in Central Europe, with a key role in the affairs of the Empire.[36] Bohemian prominence derived not only from its strategic position in Central Europe and its considerable mineral wealth, but also from the ambition of its gifted rulers. At various times they sought to extend their dynastic rule into Austria, Silesia, Poland, Hungary and Brandenburg. This involvement in the political affairs of Europe had the effect of stirring Bohemia's economic development and intellectual awareness. It led, for example, to the foundation of the Charles University in Prague in 1348 – the first university north of the Alps and east of the Rhine. This university was seen as both an imperial and a Czech institution, serving four nations – Czech, Saxon, Bavarian and Polish.[37]

Sadly, Bohemia's position as one of the Empire's most dynamic and prosperous states did not last. In the early fifteenth century, the Czech lands were wracked by a series of bitter conflicts known as the Hussite rebellion. The Hussite upheaval was 'perhaps the most important single development in Czech history'.[38] Its causes were complex and diverse, but two strands stand out. First, religious and spiritual issues: the Hussite movement was inspired by Jan Hus, a preacher who spoke out against the corruption and worldliness of the clergy and the Catholic Church, themes later taken up by Luther and the Reformation. Second, ethno-linguistic: the Hussites tapped a powerful seam of anti-German feeling, thereby strengthening the emergence of a Czech national consciousness. Despite early battlefield victories, the Hussite rebellion eventually fell apart through internal divisions, leaving Bohemia greatly weakened.[39] For the remainder of the fifteenth century, Bohemia was regarded as a hotbed of heresy and treated as a leper by its neighbours. This meant that the Czech lands were to some extent marginalised during the Italian Renaissance in a way that was not the case for Catholic Poland or for Hungary under Mátyás Corvinus (also known as Mátyás Hunyardi).[40]

Two centuries later, Bohemia was once again to seize the limelight in Central Europe. In 1618, when asked to vote on the succession, Protestant nobles refused to accept a Catholic, Ferdinand of Habsburg. Instead, some of them perpetrated what became known as the 'Second Defenestration of Prague'.[41] This precipitated the Thirty Years' War, a war which resulted in the devastation of vast swathes of Central Europe.[42] The Bohemian Protestant Army itself was routed at the Battle of the White Mountain in 1620. This defeat led to the wholesale persecution of Czech Protestantism and the eradication of an independent Bohemia and Moravia. For the next three centuries, they were merely a province of the Habsburg Empire.

In the nineteenth century, two developments occurred in the Czech lands that proved of far-reaching significance. First, Bohemia emerged as the most important industrial province of the Habsburg Empire. As the industrial revolution began transforming the face of Europe, Bohemia – and, to a lesser extent, Moravia – became important producers of iron and steel, along with agricultural machinery, railway rolling stock, chemicals, armaments, glass and porcelain. Second, a Czech national movement developed. This found expression in a variety of different forms, including the music of Bedrich Smetana and Antonin Dvorak, and – by way of contrast – in the armed uprising of June 1848. The 1848 uprising was savagely repressed. Austrian retribution included a ban on the use of the Czech language in schools and newspapers, in favour of German. When the Austro-Hungarian Dual Empire was created on 8 June 1867, Bohemia and Moravia were left as provinces of Austria, although the Czech language was reinstated in schools and official documents. The Czechs were therefore left as a subject people in a multinational empire dominated by the Germanic language and culture of Austria.

During World War One, Czech and Slovak nationalist leaders met in Pittsburgh, Pennsylvania, to discuss the post-war arrangement for their two peoples.[43] It was agreed that a Czechoslovak Republic would be created out of the ruins of the Habsburg Empire, in which the Slovaks would be granted considerable autonomy. On 28 October 1918, the new country was born. It was formed from the historic Czech lands of Bohemia and Moravia, along with Slovakia and Ruthenia, which had formerly been under Hungarian administration. The President of this new republic was Tomáš Masaryk, a distinguished American-educated liberal intellectual. He preached the values of tolerance and reason, and set out to 'create an island of democracy in the centre of Europe'. In doing so, he faced two major problems. First, Czechoslovakia was a multinational state: it was composed of 46% Czechs, 28% Germans, 13% Slovaks, 8% Hungarians and 3% Ruthenians. However, the 1920 constitution created a unitary state, with Czechs in all key administrative positions. This was a particular source of dissatisfaction amongst both the 3.5 million Germans (who were concentrated in the Sudetenlands around the western rim of Czechoslovakia), and with the Slovaks.[44] Second, Czechoslovakia was surrounded by hostile and revanchist states, notably Germany and Hungary, but also Poland and the USSR.

On the other hand, Czechoslovakia had two things in its favour. Although it inherited only one-quarter of the population and one-fifth of the territory of the old Austro-Hungarian Empire, it found itself with two-thirds of its industrial capacity. It was therefore an economically viable state, with a strong manufacturing and engineering sector. Second, the new republic was blessed with competent and decent leaders, in the shape of Tomáš Masaryk and Edvard Beneš. They were both important assets for their country, despite their failure to deal with the minorities problem. These two factors help explain why Czechoslovakia was able to remain an island of liberal democracy and relative political stability throughout most of the period between the wars. It is perhaps symbolically significant that whereas Poland was ruled by a military strong-man in the inter-war years, Czechoslovakia was ruled by liberal intellectuals.

Sadly, this bastion of liberal democracy and economic development in East Central Europe was to perish at the hands of German and Hungarian aggression, with the shameful complicity of the British and French governments. In September 1938, declaring that the crisis over the Sudetenland was 'a quarrel in a far-away country between people of whom we know nothing' (and apparently cared even less), the British Conservative Prime Minister Neville Chamberlain agreed at Munich to the Nazi dismemberment of Czechoslovakia.[45] After this, Czechoslovakia's days were numbered: the Poles successfully demanded the return of Teschen; Hungary was awarded Ruthenia and parts of Slovakia by the Axis powers; with German support, a clerical–fascist puppet state was established in Slovakia on 14 March 1939; and next day, German troops entered Prague and declared Bohemia and Moravia *Reich Protektorat*.

Liberation in 1945 found Czechoslovakia occupied by the Red Army. Yet in contrast to Poland, there was significant popular sympathy for the Russians – fellow Slavs who were widely regarded as liberators, and contrasted favourably to the Western powers who had betrayed the country at Munich. Czechoslovakia also possessed a strong and politically influential communist party. In free elections in 1946, the party won 38% of the popular vote, and was the key force in a 'popular front' style coalition government.[46] Unfortunately, whatever popular support for the communists and empathy with the Russians had existed in 1945–47, it quickly evaporated following the February coup of 1948. The communist seizure of power was followed by a long period of oppressive Stalinisation, and for two decades Czechoslovakia stagnated under the iron grip of Antonin Novotny.

Then in 1968 an event occurred which captured the imagination of a generation. Alexander Dubcek, a reform communist, led a popular movement aimed at creating 'Socialism with a human face'. Tragically, the 'Prague Spring' (as it was known) was crushed by Warsaw Pact tanks. This all too brief experiment in democratic socialism was followed by a stifling process of Brezhnevite 'normalisation'.[47]

Just over two decades later, Czechoslovak communism collapsed in a 'velvet revolution'. Gorbachev's commitment to *glasnost* and *perestroika* undermined the ideological legitimacy of Husak's authoritarian communism, and as neighbouring communist regimes toppled one by one, and as thousands of ordinary citizens poured out on to the streets in a determined expression of 'people's power', the Czechoslovak communist party negotiated a rapid hand-over of power.[48] The new president of the Republic was Václav Havel. Together with his trusted associate from the Charter 77 dissident movement, the new Foreign Minister Jirí Dienstbier, Havel gave Czechoslovakia's foreign policy a distinctly moralistic flavour. This moralism was particularly pronounced between 1990 and 1992, and was evident from their principled opposition to arms sales;[49] their championing of a CSCE-based collective security system for Europe; and their offer to mediate in the Middle East conflict.[50]

Unfortunately, Czechoslovakia's 'velvet revolution' was followed by a 'velvet divorce', as the Federation dissolved into its Czech and Slovak components at midnight on 31 December 1992. Although only two-thirds the size of the former CSFR, the economic prospects for the Czech Republic look relatively favourable – not only when contrasted with those of Slovakia, but also when compared with the other Visegrad states. Indeed, the Czech Republic has emerged as an island of political stability and a pioneer in market-orientated economic reforms in the region (largely due to the avidly Thatcherite Prime Minister, Václav Klaus).[51] Prospects for foreign investment are good, and the rate of unemployment is one of the lowest in Eastern Europe. On the negative side, environmental problems remain serious, and crime has escalated. Both of these developments have important cross-border and regional dimensions.[52]

The foreign policy of the Czech Republic revolves around three key goals: incorporation of the Republic into the structures and organisations of the democratic West; collaboration in Central Europe; and partnership with – not subservience to – Germany.[53] As their previous history indicates, the future of the Czech lands will be very much tied up with Germany. This will certainly be the case for the country's economic development, but social, political and cultural affairs will also be much influenced by the German-speaking lands to their north and west.[54]

Slovakia

With a population of 5.26 million and a territory of 49,035 square kilometres, Slovakia is the smallest of the four Visegrad countries. It is also the poorest and least stable politically. Slovakia came into existence on 1 January 1993, following the peaceful dissolution of the CSFR. Although Czechs and Slovaks are both Slavs whose language derives from a common stock, there are many cultural differences between the two peoples and a common 'Czechoslovak' state was a somewhat artificial creation.

The Czechs and Slovaks are Slavic peoples who came to the region during the fifth, sixth and seventh centuries. Along with Slavs in western Poland and the Pannonian basin, they formed a loose confederation grandly called the 'Great Moravian Empire'. This collapsed in AD 896 under the shock of the devastating Magyar invasion (see under 'Hungary', below). The Magyars seized Slovakia, and for the next thousand years Czechs and Slovaks followed separate paths. First, whereas the Czechs were strongly influenced by Germany and the Habsburg Empire, the Slovaks were for most of their history ruled by the Hungarians and subject to a policy of forced 'Magyarisation'. Today the Czech lands have a small German minority, whilst approximately 10% of Slovakia comprises Hungarians. Secondly, whereas Bohemia and Moravia were at the forefront of industrialisation in Central Europe from the 1870s onwards, Slovakia remained largely rural, agrarian and backward. Following the communist takeover, Slovakia experienced rapid industrialisation. Unfortunately, this has left it with outdated and inefficient 'smokestack' industries, along with a substantial armaments industry. Slovakia also remains less urbanised than the Czech lands.[55] Thirdly, the Slovaks, like the Poles, are strongly Roman Catholic. The Czechs turned to Hussite Protestant ideas after

1410. They were forcibly re-Catholicised after the 1620 Battle of the White Mountain, but 'while Catholicism is the major religion in both parts of Czechoslovakia, the Czech Republic is notably more secular than Slovakia'.[56] Last but not least, the Czechs are great beer drinkers, whilst the Slovaks tend to prefer wine.

The Slovaks belong to that group of communities known in the nineteenth century as 'nations without a history'. Having been militarily defeated and politically subordinated by the Magyars, the Slovaks lacked their own indigenous ruling class. In an essay written in 1968 and entitled *Where Are Our Castles?*, the Slovak writer Vladimir Mináč pointed out that Slovakia was strewn with castles, fortresses, manor houses and lordly dwellings. However, these castles and mansions were occupied by Hungarian nobility, whilst the Slovak peasants round about dwelt in *drevenice*, wooden huts held together with straw and dung. Reflecting on this essay, Claudio Magris has written that,

> In the castle of Oravsky Podzamok, in the Otava valley, there is a picture revealing the white complexion and plump hands of the Celssimus Princeps Nicolaus Esterhazy [a Hungarian noble], while the hands of the peasants in the village beneath the castle even today are the colour of earth, wrinkled and knotty as the roots of trees writhing among the stones. The difference between those hands is a symbol of the history of these peoples. The Slovaks have for centuries been a downtrodden people, the obscure substratum of their country, not unlike the straw and dried dung which hold their huts together. We have no history, writes Mináč, if this is made up solely of kings, emperors, dukes, princes, victories, conquests, violence and pillage. In a poem by Petöfi, the national poet of Hungary, the Slovak is depicted, though in a good-natured way, as a red-nosed tinker in a washed-out smock.[57]

When Slovak nationalism began to stir in the nineteenth century, it immediately came up against the intolerance and repression of the Hungarian overlords.[58] Given the relatively backward nature of Slovak society – a society largely undisturbed by the elemental forces unleashed by the industrial revolution and the associated process of modernisation – Slovak nationalists saw their nation as one of the original, genuine cradles of an ancient Slavic civilisation. The very backwardness of Slovakia, they believed, had preserved uncontaminated the purity and integrity of their Slavic essence. It is therefore not surprising that Slovak nationalism was strongly influenced by Pan-Slavic ideas, and that it was in Slovakia that messianic Slavophilism found its first expression, both earlier and more vigorously than among the Czechs.[59] When nationalist and democratic revolutions erupted throughout Europe in 1848, the Slovaks presented their Hungarian masters (themselves in revolt against the Austrian Habsburgs) with the so-called 'claims of Liptovský Mikuláš'. This called on the Hungarians to recognise some basic rights for the Slovak people. It was answered by arrests and other repressive measures.

After 1848, the Habsburgs sought to repair their relations with the Hungarians and consequently abandoned the Slovaks to their tender mercies. Repression of the Slovaks was intensified after the creation of the Dual Monarchy in 1867. A Hungarian law of 1868 defined the Slovaks as a mere folk survival within the Magyar nation and denied them their own separate national identity. This meant that the Slovak language was repressed, and an independent cultural life severely constrained. Hungarian social and economic dominance condemned the Slovaks to what Marx dismissed as the 'idiocy of rural life', preventing the emergence of an indigenous Slovak professional and entrepreneurial class. One consequence of this was widespread emigration, largely to America. In this hostile environment, the survival of the Slovak language and a nascent sense of national identity was due in no small part to the Church – both Catholic and Evangelical – which set up schools and preserved the use of the language. This long history of enforced Magyarisation and Hungarian persecution has left a legacy of Slovak resentment of their former overlords which persists down to the present.[60]

The outbreak of the Great War in 1914 provided the Slovaks with their first real chance of winning independence from their Hungarian oppressors. However, rather than opting for an independent Slovak nation state, Slovak nationalist leaders chose to cooperate with their fellow Slavs from Bohemia and Moravia in the Czechoslovak National Council, established in Paris in 1915. With the support of the victorious Allied powers, this led to the creation in 1918 of the Czechoslovak Republic. This republic was meant to be federal in character, with equal rights for the Slovaks. But, as we have already noted, from the very start Czechs dominated the new state. Resentment at this, and at the perceived condescension of the Czechs, mounted amongst Slovaks in the inter-war years. This resentment was exploited craftily by Hitler, and in March 1939 an independent Slovak state was proclaimed. This new state was little more than a German dependency with a reactionary, authoritarian and pro-Nazi government under Monsignor Tiso.[61] The constitution of 21 July 1939 created a one-party state run along corporatist lines, with most industries under German control. Slovak troops fought alongside the Wehrmacht in Russia, and nearly three-quarters of Slovak jews were deported by the regime to death camps.

With liberation in 1945, the Czechoslovak state was re-established. After the crushing of the Prague coup, a federal constitution was introduced, and great effort was made to industrialise Slovakia. Indeed, whilst 'normalisation' led to the suffocation of Czech culture and society, Slovakia paradoxically experienced some positive changes. Writing on the eve of the collapse of communism, Claudio Magris noted that, 'the totalitarian restoration of 1968, while it was certainly savage in repressing civil liberties and the rights of the individual, nevertheless increased the political weight of the local population, either as a result of political calculation or out of faith in the Pan-Slavic (and therefore pro-Russian) tradition of the country'. Indeed, he argued, 'Slovakia today is therefore at one and the same time beneath an iron heel and in a phase of historical regeneration, with an expanding role in affairs'. In contrast to the sense of 'neglect and death' in Prague, 'Bratislava, in spite of everything, is sanguine and cheerful, a vital world in an expansive phase, looking not to the melancholy of the past, but to growth and the future'.[62]

With the disintegration of the Husak regime in 1989, political developments in Slovakia began diverging from those in the Czech lands. Whereas elections in Bohemia and Moravia in June 1992 brought to power a centre-right government committed to radical market-orientated reforms under Václav Klaus, those in Slovakia led to the creation of a nationalistic centre-left government under Vladimir Meciar. Failure to resolve a series of legal, political and economic differences led to an agreement to dissolve the federation at the end of 1992, despite there being little public enthusiasm for such a drastic step.

The new Slovak Republic was immediately faced with fundamental questions concerning its foreign and security policy orientation. It was not initially clear whether Slovakia would continue with the broad thrust of the CSFR's external relations –

namely integration in Western organisations and structures – or whether it would place greater emphasis on cultivating closer links with its eastern neighbours. The problems of foreign policy reorientation were complicated by the relative inexperience of Slovak diplomats and foreign policy specialists, given the dominance of Czechs in the former Czechoslovak Ministry of Foreign Affairs. Consequently in the first months of independence, the Slovaks issued conflicting signals regarding their external orientation. Yet by mid-1993, integration in Western organisations, especially the EU and NATO, had emerged as a key plank of Bratislava's foreign and security policies.[63] In pursuing this aim, however, Slovak foreign-policy makers faced an uphill struggle, primarily because of Bratislava's poor image abroad – an image tarnished by its policies towards its ethnic minorities, its environmental record, and the worrying trends of a slide into authoritarianism by the Meciar government.

The new Slovak Republic thus faces daunting problems. Large parts of its economy are internationally uncompetitive; the domestic political scene is worryingly fragmented; the legitimacy of constitutional opposition and press freedom is not universally accepted; relations with the Hungarian minority are tense; discrimination against Gypsies is rampant; and the country remains locked into a debilitating dispute with Hungary over the Gabcikovo-Nagymaros hydroelectric dams along the Danube.[64] The country did manage to gain admittance to the Council of Europe in June 1993, but only after promising to repeal laws that discriminated against ethnic Hungarians (notably by banning the use of non-Slovak Christian names on official documents). The prospects facing Slovakia are therefore somewhat bleak. There are no simple or obvious solutions to its mounting domestic problems, and its international situation is unhealthily complicated. Of the four Visegrad countries, it is undoubtedly Slovakia which is confronted with the most intractable and potentially debilitating problems.

Yet Slovakia is important within East Central Europe for two main reasons. First, it is the only one of the Visegrad group that borders on all the other three; it could therefore play a pivotal role within Visegrad. Second, Slovakia is the most 'Eastern' of the Visegrad states, and has cultivated close relations with both Ukraine and Russia. Slovakia could therefore play a positive 'bridging' role between the West and the CIS states, helping to forge a more united and integrated Europe. If, on the other hand, Bratislava chooses to distance itself from the other Visegrad states, or is cold-shouldered by them, then the Czech–Slovak border could become the new East–West dividing line in Europe.[65]

Hungary

In the late ninth century, a nomadic tribe of horsemen came thundering out of Asia.[66] They smashed the Great Moravian Empire and settled on the plains of Hungary. These were the Magyars, known as the On-Ogurs, or 'People of the Ten Arrows'. They were of Finno-Ugric descent, and had an agglutinate language that was utterly incomprehensible to the Slavs around them. Led by Árpád, the founder of the Hungarian native dynasty, the Magyars settled in the Carpathian basin, 'almost exactly in the centre of the European continent'.[67] For the next sixty years they raided the Danube and Elbe valleys, reaching as far as France and Lombardy. Yet resistance to their incursions stiffened, and following a major defeat at German hands in 955, they abandoned their nomadic and raiding existence, and adopted a settled way of life.[68] This transformation was reinforced at the turn of millenium, when Hungary adopted Christianity. In 1001, Pope Sylvester I gave a royal crown to Stephen, symbolising the entrance of the Magyars into medieval Christendom.

Like the other peoples of the region, the Hungarians were acutely sensitive to threats to their security emanating from Asia. In 1241, the Hungarian kingdom was nearly annihilated by the Mongol horde. The Magyars recovered from this catastrophe, but became increasingly concerned about the growing threat from the expanding Ottoman Empire. The Turkish defeat of the Serbs at Kosovo in 1389 opened the way for the Ottoman armies to launch an invasion of the Pannonian basin. For over a century, the Hungarians conducted a bitter struggle with the Turks. During this period, Hungary flourished, especially during the thirty-two-year reign of Mátyás Corvinus (1458–90). He was a great Renaissance monarch, a patron of the arts, a reforming political leader and an inspired military commander (it was he who created the Hussars, the famous light cavalry distinguished by wolf skins slung rakishly over their left shoulders, who would eventually be mimicked by every major military power in Europe). In 1526, however, Hungary suffered the greatest setback of its history: on the field of Mohács, the Hungarian army was wiped out by the Ottoman Turks. After 500 years, the Hungarian state ceased to exist.[69]

The old Magyar kingdom was divided into three parts: in the west, 'Royal Hungary' went to the Habsburgs; the central area became 'Turkish Hungary'; and Transylvania (the *Erdély*) was left as a small Turkish vassal state. The Ottoman Empire, driven by its potent military machine, continued to expand until in 1683 the Turks laid siege to Vienna. Vienna was only saved by the arrival of Polish cavalry – including the famous winged Hussars – led by Jan Sobieski. Three years later, the Austrians defeated the Turks at Mohács. By the 1699 Treaty of Karlowitz, Hungary and Transylvania were given to the Habsburgs.[70] Hungary thus swopped occupation by the Turks for occupation by the Austrians, and soon discovered that 'their rule was by no means more benevolent than the Turks'.[71]

Nevertheless, despite centuries of foreign domination, the Hungarians retained a strong sense of their Magyar culture and identity. Nationalist uprisings took place in 1703 and 1848: the latter uprising, led by Lajos Kossuth, was crushed only by the arrival of Russian troops. Eventually in 1867 the Habsburgs agreed to create a Dual Monarchy, and gave the Hungarians rule over half of the Empire. For Hungary this meant the beginnings of a 'golden age', but for the Slovaks, Romanians, Jews, Gypsies and others under Hungarian domination, it was a period of often acute national persecution. The Hungarians, for so many years the victims of discrimination and cultural oppression, now acted in a high-handed, arbitrary and domineering manner towards the minority groups under their sway – minority groups who collectively, until about 1900, constituted over half the population in Hungarian-ruled lands.[72] This illustrates what Susan Strange has called 'the trouble with freedom', namely that 'it often involves a zero-sum game: more freedom for me means less for you; national liberation for one ethnic group may mean enslavement for others'.[73] Piotr Wandycz has also noted that often in the history of East Central Europe 'freedom had a price which had to be paid by somebody: a nation, a class, or an individual'.[74] In this case, the national 'freedom' of the Magyars after 1867 was paid for by the denial of national rights and liberties to their subject peoples.

Unfortunately for the Hungarians, this was to rebound on them in the twentieth century. Hungary ended up on the losing side in the Great War of 1914–18. Many of the national groups who had suffered from 'Magyarisation' in the Dual Empire now sought independence. The result was the 1920 Treaty of Trianon – a treaty which most Hungarians still regard as a national tragedy. Hungary lost 68% of its pre-war territory and 59% of its population. Nearly one-third of all Magyars found themselves living outside of Hungary, mostly in the new Romanian, Yugoslav and Czechoslovakian states on Hungary's borders. This truncated Hungarian state was immediately wracked by domestic strife. A short-lived communist insurrection was replaced by an authoritarian conservative regime led by Admiral Miklós Horthy.[75] Horthy's repressive government, fuelled by nationalist fervour and determined to regain Hungary's lost territory, was subsequently to ally itself with the rising power in the region – Nazi Germany.[76]

At first, this unholy alliance paid off. With Hitler's support, Hungary took southern Slovakia and southern Ruthenia from Czechoslovakia in 1938; northern Transylvania from Romania in 1940; and parts of northern Yugoslavia in 1941.[77] By the end of 1941, Hungary had doubled in size and population. Once again, however, Hungary had allied itself with the losing side. Much of the Hungarian Army was sent to the eastern front, where it perished at Voronezh. In February 1945, Budapest was occupied by the Red Army, and in 1947 a treaty was signed which restored to Hungary its pre-war borders (with the minor exception of a small rectification in Czechoslovakia's favour). Hungary itself fell victim to a classic exercise in 'salami tactics' by the small but highly organised communist party, and by the late forties was in the grip of a series of ruthless Stalinist purges.[78]

The tragic and doomed uprising in 1956 marked a watershed in the history of Hungarian communism. Having crushed the uprising with the help of Soviet tanks, the party, under its leader Janos Kádár, embarked on a programme of national reconciliation and compromise. Adopting the slogan, 'he who is not against us, is with us', Kádár encouraged a tacit social contract with the people whereby rising living standards were traded for political docility. The result was the emergence of a 'goulash communism' which made Hungary 'the happiest barracks in the Soviet bloc'. When this relatively tolerant and open communist system experienced growing economic problems in the late 1980s, the leadership, emboldened by Gorbachev's reform programme, opted to transform their country into a pluralist liberal democracy with a market economy. The result was what Timothy Garton Ash has called a 'refolution':[79] a peaceful and gradual transfer of power, without mass protests or social upheaval.

The first 'post-refolution' government of Prime Minister Ántáll pursued three main foreign policy objectives: integration into Europe; good relations with Hungary's neighbours; and support for Magyar communities abroad. However, balancing these three objectives has not been easy. For example, too much support for Hungarian minorities in neighbouring states could tend to undermine bilateral relations with these neighbours, and might also create a bad impression in the West, thereby undermining the prospects for integration. The dilemmas posed for Hungarian foreign policy by these three sometimes conflicting objectives became a major issue in the July 1994 elections. The winner of elections, the MSP (Hungarian Socialist Party), had accused the Ántáll government of concentrating on the issue of minorities to the detriment of the other goals.[80] Nonetheless, it remains to be seen how the MSP government of Gyula Horn manages to reconcile these three foreign policy objectives.

Despite these domestic controversies, Hungary has sought to play an active role in the wider international community: from 1992–93 it served a two-year term as a non-permanent member of the UN Security Council; it contributed small groups of observers to UN missions in Cambodia, Cyprus, Georgia, Mozambique and Uganda; it took over the Chair of the CSCE from Italy in the autumn of 1994; and it has continued to play a full role in regional fora such as the Visegrad group and the Central European Initiative.

Yet the memory of the Treaty of Trianon continues to haunt Hungary. The government's policy towards Hungarian minorities in neighbouring lands remains a sensitive and controversial issue, both domestically and internationally. Support for an outright irredentist policy within Hungary is very limited – reflecting the changed political and moral climate within Hungarian society in an age of democracy and European integration. As J. F. Brown has argued, 'irredentism is no longer considered a viable proposition in either Hungary itself or in the lost lands of St. Stephen'. This is not only because of its impracticality but also because of its immorality.

'Hungary's behaviour in the 1930s and during war; the suffering it caused to other countries and to itself, the lasting damage it did to Hungary's name – the bad memory of all of this led to a considerable moral revulsion against irredentism'.[81]

Hungary's more recent policy towards the issue of minority rights for Magyar communities has been to internationalise the issue. Budapest has been a vigorous proponent of a more robust minority rights regime in Europe, and has raised the issue of minority rights in multilateral fora such as the Council of Europe, the EU and the OSCE. Unfortunately, some ill-considered remarks by leading Hungarian politicians have generated suspicions about Hungary's 'real' ambitions.[82] Bratislava, Bucharest and Belgrade have all expressed their concerns about Hungarian 'revisionism', although this is a danger that exists more in the minds of Hungary's neighbours than it does in the hearts of the Hungarian people.

Having said this, the Hungarian government's occasional lack of clarity and consistency on the question of borders and the minority issue reflects underlying political struggles going on within Hungary for the 'soul' of the Magyar nation. Hungarian domestic politics is dominated by the struggle between the country's two great traditions: the populists, who tend to be conservative, nationalist, traditionalist, anti-intellectual, anti-semitic and inward-looking; and the urbanists, who tend to be more liberal, intellectual, cosmopolitan and outward-looking.

This domestic political conflict, which does not correspond to the left–right divide of many West European countries, has great implications for Hungary's foreign policy. The urbanists tend to believe that it is essential to combine Hungarian culture with European values and ideas. The populists tend to believe that Hungarian culture can survive only by remaining pure: this approach could leave Hungary isolated, neurotic, defensive, and susceptible to demagogic nationalists. Hungary's foreign policy dilemmas are also aggravated by its sensitive geopolitical situation. Hungary has the misfortune to be surrounded by the former Yugoslav states of Slovenia, Croatia and Serbia, along with Romania, Ukraine and Slovakia. All of these states, to a greater or lesser extent, are experiencing economic dislocation, political instability and resurgent nationalism. Hungary's new democratic leadership must therefore tread carefully if it is to manage its foreign policy dilemmas successfully.

Conclusion

East Central Europe has had a stormy and eventful history. After
adopting Catholicism at the end of the first millenium, the medieval
kingdoms of Hungary, Poland and Bohemia formed the eastern
bulwark of European Christendom. From the sixteenth century
onwards, the region became the battleground for expansionist
empires – the Ottoman, Habsburg, Russian and Prussian. Eventually,
weakened by internal disputes and petty rivalries, all three of the
once powerful kingdoms of East Central Europe succumbed to the
expanding multinational empires on their borders.

It was only in the wake of the 1914–18 cataclysm that the
imperial yokes were lifted. The new states that emerged in the region
were saddled with enormous domestic and international problems.
With the partial exception of Bohemia and Moravia, all were
economically backward and prone to various forms of authoritarian
populism. Poland and Czechoslovakia were weakened by dissatisfied
national minority communities, and all three states were locked into
debilitating ethnic and territorial disputes with their neighbours. This
left them vulnerable to predatory neighbours – which by the 1930s
meant Nazi Germany.

World War Two was the second great watershed in the modern
history of the region. As the Nazi war machine first faltered and then
cracked in the face of ferocious onslaughts from the Red Army,
Soviet power was extended into much of Eastern Europe and the
Balkans. After a temporary flirtation with 'national roads to
socialism' in Eastern Europe from 1944 to 1947, a Stalinist
Gleichschaltung took place from 1948–49 onwards. From that point
on, 'despite various mutations, Soviet influence remained the
fundamental fact of life until the revolutions of 1989'.[83]

The *annus mirabilis* of 1989 constitutes the third great caesura in
modern European history. Timothy Garton Ash has suggested that
the history of Central Europe from 1949 could be written as:

> the story of attempts by European peoples to become once again the
> subjects rather than the objects of history. For Poles, Hungarians and
> Czechs this meant primarily the attempt to regain control over their
> own internal affairs, for to regain control over their external affairs
> was hardly to be dreamed of. It meant endeavouring to restore, by
> reform or revolution, what might be called 'internal sovereignty',

with citizens becoming willing, participant and enfranchised subjects rather than unwilling, non-participant and disenfranchised objects of state policy.[84]

For East Central Europe, therefore, the 1989 revolutions signified the rebirth of history, rather than its end. This 'rebirth of history in Eastern Europe', Misha Glenny has written, 'will enable the people to participate actively in determining their own fate, in most cases for the first time in half a century'.[85] The inspiration for the revolutions of 1989 came largely from the West – from the model of Western liberal democracy and social market economies which increasingly permeated the consciousness of the peoples of Central Europe as the 'Iron Curtain' became more porous. This gave them a unique quality. Unlike previous revolutions, they did not seek to establish something new and 'revolutionary'. Rather, they sought to 'rejoin' the European mainstream. In Jürgen Habermas's phrase, they constituted *die nachholende Revolution* ('the catching-up revolution').[86]

Nonetheless, this should not obscure their profound and far-reaching significance. The Visegrad peoples have won not only their internal sovereignty but also their external sovereignty. This they are now exercising in order to return to Europe. At the same time, the end of the Cold War has reopened the 'post-Habsburg' problem of political arrangements in East Central Europe, a problem apparently settled by Cold War bipolarity. A more multipolar economic and political system has emerged in Central and Eastern Europe, reminiscent to some extent of the 1920s, or even the 1880s.

Yet Europe on the eve of the twenty-first century is in many significant respects fundamentally different from the Europe of the nineteenth or early twentieth centuries. Western Europe has been transformed by post-industrialism, complex interdependence and globalisation. New institutions for multilateral cooperation have been created, and the political culture of Western and much of Central Europe has been transformed by the spread of democratic values. Within the wider transatlantic area, a *pluralistic security community* has emerged, in which war, and the threat of war, no longer play a part in state-to-state relations.[87] These transformations have already begun to exert a powerful influence on the politics and international relations of the new democracies of East Central Europe. This means that the Visegrad countries have regained their national sovereignty in the context of a continent being profoundly reshaped by both informal integration and multilateral institutions – developments which are transforming the very nature and meaning of 'sovereignty' itself.[88]

International relations in this region in the next century will therefore exhibit elements of both historical continuity and change. The French philosopher André Glucksman said in the autumn of 1989 that 'leaving communism means re-entering history'. Responding to this, Ferenc Gazdag has argued that developments in Central and Eastern Europe,

> can only be understood in the light of history. But history is being remobilized, and in a different way in every country, depending on what point in time the organic evolution was broken off in the given country. Today, our duty is not only to settle the problems of the present, but also those left over from the past.[89]

Endnotes

1   P. Wandycz, *The Price of Freedom*, London, Routledge, 1992, p. 11.
2   *Ibid.*, p. 10.
3   Norman Davies, *God's Playground: A History of Poland*, 2 vols, New York, Columbia University Press, 1982.
4   Robert Marshall, *Storm From the East. From Genghis Khan to Khubilai Khan*, London, BBC Books, 1993, pp. 108–15.
5   On the military aspects of this struggle see Wieslaw Majewski, 'The Polish art of war in the sixteenth and seventeenth centuries', in J. K. Fedorowicz, ed. and trans., *A Republic of Nobles. Studies in Polish History to 1864*, Cambridge, Cambridge University Press, 1982, pp. 179–97.
6   'The function of the wings has been (and will probably always be) a source of speculation and curiosity. Theories have included their being a defence against sword-cuts, or against lassoes; a souvenir worn only by veterans of wars against the Turks; or an attempt to make the wearers look like angels! Aside from the obvious motive, of simply wanting to look splendid, by far the most likely answer now appears to be that they were used as a device for scaring the enemy, especially the enemy's horses – not by any whistling sounds that they are alleged to have made, but by sheer visual impact. The wearing of wings is linked so closely with the wearing of furs that it would seem that the furs, wings and fluttering pennants were, in fact, all part of the same device.' Richard Brzezinski, *Polish Armies 1569–1696*, London, Osprey, 1987, p. 15.
7   G. R. Potter *et al.*, *The New Cambridge Modern History*, 7 vols, Cambridge, Cambridge University Press, 1957–70, vol. 1, p. 585.
8   Some international relations commentators, like Gentz and Burke, have argued that the partition of Poland was 'an aberration and a departure from

the true principles of the balance of power, which enjoined respect for the independence of all states, large and small alike'. Hedley Bull, however, argues that 'The principle of the preservation of the balance of power has undoubtedly tended to operate in favour of the great powers and at the expense of the small. Frequently, the balance of power among the great powers has been preserved through partition and absorption of the small'. He thus concludes that 'The partition of Poland was not a departure from the principle of balance of power but an application of it'. See Hedley Bull's classic text, *The Anarchical Society*, London, Macmillan, 1977, pp. 107–8.

9   Brian M. Downing, *The Military Revolution and Political Change: Origins of Democracy and Autocracy in Early Modern Europe*, Princeton, Princeton University Press, 1992.

10   *Ibid.*, p. 144.

11   Indeed, these clan affiliations were deemed so important that a knight assumed as his last name a part of his clan's battle cry.

12   The constitutional problems of the Polish diet, or *Sejm*, were typified by the institution of the Liberum Veto. Not only was the *Sejm* larger (and therefore even more unwieldy) than any other European diet, but its proceedings and decisions could be undone by a single unexplained shout of '*Nie pozwalam*' ('I do not allow it'). This absurd constitutional device paralysed effective administration and prevented any attempt at reforming the Polish state.

13   Downing, *op. cit.*, p. 145.

14   The Treaty of Westphalia was one of the most important events demarcating the medieval from the modern period in European history, but as Lynn Miller notes, 'Like all such historical benchmarks, Westphalia is in some respects more a convenient reference point than the source of a fully formed new normative system. Some elements that characterize the modern world, separating us from the Middle Ages, were well established long before 1648; others did not emerge until many years after. Still, the Peace of Westphalia created at least the foundations of a new European system – one that would not become truly a world system until the second half of the twentieth century – out of the ruins of the political structures and idealized rationale for them that had existed more or less unchanged in Europe for the preceding thousand years.' Lynn H. Miller, *Global Order: Values and Power in International Politics*, 3rd edn, Boulder, Westview, 1994, p. 20.

15   Downing, *op. cit.*, p. 156.

16   See Geoffrey Parker, *The Military Revolution: Military Innovation and the Rise of the West, 1500–1800*, Cambridge, Cambridge University Press, 1988; Michael Duffy, *The Military Revolution and the State 1500–1800*, Exeter, Exeter University Publications, 1980; and Jeremy Black, *A Military Revolution? Military Change and European Society 1550–1800*, London, Macmillan, 1991.

17   Downing, *op. cit.*, p. 155. Peter Englund, in his powerful and moving book *The Battle of Poltava: The Birth of the Russian Empire*, London, Victor Gollancz, 1992, has written of the Great Northern War (1700–21), 'The war prolonged the martyrdom of Poland. This pitiable country was now having to pay for its military and political weakness; again it became the battlefield of two great powers. On the one hand was a large Swedish army determined to

eat its way through an already substantially destitute countryside, and on the other a multitude of Russian forces with only one aim: to destroy as much as possible before their enemy arrived. On crossing the Silesian border the Swedish troops were at once confronted with thorough devastation. The Russians had burnt villages and towns, poisoned wells and terrorized the civilian population. For those who had grown used to the sumptuous billets in Saxony it was like being thrown straight out over an abyss. Poland was the grain of corn between two millstones' (pp. 42–3).

18 Davies, *op. cit.*, vol. 1, p. 515.
19 Downing, *op. cit.*, p. 154.
20 Wandycz, *op. cit.*, p. 10.
21 Emboldened by France (who saw a strong Poland as a barrier to Russo-German collusion), this new Polish state attempted to turn itself into a major power at the expense of the Germans, Russians, Ukrainians, Lithuanians and Czechs. Their ambitions and their aggressiveness were disapproved of by both President Woodrow Wilson and the British government. London was particularly concerned that Poland's territorial ambitions in the East could only be satisfied at the expense of peoples of mostly non-Polish stock. Hence they proposed the 'Curzon line', an attempt to define a realistic and just delineation of Poland's eastern border. In the end, Poland's military victories over the Red Army meant that the country's eastern border stretched 200 km beyond the 'Curzon line', and included about three million non-Poles. See C. J. Bartlett, *The Global Conflict. The International Rivalry of the Great Powers, 1880–1990*, 2nd edition, London, Longman, 1994, pp. 108 and 121.
22 The Belorussian, Ukrainian and Lithuanian minorities constituted majorities in a number of Poland's eastern provinces and northern areas. For details see Jerzy Tomaszewski, 'The national question in Poland in the twentieth century', in Mikuláš Teich and Roy Porter, eds, *The National Question in Europe in Historical Perspective*, Cambridge, Cambridge University Press, 1993, pp. 293–316 (p. 306).
23 'As the fragile structures of the new order of international relations, epitomised by the League of Nations, began to collapse, the new countries of eastern Europe became the objects of an increasingly deadly game of territorial revision, in which the two former great powers in the region ultimately colluded to devastating effect, in 1939'. David Kirby, *The Baltic World 1773–1993. Europe's Northern Periphery in an Age of Change*, London, Longman, 1995, p. 290.
24 Misha Glenny, *The Rebirth of History. Eastern Europe in the Age of Democracy*, London, Penguin, 1990, p. 50. More than six million Poles were killed during World War Two – a casualty rate of 18%. This compares with 0.2% in the USA, 1% in the UK, 7.4% in Germany and 11.2% in the Soviet Union. Fewer than 100,000 of these deaths occurred in the 35 days it took for the Wehrmacht to overwhelm the Polish army. The rest, including most of Poland's three million Jews, died in brave but futile uprisings, were murdered by the German occupiers, or perished in the concentration camps. Wandyzc, *op. cit.*, also notes that, 'Population losses were proportionally the highest in Europe, and they comprised wartime dead, postwar deportees to the USSR, and the political emigration in the West. In comparison with the prewar 35

million, Poland's population within the new borders in 1945 stood at 24 million inhabitants. The loss of $625 per capita, the destruction of 85% of Warsaw and some other cities, enormous cultural losses, all caused Poland to hold a number of grim records' (p. 238).

25 For details see Susanne Lotarski, 'The communist takeover in Poland', in Thomas T. Hammond, ed., *The Anatomy of Communist Takeovers*, New Haven, Yale University Press, 1975, pp. 339–67; and Norman Davies, 'Poland', in Martin McCauley, ed., *Communist Power in Europe 1944–49*, London, Macmillan, 1977, pp. 39–57.

26 See Timothy Garton Ash, *The Polish Revolution*, London, Granta, 1991; Neal Ascherson, *The Polish August. What Has Happened in Poland*, London, Penguin, 1981; and Janusz Ziolowski, 'The roots, branches and blossoms of Solidarnosc', in Gwyn Prins, ed., *Spring in Winter. The 1989 Revolutions*, Manchester, Manchester University Press, 1990, pp. 39–64.

27 'Continuity of direction – change in style and emphasis: this has been the hallmark of the foreign policies pursued by the post-communist parties that have gained power. Their paramount goal – integration with the West – is no different from that of their anti-communist predecessors'. Gabriel Partos, 'Who's afraid of post-communism?', *The World Today*, February 1995, pp. 28–32.

28 Jan B. de Weydenthal, 'Polish foreign policy after the elections', *RFE/RL Research Report*, 2, no. 41, 15 October 1993, pp. 17–19 (p. 17).

29 Janusz Stefanowicz, 'Central Europe between Germany and Russia. A view from Poland', *Security Dialogue*, 26, no. 1, 1995, pp. 55–64.

30 'The emergence of an independent Ukraine, Belarus and Lithuania presents the opportunity to rationalize relations along the Berlin–Warsaw–Moscow axis. The political pluralization of the territory between the Baltic and the Black Sea heads off the threat that Poland might be crushed between the two huge powers on either side. It also gives Polish politics greater room for manoeuvre. Needless to say, all this should foster in us a greater sense of added responsibility. For example, Poland's meddling in Ukrainian–Russian disputes would be suicidal.' Jerzy Marek Nowakowski, 'Germany, Russia and the Polish question', *East European Reporter*, 5, no. 5 (September/October 1992), pp. 26–8 (p. 28).

31 It is interesting to note that these two key institutions of medieval Europe also played a seminal role in the early development of international relations theory. As Torbjörn Knutsen has argued, it was within the conflict between the Catholic Church and the Holy Roman Empire that 'the seeds of International Relations theory germinated. They caused lasting theoretical debates about the nature of power and the division of political authority between religious and secular actors over the Christian world.... The debate about these questions is the closest there was to International Relations theorising in the High Middle Ages.' For further details see Dr Knutsen's informative and highly readable study, *A History of International Relations Theory*, Manchester, Manchester University Press, 1992, p. 17.

32 Philip Longworth, in *The Making of Eastern Europe*, London, Macmillan, 1992, argues that this was 'a political step devoid of the spiritual content with which it was subsequently invested, for its purpose was to obtain sanction for

an ecclesiastical organization, headed by its own archbishop, which would be independent of the German hierarchy and hence beyond the control of German secular rulers' (p. 283).

33   Quoted in *Eastern Europe*, Time Life Library of Nations, Amsterdam, Time Life Books, 1986, p. 42.

34   Milan Hauner, 'The Czechs and Germans: a one-thousand-year relationship', in Dirk Verheyen and Christian Soe, eds, *The Germans and Their Neighbours*, Boulder, Westview, 1993, pp. 251–78 (p. 259).

35   Arnošt Klíma, 'The Czechs', in Mikuláš Teich and Roy Porter, eds, *The National Question in Europe in Historical Perspective*, Cambridge, Cambridge University Press, 1993, p. 231.

36   Indeed, the Golden Bull of 1356 formally made the King of Bohemia the first of the imperial electors, and the Bohemian King Charles IV was also to reign as the Holy Roman Emperor, turning Prague into a great Central European capital.

37   Donald Matthew, *Atlas of Medieval Europe*, Oxford, Andromeda Books, 1991, pp. 189–90.

38   Wandycz, *op. cit.*, p. 43.

39   For details of the Hussites' extraordinary military feats, see Jon Swan, 'Brother Zizka's wagon-fort strategy', *Military History Quarterly*, 5, no. 4, summer 1993, pp. 44–7.

40   C. F. Black *et al.*, *Cultural Atlas of the Renaissance*, Oxford, Andromeda Press, 1993, pp. 137–9.

41   Windows have played an important part in Czech history. In 1414, after the martyrdom of Jan Hus, a procession of his supporters was stoned from the town hall in Prague. The incensed Hussites stormed the building and threw their assailants out of the windows. When news of this event – known as the First Defenestration of Prague – reached the Holy Roman Emperor, Václav IV, he was seized with a fatal attack of apoplexy. Bohemia was subsequently to be ravaged by the Hussite Wars. The Second Defenestration of Prague had even worse consequences: some Protestant nobles threw two Catholic governors and their clerks out of the windows of Prague Castle into the moat below. Their fall was actually broken by a heap of rubbish and, unharmed, they escaped to Vienna to tell their story. This event was to precipitate the carnage and blood-letting of the Thirty Years' War. The Third Defenestration of Prague occurred on 10 March 1948. During the closing stages of the communist takeover in Czechoslovakia, Jan Masaryk, the popular foreign minister and son of Tomáš Masaryk, fell – or more likely was pushed – out of a window. His body was found in the courtyard of the Foreign Ministry, which is situated at the crest of Prague's Charles Hill. The death of Jan Masaryk removed one of the last hindrances to the complete communist takeover of Czechoslovakia.

42   Herbert Langer, *The Thirty Years' War*, New York, Hippocrene Books, 1980.

43   David Kelly, 'Woodrow Wilson and the creation of Czechoslovakia', *East European Quarterly*, 26, no. 2, June 1992, pp. 185–207.

44   Longworth, *op. cit.*, pp. 68–9.

45   On the 'Munich betrayal' see John Hiden, *Germany and Europe 1991–1939*, 2nd edn, London, Longman, 1933, pp. 100–1, 162–7.

46 Martin Myant, *Socialism and Democracy in Czechoslovakia, 1945–48*, Cambridge, Cambridge University Press, 1981; Jon Bloomfield, *Passive Revolution. Politics and the Czechoslovak Working Class, 1945–48*, London, Allison and Busby, 1979; and Frantisek August and David Rees, *Red Star Over Prague*, London, The Sherwood Press, 1984.

47 Milan Simecka, *The Restoration of Order. The Normalization of Czechoslovakia, 1969–76*, London, Verso, 1984. For an 'official' Marxist-Leninist account of this depressing period in post-war Czechoslovak history see *An Outline of the History of the CPCz*, Prague, Orbis Agency, 1980.

48 For details see Gale Stokes, *The Walls Came Tumbling Down. The Collapse of Communism in Eastern Europe*, Oxford, Oxford University Press, 1993, pp. 131–67; and Nigel Hawkes, ed., *Tearing Down the Curtain. The People's Revolution in Eastern Europe*, London, Hodder & Stoughton, 1990, pp. 100–23.

49 Paul Laurent, 'Czech and Slovak arms sales policies: change and continuity', *Arms Control. Contemporary Security Policy*, 14, no. 2, April 1993, pp. 151–80.

50 John Feffer, *Shock Waves: Eastern Europe After the Revolutions*, Montreal, Black Rose Books, 1993, pp. 175–90.

51 The public image of the Czech Republic has been tarnished somewhat by a series of corruption and sleaze allegations which surfaced in late 1994. See Steve Kettle, 'Of money and morality', *Transition*, 1, no. 3, 15 March 1995, pp. 36–9

52 Otto Pick, 'The Czech Republic – a stable transition', *The World Today*, November 1994, pp. 206–8.

53 *Czech National Interests*, Prague, Institute for International Relations, 1993, p. 15.

54 Sixty-two per cent of the Czech Republic's borders are with German-speaking Europe.

55 In 1989, approximately 2,530,000 Czechs and only 676,000 Slovaks lived in cities with over 100,000 inhabitants. Moreover, Slovak towns tend to be smaller than Czech towns, and to have less diverse – and therefore less robust – local economies. See Karen Henderson, *Czechoslovakia: The Failure of Consensus Politics*, Leicester University Discussion Papers in Politics, August 1993, p. 16.

56 K. Henderson, *op. cit.*, p. 15.

57 Claudio Magris, *Danube*, London, Collins Havill, 1990, p. 222.

58 Emil Niederhauser, 'The national question in Hungary', in Mikulás Teich and Roy Porter, eds, *The National Question in Europe in Historical Perspective*, Cambridge, Cambridge University Press, 1993, pp. 248–69 (pp. 255, 259).

59 See Peter Brock, *The Slovak National Awakening*, Toronto, University of Toronto Press, 1976.

60 Indeed, much of the Slovak national identity was formed and developed in opposition to Hungary. The Slovak writer referred to earlier by Claudio Magris, Vladimír Minác, articulated the Slovak sense of hurt and resentment in the following terms: 'Should one touch healed wounds? Are the wounds really healed? National antagonism is a tough flower; if we do not talk about it, that does not signify it does not exist. Our relationship to the Hungarians

not only moulded our national life but also formed our way of thinking; it formed the soul of the nation'. Quoted by J. F. Brown, *Eastern Europe and Communist Rule,* Durham, Duke University Press, 1988, p. 433.

61   Josef Tiso – whose government implemented anti-Jewish legislation and who celebrated the brutal crushing of the Slovak uprising in August 1944 with a mass of thanksgiving at Banská Bystrica – was hanged for war crimes on 18 April 1947. For some Slovak nationalists, however, he remains a Slovak martyr. For further details see Owen Chadwick, *The Christian Church in the Cold War,* London, Penguin, 1993, pp. 61–2.

62   Magris, *op. cit.,* p. 226.

63   Sharon Fisher, 'Slovakia's foreign policy since independence', *RFE/RL Research Report,* 2, no. 49, 10 December 1993, pp. 28–34.

64   Sharon Fisher and Stefan Hrib, 'Political crisis in Slovakia', *RFE/RL Research Report,* 3, no. 10, 11 March 1994, pp. 20–6; Jan Obrman, 'The Slovak government versus the media', *RFE/RL Research Report,* 2, no. 6, 5 February 1993, pp. 26–30; and Sharon Fisher, 'The Gabcikovo–Nagymaros controversy continues', *RFE/RL Research Report,* 2, no. 37, 17 September 1993, pp. 7–12.

65   'If Slovakia is not allowed to participate fully in the Visegrad Group and provide a political, economic, and social bridge to Ukraine, thereby facilitating the evolution of a united Europe, then the Velvet divorce risks dividing Slovakia and Ukraine from the West.' Jeffrey Simon, *Czechoslovakia's 'Velvet Divorce', Visegrad Cohesion, and European Fault Line,* McNair Paper 23, Washington, DC, Institute for National Strategic Studies, 1993, p. 22.

66   Following recent archaeological excavations at a graveyard near Urumchi (the capital of Xinjiang province in the north-west of China), the Hungarian ethnographer Istvan Kiszely now believes that the ancient Magyars left Xinjiang no later than the fifth century and fell into a pattern of settling briefly, then moving westwards. As centuries passed, they mixed with the ancient Finns in Siberia where their unusual language (which belongs to the Ural-altaic group) evolved. He also suggests that their historical ancestors are the Ugars, of whom no more than 9,000 survive today. 'Hungarians go far, far east in search of their roots', *The Guardian,* 8 February 1995.

67   Hans-Georg Heinrich, *Hungary. Politics, Economics and Society,* London, Pinter, 1986, p. 1.

68   Between 899 and 955 the Magyars carried out at least 32 raids. Most were directed at the Holy Roman Empire, but France and Italy were also attacked. The Magyars themselves formed a kind of 'military republic' linking several tribes. Within it, only men fit for war exercised political rights. They fought primarily on horseback, armed with sword, spear and bow, and were lightly armed. Their enemies regarded them with terror, and they were suspected of drinking the blood of their victims. At the same time, westerners also admired their solidarity in combat: they always attempted to recover captured companions and were anxious to burn their war dead in order to carry home their ashes. For further details see Philippe Contamine, *War in the Middle Ages,* London, Basil Blackwell, 1984, pp. 32–5; and Sir Charles Oman, *A History of the Art of War in the Middle Ages,* Vol. 1: *378–1278 AD,* London, Greenhill Books, 1991, pp. 116–25.

69   See David Nicolle, *Hungary and the Fall of Eastern Europe, 1000–1558*, London, Osprey, 1988.

70   Istvan Lazar, *Hungary: A Brief History*, Budapest, Corvina, 1990.

71   Hans-Georg Heinrich, *op. cit.*, p. 6.

72   For full details see Emil Niederhauser, *op. cit.* p. 258.

73   Susan Strange, *States and Markets*, 2nd edn, London, Pinter, 1988, p. 18.

74   Wandycz, *op. cit.*, p. 11.

75   Admiral Horthy, Regent of Hungary, remains a controversial figure. In September 1993 he was reburied in a televised funeral in a manner more appropriate to a national hero: his funeral was attended by over 20,000 people, including eight ministers and nearly half the cabinet. The many victims of the Horthy regime were commemorated in emotional demonstrations organised by liberal and Jewish organisations on the eve of the funeral. The attempt to rehabilitate Horthy – admiral of a landlocked state, and regent of a country without a king – has been viewed with suspicion by some of Hungary's neighbours. They worry that a revival in nationalist passions within Hungary might lead to a revisionist foreign policy aimed at reversing the Trianon settlement. See 'Ugly memories', *The Economist*, 11 September 1993, pp. 43–4.

76   See M. D. Fenyo, *Hitler, Horthy and Hungary: German–Hungarian Relations, 1941–44*, New Haven, D. H. Back Press, 1972.

77   For details, see Hugh Seton-Watson, *Eastern Europe Between the Wars, 1918–1941*, New York, Harper and Row, 1967.

78   The phrase 'salami tactics' was used by the Hungarian communist leader Mátyás Rákosi to characterise the gradual but relentless concentration of political power into the hands of the Party. For details see Paul Ignotius, 'The first two communist takeovers of Hungary: 1919 and 1948', in Thomas T. Hammond, ed., *The Anatomy of Communist Takeovers*, New Haven, Yale University Press, 1975, pp. 385–98; and Bogdan Szajkowski, *The Establishment of Marxist Regimes*, London, Butterworth, 1982, pp. 69–71.

79   Timothy Garton Ash, *We the People: The Revolution of 1989*, Harmondsworth, Penguin, 1990, p. 14.

80   Alfred A. Reisch, 'The new Hungarian government's foreign policy', *RFE/RL Research Report*, 3, no. 33, 26 August 1994, pp. 46–57.

81   Brown, *op. cit.*, pp. 437–38.

82   Prime Minister Ántáll declared, 'I wish to be the head of government for ten million Hungarian citizens, but I wish to be the Prime Minister of fifteen million Hungarians emotionally as well as spiritually'. Foreign Minister Géza Jeszenszky has also raised the issue of reshaping Europe 'like the Vienna Congress had to do it in 1814–15 or like the Paris Conference did in 1919'. Quoted in Gabriel Munuera, *Preventing Armed Conflict in Europe: Lessons From Recent Experience*, Chaillot Paper 15/16, Paris, WEU Institute for Security Studies, 1994, p. 13.

83   David Reynolds, 'Thawing history: Europe in the 1990s and the pre-Cold War patterns', in Colin Crouch and David Marquand, eds, *Towards a Greater Europe? A Continent Without an Iron Curtain*, Oxford, Blackwell, 1992, pp. 9–33 (p. 18).

84   Timothy Garton Ash, *In Europe's Name. Germany and the Divided Continent*, London, Vintage, 1994, p. 22.
85   Glenny, *op. cit.*, p. 234.
86   Quoted by Fred Halliday, 'The end of the Cold War and international relations: some analytic and theoretical conclusions', in Ken Booth and Steve Smith, eds, *International Relations Theory Today*, Cambridge, Polity, 1995, pp. 38–61 (p. 41).
87   The concept of a 'pluralistic security community' derives from Karl Deutsch, S. A. Burrell, R. A. Kahn, *et al.*, *Political Community in the North Atlantic Area*, Princeton, Princeton University Press, 1957. Such a community exists when the likelihood of force between two or more states has virtually disappeared. This state of affairs can be said to exist when there are no military plans or deployments targeted against the other members of the community; when there is no expectation of war between these states; and when there is mutual acceptance and regular observance of the basic rules of international law. The implications of this concept, and its relevance for understanding the changing fabric of international relations in Europe, will be explored in subsequent chapters of this book.
88   See for example Joseph A. Camilleri and Jim Falk, *The End of Sovereignty. The Politics of a Shrinking and Fragmenting World*, Aldershot, Edward Elgar, 1992; Cynthia Weber, *Simulating Sovereignty. Intervention, the State and Symbolic Exchange*, Cambridge, Cambridge University Press, 1995; Marianne Heiberg, ed., *Subduing Sovereignty. Sovereignty and the Right to Intervene*, London, Pinter, 1994; and Neem Inayatullah and David Blaney, 'Realizing sovereignty', *Review of International Studies*, 21, no. 1, January 1995, pp. 3–20.
89   Ferenc Gazdag, 'Does the West understand Central and Eastern Europe?', *NATO Review*, December 1992, pp. 14–19 (p. 16).

Chapter Three

Geopolitics, culture and nationalism

> There was much in the history of Eastern Europe that overlapped
> with that of Western Europe and, to this extent, Eastern Europe is
> quintessentially a part of the broad pattern of shared experiences and
> values in the European arena. To a greater or lesser extent, especially
> in Central Europe, where Eastern Europe had adopted Western
> Christianity, these societies shared in aspects of feudalism, mediaeval
> Christian universalism, the Renaissance, the Reformation and
> Counter-Reformation and the Enlightenment. Yet each one of these
> was shared slightly differently, less intensively, less fully, with the
> result that East European participation in the European experience
> was only partial ...; how far any one society took part was
> determined by geography and politics, with the two often reinforcing
> each other. (George Schöpflin[1])

In the previous chapter, we examined the formative historical
developments which have shaped the texture of international politics
in the lands between the Neisse and the Bug. In this chapter, our
concern is with the impact on the region of geopolitics, culture and
nationalism, and our purpose is to identify what gives East Central
Europe its distinctive character within the wider international system.
These three factors – geopolitics, culture and nationalism – all play
a decisive role in determining the pattern of international relations in
the region. This chapter begins by analysing the geopolitics of East
Central Europe, concentrating on its location between Germany and
Russia, and its relative proximity to Asia. It then considers the
evolution over the last millennium of East Central Europe's
distinctive cultural identity, before moving on to an evaluation of the
significance of the ethno-national heterogeneity of the region for the
nationalist project in East Central Europe. Before concluding, the
chapter identifies the four key factors (economic development,

societal structure, political development and culture) which give the region its unique identity within the global system.

Geopolitics: geography and security

The character of East Central Europe has been much influenced by its physical, economic and human geography.[2] Clearly, geography alone does not determine the fate of nations – even though no less a figure than Napoleon Bonaparte went so far as to assert 'the policy of a state lies in its geography'. Nonetheless, it does provide an important context within which foreign policy options are weighed and considered. Moreover, as one writer has pointed out,

> In this political context, 'geography' means more than topological irregularity or climatic variation, more than distribution of mineral resources or configurations of human settlement, and even more than patterns of commerce and finance or networks of transport and communication. It signifies the almost a priori spatial frame of reference, which is usually centred on an imagined point of origin within the core area of a country from which the activities of that society are organized and proceed. The foreign thrusts as well as the domestic initiatives of a regime and nation are thus guided.[3]

The study of the interaction between geographical space and politics constitutes a distinctive theoretical approach within the social sciences known as geopolitics. Its origins lie with two politically engaged geographers writing at the turn of century, Karl von Haushofer and Sir Halford MacKinder. They were interested in the impact of rapid technological innovation on the spatial dynamics underlying the changing balance of global power. Both writers have been subsequently – and rightly – criticised for their part in legitimising imperial conquest. Nonetheless, they did perform a valuable service by opening up new lines of enquiry for students of international politics. MacKinder's writings are also of interest because of his comments on the geopolitical importance of Eastern Europe. His thesis was that the global system was dominated strategically by what he called the 'world island', that is, Eurasia and Africa. The key to control over this world island – what MacKinder, after Haushofer, identified as the geographical pivot, or 'heartland' of the world – was, he argued, Eastern Europe. He thus coined the aphorism, 'he who controls Eastern Europe controls the World Island, he who controls the World Island controls the world'.[4]

Geopolitics, as a distinctive branch of contemporary international relations theory, has been defined in one recent study as follows:

> Briefly stated, geopolitics is the applied study of the relationship of geographical space to politics. Geopolitics is therefore concerned with the reciprocal impact of spatial patterns, features, and structures and political ideas, institutions, and transactions. The territorial frameworks within which such interrelationships are played out vary in scale, function, range, and hierarchical level from the national, inter-transnational, and continental-regional to the provincial and local. The interaction of spatial and political processes at all these levels creates and moulds the international geopolitical system.[5]

The distinctive geopolitics of the Visegrad region derive from Eastern Europe's perceived location on the borderlines between Europe and Asia. For two millennia, the lands to the east of the Rhine and Danube rivers have constituted the borderlands of European civilisation. For the Roman Empire, the Rhine and Danube rivers provided defendable natural borders. The lands to the east were left either outside the Empire, or constituted part of its military borders – as with Pannonia (latter-day Hungary).[6] With the emergence of medieval Christendom, the kingdoms of Poland, Hungary and Bohemia found themselves serving as the bulwark of European civilisation against perceived threats from Asia and the East.

Thus one important feature of the region's spatial location is its relative proximity to Asia. The steppes of Central Asia and the mountains of Anatolia were for centuries the source of a series of threats to Europe. The Huns, Visigoths, Vandals, Mongols and Turks who thundered out of Asia brought death and destruction in their wake.[7] The impact of this was felt most immediately and most painfully by the peoples of Eastern Europe. Indeed, this region acted as a buffer zone for Central and Western Europe, absorbing many of the shock waves from Asia before they could cause major disruption to the lands west of the Rhine and the Danube. In geopolitical terms, therefore, Eastern Europe constituted a 'crush zone' or 'shatterbelt' between Christian Europe and the Eurasian heartland.[8]

East Central Europe has been especially vulnerable to invasion because of its physical topology (see Map 3, p. xviii). Much of the region is covered by broad plains, which provide few natural barriers to invasion.[9] Most of Poland is covered by the North European Plain. Indeed, the name 'Poland' comes from the Slavic word 'Pole', meaning 'field'. Bohemia is situated on the Hercynian plateau, whilst much of Hungary lies in the Pannonian basin. The only significant Alpine-type fold mountains are the Carpathians, which run through Slovakia and parts of northern Hungary and southern Poland. Unfortunately, they lie on an east–west axis and therefore provide little protection from invading armies from the east.

East Central Europe's socio-economic development has been shaped by another major geographical feature, the Danube. In Western Europe, the Rhine became an important trading conduit, linking Switzerland, France, Germany, Belgium and Holland. The Rhine empties into the Atlantic, thereby linking the heartlands of Western Europe with global trading routes and colonies. This proved an important means of facilitating economic development and stimulating political modernisation at the close of the fifteenth century. Unfortunately for Eastern Europe, the Danube, which flows from Bavaria, through Austria, Slovakia, Hungary, Serbia and Romania to the Black Sea, could not play an analogous role.[10] Its utility for trade was impeded by the expansion of the Ottoman Empire into the Balkans after the fall of Constantinople in 1453. This meant that the Danube flowed through the Ottoman Empire and emptied into what was effectively a Turkish lake. This did not offer the sort of trading opportunities which encourage economic growth and modernisation.[11] Moreover, Eastern Europe also suffered when, at the start of the sixteenth century, the trade route linking Europe and China via the Middle East (which prior to 1500 had predominated in the Eurasian trade nexus) was replaced by a trans-oceanic nexus – dominated by the West European maritime powers – based on new logistical capabilities.[12] The fall of Constantinople had particularly dire consequences for Poland: it severed Polish trade with the Levant, leading to the rapid decline of many once-thriving Polish towns.[13] At the same time, Poland failed to secure control over the Baltic ports, even after winning suzerainty over East Prussia in the early fifteenth century. With the ceding of the region to Brandenburg in 1660, Poland's maritime opportunities declined even further.[14]

In a number of ways, therefore, geography has not been kind to the peoples of East Central Europe. However, with the end of the

Cold War and the emergence of a new chapter in world politics, this
may be changing. East Central Europe could well be emerging as a
crucial 'gateway region' within the international system. Saul Cohen,
a contemporary theorist of geopolitics, has defined gateway regions
as those which stimulate socio-economic and political interaction; act
as a link in an increasingly interdependent world; and 'facilitate the
boundaries of accommodation'. Cohen regards the whole of Central
and Eastern Europe as a gateway region, 'fully open to economic
forces from the East and West.... The promise of the gateway region
is that it will facilitate the transfer to economic innovation from west
to east and, ultimately, the reverse'. He argues that 'A gateway region
has "hinges" – key states that take the lead as economic and social
mediators in opening up the region in both directions'. In the context
of the Central and East European gateway, it may well be the
Visegrad countries which fulfil this 'hinge' function, given the
intensity of their economic and social interactions with both East and
West, and their traditional role on the crossroads of Europe and
Asia.[15] This is an issue to which we will return at the end of chapter
six ('Relations with the East').

Culture: between East and West?

The defining cultural affinities of East Central Europe were laid in
the fourth century by Emperor Constantine the Great. In 395 AD he
divided the Roman Empire into East and West. This decision was to
have a profound cultural, social and political impact on the future of
the European continent. The culture and social structures of the
Eastern, Byzantine Empire shaped the subsequent development of the
Orthodox heritage. The influence of this continues to be felt today in
the mainly Slavic lands of Russia, Ukraine, Bulgaria, Serbia and
Macedonia, along with the non-Slavic but Orthodox lands of
Romania, Greece and Armenia. In the West, a Romano-German
heritage was to develop, shared by both Catholics and Protestants
even after the Reformation. As these early divisions between
Orthodox East and Catholic West took shape, the lands of Poland,
Bohemia, Moravia and Hungary were subject to influences from both
East and West. Their conversion to Christianity had begun in the late
ninth century with the missions of Cyril and Methodius to Moravia.
Eastern Orthodox Christianity also had a significant impact on

Bohemia, Hungary, Croatia and parts of Poland in the early medieval period. Yet in most respects they were all very Western in culture and religion, primarily because they looked to Rome for spiritual leadership.

East Central Europe, whilst not always involved in the mainstream of European developments, has nevertheless been affected by all the great historical experiences of European civilisation – feudalism, medieval Christian universalism, the Renaissance, the Reformation, the Counter-Reformation and the Enlightenment. The same is not true of the lands to their east and south, which were initially marked by the cultural influences of Byzantium and Orthodox Christianity, and which were later largely subsumed by Moscovy-Russia and the Ottoman Empire.

At the same time, East Central Europe has provided a buffer and a protective zone for the rest of Europe from many of the destructive threats coming from the east. As we have already noted, whenever hordes of nomadic warriors descended on Europe from the steppes of Asia, their impact was felt most immediately and most harshly in the lands of Eastern Europe. This was most dramatically the case with the Mongol invasions of the thirteenth century, which caused untold suffering and destruction to the peoples of Poland and Hungary – a trauma which is still remembered each day in Cracow.[16] Later in the fourteenth century, the threat came from the Ottoman Empire. Turkish armies defeated the Serbs in 1389, the Hungarians in 1526, and by 1529 were at the gates of Vienna. By the mid-sixteenth century, only Poland and Bohemia were holding out against the Muslim invasion. In contrast, Western Europe had freed itself of foreign occupation in 1492, when the Moors were finally expelled from Granada and Andalusia.

These historical experiences have made a deep impression on the self-perception of the peoples of East Central Europe. To begin with, they have long regarded themselves as lying at the geographical centre of Europe. Geographically, Prague lies equidistant between Madrid and Moscow, but it is often forgotten that Prague lies to the west of that quintessentially Central European city, Vienna. The citizens of Warsaw and Budapest also vigorously lay claim to being at the geographical heart of Europe. Second, they tend to regard themselves as the bulwark of Christian civilisation, the *antemurale Christianitatis*. Their long struggles against the Mongols and Turks have left them with the strong self-perception that they have for centuries been the staunchest and most exposed defenders of Christendom, and that their eastern frontiers mark the frontiers of European Christian civilisation against 'Asia' and the East.[17]

Yet their eastern frontiers were never territorially rigid and culturally impenetrable. Rather than simply being barriers against the peoples and influences from the East, the lands of East Central Europe functioned as a cultural crossroads – a European 'melting pot'. The influences of Byzantium, Ottoman Turkey, Orthodox Christianity and Western Asia all strongly permeated Poland and Hungary.[18] This influence was especially marked in their eastern provinces (what is today Belarus, Ukraine and Transylvania), and can still be seen in the architecture, national dress, food and culture of East Central Europe – all of which contain strong elements of 'orientalisation'.[19]

The permeability of the region's borders to influences from both East and West has led to some novel conceptualisations of the place of East Central Europe in the wider continent. A key role early on in this debate was played by émigré intellectuals from the region. Writing in the 1950s and 1960s, Oscar Halecki, a Polish historian working in the USA, published two influential books: *Borderlands of Western Civilisation* and *The Limits and Divisions of European History*. He divided Europe into four distinct regions: Western, West Central, East Central, and Eastern. Two decades later the Hungarian scholar Jenö Szücs published *The Three Historical Regions of Europe*. This redefined and developed Halecki's concepts, but dropped the 'West Central' component.[20]

The discussion about the distinctiveness of East Central Europe re-emerged in the 1980s as Cold War definitions of 'Eastern Europe' began to lose conviction. The debate centred on the notion of *Mitteleuropa* ('Central Europe'), popularised by the German writer Friedrich Naumann during World War One.[21] As Misha Glenny has noted, '[t]he debate about Central Europe has been one of the most fruitful of the last twenty years but also one of the most complex and verbose'.[22] For all the participants in this fascinating debate, 'Central Europe' was defined, not by geography, but by values. 'Central Europe' was, in Györy Konrád's words, a *Weltanschauung*, not a *Staatsangehorigkeit* (i.e., a way of looking at the world rather than a question of citizenship); for Leszek Kolakowski it was a 'culturally connected area'; for Stefan Kaszynski a 'state of mind'; for Czeslaw Milosz 'a way of thinking'.[23]

For the Czechoslovak writer Milan Kundera, the use of the term *Mitteleuropa* was designed to emphasise the 'Europeanness' of the region's culture, despite its political and military domination by the 'Asiatic' Russians. Bemoaning what he saw as the 'tragedy of Central Europe', Kundera argued that *Mitteleuropa* 'is a piece of the Latin West which has fallen under Russian domination ... [and] which lies geographically in the center, culturally in the West and politically in the East'.[24]

For others, such as Konrád or Václav Havel, Central Europe possessed features which distinguished it from both Western individualism and Eastern collectivism. The values of Central Europe were different from both Western-style consumer capitalism and Soviet-style state socialism: they rejected politics and power per se, advocated non-violence, emphasised the importance of building up 'civil society' from below, and identified with that section of the Western peace movement which both denounced great power politics and human rights violations. Some have questioned whether these values are actually any different from the values of Western liberalism, namely pluralist democracy, human rights, individual liberties, tolerance, and so on. Claudio Magris, for example, has argued that 'for Konrád, as for Kundera, Mitteleuropa becomes a word that is noble, but at the same time vague and generic, an illusory master-key for each and every political aspiration'.[25] Misha Glenny has also commented (somewhat cynically) that the 'idea that a certain set of values binds these countries and some of their neighbours would be appealing if the values were not usually restricted to a small pool of intellectuals'.[26]

On the other hand, as Jacques Rupnik argued at the time when the communist dominoes were toppling across Eastern Europe, the idea of 'Central Europe' had been 'one of the major intellectual developments of the 1980s and [would] no doubt be a vital ingredient in the reshaping of the political map of Europe in the post-Yalta era'.[27] It was certainly a concept endorsed as a viable political project by Václav Havel when he addressed the Polish *Sejm* in January 1990. He spoke optimistically of there being a 'real historic chance to fill with something meaningful the great political vacuum that appeared in Central Europe after the break-up of the Habsburg Empire. We have the chance to transform Central Europe from a phenomenon that has so far been historical and spiritual into a political phenomenon'.[28]

With the benefit of hindsight, the *Mitteleuropa* debate can be seen as the most recent attempt by Central European intellectuals to conceptualise the specificities of their geopolitical and geocultural situation on the borderlands between European Christendom and the Orthodox and Muslim East. It is clear that this unique experience between East and West – between Europe and Asia – has given the East Central Europeans a distinctive character and identity. This is an issue to which we will return at the end of this chapter.

Nationalism

Nationalism and ethnicity

With the collapse of the communist regimes in 1989, nationalism has re-emerged as the single most powerful political force in East Central Europe. Although analysts dispute whether its impact is malevolent or constructive, there is no doubting its centrality to the politics and international relations of the region. Jack Snyder, for example, has warned that 'the possibility of a rising tide of nationalism poses the greatest challenge to the security of the new Europe'.[29] In the context of economic dislocation, social tension and political uncertainty, nationalism is a particularly potent force. It can be, and all too often has been, associated with authoritarianism, anti-Semitism and intolerance. On the other hand, a sense of national solidarity can help societies withstand the pressures of wholesale transformation, and generate a greater degree of civic pride and communal cohesion. As Judy Batt, one of the most perceptive writers on East Central Europe, has argued,

> nationalism has played an ambiguous, at times disastrous, role in Eastern Europe's political development, appearing as a form of fascism, exhibiting the parochial, intolerant, anti-semitic traditionalism that has yet to be firmly laid to rest in the region.
> However, in the current circumstances, not only can nationalism not be simply ignored or suppressed, but its potential positive contribution should be recognized. Nationalist politics provides the emotional appeal that can win wide allegiance from a fragmented, atomized society, overcome the deep sense of humiliation inherited from the experience of communist dictatorship, and provide convincing reasons why people should once again be asked to tighten their belts and to display political altruism.[30]

In order to understand the nature and potential of nationalism in East Central Europe today, it is necessary to consider both the general features of nationalism as a political force, and to analyse the specific features of nationalism as it has developed in this region over the last two hundred years. Nations themselves are highly complex and diverse social collectivities. Their complexity and diversity are inevitably reflected in the essential uniqueness and historical contingency of different nationalist political movements. Consequently, as Thomas Simons has noted, 'nationalism, like dependence, has had its own "long march" through the experience of Eastern Europe. It has never been a "given". It is always a contingent and specific phenomenon like all the rest, changing its form, its weight, and its impact over time, and depending on circumstance'.[31]

Any analysis of nationalism must begin with a definition of what is meant by that essentially contested term, the 'nation'. Stalin defined the concept as 'an historically constituted, stable community of people, formed on the basis of common language, territory, economic life, and psychological make-up manifested in a common culture'.[32] More recently, Anthony Smith has defined a nation as 'a named human population sharing an historic territory, common myths and historical memories, a mass, public culture, a common economy and common legal rights and duties for all members'.[33]

Defining 'nationalism' is no less contentious than defining what constitutes a 'nation'. Elie Kedourie's oft-quoted definition is of a doctrine which 'holds that humanity is naturally divided into nations, that nations are known by certain characteristics which can be ascertained, and that the only legitimate type of government is national self-government'.[34] Although different definitions of nationalism emphasise different aspects, there is broad agreement that the *subjective* dimension is of considerable significance. Anthony Giddens, for example, sees nationalism as 'primarily psychological';[35] Benedict Anderson describes nations as 'imagined communities';[36] similarly, Hans Kohn has described nationalism as 'that state of mind in which the supreme loyalty of the individual is felt to be due to the nation-state'.[37]

One issue which has generated considerable controversy in the contemporary literature on nationalism is the extent to which national identity is an artificial, modern construct, rather than an identity built on a pre-existing, pre-modern, perennial *ethnie*. Some, like Eric Hobsbawn,[38] emphasise the strong link between the nation and 'modernity', and argue that the emergence of nationalism as a political movement was intimately related to the transition from basically rural, agricultural and traditional societies to complex, modern industrialised societies, and involved the creation of invented traditions. Others, like Anthony Smith and John Armstrong, have drawn attention to the importance of pre-modern ethnic identities – with their myths, memories and traditions – for the articulation of the modern project of nation-building and political nationalism.[39]

Both of these schools of thought offer important insights into the nature of national identity. A full understanding of nationalism needs to take into account both the importance of pre-modern ethnic traditions and identities, as well as the role of political organisations and movements in constructing a sense of nationhood. National identity, Ole Waever has suggested, is 'a discursive construction, but yet it has to work on raw material – there has to be a reservoir of myths, stories, old battles and historic figures. This past is neither determining nor trivial for contemporary national movements and identifications'.[40] In East Central Europe, therefore, the nationalist movements of the late nineteenth century drew heavily on past glories, myths and symbols, but gave them a new interpretation, meaning and significance.

The evolution of national identity

From their very earliest days, the new Christian kingdoms of East Central Europe were multinational in character. Waves of migration from the east left a large number of intermingled ethno-linguistic groups within fairly fluid state borders. The late medieval era saw the emergence of a number of large dynastic states composed of many different ethnic groups. The Polish–Lithuanian Commonwealth was one, the Hungarian kingdom was another. In these multi-ethnic kingdoms, the source of political legitimacy was dynastic and divine. National sentiments had no particular political importance, and were certainly not seen as the source of political authority, nor as the primary identity of the people.[41]

In Western Europe in the pre-modern era, kingdoms were also composed of a heterogenous mix of different ethnic and linguistic groups, and political legitimacy was seen as deriving from God and the monarch. The difference was that in the West strong centralised states emerged which were able to impose a greater uniformity on their inhabitants and to create an embryonic sense of nationhood.[42] In France and England, for example, strong centralised and bureaucratic states were created by the post-medieval, absolutist monarchies of the Tudors and later Valois. These states began a process of social and political engineering which sought to integrate potentially conflicting interests into a competitive, but peaceful, union based on perceived common interests. This process of social engineering was able to build on a common language, shared experiences and cultural compatibilities, but nonetheless involved a conscious use of centralised state power (through education, fiscal policy, 'national' symbols, etc.) to foster the notion of being part of a distinct political community. In this way, these states began the task of laying the foundations for the subsequent forging of the modern French and British 'nations' in the eighteenth and nineteenth centuries.[43]

The centralising and integrative functions of these post-medieval West European states became significant with the onset of 'modernity', a process associated economically with the Industrial Revolution and politically with the French Revolution. The Industrial Revolution provided the catalyst for a series of social and economic changes which replaced the fixity of location within a stable and stratified social structure with a process of constant and unremitting change, innovation and fluidity. In this age of rapid technological development and social flux, the individual's concept of time, order and legitimacy were all irrevocably changed: the formerly religious, stable and structured society of the High Middle Ages gave way to one where space and identity depended on politically created patterns and structures. In Karl Marx's memorable phrase, 'all that is solid melts into air'. As Gellner has suggested, in modern societies characterised by high levels of occupational mobility and unceasing innovation, the 'mystical symbolism of a religion' is less and less able to provide the cultural and ideological cement to hold a dynamic society together. Nationalism, he argues, was thus in part an attempt to create a new basis for societal cohesion and political community in an age of dynamic change and fluidity.[44]

In political terms, the modern emergence of national identity as a central source of legitimacy and authority was closely bound up with the French Revolution. Indeed, in the process of nation-building, the French Revolution constitutes a profound watershed. Having executed their king and established the Republic, the revolutionaries of Paris had to look for a new source of authority, neither dynastic nor divine. The answer was the popular legitimacy of the 'nation' – a concept which had its roots in popular traditions, a common language and a defined territory, but which was also created through the introduction of new symbols, institutions and structures (not least, conscription in the 'national' armies of France). '*Le national*', Douglas Johnson has written, 'replaced *le roi* in the hierarchy of the state'.[45]

'Western' and 'Eastern' concepts of nationalism

When nationalism as a political movement emerged in Western Europe, it did so in a context where distinctive political communities had already been forged by the strong, integrating states of the pre-modern era. Nationalism developed within existing state structures, and a population existed which fitted the 'national' territory. In this context, nationalism functioned as a political movement aimed at transforming existing dynastic states into 'people's states'. In Western Europe, therefore, nationalism took the form of 'civic nationalism'. Nationality was defined primarily by territoriality and legal definitions of citizenship, and was thus closely linked to concepts of constitutional government, liberal democracy and citizenship with civic freedoms.[46]

In stark contrast, when nationalist movements emerged in Central and Eastern Europe (largely as a product of forces unleashed by the Napoleonic wars), they did so in the context where neither the state nor homogenous political communities existed. They were therefore inspired by a very different concept of nationhood – one defined in ethnic terms. Nationalist movements in Poland, the Czech lands, Slovakia and Hungary emerged in opposition to the multinational empires within which they felt trapped. Consequently their notion of nationhood could not be bound up with territoriality and legal concepts of citizenship. Instead, their notion of national identity was influenced by the Romantic movement and German idealism, and conceived in terms of ethnicity, culture and language. In contrast to Western nationalism, which was influenced by the universalism of the Enlightenment and informed by an ontological individualism, Eastern or 'Romantic nationalism' emphasised the worth and distinctiveness of individual cultures and languages, and embodied a more organic conception of the ethnic or *Volk* community as the basis of the nation.[47]

This 'ethnic nationalism' involved a much clearer distinction between *citizenship* and *nationality* than in English- or French-speaking countries. Because the existing state was often in the hands of foreign rulers, societal institutions became the mainstay of national identity. Thus whereas in the West an autonomous civil society became the bedrock of pluralism, individual liberty and democratic government, in East Central Europe it was perceived as the principal defender of nationhood. Moreover, as 'national identity' became an instrument of exclusivity, society in Eastern Europe was all too often coloured by an illiberal and intolerant attitude towards 'non-national' or 'anti-national' forces – in particular minority groups such as Jews, Germans or Gypsies.[48]

Hans Kohn played an influential role in exploring this essential difference between Western and Eastern concepts of nationalism. He suggested that while West European nationalism 'corresponded to changing social, political and economic realities, it spread to Central and Eastern Europe before a corresponding social and economic transformation'. This, he believed, had resulted in two very different types of nationalism: 'one based upon liberal middle class concepts and pointing the way to a consummation in a democratic world society, the other based upon irrational and pre-enlightenment concepts tending toward exclusiveness'.[49]

The nationalism which developed in East Central Europe in the late nineteenth century was thus much more bound up with ethnicity, language and culture than Western nationalism, which tended to link nationality to territoriality and citizenship rights. Piotr Wandycz has argued that the reason for this should not be attributed simply to the greater ethno-national heterogeneity of the region. Instead, he suggests, the crucial reason for the difference between 'Western' and 'Eastern' nationalism is that for much of Central and Eastern Europe, the process of building states and nations was interrupted by foreign invasion and occupation:

> It was the interruption of statehood, in Poland's case through the partitions, that vitiated the process of nation forming along the Western lines. The result was an evolution toward a different concept of nationhood, colored by the romantic outlook, conceived in terms of ethnicity and cultural-linguistic criteria. It promoted the rise or revival of nations that either never had their own statehood

(Slovaks) or had lost it at early times. In that sense it was not so much the multi-ethnic character of the historic Poland, Hungary, or Bohemia, as the interrupted statehood that brought the nationality issue to the fore.[50]

The interruption of statehood thus left the ethno-national topology of the eastern half of the continent much more diverse and heterogenous than in the West.[51] The distribution of divergent ethnic, cultural, linguistic and religious communities across this part of the continent often seems to be as random as the patterns produced by shaking a kaleidoscope. Different communities and peoples are scattered widely across the region, producing a rich tapestry of intricately intermingled groups. Some of this cultural richness has diminished as a result of the tragedies and suffering of the twentieth century: Jewish communities were almost wiped out by the Holocaust, whilst many Germans were expelled from Slavic lands at the end of World War Two. Yet even today, the heterogeneity of the region makes it virtually impossible to draw up uncontentious borders of would-be nation states in ways that do not exclude some nationals and include other national minorities.

In the past, this ethno-national complexity has produced many bitter disputes. However, there is no reason for assuming that past nationalist animosities in East Central Europe will inevitably re-emerge. As we have seen, nationalism as a political project can and has varied significantly in different economic, social and inter-national contexts. As East Central Europe prepares to enter the twenty-first century, there is already growing evidence to suggest that the political complexion of nationalism in the region will be significantly different in character from the nationalism of the nineteenth and early twentieth centuries.

East Central Europe and the 'new nationalist myth'

When nationalist movements developed in Central and Eastern Europe in the nineteenth century, they did so in the context of an anarchic, multipolar balance of power, in which parliamentary forms of government were the exception not the rule, and in which ideas of democracy and human rights were regarded as dangerously subversive. However, nationalism in post-communist East Central Europe has re-emerged in the context of a continent transformed by

the processes of democratisation, globalisation, complex interdependence and institutionalised multilateral cooperation. Moreover,
there have been profound changes in the domestic politics and
societies of the Visegrad countries in the post-war period. As Judy
Batt has written, 'the underlying motive force of these countries'
development since the Second World War, culminating in 1989', has
been 'the steady maturation of the popular will to "rejoin the West",
to live under democratic government and to work in a free
economy'.[52] This changed international and domestic context in
which nationalism has re-emerged in East Central Europe has
modified the political character of nationalism in the region. As
Victor Zaslavsky has argued, a 'new nationalist myth' has emerged
in Eastern Europe: 'It is the myth of belonging to European culture,
the myth of return to real or imaginary European roots, the myth of
normal development brutally interrupted by the Bolshevik experiment or the Russian aggression or both.'[53]

This 'myth' of belonging to Europe was very evident in the
intellectuals' debate on *Mitteleuropa* in the 1980s, and its roots can
be traced back through the history of East Central Europe to early
medieval Christendom. The new nationalist myth acquired popular
endorsement in the heady days of autumn 1989. There was subsequently a widespread popular consensus for a return to Europe which
continues to unite almost all parts of the new political spectrum in
the Visegrad four. Domestically, it has inspired a far-reaching reform
programme aimed at producing liberal democratic market
economies; internationally, it attracts them towards the West and
towards the processes of European integration. As Peter Frank has
argued, the widely held perception that the countries of the region
constitute 'part of a broad European cultural tradition to which they
hope to return' may well be a myth. Nonetheless, 'myths can be very
powerful and if this one is capable of encouraging self-restraint and
the maintenance of peace in the region, good luck to it!'[54]

The new nationalist myth in Eastern Europe thus attempts to
define contemporary national identity in terms of European values
and a European cultural heritage. The desire to return to Europe and
embrace European values has led to a growing acceptance in much
of East Central Europe of liberal democracy, human rights,
multilateral cooperation and European integration. Consequently,
traditional Eastern nationalism of the sort discussed above is being
tempered and constrained by political and moral values derived from

the mainstream of Europe's Enlightenment and liberal humanist traditions. In this way, a more complex national identity is being created from an amalgam of traditional nationalist identities and contemporary 'European' values and attributes.

Developing this theme further, it could be argued that what may be emerging in East Central Europe is a shift towards multiple loyalties, with the primary focus on the nation being supplemented by European and regional affiliations above and below the existing state. This has certainly been the pattern of development in Western Europe in the last few decades.[55] Loyalties have not been transferred simply from one dominant focus to another: rather, identities have been become diffused among different levels of community – local, national, European – by a process of cultural, economic and societal interaction and transnational exchange.[56]

This is the reverse of the process which gave rise to the modern state. As Martin Wight has argued, in medieval Christendom, individuals had an inner web of customary loyalties to an 'immediate feudal superior' and an outer web of 'customary religious obedience to the Church under the Pope'. With the rise of the modern state, a 'revolution in loyalties' occurred, in which an 'inner circle of loyalty expanded' and 'an outer web of loyalty shrank'.[57] Henceforth, with the onset of modernity, the primary focus of loyalty and identity became the nation state.

However, in post-war Western Europe, there has been a noticeable shift towards multiple loyalties, and it is this process which may now be occurring in East Central Europe. This shift towards multiple loyalties is being encouraged by three underlying secular trends: first, a strengthening of the normative framework of the European society of states, particularly in terms of the growing acceptance of internationally defined standards of basic human rights (expressed through the UN, the OSCE and the Council of Europe);[58] second, an increasing awareness of the need for multilateral action to tackle transnational problems such as environmental and ecological degradation, structural unemployment and regional inequalities; and third, the impact of economic and technological globalisation on traditional notions of state sovereignty.[59]

Thus there is good reason for believing that continuing progress in integration in multilateral European institutions, coupled with an acceleration of the impact of globalisation and interdependence on the region, might well modify the political character of nationalism in significant respects. In particular, it might impart to national identity in East Central Europe a more liberal, tolerant and accommodating complexion, in which concepts of civic nationalism take precedent over those of ethnic nationalism. The European idea, George Kolankiewicz notes, 'has acted successfully as a political-cultural as well as an economic template'. Consequently, 'Respect for citizenship rights, civil, political and social, is now a priority for all parties and extremism has been largely marginalized'.[60] The process of European integration and global interdependence is thus intensifying a longstanding struggle for the 'soul' of nationalism in the region. At its most polarised, this struggle is between liberal cosmopolitans on the one side (who are seeking to define national identity in terms of pluralist democracy, an open civil society and European values), and traditionalists and conservatives on the other (who seek reassurance in the verities of an imagined past, and who are attempting to define the nation in terms of ethnic purity, cultural exclusivity and national solidarity).[61]

This struggle between competing visions of national identity in an era of European integration and economic globalisation has transformed the nature of domestic politics in much of post-communist Europe. At a conference of East Central Europeans in Bratislava in April 1990, the veteran dissidents and human rights activists Adam Michnik and György Konrád both warned that national bigotry and inter-communal violence represented the biggest threat to the peaceful and democratic evolution of the region. Michnik went on to argue that the central political cleavage in Eastern Europe was no longer between left and right, but between those – primarily urban-based, secular, liberal progressive groups – who spoke of a 'European potential' and who favoured an outward-looking and liberal approach, and proponents of an inward-looking and parochial obscurantism who emphasised the need for a revival of pre-communist, national traditions and cultures (often linked to the more conservative trends in Catholicism).[62] The former group were active in fostering and propagating the new nationalist myth of a European nationalist identity, and provided the political bedrock of support for an open civil society and a democratic polity. This more liberal and outward-looking group also advocate 'a more western-orientated politics which stresses the rapid transition to a market economy as the only real way to solve economic problems'.[63] The latter group sought to protect the nation from 'contaminating' external influences, and tended to pursue a populist politics which was wary of radical economic reform. 'This politics is often rather anti-western and sometimes echoes national themes such as anti-semitism'.[64]

This division in the domestic politics of the Visegrad countries between outward-looking liberals and inward-looking conservatives remains decisive – even more so in the light of the re-emergence of post-communist parties and their electoral successes in Poland and Hungary. Gabriel Partos writes:

> The initial record of the post-communist Governments suggests that the once-sharp distinction between ex-communists and the rest of the political establishment is becoming increasingly irrelevant. There has been considerable cooperation across the old divide. The main division that cuts across East-Central Europe's new political land-scape is between parties that support radical or extreme forms of nationalism, intolerance and authoritarian rule as against those that espouse broadly liberal and pluralistic values.[65]

The demise of communist authoritarianism in the region, therefore, does not simply mean the rebirth of history, with its legacy of nationalist conflicts and cultural intolerance. Rather, national identities are being redefined in the context of a Europe transformed by political integration and economic globalisation. More than at any previous time in the long history of East Central Europe, domestic developments are intimately bound up with broader developments in Europe and the wider international system. This has introduced a new and complex dynamic into the politics of the region. As Gale Stokes has argued, although the more intolerant and ethnically based nationalism of Eastern Europe continues to exert its baleful influence,

> it is not impossible that the twenty-first century style of nationalism will be less disruptive and more protective of the status quo. The international agreements of the last half of the twentieth century have produced standards of minority treatment and of border inviolability that could, when backed by an international structure analogous to the European Community, reduce twenty-first century nationalism to a form of patriotism not inconsistent with political stability. In the European Community today, for example, it is possible for a Florentine to be a city booster, a Tuscan patriot, an Italian citizen, and an advocate of European unity all at the same time, or at least at different times as the situation demands.[66]

The impact of European political integration and economic globalisation on the domestic politics of East Central Europe, along with the changing nature of national identity in the region, is an important issue which is vital for understanding contemporary developments in the region. We will return to this important theme in the concluding chapter of this book.

The distinctiveness of East Central Europe

In this chapter we have considered the impact of geography, culture and nationalism on East Central Europe. One further question needs to be addressed: what gives the region its distinctive character and identity? Here, four factors are of particular significance: economic development, social structure, political development, and culture.

Economic development

East Central Europe has always been less developed than the countries to its west, and has been marginalised in relation to the economic heartlands of Western Europe and Germany. From at least the fourteenth century, the region has constituted part of the European economy's 'semi-periphery' (with the partial exception of Bohemia, which belonged to the 'centre', and of the eastern provinces of Poland, Hungary and Slovakia, which have been part of the 'periphery'), a status they share with Spain and Portugal, parts of southern and western France, Brandenburg, Ireland and the Italian south.[67] Until well into this century, the economies of the region have been primarily agrarian in character, characterised by what Joseph Rothschild has described as 'a vicious cycle of rural undercapitalization, underproductivity, underconsumption, under-employment, overpopulation, and pervasive misery'.[68] The inefficient and low-productivity peasant economies of East Central Europe proved a crippling handicap. Thus when the peoples of the region gained their independence from the multinational empires which collapsed at the end of the Great War, they found it hard to survive the economic travails of the inter-war years. 'By virtually every relevant statistical index', Rothschild notes, 'East Central Europe was less productive, less literate, and less healthy than West Central and Western Europe. A potentially rich region with poor people, its interwar censuses record not so much a distribution of wealth as a maldistribution of poverty'.[69]

Today, East Central Europe remains relatively backward when compared with the more prosperous economies of the EU. However, the Visegrad states – with the partial exception of Slovakia – constitute a distinct group within the post-communist East. When compared with their neighbours to their east and south, the East Central Europeans stand out by virtue of their progress in terms of marketisation and privatisation; the relative success of their economic reforms; and their generally more developed industrial and service sector.[70] It is thus no surprise that the Visegrad four are widely regarded as being the most promising candidates from the East for early membership of the EU.

Social structure

The second distinguishing feature of East Central Europe is its societal structure, which derives in large part from its relative economic backwardness. The societies of this region tended to be characterised by major cleavages between classes and strata, with a wide gap between rich and poor. The most obvious social cleavage has been between the urban elite and the peasant masses. The large and under-capitalised agrarian sector created an impoverished peasantry. Moreover, as the West moved towards proto-industrialisation from the fifteenth century onwards, the peasantry developed into a more stratified group, which included the emergence of a class of small-scale capitalist farmers. East Central Europe, on the other hand, experienced a 'second serfdom', which perpetuated the low productivity of the agrarian sector and reinforced the conservative ethos of the peasantry.[71] The agrarian character of East Central European society has proved enduring, and continues to influence political behaviour and attitudes. The limited development of commerce and industry in the region also meant that these societies lacked a strong and influential middle class – the class which provided the social basis for the development of parliamentary democracy in much of Western Europe.

During the post-war years, the communists sought to modernise Eastern Europe by collectivising agriculture (although this was not achieved in Poland) and by developing a heavy industrial base. The result has been the creation of a strong urban working class, employed in what have become uncompetitive 'smokestack' industries. This has left East Central Europe with a larger and more homogenous urban working class, along with a much more traditionally structured class system, than that which now exists in the 'post-industrial' societies of the West.[72]

At the same time, communist 'totalitarianism'[73] prevented the full and free development of 'civil society' in East Central Europe, and impeded the development of an independent middle class. The lack of a mature civil society and of a prosperous middle class today is hampering the task of democratic consolidation. Nonetheless, when compared with their eastern and southern neighbours, the countries of East Central Europe – again with the possible exception of Slovakia – have a more developed and variegated social structure. Within the post-communist world, it is in these countries that civil society is most advanced. Once again, in terms of social structure, East Central Europe emerges as a distinct region – distinct both from the more developed West, and from the relatively less developed post-communist states to their south and east.

Political development

The political distinctiveness of the region stems in part from its economic and social characteristics. Politics in East Central Europe reflects the region's relative economic backwardness and more traditional class-based social structure. There tends to be a large gulf between the political elite and the mass of the population, which in turn provides opportunities for demagogues and populists. The political culture is less developed than in Western Europe and North America, in the sense that notions of consensus-building, tolerance and compromise are less widely accepted. The ethos of citizen participation in the public life through a network of social, economic and political organisations and interest groups is not as widespread as in mature Western liberal democracies. Statist and dirigiste traditions are more deeply ingrained in the region than in the West. Consequently, ideas associated with the classical liberal tradition, and with the methodological individualism which underpins it, are much weaker in East Central Europe than in the West. Instead, as Svetozar Pejovich has argued, 'the ethos in Eastern Europe has a strong bias towards communalism'.[74] Nationalism and the politics of ethnicity also play a central role in the political life of East Central Europe. As we have already noted, one of the most distinctive features of this part of Europe is the central importance of nationalism to all areas of life, from its culture to its patterns of political behaviour. Finally, in the post-communist period, political life in the region has been coloured by a high degree of instability, reflecting the fluidity of the party systems and the still inchoate and embryonic structure of interests in society.[75]

Yet, once again, it is in East Central Europe that the best chances of democratic consolidation in the post-communist East exist. When compared with countries like Russia, Romania or Croatia, the Visegrad states can be seen as having relatively stable and pluralist political systems – although with the now familiar question mark over Slovakia, whose democratic credentials are much weaker than those of its fellow Visegrad partners.

Culture

The fourth distinguishing feature of the region is its unique cultural make-up. East Central Europe possesses a rich and varied culture, reflecting its position on the borderlands of East and West. The Slavs and Magyars of East Central Europe have been exposed to cultural and spiritual influences from Latin Christendom, the Ottoman Empire and the Orthodox countries to its east. The culture of the region has also been enriched by the Jews and Germans who settled in towns and villages throughout these lands. Of particular cultural and political significance was the adoption of the Roman, rather than the Orthodox, version of Christianity. These Catholic countries looked to Rome for spiritual guidance and with this came a more Western outlook. This is reflected in the architecture, art, food, costume and attitudes of the East Central Europeans when compared with their fellow Slavs to the east and south. The cultural diversity and richness of East Central Europe has been well captured by Claudio Magris. Referring to Prince Metternich's lapidary formulation that immediately across the Rennweg one is already in Asia, he goes on to remark that,

A moment spent in a Budapest pastry-shop or bookshop will give the lie to anyone who thinks that an indistinct sort of Asiatic womb begins just east of Austria. When we enter the great Hungarian plains we are certainly entering a Europe that is in part 'other', a melting-pot composed of elements rather different from those that form the clays of the West. The poetry of Endre Ady, the greatest Hungarian poet of the twentieth century, is darkly oppressed by the age-old burden which, as has been said, weighs on the Hungarians; that is, the necessary and often impossible choice between East and West....

Hungary was a whole range of different cultures, a mosaic in which diverse sovereignties flourished, and occasionally intersected: the Habsburg territories, the *villayet* or Turkish districts, the principality of Transylvania.[76]

Although Magris is here writing specifically of Hungary, his words apply equally well to Poland, Slovakia or the Czech lands, where cultural diversity, a mix of Eastern and Western elements, is very much in evidence.

Conclusion

Thus far in this book, we have considered the extent to which history, culture, geography, ethnicity and nationalism have combined to give politics in East Central Europe a distinctive flavour and texture. This provides us with an essential background for analysing the changing dynamics of international politics in this region. Later in this book, we will consider the impact on the Visegrad countries of changes in the wider global system, focusing in particular on globalisation, institutional integration and complex interdependence. However, at this stage, it is important to recognise the extent to which international relations in this region have been influenced by domestic factors. 'A constant theme in the politics of east central Europe in the twentieth century', Judy Batt has written, 'has been the close linkage between domestic developments and the external environment. This arises from what is often referred to as the region's "geopolitical predicament", which is one of vulnerability to external pressures and endemic challenges to the internal integrity of the state'.[77]

This vulnerability to external pressures has been accentuated by changes in the wider global system in the late twentieth century. 'The linkage between domestic and international affairs', Joseph Frankel has observed, 'has grown greatly in both directions. On the one hand, rapidly growing domestic needs and demands have become increasingly dependent upon international politics; on the other, international politics has become increasingly affected by domestic conflicts'.[78] Thus understanding the changing pattern of international politics in East Central Europe is possible only if one takes into consideration the cultural specificities and unique historical experiences that have coloured the nature of politics in individual states in the region. As Fred Northedge has noted,

> in the end, the nature of [an individual] state and its attitude towards other state-members of the international system will elude us unless we have done something to penetrate its unique cast of mind, the product of quite unique historical experiences.[79]

Endnotes

1   George Schöpflin, *Politics in Eastern Europe*, Oxford, Blackwell, 1993, p. 11.
2   For details see David Turnock's two volumes, *Eastern Europe. An Economic and Political Geography*, London, Routledge, 1989; and *The Human Geography of Eastern Europe*, London, Routledge, 1989.
3   Alan K. Henrikson, 'The power and politics of maps', in George J. Demko and William B. Wood, eds, *Reordering the World: Geopolitical Perspectives on the 21st Century*, Boulder, Westview, 1994, pp. 49–70 (p. 49).
4   For recent exposition of the geopolitical ideas of Haushofer and MacKinder, see Milan Hauner, *What is Asia To Us? Russia's Asian Heartland Yesterday and Today*, London, Unwin Hyman, 1990, pp. 135–46.
5   Saul B. Cohen, 'Geopolitics in the new world era: a new perspective on an old discipline', in George J. Demko and William B. Wood, eds, *Reordering the World: Geopolitical Perspectives on the 21st Century*, Boulder, Westview, 1994, pp. 15–48 (p. 17).
6   Arther Ferrill, 'The grand strategy of the Roman Empire', in Paul Kennedy, ed., *Grand Strategies in War and Peace*, New Haven, Yale University Press, 1991, pp. 71–86.
7   C. Northcote Parkinson, *East and West*, London, John Murray, 1963.
8   Cohen, *op. cit.*, p. 32.
9   'The nations of Western Europe can be more peaceful than those of the East because they are endowed with more defensible borders: the French, Spanish, British, Italian, and Scandinavian nations have natural defenses formed by the Alps and the Pyrenees, and by the waters of the English Channel, the Baltic, and the North Sea.... In contrast, the nationalities living on the exposed plains of Eastern Europe and western Asia contend with a harsher geography: with few natural barriers to invasion, they are more vulnerable to attack, hence are more tempted to attack others in preemptive defense. They are therefore more likely to disturb the status quo, or to be victims of other disturbers.' Stephen van Evera, 'Hypotheses on nationalism and war', *International Security*, 18, no. 4, spring 1994, pp. 5–39 (p. 21).

10   A. Hyde-Price, 'Eurasia', in Caroline Thomas and Darryl Howlett, eds, *Resource Politics. Freshwater and Regional Relations*, Buckingham, Open University Press, 1993, pp. 149–70.

11   Michael G. Roskin, *Rebirth of East Europe*, New Jersey, Prentice Hall, 1991, p. 8.

12   B. K. Gills, 'International relations theory and the processes of world history: three approaches', in H. C. Dyer and L. Mangasarian, eds, *The Study of International Relations: The State of the Art*, London, Macmillan, 1989, pp. 103–54 (pp. 109, 114).

13   For details see J. Hussey, ed., *The Cambridge Medieval History*, vol. 8, Cambridge, Cambridge University Press, 1975, pp. 582–3.

14   P. Anderson, *Lineages of the Absolutist State*, London, Verso Books, 1974, pp. 288–9.

15   Cohen himself suggests that the 'hinges' of this gateway region will be the eastern part of Germany, Slovenia and the Baltic states. For the discussion on gateways, see his chapter in Demko and Wood, *op. cit.*, pp. 38–46.

16   'In the centre of the main square in Cracow stands St Mary's church, considered one of the most important churches in Poland. Every hour on the hour, a trumpeter from the Cracow fire department presents himself at the balcony of the main tower and blows an alarm. This ceremony has taken place each day, almost continuously since the middle of the thirteenth century. It commemorates the destruction of the city, for the trumpeter is blowing a call to arms, a signal that the enemy has been sighted and is at the gates. As the trumpeter sounds his haunting melody he comes to an abrupt halt midway through the call – at precisely the moment, so legend has it, when the Mongol arrow struck.' Robert Marshall, *Storm From the East*, London, BBC Books, 1993, p. 9.

17   As the then Polish Prime Minister Tadeusz Mazowiecki said in his speech to the Council of Europe in Strasbourg on 30 January 1990, 'The idea of being the "ramparts of civilisation" and, by the same token, of Europe, has remained alive in Poland throughout three centuries.' T. Mazowiecki, 'Belonging to Europe', reprinted in Adam Daniel Rotfeld and Walther Stützle, eds, *Germany and Europe in Transition*, Oxford, Oxford University Press for SIPRI, 1991, pp. 131–4 (p. 131).

18   'The nationalistic passion of the Magyars, which runs with heroic and ferocious fury all through Hungarian history, is born from a land in which wave after wave of invasions and immigrations, Huns and Avars, Slavs and Magyars, Tartars and Kumans, Jazigs and Pechenegs, Turks and Germans are superimposed and deposited one upon another in layer after layer. The migrations of peoples bring devastation, but also civilization, like the Turks, who not only brought plunder but also the culture of Islam. They produce mixtures, the secret roots of every nationalism and its obsession with ethnic purity.... Hungary was a whole range of different cultures, a mosaic in which diverse sovereignties flourished, and occasionally intersected: the Habsburg territories, the *villayet* or Turkish districts, the principality of Transylvania'. Claudio Magris, *Danube*, London, Collins Harvill, 1990, pp. 242–3.

19   A good example of the many varied cultural influences on the region is provided by its cuisine. For a well written and mouthwatering introduction to

the dishes of East Central Europe, see Lesley Chamberlain, *The Food and Cooking of Eastern Europe*, London, Penguin, 1989.

20   P. Wandycz, *The Price of Freedom. A History of East Central Europe From the Middle Ages to the Present*, London, Routledge, 1992, p. 3.

21   Naumann's book on *Mitteleuropa* was published in 1915 and sought to justify German hegemony over Central and Eastern Europe. The concept of *Mitteleuropa* as a cultural-historical phenomenon was taken up by German writers (beginning with Karl Schlögel) in the 1980s, and developed into a political strategy for developing *Ostpolitik* by some on the left. Yet there was a profound tension between the German proponents of *Mitteleuropa* and the use of the term in East Central Europe. As Timothy Garton Ash notes, 'the immediate political thrust of the East European revival of the concept was clearly to get further away from the East – meaning above all the Soviet Union – and closer to the West. The political thrust of the German Social Democratic revival of the concept of *Mitteleuropa* was to pull away from the West – or at least, from the Western Alliance and the United States'. Garton Ash, *In Europe's Name. Germany and the Divided Continent*, London, Vintage, 1994, p. 317. See also his article 'Mitteleuropa?', *Daedalus*, 119, no. 1, winter 1990, pp. 1–21.

22   Misha Glenny, *The Rebirth of History. Eastern Europe in the Age of Democracy*, London, Penguin, 1990, p. 185.

23   George Schöpflin and Nancy Woods, eds, *In Search of Central Europe*, Cambridge, Polity, 1989.

24   Milan Kundera, 'The tragedy of Central Europe', *New York Review of Books*, 26 April 1984, pp. 33–8.

25   Magris, *op. cit.*, p. 268.

26   Glenny, *op. cit.*, p. 185.

27   J. Rupnik, 'Central Europe or *Mitteleuropa*?', *Daedalus*, 119, no. 1, winter 1990, pp. 249–78.

28   Václav Havel, 'Return to Europe', *East European Reporter*, 4, no. 2, March/April 1990, pp. 17–19.

29   J. Snyder, 'Controlling nationalism in the new Europe', in A. Clesse and R. Ruhl, eds, *Beyond East–West Confrontation: Searching for a New Security Structure in Europe*, Baden-Baden, Nomos, 1990, p. 58.

30   J. Batt, *East Central Europe from Reform to Transformation*, London, Pinter, 1991, p. 50.

31   Thomas Simons, *Eastern Europe in the Postwar World*, 2nd edn, London, Macmillan, 1993, p. 235.

32   J. V. Stalin, 'Marxism and the national question', quoted in Graham Smith, ed., *The Nationalities Question in the Soviet Union*, London, Longman, 1990, p. 3.

33   Anthony D. Smith, *National Identity*, London, Penguin, 1991, p. 14. There is of course a plethora of definitions of nationalism. In his book, *Nationalism*, London, Edward Arnold, 1985, Peter Alter quotes two writers on nationalism: Eugen Lemberg, a sociologist and historian, who defined nationalism as 'A system of ideas, values and norms, an image of the world and society ... which makes a large social group aware of where it belongs and invents this sense of belonging with a particular value'; and Theodor Schieder, for whom nationalism was 'a specific integrative ideology which

always makes reference to a "nation" in one sense or another, and not merely to a social or religious type of group' (p. 8). Alter himself said of nationalism that as a 'largely dynamic principle capable of engendering hope, emotions and action, it is a vehicle for activating human beings and creating political solidarity amongst them for the purpose of achieving a common goal' (p. 9).

34 Elie Kedourie, *Nationalism*, 4th edn, Oxford, Blackwell, 1993, p. 1.
35 A. Giddens, *The Nation-State and Violence*, Berkeley, University of California, 1987, p. 116.
36 B. Anderson, *Imagined Communities: Reflections on the Origin and Spread of Nationalism*, revised edn, London, Verso, 1991.
37 Quoted in Stephen Griffiths, 'Nationalism in Central and South-Eastern Europe', in Colin McInnes, ed., *Security and Strategy in the New Europe*, London, Routledge, 1992, p. 63.
38 Eric Hobsbawn, 'Mass-producing traditions: Europe 1870–1914', in Eric Hobsbawn and Terence Ranger, eds, *The Invention of Tradition*, Cambridge, Cambridge University Press, 1983, pp. 264–5, 271–8.
39 J. A. Armstrong, *Nations before Nationalism*, Chapel Hill, University of North Carolina Press, 1982; and A. D. Smith, *The Ethnic Origins of Nations*, Oxford, Blackwell, 1986.
40 O. Waever, *et al*, *Identity, Migration and the New Security Agenda in Europe*, London, Pinter, 1993, p. 27. From a historian's perspective, Arnošt Klima has written that 'Whereas modern nationalism and the process of solving the national question was very closely linked with the beginnings of capitalism one should be aware of the fact that the foundations of the development of nations had already been laid during the Middle Ages'. Nonetheless, he also stresses that the 'modern nation is inseparably connected with the rise of capitalism and differs substantially from the medieval nation which consisted of the privileged strata of society'. Klima, 'The Czechs', in Mikuláš Teich and Roy Porter, eds, *The National Question in Europe in Historical Perspective*, Cambridge, Cambridge University Press, 1993, pp. 228–47 (pp. 228, 232).
41 'From its beginnings', Emil Niederhauser has pointed out, 'medieval Hungary was a multiethnic state'. Indeed, 'By the end of the eighteenth century, the Hungarians were in an ethnic minority in comparison to the other nationalities, though individually these were of a smaller number, allowing the Hungarians to retain their relative majority'. Nevertheless, 'Traditional society is always more sensitive to social and political differences than it is to ethnic and linguistic differences. Therefore this multinational combination did not create conflicts.... The real national question in the modern sense of the word arose only in the late eighteenth century, under the influence of the French Revolution'. Niederhauser, 'The national question in Hungary', in Mikuláš Teich and Roy Porter, eds, *The National Question in Europe in Historical Perspective*, Cambridge, Cambridge University Press, pp. 248–69 (pp. 248–9).
42 Roskin, *op. cit.*, p. 12.
43 See for example Linda Colley's excellent study, *Britons. Forging the Nation 1707–1837*, London, Pimlico, 1992.

44   For a recent elaboration of this perspective see Ernest Gellner, *Encounters With Nationalism*, Oxford, Blackwell, 1994.

45   Douglas Johnson, 'The making of the French Nation', in Mikuláš Teich and Roy Porter, eds, *The National Question in Europe in Historical Perspective*, Cambridge, Cambridge University Press, pp. 35–62 (p. 48). James Mayall, in *Nationalism and International Society*, Cambridge, Cambridge University Press, 1990, also emphasises the importance of the 'substitution of a popular for the prescriptive principle of sovereignty' for the international society of states (p. 149).

46   Uri Ra'anan has argued that 'allegiance to the state, residence therein, and submission to its jurisdiction, are the hallmarks of the Western idea of nationality – to the point where, in American English, one speaks of a "national" of a country when, actually, one means a "citizen". The two terms have become synonymous. It is an individual's place of residence and his passport that largely determine his nationality in the West, i.e., primarily territorial and juridical criteria.... For the same reasons, "state" and "nation" have tended to become almost synonymous in the English language, to a degree that causes many to refer to "national interests" when, in fact, they mean "state interests", while others speak simplistically of a world of "nation-states"'. Uri Ra'anan, 'Nation and state: order out of chaos', in Uri Ra'anan, Maria Mesner, Keith Armes and Kate Martin, eds, *State and Nation in Multi-Ethnic Societies: The Break-Up of Multinational States*, Manchester, Manchester University Press, 1991, p. 11.

47   Ra'anan argues that for the 'Eastern' concept of national identity, 'it is not *where* an individual resides and which state has jurisdiction over him that determines his nationality, but rather *who* he is – his cultural, religious and historic identity, i.e., his ethnicity, a heritage received from his ancestors and carried with him, in mind and body, irrespective of his current place of domicile. Consequently, one is dealing here with *personal* (as opposed to the Western *territorial*) criteria of nationality'. He goes on to distinguish between two non-Western concepts of nationality, which are related but slightly differing: 'the Eastern (covering roughly Europe east of the Rhine) and the Southern (covering the southern and eastern rims of the Mediterranean, i.e., the successor states of the Ottoman Empire). Both are based upon personal rather than territorial criteria, but the Eastern approach tends to focus upon cultural touchstones of ethnicity (including ancestral language and name), whereas, in the Southern view, religion is one of the primary hallmarks of nationality, so that the existence of a separate religious community frequently is a precondition for the successful development of full-blown nationhood'. Ra'anan, *op. cit.*, pp. 13, 14.

48   'Nationalism in the west arose in an effort to build a nation in the political reality and struggle of the present without too much sentimental regard for the past; nationalists in central and eastern Europe created, often out of myths of the past and the dreams of the future, an ideal fatherland, closely linked with the past, devoid of any immediate connection with the present, and expected to become sometime a political reality'. P. Sugar and I. Lederer (eds), 'Introduction', in *Nationalism in Eastern Europe*, Seattle, University of Washington, 1969, p. 10.

49   Hans Kohn, *The Idea of Nationalism: A Study in its Origins and Background*,
     New York, Macmillan, 1944, p. 457. For an exploration of the implications
     of this distinction between 'Western' and 'Eastern' nationalism for the
     development of the state, see Kenneth Dyson, *The State Tradition in Western
     Europe: A Study of an Idea and Institution*, Oxford, Martin Robertson, 1980,
     pp. 157–83.
50   Wandycz, *op. cit.*, pp. 7–8. George Schöpflin has suggested that the distinctive
     character of nationalism in Eastern Europe can also be attributed to the 'very
     particular role played by intellectuals' in the region. He argues that 'Because
     society was weak, the rise of a secular intellectual stratum with the
     Enlightenment produced a social configuration palpably different from that of
     Western Europe. While in the West the intellectuals had to contend with a
     reasonably well-established bourgeoisie and a confident ruling stratum in
     their attempts to secure their authority, further east they were virtually
     unchallenged. Consequently, when the intellectuals encountered nationalism,
     they were able to construct a programme that fused their claim to be moral,
     political and social legislators with the claim for national independence. This
     gave Central and East European politics a very striking quality, in that the
     ethnic and civil agendas of politics were consistently confused and collective
     and individual freedoms were combined and sometimes confounded'.
     Schöpflin, 'Culture and identity in post-communist Europe', in Stephen White,
     Judy Batt and Paul Lewis, eds, *Developments in East European Politics*,
     London, Macmillan, 1993, pp. 16–34 (p. 18).
51   'While Eastern Europe, in the sense of the lands lying to the east of the
     predominantly German- and Italian-speaking areas, had roughly the same area
     as the western portion, it contained three times as many different nationalities.'
     Paul Lewis, *Central Europe Since 1945*, London, Longman, 1994, p. 28.
52   Batt, *op. cit.*, p. 104. It should be noted that Judy Batt's more optimistic
     assessment of the underlying trends in political culture and democratic values
     in East Central Europe – which I share – is not universally accepted. George
     Schöpflin, one of Britain's most interesting and informed writers on East
     European politics, has suggested that the 'nature of popular values, as these
     surfaced in Hungary in 1956, in Czechoslovakia in 1968 and in Poland in
     1980–81, could be read as well disposed towards reciprocity and democracy.
     Yet with the benefit of hindsight this was too simplistic. The popular values
     that emerged during these upheavals pointed in another direction, that of
     homogeneity and oversimplification. One of the clearest expressions of this
     was during the Solidarity period, understandably given that it lasted longest.
     The Solidarity programme, adopted at the congress of September–October
     1981, was a clear indicator of this tendency. Attitudes were essentially
     structured by a very strong sense of good and evil, with society cast in the
     role of the former, and "them", the party-state, in the role of the latter.'
     Schöpflin in *Developments in East European Politics*.
53   Victor Zaslavsky, 'Nationalism and democratic transition in postcommunist
     societies', *Daedalus*, 121, no. 2, spring 1992, pp. 97–121 (p. 110).
54   Peter Frank, 'Stability and instability in Eastern Europe', in *European Security
     After the Cold War*, Adelphi Paper 285, London, Brassey's for the IISS, 1994,
     pp. 3–14 (p. 11).

55   William Wallace, *The Transformation of Western Europe*, London, Pinter for the RIIA, 1991, pp. 33, 56.

56   For a self-consciously radical, 'post-positivist' analysis of identity see Marysia Zalewski and Cynthia Enloe, 'Questions about identity in international relations', in Ken Booth and Steve Smith, eds, *International Relations Theory Today*, Cambridge, Polity, 1995, pp. 279–305. In his book, *Culture and Imperialism*, London, Vintage, 1993, Edward Said argues that 'Gone are the binary opposites dear to the nationalist and imperialist enterprise. Instead we begin to sense that old authority cannot simply be replaced by new authority, but that new alignments made across borders, types, nations, and essences are rapidly coming into view, and it is those new alignments that now provoke and challenge the fundamentally static notion of *identity* that has been the core of cultural thought during the era of imperialism' (p. xxiii).

57   Martin Wight, *Power Politics*, London, Leicester University Press, 1978, p. 25.

58   Marianne Hanson, 'Democratisation and norm creation in Europe', *European Security After the Cold War, Part One*, Adelphi Paper 284, London, Brassey's for the IISS, 1993, pp. 28–41.

59   Antony McGrew and Paul Lewis, *et al.*, *Global Politics*, Cambridge, Polity, 1992; Martin Shaw, *Global Society and International Relations*, Cambridge, Polity, 1994; and Joseph A. Camilleri and Jim Falk, *The End of Sovereignty? The Politics of a Shrinking and Fragmenting World*, Aldershot, Edward Elgar, 1992.

60   George Kolankiewicz, 'Consensus and competition in the Eastern enlargement of the European Union', *International Affairs*, 70, no. 3, 1994, pp. 477–95 (p. 481).

61   See for example George Schöpflin, in *Developments in East European Politics*, pp. 16–35.

62   Adam Michnik, 'The two faces of Europe', *New York Review of Books*, 19 July 1990, p. 7.

63   John Breuilly, *Nationalism and the State*, 2nd edn, Manchester, Manchester University Press, 1993, p. 352.

64   *Ibid.*, p. 352. See also T. Szayna, 'Ultra-nationalism in Central Europe', *Orbis*, 37, no. 4, autumn 1993, p. 527.

65   Gabriel Partos, 'Who's afraid of post-communism?', *The World Today*, February 1995, pp. 28–32 (p. 31).

66   Gale Stokes, *The Walls Came Tumbling Down: The Collapse of Communism in Eastern Europe*, Oxford, Oxford University Press, 1993, p. 257.

67   Immanuel Wallerstein, *The Modern World System*, 3 vols, New York, Academic Press, 1974, 1980, 1989.

68   Joseph Rothschild, *Return to Diversity: A Political History of East Central Europe Since World War II*, Oxford, Oxford University Press, 1989, p. 13.

69   *Ibid.*, p. 13.

70   Andrá Köves, *Central and East European Economies in Transition. The International Dimension*, Boulder, Westview, 1992; and Laszlo Valki and Laszlo Csaba, 'Economic and social stability in Central and South-Eastern Europe: preconditions for security', in *European Security After the Cold War, Part One*, Adelphi Paper 284, London, Brassey's for the IISS, 1994, pp. 42–59.

71   Joseph Rothschild has suggested that the 'characteristic political behaviour' of
      the typical peasant in Eastern and East Central Europe is expressed by 'long
      periods of submissiveness interspersed with bouts of *jacquerie* violence'. This,
      he argues, 'indicates profound, albeit understandable, apathy, alienation, and
      rancour. Excluded from the general progress of Europe, he felt himself to be
      both the guardian and the victim of anachronistic values and institutions,
      whose very anachronism undermined and negated the potential power of the
      peasantry as the area's most numerous class'. *Op. cit.*, p. 14.
72   'Communism proved to be, *inter alia*, a method for building up a nineteenth-
      century industry, with super-large enterprises using relatively straightforward
      technology. The ideal was always the male manual worker using simple
      technology as portrayed under Stalinism; this did not change symbolically in
      any major way later. In this sense the working class that emerged from
      communism was relatively homogenized, confused and economically
      increasingly threatened by the collapse of these economies. It disliked
      differentiation, whether in material or in status terms, and was characterized
      by a kind of negative egalitarianism. Equally it was, with some exceptions,
      strongly anti-intellectual, impatient with the complex solutions offered by the
      new governments and politically inexperienced, making it vulnerable to
      demagogic manipulation'. George Schöpflin, in *Developments in East
      European Politics*, p. 271.
73   'Totalitarianism' is a concept which originated in the early Cold War years to
      describe the political systems of both communism and fascism. The classic
      totalitarian model of Friedrich and Brzezinski contains six defining features of
      a totalitarian state: a messianic ideology; a single party, typically led by one
      man; terroristic police control; a monopoly of the means of communication;
      state control of the essential mechanisms of economic activity; and an
      effective monopoly of the instruments of coercion. By the late sixties and early
      seventies, the concept of 'totalitarianism' had been widely criticised for its
      analytical weaknesses and Cold War political assumptions. I am using it here
      simply to draw attention to the fact that communist political systems sought
      to exercise total control over virtually all aspects of public life, thereby
      impeding the formation and development of the sort of autonomous civil
      society which characterises Western liberal democracies.
74   Svetozar Pejovich defines classical liberalism and methodological individ-
      ualism as follows: '*Classical liberalism* usually is taken to mean individual
      liberty, openness to new ideas, tolerance of all views, and a government under
      law. *Methodological individualism* is a method for understanding social
      phenomena. Its main postulate is that the individual is the only decision
      maker. That is, governments, universities, corporations, and other entities do
      not and cannot make decisions, only individuals can and do. To understand
      the behaviour of any social, economic, or political entity, it is necessary to
      identify incentive structures under which individuals operate.' He also argues
      that, 'It is frequently said that there was more a Western tradition in
      Czechoslovakia, Slovenia, and perhaps Hungary, than in other Eastern
      European countries. That is certainly true. However, classical liberalism,
      which is only part of the Western tradition, does not have deep roots in the
      region.' See his article, 'Institutions, nationalism, and the transition process in

Eastern Europe', *Social Philosophy and Policy*, 10, no. 2, summer 1993, pp. 65–78 (p. 70).

75 For further details see Sten Berglund and Jan Äke Dellenbrant, eds, *The New Democracies in Eastern Europe. Party Systems and Political Cleavages*, 2nd edn, Aldershot, Edward Elgar, 1994; and Stephen White, Judy Batt and Paul Lewis, eds, *Developments in East European Politics*, London, Macmillan, 1993.

76 Magris, *op. cit.*, pp. 242–3.

77 Judy Batt, 'The political transformation of East Central Europe', in Hugh Miall, ed., *Redefining Europe. New Patterns of Conflict and Cooperation*, London, Pinter, 1994, pp. 30–47 (p. 30).

78 J. Frankel, *International Relations in a Changing World*, Oxford, Oxford University Press, 1988, pp. 219–20.

79 Quoted by Steve Smith, 'Foreign policy analysis: British and American orientations and methodologies', *Political Studies*, XXXI, 1983, pp. 556–65 (p. 561).

Chapter Four

Regional conflict and cooperation: I. Bilateral relations

> The end of the Cold War and the changes set in motion in 1989 have not been restricted in their consequences to the transformation of the political and socioeconomic orders of individual states or to re-evaluation of their status within a broader Europe and relations with the West. They also affect ... relations between states within that region as well as the lines of ethnic division that run within and across those sovereign territories.... Relations both within and between the states of Eastern Europe, and the peoples that live within them, have thus become subject to considerable uncertainty and raise further questions about political order and the security both of that region and of Europe as a whole. (Paul G. Lewis[1])

Having considered the history, geography, cultural distinctiveness and national identity of the Visegrad countries, it is now time to focus more directly on the international politics of the region. The specific concern of this chapter is the evolving pattern of bilateral relationships within East Central Europe. Relations between the four states and many peoples of this culturally diverse region are rich, varied, complex and intense. They span a spectrum ranging from cooperation to conflict. They also exhibit elements of continuity and change, with the partial re-emergence of historical patterns of cooperation and conflict, along with the appearance of new dynamics in inter-state relations – largely as a consequence of the changing character of international relations in a Europe being reshaped by democracy, economic development, complex interdependence and globalisation.

The fabric of international relations in the region is composed of many strands: intergovernmental and transnational, formal and informal. Throughout East Central Europe, there are formal exchanges between governments, ministries and officials; between local authorities in neighbouring countries; and between government officials in one country and non-governmental organisations in other countries. There is also a myriad of informal relations between enterprises, churches, professional associations, trades unions, nationalist organisations and citizens' movements.[2] In this more interdependent pattern of regional relations, political coalitions operate across states as well as within them. Regional international relations therefore take place within a complex multilayered structure consisting of governments, state bureaucracies, trans-national organisations, local communities and other social collectivities.

In this chapter, we will assess the health and prognosis of bilateral relations in East Central Europe. We will begin by considering the historical legacy of regional conflict and cooperation, focusing primarily on the inter-war years. We will then outline the post-Cold War agenda of regional relations, seeking to assess to what extent new issues have replaced more traditional concerns. Finally, we will consider how bilateral relations have developed between the Visegrad countries in the years since 1989.

Historical patterns of cooperation and conflict

When, in 1990–91, the new post-communist elites of East Central Europe wanted to develop a limited form of regional cooperation, they had few modern precedents to follow. Instead, they had to look back to 1335. In this year the kings of Poland, Bohemia and Hungary met at Visegrad, a sumptuous Gothic palace on the banks of the Danube protected by an imposing citadel and powerful riverside fortifications. There they reached agreement on a number of issues, the most significant being economic cooperation.[3] This medieval example of regional summitry – one of the few serious attempts at regional cooperation in the history of this troubled area – was to provide symbolic inspiration for Walesa, Havel and Ántáll in February 1991 when they met at Visegrad and announced their intention to cooperate in rejoining Europe.

Sadly, regional cooperation in East Central Europe has been the exception rather than the rule. The history of this part of Europe is replete with conflicts between neighbouring states and communities.

This was certainly true of the inter-war years. The new states of Czechoslovakia, Hungary and Poland immediately found themselves in a hostile environment. Surrounded by enemies, they had to struggle hard to assert their territorial boundaries and preserve their newly acquired sovereignty.

The key problem in inter-war East Central Europe was disputed borders and disgruntled national minorities. This problem poisoned relations between Poland and Czechoslovakia for decades after 1919, following Czechoslovakia's forceful seizure of a part of Silesia. This area (known as Teschen or Těšín to the Czechoslovaks, and as Cieszyn to the Poles) was predominantly inhabited by Poles, but was of great economic and strategic value to the Czechoslovaks.[4] However, the most acute bilateral problems in the region involved Hungary and its neighbours. As a result of the 1920 Treaty of Trianon, Hungary lost almost two-thirds of its pre-war territory and three-fifths of its population. It was thus left with a burning sense of injustice and was instinctively hostile to its neighbours – particularly Czechoslovakia, Yugoslavia and Romania – who had gained what was formerly Hungarian territory. As one historian notes,

> Almost every third ethnic Magyar found himself now living under Romanian, Czechoslovak, Yugoslav, or Austrian rule. Hungary was fully independent at last but under conditions that amounted to a national disaster. Small wonder that extreme bitterness prevailed and the cry 'nem, nem, soha' ('no, no, never') reverberated throughout the truncated land. The Hungarians became obsessed with a revision of Trianon, revisionism shaping to a large extent Budapest's external and domestic politics.[5]

In the inter-wars years, therefore, regional relations were dominated by a balance-of-power logic and power-political considerations – in other words, traditional realist concerns. This militaristic and realpolitik mentality reflected the structure of the European states system at this time, and was aggravated by economic problems (which worsened already severe social tensions); by political instability and the lack of viable democratic institutions (with the partial exception of Czechoslovakia); and by the mood of ultranationalism which gripped this region in the inter-war years.

Regional cooperation was thus barely existent during the 1920s and '30s. The only form of regional cooperation which did emerge was directed against Hungary. This was the 'Little Entente' (sometimes referred to as the 'Triple Entente'). The Little Entente was a defensive military alliance established in 1920–21 between Czechoslovakia, Yugoslavia and Romania – countries which felt threatened by Hungary's barely concealed revisionist aspirations. It was sponsored by France, and strengthened in December 1932 by the creation of a permanent secretariat.[6]

The Hungarian threat to regional security was superseded in the 1930s by an even more serious and alarming threat. With Hitler's seizure of power in 1933, Nazi Germany began its search for *Lebensraum* in the East.[7] This aggressive policy focused initially not on Poland but on Czechoslovakia, which was regarded by the Nazis as 'the keystone of Germany's "encirclement" that would have to be dislodged first to collapse the arch.'[8] Germany's willing ally in this plan for conquest and subjugation was Hungary. Germany's first moves were economic: by offering preferential trade terms to Czechoslovakia's allies, Romania and Yugoslavia, Hitler hoped to weaken the cohesion of the Little Entente. In the context of the Great Depression, this proved remarkably successful.[9]

In 1936 Czechoslovakia, worried by Berlin's increasingly assertive foreign policy, proposed bringing Austria, Italy, Hungary and Poland into a new zone of economic cooperation with the countries of the Little Entente, in order to create a regional counterweight to Germany. However, only Austria proved receptive. Fascist Italy chose to join the 'Axis Pact'; Hungary had already decided to pursue its revisionist aims through an alliance with Nazi Germany; Yugoslavia and Romania had been seduced by Germany's preferential trade terms; and Poland – a natural ally of Czechoslovakia against an expansionist Germany – was cool towards Prague not only because of the dispute over Teschen, but also because Czechoslovakia had refused to allow Poland to join the Little Entente, and because it provided sanctuary for Polish political dissidents. Moreover, Poland had already signed a non-aggression pact with Germany.[10]

Following this failed attempt at economic cooperation, Czechoslovakia proposed that the Little Entente's military alliance against Hungary be applied to 'any aggressor'. Unfortunately, by this stage, Romania and Yugoslavia had already made their own security arrangements, and did not want to commit themselves to the defence of Czechoslovakia against their increasingly important economic partner, Germany. In the end, Prague turned to the Soviet Union and France, concluding military pacts with these two states in May 1935.

Czechoslovakia's obvious regional partner against German expansionism was Poland, but short-sighted national concerns made this impossible. As Philip Longworth has written, 'If Poland and Czechoslovakia had shown a common front against him, it is doubtful if Hitler could have realized his imperial ambitions in Eastern Europe.'[11] But as another historian comments, while many good reasons for cooperation existed, 'the two states never closed ranks. Prague did not want to jeopardize its position by siding with Poland, which was threatened by both Germany and the USSR. When in the mid-1930s the situation changed to Czechoslovak disadvantage, Prague's advances met with a cool reception in Warsaw.'[12]

Not only did Warsaw fail to stand by Prague in its hour of need, but when Germany, with British and French collusion, dismembered Czechoslovakia in 1938, Poland greedily fell upon its prostrate neighbour. Mercilessly taking advantage of Prague's misfortune, the Warsaw government demanded the return of the disputed territory of Teschen. With the effective destruction of the Czechoslovak state, the way lay open for Hitler to turn his attention to Poland, now without any regional allies. Poland had stabbed a fellow Slavic country in the back and, in doing so, had undermined its own moral standing when faced with German territorial demands the following year. The Poles and Czechoslovaks had ignored Benjamin Franklin's warning to the Continental Congress: 'Either we all hang together or we all hang separately'.[13] By failing to bury their differences and cooperate, the East Europeans helped to open the way for the cataclysm of fascist rule and total war, followed by communist subjugation.

If regional relations in the inter-war years were dominated by irredentist disputes and nationalist rivalries, relations during the Cold War were little better. A fractious nationalism was replaced by the deadening hand of Moscow. We will consider the nature and internal functioning of the Soviet bloc in chapter six. Suffice it to note here that the Soviet Union prevented the development of autonomous and organic regional relations within Eastern Europe. Instead it imposed an institutional structure for regional policy coordination dominated by loyal local communists and designed to service the interests of Moscow. It was only in the late 1970s and 1980s that regional patterns of cooperation and discord began emerging within the Warsaw Pact. At this time, the main bones of contention were the importance attached to preserving detente with the West, and the desirability of economic and political reform. Thus when the East Central European states regained their national freedom in 1989–90, they were faced with the task of reformulating relations with their regional neighbours largely from scratch – with few positive historical examples to guide them.

The changing agenda of regional relations

The contemporary pattern of regional relations in East Central Europe contains elements of both historical continuity and change. Many traditional cultural and ethno-linguistic relationships have persisted, as have a number of enduring facts of geopolitical life in the region. But European international relations have also been transformed in the post-war period by globalisation, interdependence and democratisation. Thus although some historical patterns of regional cooperation and conflict may well have re-emerged, they have done so in the context of a European states system fundamentally different from that of the inter-war years.

Seven major changes have transformed the context of regional relations in East Central Europe. The first three are all related to wider changes in the European states system. First, the end of the Cold War has created an external environment which is generally supportive of the domestic reform projects of the Visegrad countries. With the collapse of bipolarity, a new 'concert of Europe' has emerged, which represents a fundamentally different international arrangement to that of the Cold War.[14] As US Secretary of State Warren Christopher has noted, we are now living in 'a unique historical moment, when none of the great powers views any other as an immediate military threat'.[15] Moreover, the power politics and balance-of-power mentality of pre-war Europe has been steadily eroded by the spread of complex interdependence, institutionalised multilateral cooperation and liberal democratic forms of government.[16] Although these changes have been concentrated on Western Europe, their impact has been felt throughout much of Central and Eastern Europe – especially East Central Europe, given the region's geographical proximity and the intensity of its economic and cultural relations with the West.

The second factor derives from the first: East Central Europe is no longer directly threatened by hostile great powers using states in the region as pawns in a wider balance-of-power contest. Germany has been a generous patron of economic and political reform in the East, and thus constitutes a benign regional hegemony. Russia remains more problematic: Moscow remains a long-term security concern for the Visegrad countries given its geopolitical weight, military capabilities and political instability. Yet diplomatic relations with Russia have been put on a new and more cooperative footing, and Moscow presents no immediate threat to its former Warsaw Pact allies. As former Polish Defence Minister Janusz Onyszkiewicz, has said, Poland does not fear a Russian attack – 'We see that as a virtual impossibility'.[17]

Third, Europe now possesses an institutionalised multilateral framework for regular consultation and cooperation. This consists of the OSCE and the Council of Europe, both of which provide the institutionalised basis for a new normative order in Europe. This normative order has been constructed around the classical liberal notions of democracy, human rights and the peaceful settlement of disputes. Violation of these norms, which has occurred in the Balkans and parts of the former Soviet Union, can take place only at the cost of political, diplomatic and economic sanctions to the perpetrators.[18]

Fourth, there are no major irredentist disputes in East Central Europe. Some Hungarian officials and politicians have on occasion made ambiguous comments on the borders laid down at Trianon. Nonetheless, the weight of evidence suggests that no political force of any consequence in Hungary is seeking to revise Hungary's internationally recognised borders. Thus, despite occasional grumbles, all four states recognise the legitimacy of existing territorial borders, and are not seeking to change them.

Fifth, the question of national minorities is no longer as intense and emotive as it was in the inter-war years. The treatment of the Hungarian minority in Slovakia remains a controversial issue, and the treatment of their respective national minorities is a sensitive issue for the Czech and Slovak republics. On the whole, however, aggrieved minority communities do not present the inflammatory problems they did in the inter-war years. Paradoxically, this is in part due to the success of 'ethnic cleansing' during World War Two and its immediate aftermath, when the Jewish communities throughout the region were brutally decimated and Germans were expelled from much of Silesia, Pomerania and the Sudetenland. Ethnic homogeneity was also increased by post-war border changes: the accession of sub-Carpathian Ukraine (also known as *Zakarpattya*) to the USSR removed most Ruthenians from Czechoslovakia, whilst the shifting of Poland's borders nearly 200 kilometres to the west meant that Poland lost most of its former Ukrainian and Belarussian minorities.

Sixth, all four Visegrad countries have liberal democratic institutions – however fragile and occasionally compromised by scandal. They are also developing open and pluralist civil societies. As a number of international relations analysts have argued, the spread of democracy and liberal democratic values has important ramifications for diplomatic and inter-state practice. Democracies, it is argued, do not tend to fight each other. Thus the spread and consolidation of democracy will reinforce peaceful and cooperative patterns of inter-state behaviour.[19]

Finally, the international economic context has changed. Not only is the European economy in a far healthier condition than it was during the years of the Great Depression, but it has been transformed by the forces of economic integration and globalisation. As we shall see, this has important consequences for regional politics in the Visegrad area.

Bilateral relations

Polish–Czech relations

Relations between Poles and Czechs have for centuries been difficult, if not downright bad. This has left a legacy of mutual suspicion which continues to influence contemporary popular attitudes. Many Czechs regard their Polish neighbours as narrow-minded nationalists with an unhealthy streak of clericalism. Similarly, many Poles regard the Czechs as 'Slavic Prussians', permeated by German civilisation and attitudes.[20]

In the inter-war years, Polish–Czechoslovak relations were poisoned by the dispute over Teschen. After the war, Poland regained most of this lost territory. Yet no real process of national reconciliation (comparable to that between France and the BRD) took place between the two countries. Instead, existing popular stereotypes remained, and intensive interaction between the two countries took place only at the level of communist elites. However, one development which was significant for the future was the development of links between the dissident movements in *Mitteleuropa*. From the late 1970s, contacts were established between Charter 77 in Czechoslovakia and the Polish Workers' Defence Committee (KOR).[21] This was subsequently to bear fruit after 1989 because the generation of dissidents who had cooperated together in the anticommunist underground subsequently moved into policy-influential positions.[22]

Despite these tentative links between human rights organisations in Poland and Czechoslovakia, relations between the two countries after 1989 got off to a bad start. Some Poles were upset that President Havel chose to make his first official visit abroad to Germany rather than Poland. It was also apparent that relations between Havel and Walesa have lacked warmth and empathy. Moreover, Czechoslovakia angered Warsaw by refusing to open up its border with Poland to unrestricted traffic, despite having done so with all its other neighbours. Prague's concern was that to do so would leave Czechoslovakia vulnerable to the black market activities of Polish criminal elements. This issue generated growing bitterness, and towards the end of 1990 Polish officials began arguing that Prague's refusal to open up its border with Poland amounted to a violation of human rights.

Happily, Polish–Czechoslovak relations improved steadily throughout 1991. Travel restrictions were finally lifted in May 1991. A Treaty of Friendship and Cooperation was also signed in 1991, and political and diplomatic exchanges intensified. This led to the beginnings of a new warmth in Polish–Czechoslovak relations.

This growing warmth in bilateral relations between Warsaw and Prague was not significantly damaged by the break-up of the Czechoslovak Federation. Poland and the Czech Republic continue to share a number of foreign policy objectives – most importantly, membership of the EU and NATO. Nevertheless, Polish–Czech relations are not without their problems. There are some minor disputes concerning travel restrictions, exchange rates and ecological issues (which are bound up with the pollution of the Oder and with environmentally damaging industrial plants in the Kudowa and Stonawa border region). There is also a 50,000-strong Polish community in the Ostrava region of the Czech Republic, and some disgruntlement over a small slither of the Teschen region which remains under Prague's sovereignty – although neither of these issues is a source of serious inter-governmental controversy. More significantly, Prague and Warsaw are economic competitors, both seeking to develop privileged relations with Western governments and firms.[23] There are also differences in emphasis in terms of security policy: Poland tends to be more Atlanticist and pro-NATO in orientation, whilst the Czech Republic is more 'European', focusing primarily on the EU and the WEU. Nevertheless, bilateral relations have not been disrupted by any serious controversies, and over recent years have begun to exhibit growing warmth as bilateral exchanges have broadened and intensified.

One particularly heartening aspect of Polish–Czech bilateral relations has been the development of cross-border cooperation at the local level.[24] In September 1992 more than 140 Czech and Polish communities set up a 'voluntary international association', with main offices in Katowice and Ostrava. The aim has been to cultivate good cross-border relations between the Polish industrial area of Upper Silesia and neighbouring Moravian communities in the Czech Republic. Joint projects involving economic and environmental cooperation have been drawn up, and there have been calls for new border crossings to be opened in order to facilitate cross-border commerce and tourism. A number of working commissions have been created, and it is hoped that a joint regional council and an elected executive leadership can be created.

Such cross-border cooperation has helped erode lingering suspicions between Czechs and Poles. As Jan Olbrycht, the Mayor of the Polish half of the ethnically mixed Czech–Polish city of Cieszyn (Teschen) has noted, although 'Polish–Czech contacts have never been easy, the fact that we cooperate at the moment means that both sides are thinking openly and along rational lines [in an effort to] overcome certain negative attitudes'. He continued by pointing out that cooperation between the local authorities in the divided city had already made 'life in Cieszyn more dynamic', and that the Czechs were now proposing to establish an international bank to service financial transactions between the two countries.[25] Contacts between Polish and Czech firms along the border are also becoming more frequent and productive. Such examples of informal cooperation may provide the foundations for a closer and more institutionalised relationship between the two states in future decades.

Polish–Slovak relations

The break-up of the CSFR left the new Slovak state facing an unpropitious external environment. Bratislava faced complicated bilateral relations with virtually all of its neighbours. The one significant exception was Poland. Indeed, relations with Warsaw have been the most uncomplicated and cordial of relations with all its neighbours. There are no major problems with borders or minority communities, and no significant historical grudges. Local Slovak officials have long been keen on expanding cross-border relations, but before the break-up of the Federation, they were hampered by financial and administrative restrictions imposed upon them by the central Czechoslovak authorities in Prague. Since January 1993, however, cross-border exchanges have mushroomed.[26]

Relations between the two states are of course asymmetrical: Poland is about seven times larger than Slovakia in terms of population and territory, although their gross domestic product per person is only marginally different.[27] On the other hand, two things unite them: they are both Slavic nations, and they are both strongly Roman Catholic.[28] This provides the basis for a close cultural and religious relationship, which may well have an important political significance as regional relationships mature. Bratislava and Warsaw also share a commitment – along with Hungary – to closer regional cooperation. This was underlined by Slovak President Kovác in January 1994 on the occasion of his first visit to Poland.

Polish–Hungarian relations

Poland and Hungary do not share a common border, and therefore are not neighbours in the strict sense of the term. Nonetheless, they are close regional partners, sharing a special relationship that stretches back centuries. Perhaps because they are not contiguous neighbours – and therefore have had no border disputes nor bilateral minority problems – Poles and Hungarians traditionally have enjoyed friendly relations. This friendship can be traced back centuries and was renewed in 1956 when both Poles and Hungarians struggled to loosen the bonds of Soviet domination. 'Poland and Hungary', Misha Glenny has observed, 'have a history of popular friendship that stretches back into the last century and beyond. In 1956, when the two countries became the first in Eastern Europe to revolt, the slogan "Long Live Polish–Hungarian Friendship" was one of the most memorable'.[29]

Polish–Hungarian friendship persisted throughout much of the Cold War. In the 1970s, and more prominently in the 1980s, Poland

and Hungary had reform-minded communist leaderships, who cultivated an informal alliance within the councils of the Warsaw Pact and the CMEA. Cooperation also developed between dissident groups in the two countries, often on a trilateral basis along with the Czechoslovaks. This was to bear fruit after the peaceful transfer of power to former dissident activists in 1989 and 1990. For example, after some initial problems in their bilateral relationship emerged, the prime ministers of the two new democracies agreed to establish a committee to identify and resolve any further bilateral problems.

Since then, relations between Warsaw and Budapest have blossomed. Indeed, following an official visit to Poland, Hungarian Foreign Minister Jeszenszky described Hungarian–Polish relations as the best in Europe (although he added that economic ties could be improved).[30] Hungary and Poland cooperate closely together within the Visegrad group, and have emerged as the driving force behind this regional initiative. They also took the lead in setting up the Carpathian Euroregion in February 1993. Poland and Hungary are, of course, rival suitors for Western investment and for Western favours: nonetheless, their bilateral relations are good, and the two countries contribute to developing multilateral relations in the wider region.

Czech–Slovak relations

The break-up of the Czechoslovak Federation at the end of 1992 created a new and complicated bilateral relationship in the heart of *Mitteleuropa*. The reasons for the failure of the Federation are to be found in both Czechoslovakia's early history and its more recent past. The original Czechoslovak state was created in 1918 to provide mutual protection for two small Slav nations facing a hostile external environment (in the shape of Germany and Hungary).[31] However, during the inter-war years, Slovak dissatisfaction with perceived discrimination and Czech condescension undermined the legitimacy of the Czechoslovak state in Slovak eyes. Some have suggested that the re-established Czechoslovak state would not have survived long into the post-war world had it not been for the imposition of communist and Soviet control in 1948. The creation of a federation in 1969 went some way to assuage Slovak discontent, but with the overthrow of the communist regime, ethnic tensions reappeared. Three issues were illustrative of the growing political distance between Czechs and Slovaks in post-communist Czechoslovakia: the 'hyphen controversy' (April 1990); policy towards the Hungarian national minority (October 1990); and the issue of arms sales (January 1990).[32]

In the end, the break-up of the Federation can be attributed to the uncertainties engendered by the process of post-communist transformation – especially concerning the pace and direction of economic reform. This in turn fuelled political differences, which came to a head in the 1992 Federal elections. Whilst the Czechs elected a centre-right government under Václav Klaus committed to rapid marketisation and integration in the West, the Slovaks elected a left/nationalist government led by Vladimir Meciar, which had a more dirigiste economic policy and a foreign policy aimed at balancing Slovakia's Eastern and Western interests. The 1992 elections thus produced divergent political forces which led the Federation inexorably down the road to the 'velvet divorce'. Despite the fact that separation was not strongly supported by citizens in either state, the political divergence between the Czech and Slovak parliaments created by the 1992 elections led to a blockage of Federal constitutional structures, and consequently to a failure of the 'consociational democracy' that alone could have kept the CSFR together.[33]

The break-up itself was effected with unusual civility. In stark contrast to the disintegration of Yugoslavia and the USSR, the break-up of the CSFR took place peacefully and by mutual agreement. The two states that emerged on 1 January 1993 had no territorial claims on each other, and harboured no major historical grudges. However, as one might expect, bilateral relations were complicated by the details of the 'velvet divorce'. The biggest problems were the division of Federal property, economic relations and the issue of citizenship rights.

The division of Federal assets proved complicated and con-troversial. Disputes over this thorny problem soured relations in the first months after separation. Nonetheless, by the end of 1993, Czech officials stated that 95% of the property had been amicably divided.[34] One important aspect of this was the division of military assets. Given the offensive posture of Warsaw Pact deployments in former Czechoslovakia, 80% of military facilities and airfields were in Bohemia and Moravia. It had been agreed that the armed forces would be divided on a 2:1 basis (reflecting the relative size of the two populations), but this proved difficult to implement in practice. Slovakia also found itself without any air defence system, and facing the task of creating a military command structure virtually from scratch.[35]

Economic issues had been at the heart of the political impasse leading to the break-up of the Federation, and it is therefore not surprising that they were the cause of much dispute throughout most of 1993. The October 1992 agreement to maintain a single currency and a customs union after the break-up of the Federation on 1 January 1993 lasted only thirty-eight days, collapsing in February 1993, and leading to a host of new customs and tax regulations.[36] This in turn contributed to a marked deterioration in bilateral trade: in the first five months of 1993, Czech–Slovak trade declined by 8.8 billion koruny – a fall of approximately 40%.[37] This was more serious for Slovakia, which possesses an economy dominated by uncompetitive 'smokestack' industries and a large armaments industry. Czech–Slovak trade relations remain asymmetrical: whilst the Czech Republic's main trading partner is now Germany, Slovakia's is still the Czech Republic.[38] Nevertheless, bilateral trade remains important for the economic health of both sides, and negotiations have continued to construct a sound basis for conducting bilateral trade on a stable and long-term basis.

The sundering of the Federation raised the problem of the future status of Czechs and Slovaks living in each other's republics. Interwoven with this issue was that of citizenship rights, and cross-border links. Following the velvet divorce, 308,000 Slovaks found themselves living in the new Czech Republic (approximately 4% of the total Czech population), whilst only 55,000 Czechs were left in Slovakia (just over 1%).[39] The Slovaks have been pressing the Czech authorities to grant dual citizenship to Slovaks in the Czech Republic, but this Prague has refused to do – despite the fact that it has dual citizenship accords with several other countries. The process of naturalisation of ethnic Slovaks in the Czech Republic has also been implemented at a very slow pace. Despite these legal complications, however, relations between ordinary Czechs and Slovaks remain generally good, with no major feelings of resentment or dislike between the two communities.[40]

Thus despite some difficult problems, the break-up of the CSFR has not led to any intractable disputes. Czech–Slovak relations deteriorated temporarily in early 1993 as conflicts flared up over the break-up of the customs union, the creation of separate currencies and the division of Federal property. But by the autumn, inter-governmental relations had warmed considerably after a series of regular meetings between leading government representatives and top officials. They strove to cement a 'special relationship', which bore fruit in the form of close bilateral cooperation in a number of multilateral fora. The Czech Republic gave strong support to Slovakia in both the Council of Europe and the Central European Initiative at a time when Bratislava was under intense criticism from Hungary for its human rights policies, and also supported the case for Slovak membership of NATO. Conversely, Slovakia lobbied hard for the Czech Republic's membership of the UN Security Council (which was finally granted in October 1993).[41]

As to the future of Czech–Slovak relations, much depends on domestic political developments in the two republics. It was evident, for example, that bilateral relations improved considerably after the fall of the first Meciar government in March 1994. As the then Slovak Foreign Minister Eduard Kukan has noted, their bilateral relationship is still 'in the building stage', and a constructive attitude on the part of both governments can make all the difference to its overall health and prospects. Although there is some nostalgia for the former Federation (especially in Slovakia), no serious political forces are calling for its re-establishment. However, even if inter-governmental relations remain good, the economic gap between the two republics is likely to widen. Their foreign policy orientation may also demonstrate some differences of tone and direction, with the Czech Republic focusing primarily on its *Westpolitik* and seeking rapid integration into the EU and NATO, whilst Slovakia attempts to balance its goal of integration in the West with good relations with its neighbours to its east and south (Ukraine, Romania and Serbia). Finally, cultural relations may also weaken, given the diverging economic and political priorities of Prague and Bratislava.[42]

One last point to note is that the future of Czech–Slovak relations will be affected by the process of European integration. If the two republics both become members of the EU, NATO, and other Western organisations, this will transform the context within which their bilateral relationship takes place. This is particularly the case as both countries become integrated into a globalising economy, with its regional hub located in Germany and the central European economy. As the then Slovak Prime Minister Moravcik said at a press conference in June 1994, membership of the EU would effectively make the division of Czechoslovakia 'only temporary', given that as EU members they would 'again have the closest possible contacts'.[43]

Hungarian–Slovak relations

'It is true', Robert Kann has commented, 'that most Slavic peoples and indeed Germanic and Romance peoples had conflicts with some of their neighbours some of the time; the Magyars had trouble with them most of the time'.[44] This is certainly true when one comes to consider relations between Magyars and Slovaks. In East Central Europe today, the most conflictual bilateral relationship is that between Budapest and Bratislava. History, economics and politics have conspired to make this relationship a sour and suspicious one. Historically, the Slovaks were for a thousand years ruled by the Hungarians, who exercised their overlordship in a domineering and arrogant manner. Even today, many Hungarians still regard southern Slovakia, which they refer to as the *Felvidék* or 'Uplands', as an integral part of Hungary.[45] Consequently the Slovaks – still seeking to assert their national identity and their independent statehood – are deeply suspicious of Hungarian policy, fearing that Budapest harbours a hidden agenda dedicated to reversing the Treaty of Trianon and re-establishing a 'Greater Hungary' at Slovakia's expense (amongst others).

This legacy of mutual distrust and ancient animosities provides fertile soil for the proliferation of bilateral disputes. Two conflicts in particular stand out: the problem of the Magyar minority in Slovakia, and the Gabcikovo-Nagymaros dams on the Danube. The disputes over these two contentious issues have not only soured Hungarian–Slovak bilateral relations, but have also threatened to derail tentative steps towards multilateral cooperation in the region.

The Hungarian minority is concentrated in the *Felvidék* along Slovakia's border with Hungary. This is an area which was given to the new Czechoslovak state in 1920 for strategic reasons, despite the existence of a substantial Hungarian community. Today the Magyar minority numbers some 600,000 (approximately 11% of Slovakia's population). Ethnic Hungarians live in eleven of Slovakia's thirty-seven districts, forming a small majority in two of them. The Magyar community is well organised and represented in parliament (although its political representation is magnified by

Slovakia's first-past-the-post electoral system).[46] As is usual in such cases, the key grievances of the Magyar minority concern access to schools and higher education in their native tongue; bilingual road signs in areas with a large Hungarian population; and use of Hungarian names and language for official purposes in local administration in parts of the *Felvidék*.

The strengthening of Slovak nationalist aspirations in 1990–91 created a growing sense of unease amongst the Hungarian minority. As has all too often been the case in this region, the assertion of national identity involved hostility towards the 'other', in this case the Magyar community. Consequently, a number of anti-Hungarian demonstrations were organised by Slovak nationalists. The Hungarian community thus looked increasingly to the Federal authorities in Prague for protection, and feared for their future in an independent Slovakia. Their fears seemed justified when the new Slovak constitution was published: rather than referring to 'We, the Citizens of the Slovak Republic', it used the controversial formula 'We, the Slovak nation' – this in a country were non-Slovaks make up 17% of the total population. New Slovak language and land laws also blatantly discriminated against ethnic Hungarians.[47]

The Slovak government's treatment of its Magyar citizens soured Bratislava's already tense relations with Hungary. Prime Minister Meciar sought to exploit anti-Hungarian sentiments, and openly voiced his 'distrust' of Hungary. In this he was given valuable political ammunition by unfortunate comments – reputedly from a senior Hungarian official – pointing out that Hungary had surrendered its Slovak territories to *Czechoslovakia*, and not to an independent Slovak state: such loose talk only fuelled Slovak fears of Hungarian irredentism.[48]

Hungary's response to the problems of the Magyar minority in the *Felvidék* has been to internationalise the problem. Budapest hopes that the international community will pressurise Slovakia to improve its treatment of the Hungarian community, and has thus raised the issue with the EU, the OSCE and the Council of Europe. Hungary also sought to block Slovakia's membership of the Council of Europe, and relented in its opposition only after intense lobbying from the Czech Republic, Poland and EU member states (who argued that greater leverage could be exercised on Bratislava from within the Council of Europe than from without). Slovakia's membership of the Council of Europe was eventually approved in June 1993, but only on the understanding that it made a series of changes to the more objectionable aspects of its policies towards ethnic Hungarians. Since then, Bratislava has removed some of its more blatantly discriminatory measures, but progress on this front in general has been half-hearted and slow.

The second major controversy facing Budapest and Bratislava is the dispute over the Gabcikovo-Nagymaros hydroelectric dam project – 'one of Europe's most ambitious and absurd river-diversion projects'.[49] Plans for such a project had first been mooted in the 1950s, but it was only in 1977 that a treaty was signed between Czechoslovakia and Hungary to create a series of dams and hydroelectric power plants on the Danube. The Czechoslovak and Hungarian authorities originally argued that this scheme would provide much-needed energy, and would improve navigation along the Danube. However, environmentalists in Hungary, Czechoslovakia and Austria opposed the project on the ground that it would irreversibly alter the ecological profile of the region, adversely affecting the sensitive hydro-geology of the Danube basin and jeopardising ground water supplies.[50] In 1984 the 'Danube Circle' was founded in Hungary in order to organise a coordinated campaign against the project, and it quickly acquired a significance beyond its immediate objective. Indeed, opposition to the Gabcikovo-Nagymaros dam project became one of the catalysts for the emergence of a wider 'civil society' in Hungary, which was ultimately to lead to the disintegration of the Kadar regime.[51]

By 1989, the Hungarian authorities were under intense domestic pressure over the issue, and finally the government decided to suspend work on its part of the project. Within Czechoslovakia, opinion on the project in Prague was divided, but in Slovakia the issue became increasingly bound up with the growing nationalist movement. In April 1991, the Hungarian parliament passed a resolution asking the government to start negotiations with the Czechoslovaks cancelling the 1977 treaty. They said it would have 'serious ecological and economic consequences' for both countries. Attempts to negotiate a solution to the imbroglio in the summer of 1992 came up against Hungarian high-handedness and rising Slovakian nationalism. As the dispute worsened, the Czechoslovak Federal Minister of Environment issued dark warnings that failure to resolve the Danubian dams controversy could result in 'armed conflict' between the two sides.[52] Finally, in March 1992, the

Hungarian parliament issued an ultimatum: unless the Slovaks halted work on the dams, Budapest would abrogate the 1977 treaty – a step finally taken in May 1992.[53] The Slovak response was to proceed with a variant of the original project (the 'C-Variant') which involved a minor diversion of the Danube upstream from Dunakiliti, where both banks lie in Slovakia.[54] Hungary in turn claimed that this act would alter the border and thus breach international law. Nonetheless, in October 1992, the diversion went ahead, leaving the original bed of the Danube nothing more than a miserable little creek.[55]

The Danubian dam affair demonstrates the powerful effect nationalism can have on the international politics of Central and Eastern Europe. Bratislava's intransigent stance on the Gabcikovo-Nagymaros dams partly reflected the new Republic's economic interest in completing the project. But at the same time, the dam issue increasingly assumed a symbolic importance far beyond its immediate economic value – it became an issue of Slovak national pride. Completing the dams project thus became entwined with Slovak national identity and the assertion of its nascent international sovereignty. This is what made the dispute so unamenable to settlement through bilateral negotiation for so long.

Faced with Slovakia's intransigence, Hungary once again attempted to internationalise the dispute.[56] In October 1992 Budapest wrote to the Danube Commission (which regulates transportation along the river); invoked the CSCE Emergency Procedure; and then wrote to the UN Security Council. In the end, it was the EU which played the key role in the peaceful defusing of the conflict – a development which underlines the increasingly important role of the EU in post-Cold War Europe.[57] The European Community had been drawn into the dispute as early as 1990, but from May 1992 it played an increasingly influential role in the mediation process. The leverage enjoyed by Brussels in this dispute stemmed from the fact that both Hungary and Slovakia were keen to secure favours from and eventual membership of the Union. The break-through in the dams controversy occurred at an EC–Visegrad Summit in London in late October 1992. In the resulting London Protocol it was agreed that the dispute would be put to the International Court of Justice (ICJ) in the Hague. This was finally done in April 1993 following a meeting between the Hungarian and Slovak prime ministers, chaired by the European Commissioner Hans Van den Broek. Both sides have agreed to respect the decision of the ICJ. Thus as Alfred Reisch notes, by turning an emotionally charged political issue into a technical and legal one, this accord 'temporarily defused one of the two major causes of Slovak–Hungarian tension'.[58]

The ups and downs of Budapest and Bratislava's relations over recent years demonstrate the influence of the wider international community on bilateral relations in East Central Europe. They also demonstrate how sensitive bilateral relations are to domestic political developments. Early tensions were very much aggravated by the confrontational attitude of Slovak Prime Minister Meciar and, to a lesser extent, by the flirtation of Hungarian Prime Minister Ántáll with the nationalist right in his own party. After the fall of Meciar in March 1994, bilateral relations noticeably improved. The new Foreign Minister Eduard Kukan stressed his government's commitment to improving relations with its neighbours, and committed himself to a process of intense dialogue with Budapest in order to tackle outstanding bilateral disputes.[59] Relations with Slovakia also became an important issue of dispute in the spring 1994 parliamentary elections in Hungary.[60] The elections were won convincingly by the Hungarian Socialist Party (the MSP, the successor to the former reformist-led communist party, the MSzMP), led by Gyula Horn (the former Hungarian foreign minister under the last MSzMP regime). The MSP recognised the importance of seeking to protect Magyar minorities abroad, but argued that it should not be the *sole* criterion for dealing with neighbours – a mistake which, they claimed, the Ántáll government had made. Instead, they argued that this foreign policy objective needed to be balanced with two other foreign policy goals: integration in European multilateral organisations, and good relations with Hungary's neighbours. They therefore called for a 'historic compromise' with Slovakia and Romania, which would seek to build mutual trust through state treaties confirming the inviolability of borders and guaranteeing minority rights.[61]

Hungary's new socialist government naturally found it more difficult translating these laudable principles into concrete policy. The new Prime Minister, Gyula Horn, made an early visit to Bratislava in August 1994 in attempt to 'win mutual trust and eliminate tensions' between the two neighbouring countries. However, although a number of agreements were signed, the draft of the bilateral state treaty was not signed.[62] Nevertheless, progress in bilateral relations continues. In February 1995, Hungary, Slovakia and Romania signed the Council of Europe's framework convention on minorities. More significantly, the long-awaited Hungarian–Slovak 'basic treaty' was signed in March 1995. This renounced all territorial claims and confirmed the existing border. It also incorporated a Council of Europe non-binding recommendation calling for 'appropriate local or autonomous authorities' in areas where ethnic Hungarians constitute a majority.[63] At the same time, Vladimir Meciar (Prime Minister for the second time from December 1994) even spoke of the positive role minorities could play in bilateral relations. 'Mutual trust and understanding', he declared, 'will make the minorities a bridge, a connecting link instead of a problem'.[64]

Whether this new mood will last is of course difficult to predict. Certainly, the issue of minority rights remains acutely sensitive throughout Central and Eastern Europe. In particular, the question of whether the rights of minority communities can best be protected through *individual* or *collective* rights has now emerged as the single most contentious human rights issue in post-Cold War Europe. Whereas most Hungarians advocate a system of collective human rights provisions,[65] Slovakia, supported by Romania and Serbia, have argued that collective rights can be divisive and generate secessionist aspirations.[66] They therefore insist that minority communities' rights can best be safeguarded by a comprehensive regime of individual human rights. This view has been supported by Václav Havel,[67] and reflects mainstream thinking within the OSCE, the UN and the Council of Europe. This issue of collective versus minority rights raises a whole host of complex philosophical and political issues, and is a question which has a pressing relevance for international relations in Europe extending far beyond Slovak–Hungarian bilateral relations.[68]

Given the emotions surrounding the disputes over minority rights and the Gabcikovo-Nagymaros dams, it is striking the extent to which Slovak–Hungarian relations have been managed in such a relatively peaceful and sober way. The inflammatory potential of both disputes has been considerably defused, and the ground prepared for mediation efforts. Two reasons account for this. First is 'the moderating influence exerted by some leaders and the ultimately sensible stance adopted by most Hungarian and Slovak politicians in coping with bilateral disputes, which has offset to a large extent their understandable inexperience in managing bilateral relations'.[69] Thus despite Meciar's frequently inflammatory comments and his nationalist rhetoric, other senior Slovak politicians have sought to defuse the situation. For example, the Slovak Defence Minister, Imrich Andrejcak, twice denied Meciar's claims that Hungary was beginning a regional arms race, whilst Slovak President Michal Kovác has established an inter-ethnic round table to engage in permanent dialogue with the Magyar minority. Moreover, even Meciar himself agreed to establish a 'hot line' with his Hungarian counterpart in July 1992.

The second reason for the successful management of Hungarian–Slovak tensions has been the constructive role played by international organisations operating in the context of a post-Cold War 'concert of Europe'. Hungary's and Slovakia's desire to join Western multilateral organisations – in particular the EU – has given the international community considerable leverage. Both states have demonstrated their respect for international law and for the authority of the ICJ in the Hague. The Council of Europe and the OSCE have also been able to facilitate the search for a peaceful resolution of Hungarian–Slovak disputes.[70] This in turn demonstrates how far Europe – or rather, Central and Western Europe – has moved from the 1930s when a Hobbesian condition of anarchy dominated by a Bismarckian realpolitik held sway in Europe. Today, the elements of 'international society' completely outweigh the elements of competition and conflict in Central and Western Europe. East Central Europe is thus already part of what Hedley Bull has termed 'international society':

> A society of states (or international society) exists when a group of states, conscious of certain common interests and common values, form a society in the sense that they conceive themselves to be bound by a common set of rules in their relations with one another, and share in the workings of common institutions.[71]

Hungarian–Czech relations

Since the break-up of the CSFR, Hungary and the Czech Republic no longer share a common border. Perhaps because they are not immediate neighbours, relations between them have been, and remain, good. Budapest and Prague are close partners within the Visegrad group, and share common democratic and European values. They also face similar problems of post-communist reform, and share many common foreign and security concerns.

On the other hand, they are economic competitors and rival suitors for the attention, support and investment of the West. There are also some differences between them on the nuances of foreign policy. For example, whilst Hungary is keen to see the Visegrad group develop into an effective forum for multilateral cooperation, the Czech government under Václav Klaus tends to regard regional cooperation as a distraction from the real task of Czech foreign policy, which he defines as rapid integration into Western organisations. Klaus also tends to be more sceptical than his Visegrad partners of other regional cooperation ventures, such as the CEI.

A more significant source of political difference between Prague and Budapest has been relations with Slovakia and the broader question of minority rights in Central Europe. On the eve of the CEI summit in July 1993, for example, Prime Minister Ántáll sent Klaus a letter. Klaus interpreted this letter as an attempt to secure Czech support for Hungary's policy of preventing Slovakia's accession to the Council of Europe until Bratislava changed its policy towards its Magyar community. Klaus strongly rejected this overture, and stressed that the Czech Republic had no intention of interfering in bilateral disputes between Hungary and Slovakia. He subsequently supported Slovakia both at the Council of Europe and at the CEI summit. The Czech government has also made it clear that it rejects the Hungarian view that the minority problem is the dominant issue in Central Europe, and has argued that detailed legislative measures to guarantee minority rights would harm rather than help European stablity.[72]

Conclusion

The end of the Cold War has led to a veritable explosion in cross-border exchanges throughout East Central Europe. During the Cold War, communist authorities in Warsaw Pact states acted as 'gatekeepers', preventing the free flow of people and ideas across borders of nominally 'fraternal socialist allies'.[73] With the disintegration of communist authoritarianism, transnational social, economic and political links have proliferated, largely on an informal basis. These informal developments have stimulated legal and political steps to regulate and formalise them, primarily through the medium of bilateral state treaties and agreements on cross-border exchanges.

Bilateral relations in East Central Europe have on the whole developed positively in the years since 1989, despite some early teething problems. Relations between Budapest and Bratislava are the exception, where serious disputes have arisen over the Danube dams and the Magyar community in southern Slovakia. In the rest of the region, bilateral relations have been generally cordial and constructive, although without the intimacy and sense of shared destiny found in areas with a more established sense of regional identity (such as the Nordic region or amongst the Benelux countries). This is because the Visegrad states remain divided over a series of economic and political issues, even though they share many problems and pursue broadly compatible foreign policy goals. The pattern of bilateral relations in the region is also distorted by the asymmetries between the Visegrad four: in particular, Poland's size means it could potentially dwarf its East Central European neighbours in any multilateral regional arrangement. Finally, within the web of bilateral relations in the region, it is interesting to note that only Slovakia borders all the other Visegrad states. Its geopolitical location could therefore give it a potentially pivotal role within the Visegrad group. However, Slovakia is also the most insecure of the four, with severe economic problems and a tendency towards what has been called 'chauvino-communism'.[74] Slovakia's future foreign and security policies will therefore have a significant impact on the evolution of bilateral relations in the region.

Bilateral relations are only some of the strands making up the web of international relations in East Central Europe. In the following chapter we will move on from bilateral relations to consider various examples of multilateral cooperation in East Central Europe, focusing on the Visegrad group, the CEI, Alpe Adria, the Baltic Cooperation Council, the Carpathian–Tisza integration scheme and Euroregions in East Central Europe. We will conclude by assessing the significance of, and the prospects for, regional cooperation and conflict in East Central Europe on the eve of the twenty-first century.

Endnotes

1   Paul G. Lewis, 'History, Europe and the politics of the East', in Stephen White, Judy Batt and Paul G. Lewis, eds, *Developments in East European Politics*, London, Macmillan, 1993, pp. 262–79 (p. 274).
2   Joseph Nye and Robert Keohane have drawn attention to the importance of these 'transnational interactions' (which they define as 'the movement of

tangible or intangible items across state boundaries when at least one actor is not an agent of government or an intergovernmental organisation'). See their edited volume, *Transnational Relations and World Politics*, Harvard, Harvard University Press, 1972.

3   For details see Istvan Lazar, *Hungary: A Brief History*, Budapest, Corvina, 1989, pp. 87–90.

4   Teschen was of vital strategic importance for Czechoslovakia because the only east–west rail link between the 'head and the tail' of the country ran across this piece of territory. Teschen also had some valuable mines, which both sides coveted. Philip Longworth, *The Making of Eastern Europe*, London, Macmillan, 1992, p. 70.

5   Piotr S. Wandycz, *The Price of Freedom*, London, Routledge, 1992, p. 204.

6   For details of the foundation and history of the Little Entente, see R. Machray's two works, *The Little Entente*, London, 1929, and *The Struggle for the Danube and the Little Entente 1929–1938*, London, 1938.

7   For details of Nazi Germany's strategy towards Eastern Europe see John Hiden, *Germany and Europe 1919–1939*, 2nd edn, London, Longman, 1993, pp. 153–67.

8   Joseph Rothschild, *Return to Diversity*, Oxford, Oxford University Press, 1989, p. 5.

9   See David Kaiser, *Economic Diplomacy and the Origin of the Second World War: Germany, Britain, France and Eastern Europe, 1930–1939*, Princeton, Princeton University Press, 1980.

10   'In January 1934 the Poles, whose apprehension had been considerable, were pleasantly surprised by the offer of a non-aggression pact. Not only did they fall for this but also they allowed the new intimacy for a time to put into the background their older links with France.' Michael Balfour, *Germany. The Tides of Power*, London, Routledge, 1992, p. 62.

11   Longworth, *op. cit.*, p. 91.

12   Wandycz, *op. cit.*, p. 205.

13   Michael Roskin, *The Rebirth of East Europe*, London, Prentice-Hall, 1991, pp. 45–7.

14   Philip Zelikow, 'The new concert of Europe', *Survival*, 34, no. 2, summer 1992, pp. 12–30. An example of this European concert is the 'Contact Group' on Bosnia, established in 1994, which brings together the US, Russia, Great Britain, Germany and France.

15   Quoted by Strobe Talbott, 'The new geopolitics: defending democracy in the post-Cold War era', *The World Today*, January 1995, pp. 5–10 (p. 8).

16   Susan Strange has written that she is more optimistic about the prospects for avoiding international conflict than some analysts, 'largely because of structural changes in the international political economy, in production, finance and knowledge, each interacting with the security structure'. *States and Markets*, 2nd edn, London, Pinter, 1988, p. 60.

17   Quoted in Dana H. Allin, 'Can containment work again?', *Survival*, 37, no. 1, spring 1995, pp. 53–65 (p. 54).

18   '[C]ontemporary international relations in Europe are characterised by an element which was largely absent from this arena until relatively recently. While norms constraining state behaviour have always been present to some

degree in inter-state relations, never before have they been codified so clearly to represent the obligations and expectations of states, both in their dealings with other states and in the way they treat their domestic populations. This latter point is a particularly noteworthy development.' Marianne Hanson, 'Democratisation and norm creation in Europe', *European Security After the Cold War, Part 1*, Adelphi Paper 284, London, Brassey's for the IISS, 1993, pp. 28–41.

19 There is a huge literature on the question of democracies and war. For an overview of the issues, see M. Doyle, 'Kant, liberal legacies, and foreign affairs', *Philosophy and Public Affairs*, 12, no. 3, 1983, pp. 205–20; and Raymond Cohen, 'Pacific unions: a reappraisal of theory that "democracies do not go to war with each other"', *Review of International Studies*, 20, no. 3, July 1994, pp. 207–24 (pp. 220–1). We will return to this important theme in the concluding chapter of this book.

20 Jan Zielonka, *Security in Central Europe*, Adelphi Paper 272, London, Brassey's for the IISS, autumn 1992, p. 41.

21 Contacts between the Polish dissident group 'KOR' (the Workers' Defence Committee) and the Czechoslovak group Charter 77 date back to August 1978, when a meeting was held on the Polish–Czechoslovak border. This resulted in the issuing of a joint communique on human rights which included the statement that 'Inalienable human dignity, a value that gives meaning to the life of individuals and nations, is today more than ever before the axis of all our thoughts about the future and the source of all our hopes.' Quoted by Tenly Adams in 'Charter 77 and the Workers' Defense Committee (KOR): The struggle for human rights in Czechoslovakia and Poland', *East European Quarterly*, XXXVI, no. 2, June 1992, pp. 219–38 (p. 234).

22 The former Czech dissident Jan Urban has written that, 'From the end of 1987, we Czech dissidents had concluded that it wasn't enough to make links with groups in the West, welcome as that was. We had to develop a broader context, and even co-operation, with dissidents in other parts of Eastern Europe. From 1988 we had occasional contact with the Polish dissidents. But now we understood that we had to think about joint approaches. So we began to meet regularly with the Poles – Adam Michnik, Jacek Kuron and others – in the mountains on the border. We filmed our woodland picnic and sent it to the Western media, who screened it on television, because we wanted to show that we were now starting a new phase of co-operation.' See his chapter, 'Czechoslovakia: the power and politics of humiliation', in Gwyn Prins, ed., *Spring in Winter: The 1989 Revolutions*, Manchester, Manchester University Press, 1990, pp. 99–136 (pp. 113–14).

23 J. F. Brown, *Hopes and Shadows: Eastern Europe After Communism*, London, Longman, 1994, p. 215.

24 Jan B. de Weydenthal, 'Cross-border diplomacy in East Central Europe', *RFE/RL Research Report*, 1, no. 42, 23 October 1992, p. 21. He notes that the imminent break-up of the Czechoslovak Federation acted as a spur to more intensive cross-border exchanges between both Poland and the Czech Republic, and Poland and Slovakia.

25 Jan B. de Weydenthal, 'Cross-border cooperation in East Central Europe', *RFE/RL Research Report*, 3, no. 2, 14 January 1994, pp. 32–5.

26   Jan B. de Weydenthal, 'Cross-border diplomacy in East Central Europe', *RFE/ RL Research Report*, 1, no. 42, 23 October 1992, p. 21.

27   Poland's population in 1992 was 38,300,000, whilst that of Slovakia was 5,260,000; Poland's territory is 312,677 square kilometres whilst Slovakia's is 49,035; and their respective gross domestic product per person in 1992 was estimated to be: Poland, $1,895; Slovakia, $1,820. Source: *The Economist*, 13 March 1993.

28   Jan Urban notes that the first major stirrings of dissident in Slovakia occurred in 1987 as a direct response to the example of the Polish Catholic Church's political activities. In 1987, he notes, 'there was an upsurge in the Catholic Church because of Poland. The Jakes/Husak regime was stupid enough to beat some of the Catholic demonstrators. And again, the people of Art became "oppositionary"'. Urban, *op. cit.*, p. 129.

29   Misha Glenny, *The Rebirth of History: Eastern Europe in the Age of Democracy*, London, Penguin, 1990, pp. 92–3.

30   Alfred A. Reisch, 'Central Europe's disappointments and hopes', *RFE/RL Research Report*, 3, no. 12, 25 March 1994, pp. 18–37 (p. 34).

31   David Kelly, 'Woodrow Wilson and the creation of Czechoslovakia', *East European Quarterly*, XXVI, no. 2, summer 1992, pp. 185–207.

32   For details see Glenny, *op. cit.*, pp. 37–44; and Gale Stokes, *The Walls Came Tumbling Down. The Collapse of Communism in Eastern Europe*, Oxford, Oxford University Press, 1993, pp. 180–1.

33   The concept of 'consociational democracy' was developed by Arend Lijphart to refer to those liberal democracies which operated in multinational societies with mutually reinforcing cleavages. He described these 'deviant cases of fragmented but stable democracies' as 'consociational democracies', the essential characteristic of which were 'not so much any particular institutional arrangement as overarching cooperation at the elite level with the deliberate aim of counteracting the disintegrative tendencies in the system.' A. Lijphart, 'Consociational democracy', *World Politics*, 21, January 1969, p. 211; and 'Typologies of democratic systems', *Comparative Political Studies*, 1, April 1968, p. 21. For an excellent analysis of the reasons for the break-up of the Czechoslovak Federation (which draws heavily on the writings of Lijphart), see Karen Henderson, *Czechoslovakia: The Failure of Consensus Politics*, Leicester University Discussion Papers in Politics, no. P93/4, August 1993.

34   Jiri Pehe, 'The Czech Republic: a successful transition', *RFE/RL Research Report*, 3, no. 1, 7 January 1994, pp. 70–5.

35   For details see Theo van den Doel, *Central Europe: The New Allies? The Road from Visegrad to Brussels*, Oxford, Westview, 1994, pp. 78–82; *Strategic Survey 1992-1993*, London, Brassey's for the IISS, 1993; and *The Military Balance 1993-1994*, London, Brassey's for the IISS, 1993, p. 66.

36   Jiri Pehe, 'The Czech–Slovak currency split', *RFE/RL Research Report*, 2, no. 10, 5 March 1993, pp. 27–32.

37   Jeffrey Simon, *Czechoslovakia's "Velvet Divorce", Visegrad Cohesion, and European Fault Lines*, McNair Paper 23, Washington, DC, National Defense University, October 1993, p. 4.

38   Sharon Fisher, 'Slovakia: the first year of independence', *RFE/RL Research Report*, 3, no.1, 7 January 1994, pp. 87–91.

39   *The Economist*, 13 March 1993.

40   The warmth between Czechs and Slovaks on a personal level can perhaps be gauged from the fact that 12% of all marriages on former Czechoslovak territory were between individuals from the two communities. Sharon Fisher, 'Czech–Slovak relations two years after the divorce', *RFE/RL Research Report*, 3, no. 27, 8 July 1994, pp. 9–17 (p. 17).

41   *Ibid.*, pp. 10–11.

42   For details of divergent public opinion attitudes see Mary Cline and Sharon Fisher, 'Czech Republic and Slovakia: views on politics and the economy', *RFE/RL Research Report*, 3, no. 27, 8 July 1994, pp. 33–9.

43   Fisher, 'Slovakia: the first year of independence', p. 17.

44   Robert A. Kann and Zdenek V. David, *The Peoples of the Eastern Habsburg Lands, 926–1918*, Seattle, University of Washington Press, 1984, p. 4.

45   As Misha Glenny notes, 'Whatever their public utterances, Hungarians who do not consider the Felvidék, southern Slovakia, to be part of Hungary belong to the rarest of species'; Glenny, *op. cit.*, p. 211.

46   Ethnic Hungarians are represented in parliament by two parties: the Coexistence Movement and the Hungarian Christian Democratic Movement (HCDM). The largest of their cultural and political organisations is CSEMADOK (the Democratic Association of Hungarians in Slovakia). In January 1994 a bitter political dispute broke out following a meeting in Komarno to discuss territorial autonomy. The meeting was organised by the Association of the Zitny Ostrov Towns and Villages (ZMOZO), which represents some 100 ethnic Hungarian mayors and local officials, along with Coexistence and the HCDM. For details see Sharon Fisher, 'Meeting of Hungarians causes stir', *RFE/RL Research Report*, 3, no. 4, 28 January 1994, pp. 42–74.

47   For details see 'Slovakia's new constitution', *East European Reporter*, 5, no. 5, October 1992, pp. 9–10.

48   Brown, *op. cit.*, p. 202.

49   Glenny, *op. cit.*, p. 93.

50   For a useful summary of the arguments for and against the dams project, see Julius Binder, 'Gabcikovo: the case for' and Judit Vasarhelyi, 'Gabcikovo: the case against', *East European Reporter*, 5, no. 5, September/October 1992, pp. 76–82. This edition of the journal also includes a chronology of the Danubian dams project, as well as a related article by Gyorgy Csepeli, 'Solving conflicts'. Another useful article is Sharon Fisher, 'The Gabcikovo-Nagymaros dam controversy continues', *RFE/RL Research Report*, 2, no. 37, 17 September 1993, pp. 7–12.

51   J. Galambos, 'Political aspects of an environmental conflict: the case of the Gabcikovo-Nagymaros dam system', in J. Käkönen, ed., *Perspectives on Environmental Conflict and International Relations*, London, Pinter, 1992, pp. 72–95.

52   J. Kramer, *Energy and the Environment in Eastern Europe*, a paper presented at the British International Studies Association conference, University of Lancaster, 16–18 December 1991.

53   Karoly Okolicsanyi, 'Hungary cancels treaty on Danube dam construction', *RFE/RL Research Report*, 1, no. 26, 26 June 1992, p. 48.

54 *Daily Telegraph*, 30 March 1992. See also B. Slocock, *Environmental Policy in Eastern Europe: The Emerging Coordinates*, a paper presented at the ECPR Joint Sessions Workshops, University of Essex, 1991.

55 Karoly Okolicsanyi, 'Slovak–Hungarian tension: Bratislava diverts the Danube', *RFE/RL Research Report*, 1, no. 49, 11 December 1992, pp. 49–54.

56 Vera Rich, 'The murky politics of the Danube', *The World Today*, August/September 1993, pp. 151–2.

57 Gabriel Munuera, *Preventing Armed Conflict in Europe: Lessons From Recent Experience*, Chaillot Paper 15/16, Paris, WEU Institute for Security Studies, June 1994, p. 10.

58 Alfred A. Reisch, 'Hungarian–Slovak relations: a difficult first year', *RFE/RL Research Report*, 2, no. 50, 17 December 1993, p. 18.

59 Sharon Fisher, 'New Slovak government formed after Meciar's fall', *RFE/RL Research Report*, 3, no. 13, 1 April 1994, p. 12.

60 Alfred A. Reisch, 'Hungarian parties' foreign-policy electoral platforms', *RFE/RL Research Report*, 3, no. 19, 13 May 1994, pp. 14–21.

61 Alfred A. Reisch, 'Consensus on Hungary's foreign policy frayed by elections', *RFE/RL Research Report*, 3, no. 20, 20 May 1994, pp. 42–8.

62 See Gabriel Partos, 'Who's afraid of post-communism?', *The World Today*, February 1995, pp. 28–32 (p. 31); and *RFE/RL News Brief*, 8 August 1994.

63 'Hungary and Slovakia treaty makes play for EU acceptance', *The Guardian*, 18 March 1995.

64 'History holds up ties with West', *The Guardian*, 2 February 1995.

65 See for example the interview with Istvan Baba, the Hungarian Deputy State Secretary responsible for Central and Eastern Europe, in *East European Reporter*, 5, no. 4, July/August 1992, pp. 55–7. He argues that '"Individual rights" sounds good but, in practice, rights to what? For, if we are talking about the right to a certain kind of education or religion then this no longer concerns only the individual. There are a number of areas where the rights of the individual are simply insufficient to guarantee the rights of minorities as such. Another example is the representation of minorities in national assemblies or local councils, which is a particular problem for the minorities living in Hungary, on account of the fact that there is no single region where they constitute a majority. In this case, the minority needs some kind of a special treatment' (p. 57).

66 Within Slovakia, the debate on collective rights for the Magyar minority has become increasingly lively, reflecting divergent views within the Slovak majority community. For example, the influential Slovak newspaper *Narodna obrada* reacted to Gyula Horn's visit to Bratislava by arguing that although Slovakia could not afford to make concessions on collective rights on its own, the Council of Europe should adopt a charter on minorities which would then be binding on all Council members. *RFE/RL News Brief*, 9 August 1994.

67 At the Council of Europe summit in Vienna in October 1993, President Havel argued that too much emphasis on minority rights could revive the evils of nationalism and even lead to the questioning of existing borders. He therefore suggested that respect for humanitarian civil rights was the best way to reduce ethnic tensions.

68 For a *tour d'horizon* of institutional and other responses to ethnic minority

claims see William Safran, 'Non-separatist policies regarding ethnic minorities: positive approaches and ambiguous consequences', *International Political Science Review*, 15, no. 1, 1994, pp. 61–80. A more theoretical reflection on minority rights is Vernon Van Dyke, 'The individual, the state and ethnic communities in political theory', *World Politics*, 29, no. 3, April 1977, pp. 343–69, and his later article, 'Collective entities and moral rights: problems in liberal-democratic thought', *Journal of Politics*, 44, no. 1, February 1982), pp. 21–40.

69 Munuera, *op. cit.*, p. 21.
70 On the role of OSCE (formerly the CSCE) see Konrad J. Huber, 'The CSCE's new role in the East: conflict prevention', *RFE/RL Research Report*, 3, no. 31, 12 August 1994, pp. 23–30.
71 Hedley Bull, *The Anarchical Society. A Study of Order in World Politics*, London, Macmillan, 1977, p. 13. The concept of 'international society' has been further developed in Hedley Bull and Adam Watson, eds, *The Expansion of International Society*, Oxford, Oxford University Press, 1984; and Adam Watson, *The Evolution of International Society. A Comparative Historical Analysis*, London, Routledge, 1992.
72 Alfred Reisch, 'The Central European Initiative: to be or not to be?', *RFE/RL Research Report*, 2, no. 34, 27 August 1993, pp. 30–7 (pp. 32–3).
73 See for example Gerald Segal, *Openness and Foreign Policy Reform in Communist States*, London, Routledge for the RIIA, 1992, pp. 1–18.
74 This describes the tendency of some former highly placed communist functionaries to seek to 'salvage some of their political power by a rapid ideological conversion to nationalism'. George Schöpflin, 'Culture and identity in post-communist Europe', in Stephen White, Judy Batt and Paul Lewis, eds, *Developments in East European Politics*, London, Macmillan, 1993, pp. 16–34 (p. 32).

Chapter Five

Regional conflict and cooperation: II. Multilateral relations

> Building on the most important elements of the European tradition, a society of people, working together in harmony, must be brought about which, supported by individual national identities, is committed to universal human values. This society – free of hatred, nationalism, xenophobia, and hostility to its neighbours – is tolerant towards the individual, the family, and towards local, regional, and national communities.
>
> It is the conviction of the signatory states that their cooperation, in view of the political, economic, and social challenges facing them and in view of their efforts for renewal on a democratic basis, is an important step towards the integration of the whole of Europe. (Visegrad Summit, 'Declaration ... on the Road to European Integration', 15 February 1991[1])

The development of new patterns of bilateral relations in East Central Europe has been accompanied by the creation of new structures for multilateral cooperation, both within East Central Europe itself, and in the wider region of Central and Eastern Europe. Indeed, one of the most striking developments since the end of the Cold War has been the re-emergence of historically rooted patterns of regional interaction and exchange. This development has been particularly evident in East Central Europe, where a major reorientation of external relations has taken place since 1989.

The effect of the Cold War on Central Europe was to tear asunder traditional patterns of regional interaction and exchange, and replace them with artificially created bloc structures. During the Cold War, attempts to rekindle previous economic, political and cultural relationships were constrained by the existence of the 'Iron Curtain'.[2] Yet deeply rooted historical relationships endured, as did distinctive regional identities. In East Central Europe, two distinctive regional identities have continued to colour attitudes towards politics and international relations. The first is constituted by Central Europe's most important waterway, the Danube. The mighty Danube river, which once marked the eastern borders of the *Pax Romanus*, runs throughout the *Mitteleuropäische* lands of the former Austro-Hungarian Empire, and helps define a geographical area with a distinctive culture, tradition and identity.[3] The second distinctive regional identity is that shared by states on the Baltic littoral. This regional identity draws sustenance from the historical experience of the medieval Hanseatic League.

Nostalgic memories of both the Hanseatic League and the Habsburg monarchy in *Mitteleuropa* have influenced the emerging pattern of international relations in Central and Eastern Europe. Multilateral structures have been created in both regions which draw on the legacy and traditions of the past whilst seeking to meet contemporary needs. At the same time, the four post-communist states of East Central Europe have responded to what they perceive to be their common interests by creating their own structures for multilateral regional cooperation. In this chapter we shall assess the significance and potential of these multilateral arrangements, beginning with the Alpe Adria Working Community, the Central European Initiative and the Council of Baltic Sea States. We shall then consider the development of Euroregions in East Central Europe, focusing in particular on the Carpathian Euroregion. Of greatest interest, however, is the Visegrad group. This is the most significant and ambitious attempt at regional cooperation in East Central Europe to date. As we shall see, its future prospects are very much bound up with the wider integration process in Europe.

The 'Alpe Adria Working Community'

One of the earliest forms of regional cooperation in Central Europe was the *Comunità di Lavoro Alpe Adria* ('Alpe Adria Working Community'). This was established in 1978 on the initiative of the Venetian local government and has grown to embrace many provinces and regions formerly within the Austro-Hungarian Empire, that is, the northern Italian regions of Venetia, Friuli-Venezia Giulia, Lombardy and Trentino-Alto Adige; the southern Austrian provinces

Styria, Carinthia, Salzburg, Upper Austria and Burgenland; the former Yugoslav republics of Croatia and Slovenia; the Free State of Bavaria; a number of Swiss cantons; and the Hungarian *comitats* of Gyor-Sopron and Vas. Although, of the Visegrad countries, only Hungary is currently involved in Alpe Adria, its value has been recognised by President Havel and the Czechs are keen to cooperate with it. Czech participation in its activities would also provide a bridge between Alpe Adria and Poland.[4]

Originally conceived as a means of linking the northern and southern Alpine regions, it now sees its role more in terms of providing a bridge between East and West. The purpose of Alpe Adria today is to facilitate the growth of contacts and exchanges throughout the area, particularly in border regions. In this way it is hoped that borders can be made more permeable, allowing cooperation across the region to blossom. Alpe Adria seeks to encourage policy coordination in a wide range of areas: trans-Alpine communications, harbour traffic, production and transportation of energy, agriculture, forest use, water use, tourism, protection of the environment, conservation of the cultural and recreational landscape, territorial structure, urban development, cultural links and contact between scientific institutes. Such transnational cooperation and exchange clearly depend on an efficient transport infrastructure, and consequently developing such an infrastructure has been identified as a major task for Alpe Adria. The creation of Alpe Adria has also encouraged more intensive contacts between various interest groups in the region, particularly economic elites.

It is important to understand that Alpe Adria is not meant to be a supranational body taking legally binding decisions. It was conceived as a means of policy *coordination*, and thus has a very limited organisational structure. A conference of presidents of the regions meets annually, but it can only make *recommendations*. It is serviced by a small permanent executive body, the *Commissione Alti Dirigenti*, and by six commissions. These commissions, which are attached to the administration of local governments on a rotational basis, carry out studies and issue joint reports. As Paolo Perulli notes, the activities of the Alpe Adria 'have been more on a level of information than real definition of strategies or common area problems. It can be considered that this work is active in the breaking down of barriers of knowledge between members, and in the creation of a common image at an international level.'[5]

Alpe Adria thus has two main functions – first, policy co-ordination, and second, external lobbying and promotion. It seeks to fulfil its first function by improving information exchange, which it is hoped will both encourage and facilitate the coordination of policy in the region. Thus, for example, by publishing lists of enterprises and institutions willing to cooperate in the fields of applied research, the diffusion of technology and cross-border manufacturing production, it hopes to encourage new forms of cooperation and technology transfer within the Alpe Adria region.

Alpe Adria's second function – external lobbying and promotion – has becoming increasingly important, and is focused primarily on the EU. Much of the energy of Alpe Adria is now directed towards securing grants and structural funds from the European Commission, particularly for infrastructure projects in the region. This promotional and lobbying work is especially significant given the increasing competition for funds and investment between different European regions and sub-regions.[6]

The significance of Alpe Adria for East Central Europe is that it provides a multilateral forum for practical cooperation between the post-communist democracies and their Western neighbours. It is a concrete manifestation of their return to Europe, and thus has considerable political symbolism. It also helps prepare them for their primary foreign policy goal – membership of the EU. Moreover, such regional cooperation can provide economic and political benefits, particularly for those in border regions. Transnational exchanges help make borders more permeable. In the short term, this can (and has) been an issue of political controversy, as inward-looking nationalists bemoan the perceived loss of national identity that cultural interaction and transnational exchanges inevitably involve. In the long term, however, making borders more permeable and encouraging a sense of regional identity can help defuse cross-border ethno-national tensions.

From the Pentagonale to the Central European Initiative

The success of Alpe Adria acted as a stimulus to more ambitious schemes of multilateral cooperation in the Danubian region, this time on an inter-governmental rather than a purely local authority level. The origins of this inter-governmental cooperation lie with an agreement on quadripartite cooperation between Italy, Austria,

Hungary and Yugoslavia which resulted from a meeting of foreign ministers in Budapest in November 1989. The four were later joined by Czechoslovakia and, in April 1990, the 'Pentagonale Initiative' was formally launched. The initiative included projects in the fields of environmental protection; cooperation between small and medium-sized enterprises; transport links; information and telecommunications; culture; and education and youth exchanges. The five also began coordinating their foreign policy initiatives in fora such as the UN, the Council of Europe and the CSCE Human Rights meeting in Copenhagen in June 1990 (where they presented a joint twenty-point proposal on the collective rights of minorities). The first heads of government meeting took place in July 1990, where a formal declaration setting out the objectives of the 'Pentagonale' was adopted.

From early on, Poland was keen to participate in the Pentagonale. However, when the question of Poland's application was raised by the Hungarians in July 1990, Italy was cool to the idea. Nevertheless, Poland began cooperating with two of the Pentagonale's working groups (or commissions). Then, in December 1990, Poland's request for membership finally won the support of both Italy and Hungary. One reason for this was that the international standing of both the Yugoslav Federation and the Czech and Slovak Federal Republic had been weakened by escalating nationalist discontent, and this threatened to undermine the effectiveness of the Pentagonale as a whole. Poland thus became the sixth member of the initiative in July 1991, when the Pentagonale formally became the Hexagonale.

The Hexagonale was not conceived as a security alliance, and had no formal military dimension. Hungary proposed the creation of a 'zone of confidence' between the original four, in which offensive weapons would be withdrawn from a zone of 50 kilometres (initially along the Austrian–Hungarian–Yugoslav borders), but this received a very cool reaction from its partners. Since then, security issues have not figured prominently on the agenda of this regional initiative. The primary purpose of the Hexagonale was to create new webs of international allegiances and cooperative relations. Some of its members also hoped it would provide a partial counterweight to German hegemony in *Mitteleuropa*. For most, however, the role of the Hexagonale was closely linked to the European Community. This was because the Hexagonale brought together countries who saw the Community as a central focus of their international aspirations –

either as a founder member in Italy's case, or as would-be members in the case of the other five.

The descent of Yugoslavia into the nightmare of civil war increasingly paralysed the activities of the Hexagonale. However, most of its members did not want to lose the potential for regional cooperation that the Hexagonale promised. Hungary in particular was keen to see Central European cooperation further developed, and consequently played a key role in resuscitating the organisation. Thus at a summit meeting in July 1992 the decision was taken to relaunch the now defunct Hexagonale as the 'Central European Initiative' (CEI). Membership of the CEI consisted of the former Hexagonale members, Poland, Hungary, Czechoslovakia, Austria and Italy, along with Croatia, Slovenia and Bosnia-Herzegovina. In May 1993 the Czech and Slovak republics joined as separate members. Finally, Macedonia was admitted as a member in July 1993, bringing membership of the CEI to ten. Bulgaria, Romania, Belarus and Ukraine have also expressed an interest in joining, and in May 1992 became members of a 'contact group' which met at foreign minister level. Since March 1993, they have also participated in some of the CEI's specialised working groups.

The pragmatic and flexible character of the CEI is reflected in its loose organisational structure. A conference of prime ministers meets annually, whilst foreign ministers meet biannually. These conferences are the key decision-making bodies, and issue declarations reflecting a consensus. Their agenda is prepared by the Committee of National Coordinators, which meets at least quarterly. A CEI parliamentarians committee meets at the same time as the ministerial conferences. The CEI has thirteen working groups dealing with issues such as the regional economy, transport, agriculture, telecommunications, tourism, environmental protection, information, science and technology, energy, and the development of small and medium-sized businesses. Each working group is the responsibility of one member country. In 1992 a small CEI secretariat was established at the Austrian Foreign Ministry in Vienna. A CEI project secretariat at the EBRD (European Bank for Reconstruction and Development) was established in January 1993, funded by the Italians. The CEI also has a permanent working group on minorities and a contact committee.

The broad aim of the CEI has been the same as that of its predecessor, the Hexagonale, namely to promote regional policy coordination and inter-governmental cooperation on a functional basis. Like Alpe Adria, it does this by encouraging consultation and an exchange of information, in order to facilitate policy coordination. It also draws up plans for joint projects (particularly in the transport sector). In doing so, it hopes to fulfil two long-term aims. First, it provides a bridge between East and West. Participation in the CEI and its working groups is seen as a way of bringing East European states closer to the EU, even if they have not yet signed association agreements. The CEI also hopes it can play a role coordinating Western assistance to the post-communist countries in Central and Eastern Europe. This is the purpose of its project secretariat in the EBRD.

Second, CEI members hope that regional cooperation will be useful in 'overcoming friction and misunderstanding between adjoining cultures and ethnic groups'.[7] The violent break-up of Yugoslavia and tensions between Hungary and its neighbours have made this a pressing concern. The CEI has continued with the Hexagonale's task of tackling the issue of the protection of national minorities, partly in order to give the CEI significance and status on the European scene. A key role in this respect has been played by Hungary, which assumed the presidency of the CEI at the beginning of 1993 (this office is rotated on an annual basis). Hungary has been especially keen for the CEI to take up the issue of minority rights given that 3.5 million ethnic Magyars live on the territory of Hungary's seven neighbours.

However, results on this front have been limited. In June 1990 the Pentagonale presented a joint proposal to the CSCE Copenhagen meeting on the 'Human Dimension'. The Hexagonale established an ad hoc working group on minorities in late 1990, and this became one of the CEI's permanent working groups (chaired by the Hungarians). The CEI itself submitted a communication on national minority rights to the Council of Europe summit in 1993. However, a more substantive CEI policy on the issue of minority rights has proven impossible to negotiate, given the fundamentally different approaches to this issue in the region. Whereas Hungary has pressed the CEI to agree measures designed to safeguard minority rights, Slovakia – supported by the Czech Republic – has argued that this should be left to the Council of Europe or the OSCE. The Slovaks and Czechs have argued that to agree legally binding minority rights in the CEI would create differences in legislation from region to region, thereby undermining the process of European integration.

The CEI thus provides only a limited forum for multilateral cooperation. It has yet to notch up any major practical achievements, and remains a weak consultative forum with aspirations towards policy coordination. Its work has been impeded by nationalist tensions in the region, and it failed to achieve consensus on both minority protection and a common approach at the UN Earth Summit in Rio. Growing scepticism about the usefulness of the CEI (not least on the part of Czech Prime Minister Václav Klaus) precipitated a major debate within the organisation on its rationale and goals. This resulted in a summit in Budapest in July 1993, at which a declaration was adopted outlining the common interests and goals of the CEI's members. The political section of the declaration stressed that regional cooperation was a valuable contribution to the process of European integration; pledged support for both the domestic reforms in post-communist countries and their efforts to rejoin Europe; and emphasised that minority rights were a key question for European peace and security. The economic section called for greater regional economic cooperation; underlined the need for international help in building market economies in the region; and emphasised the importance of the EU for the European integration process. The CEI still has to translate these noble sentiments into concrete policy proposals. Nonetheless, by providing an institutionalised framework for multilateral dialogue and cooperation, the CEI may help identify areas of common interest and thereby facilitate a process of consensus-building around limited policy objectives. As Hungary's late Prime Minister Ántáll noted at the Budapest summit, the CEI remains 'an important political coordination club' for an area covering one million square kilometres and inhabited by 150 million people.[8]

The CEI is also significant because of the impetus it has given to the emerging concept of a 'Europe of the Regions'. This concept has already had an impact on the EU, which now has a 'Committee of the Regions'.[9] The Declaration of Heads of Government at the CEI Summit in Vienna on 18 July 1992 specifically referred to 'the value of regional cooperation as an essential component of the evolving European architecture'. The CEI ministers also 'expressed their deep conviction that ... European institutions will have a central role in the deepening and the widening of European integration; the process of European unification will also need a complementary regional level of cooperation regarding issues of regional significance'.[10]

The future of the CEI is also bound up with the issue of widening versus deepening – a policy dilemma which is already taxing the EU. The CEI now has ten full members, and others are queuing up to join. Albania and Moldova may be offered the opportunity of participating in CEI working groups in the future, whilst Russia's application for membership is currently being examined by the Committee of National Coordinators. If the CEI continues to widen its membership, it will find itself with an even greater differentiation in terms of levels of political and economic development – from Austria at one end of the spectrum to Albania at the other. This will make it harder to achieve meaningful policy coordination and joint initiatives. One final twist to the debate on 'deepening versus widening' is the issue of the relationship of the CEI to the EU. The issue here is whether or not the CEI sees itself as an antechamber to the EU, and whether it should therefore only admit new members who have concluded association agreements with the Union.

The Council of Baltic Sea States

Moving away from the Danubian lands of *Mitteleuropa*, another area of growing regional cooperation is the Baltic. The Scandinavians have long pursued a policy of Nordic cooperation, a policy which dates back to the establishment of the Nordic Council in 1952.[11] More recently, Baltic cooperation has been energetically advocated by the Social Democratic Minister-President of Schleswig-Holstein, Bjorn Engholm. Harking back with nostalgia to the medieval Hanseatic League, he began pressing in the late 1980s for a new Hansa based on regional economic and environmental cooperation. Once again, this vision fitted in well with the notion of a Europe of the Regions, a concept strongly supported by other German *Länder*.

Current efforts to encourage closer regional cooperation in the Baltic date from September 1990, when a joint Swedish–Polish initiative led to an international conference in Ronneby. This explored the potential for regional cooperation in the fields of environmental protection (which has long been an issue of concern to the Nordic states), communications and transport infrastructure. Following the success of the Ronneby conference, a Dannish–German initiative led to a further conference on Baltic cooperation, held in March 1992. From this emerged a 'Council of Baltic Sea

States', which embraces all the Baltic littoral states: Poland, Denmark, Estonia, Finland, Germany, Latvia, Lithuania, Norway, Russia and Sweden.[12]

The Council of Baltic Sea States has two primary concerns: environmental protection, and the expansion of trade around the Baltic. Environmental problems have grown in recent years as the Baltic has become more and more polluted. Many fear that Russia and other financially hard-up post-communist regimes will continue with environmentally harmful practices unless they are given Western assistance and advice. As regards the expansion of regional trade, this, it is believed, will provide benefits for all involved – not least because it will assist the transformation of Poland, Russia and the three Baltic republics into market economies with stable democratic governments. Improved transport and communications links are widely regarded as prerequisites for boosting regional trade, and consequently discussions have begun within the Council of Baltic Sea States on this issue. In February 1994, for example, transport ministers met in Kaliningrad to discuss the establishment of a 'Via Baltica', a highway envisaged as a major thoroughfare linking the countries around the Baltic Sea.[13]

One further area where Baltic regional cooperation is urgently required is crime prevention. Cross-border criminal activity has become a serious threat to regional security over recent years. The collapse of communism in the East has weakened domestic law enforcement agencies, and generated a largely unregulated free market economy permeated by a 'get-rich-quick' ethos. This has created ideal conditions for the proliferation of mafiosa-type activities.[14] The Baltic area has suffered particularly from such criminal activities, and they have been the subject of a series of high-level conferences between the Baltic states. At an international conference in Sweden in December 1993 attended by all the Baltic states, it was concluded that 'there is a tendency towards an increase in organised crime, in the Baltic Sea area. This development has taken place in the last few years and has been particularly noticeable in 1993.... There are signs that such crime is gradually becoming more serious.'[15] In response to this problem, efforts have begun to utilise the Council of Baltic Sea States in order to coordinate crime-prevention policy and cross-border police cooperation.

The Council of Baltic Sea States thus continues the tradition of the Nordic Council in eschewing efforts to establish a supranational authority dealing with issues of 'high politics' (such as monetary union and defence). Instead it concentrates on pragmatic efforts to coordinate policy in relatively low-profile – but nonetheless important – areas such as environmental rules, transport policy, trade regulations and crime policy. For Poland, such regional cooperation provides another pathway back to Europe.

Cooperation in the Carpathians–Tisza Region

Cross-border cooperation has not only developed between the Visegrad countries and their Western neighbours. In February 1992, an agreement was signed between Poland, Hungary, the Czech and Slovak Federation and Ukraine to develop economic and environmental cooperation in their border areas. The four countries agreed to encourage the creation of cross-border ecological services and protected areas; to promote tourism; to provide mutual assistance in the event of mass migration; to investigate prospects for joint invest-ment projects; and to create duty-free zones along their border lands.

This was followed by the creation of the Carpathian–Tisza regional integration scheme, modelled directly on the *Comunità Alpe Adria*. Discussions on this scheme began in January 1992 in the Hungarian town of Nyiregyhaza. These discussions involved officials from Ukraine, Czechoslovakia, Hungary, Poland and Romania. The founding document for this scheme was signed in April 1992, and outlined proposals for cooperation in the fields of economy, information, culture, science, environmental protection and tourism.[16] Unfortunately, the signing of this document was not followed up by any substantive steps towards regional cooperation. This was partly because of the political uncertainty generated by the break-up of Czechoslovakia, but more importantly because of the growing suspicion of this sort of regional cooperation scheme on the part of Romania. The Romanian President Ion Iliescu was sharply critical of such plans, fearing that they amounted to little more than yet another Hungarian scheme to form some sort of association with Transylvania (an area of Romania with a substantial Magyar community).[17]

Nonetheless, interest in cross-border cooperation between the East Central Europeans and Ukraine continued, and after more than a year of consultations, representatives of local authorities in the contiguous border areas of Hungary, Poland, Slovakia and Ukraine met in the Hungarian town of Debrecen in February 1993. They signed an agreement establishing a 'Carpathian Euroregion', designed to facilitate cross-border cooperation on a voluntary basis amongst local communities in all four countries.[18] The immediate objective of the agreement was to streamline communications throughout the area by setting up telephone exchanges, establishing economic information centres, planning new roads, and opening more border crossing points. In the longer term, the agreement sought to encourage coordinated efforts to protect the environment; to support small businesses; and to develop contacts between different communities by cultural exchanges, cooperation between religious organisations and media reports on topics of common concern.

To fulfil these ambitious goals, the signatories created a twelve-member council which was to coordinate regional activities. The council was to be composed of three members from each country: two representing the local communities, and one from the central state administration. This council in turn would elect a general secretary, who would be responsible for directing a small permanent office. The general secretary's post was to be rotated annually amongst representatives of the participating countries (the first general secretary being a local Polish official, Adam Peziol).

The establishment of the Carpathian Euroregion might well be seen as a rather modest step forward, but its launch received considerable publicity. The foreign ministers of Hungary, Poland and Ukraine all attended, as did the then Secretary-General of the Council of Europe, Catherine Lalumière. The Council of Europe's involvement reflects the importance attached to Euroregions by this body as a means of defusing inter-ethnic conflict.[19] The Council hopes that by promoting cross-border economic transactions, cultural exchanges and transnational social interactions, mutual suspicions between neighbouring communities can be broken down. Indeed, at the signing ceremony in Debrecen, Catherine Lalumière is reported to have said, 'this agreement marks a step toward stability in your area'.[20]

'Euroregions' in East Central Europe

The creation of the Carpathian Euroregion follows the creation of Euroregions in many other parts of Europe. Euroregions have been a feature of the West European integration process for over thirty years now. The first one – the 'Regio' – was established in 1963 between Alsace in France, Baden-Wüttemberg in Germany and Basel in Switzerland. In 1972 the Association of European Border Regions was created, which now lists some thirty Euroregions in Western Europe. The EU has supported these Euroregions through the establishment of the European Regional Development Fund (ERDF), which provides some funding for infrastructural investment in selected cross-border areas. Euroregions have also been supported by the Council of Europe, which has provided guidelines and advice on their organisational structures.

With the end of the Cold War, a number of Euroregions have been established to link together border regions previously divided by the Iron Curtain. In East Central Europe the lead has been taken by Poland. In May 1992 the Polish Ministry of Foreign Affairs created a special department responsible for preparing international agreements on cross-border cooperation and providing advice to local authorities involved in such activities. The following January, Poland also signed the Council of Europe convention on cross-border cooperation between local communities of different countries.

The idea for the first Euroregion in East Central Europe came from a conference held in Zittau in the BRD in May 1991. This conference – which was supported by the Polish and German governments – involved representatives of communities in south-western Poland, the north-western part of the Czech Republic and the eastern part of Germany. Their discussions focused on the need for regional cooperation to tackle the problem of cross-border environmental pollution. In December 1991, the local authorities involved decided (again with the support of their central govern-ments) to establish a 'Neisse Euroregion', with its headquarters based in Zittau (although this seat will probably be rotated periodically between the three participating countries). The establishment of the Neisse Euroregion has been followed by a number of cross-border conferences and seminars on issues such as their common history and the regional economy. Contacts have multiplied between local businesses and institutes, and new border checkpoints have been opened to facilitate cross-border interactions. The Neisse Euroregion has also succeeded in winning financial support from the EU for an ecological study of the area.[21]

Since then, interest in creating other Euroregions has grown. In March 1993, twenty Polish communities adjoining the German state of Brandenburg called for the creation of a Euroregion along the Oder river. A third Euroregion has been proposed for the Szczecin area of northwest Poland, the German *Länder* of Brandenburg and Mecklenburg-Vorpommern, and neighbouring communities in Sweden and Denmark. A fourth has been proposed for Upper Silesia in Poland and the Moravian communities in the Czech Republic. Finally, local officials in Poland and Ukraine have been discussing the possibility of establishing a Euroregion along their common border.

The creation of Euroregions has been welcomed by many as a positive contribution to the process of European integration, and as a pragmatic contribution to the long-term task of transcending nationalist conflicts between neighbouring peoples. However, there are two potential problems involved with the development of such Euroregions. First, experience with cross-border cooperation in Western Europe suggests that it has been most effective among border communities of comparable economic performance and compatible trading interests. Where substantial levels of economic differentiation exist between neighbouring communities in different countries, transnational interaction can promote migratory move-ments and generate expressions of nationalist animosity. Given the substantial disparities in economic development between, for example, the Poles and the Germans, or the Hungarians and the Ukrainians, this does not bode well for cross-border cooperation in the region.

Second, the cultural and economic exchanges that cross-border cooperation inevitably brings in its wake are not welcomed by inward-looking nationalists. In Poland, the signing of the Debrecen agreement on the Neisse Euroregion was attacked by one *Sejm* deputy as 'suggesting the idea of [a new] partition of Poland ... so that its integration with Europe would be made easier' and of 'destroying Poland's border'. Some nationalistic Catholic groups have also condemned cross-border cooperation as a threat to Poland's identity and territorial integrity. Cross-border cooperation does indeed challenge many traditional notions of nationhood and sovereignty. As Jan B. de Weydenthal notes, debates in Poland on the implications of Euroregions raise a series of issues central to the evolution of contemporary Poland on the eve the twenty-first century:

> Faced with such political dilemmas, Poland stands on the brink of
> major policy choices that could determine its political direction for

years to come. Concerns about the implications of Euroregions and other forms of local cross-border contacts are real and cannot be dismissed. Indeed, is it not possible that the Neisse Euroregion will, in fact, undermine the 'Polishness' of an area that had for years formed an integral part of the German state? Or that the Euroregion linking Upper Silesia with the Czech Republic and Germany will strengthen latent Silesian separatism? Or that the Euroregion with Ukraine will provide a gateway for refugees from the East? In short, there are valid reasons why some Poles are worried about the country's territorial integrity. But it is also clear that the policy choices to be made on these issues are at bottom decisions about Poland and its place in the modern world. They are, in other words, choices not only about the scope and meaning of Poland's integration into Europe, but about the meaning, in Polish eyes, of Poland and of Europe itself.[22]

Visegrad: from the triangle to the Central European Free Trade Area

The Visegrad forum represents the most significant attempt at regional cooperation in East Central Europe to date. Its origins can be traced back to the first months following the implosion of communist power in Eastern Europe. In January 1990, President Havel visited Poland and Hungary and called on the three countries to coordinate their return to Europe. Later, in April 1990, the leaders of the three countries (along with observers from Austria, Italy and Yugoslavia) met in Bratislava to exchange views on the 'new European order'. At this stage, however, the only concrete proposal for expanding regional cooperation was the decision to expand the Quadrilateral into the Pentagonale by the inclusion of Czechoslovakia. Ideas of trilateral regional cooperation within East Central Europe were floated, but did not produce any substantive results. This was partly due to continuing political uncertainty in Poland and Hungary, and partly because all three governments were more interested in establishing close ties with Western governments and institutions. Throughout most of 1990, therefore, the main thrust of regional policy was developing new relations with the West and dismantling the moribund structures of the dying 'Soviet empire', rather than constructing new regional arrangements for multilateral cooperation.

This began to change in early 1991, largely as a result to two international developments. First was the Soviet use of force in Lithuania in January 1991. This provided an ominous warning that the USSR in its death throes was politically unstable and remained a major threat to the security of the new democracies in Central and Eastern Europe. Second, it became clear that the West, however lavish its praise of the new post-communist governments might be, was going to make only limited trade concessions to the East Central Europeans, and was certainly not going to make substantial contributions to the costs of economic restructuring. At the same time, EC countries made it clear that they regarded trilateral cooperation between Prague, Warsaw and Budapest as an important indication that these countries were able to work together in a multilateral framework.[23] Trilateral cooperation, it was implied, was a prerequisite for entry into the EC and other Western organisations.

Regional cooperation also had a domestic political drive behind it. Many of the more liberal-minded and cosmopolitan intellectuals from the former dissident movement believed that regional cooperation could help overcome the detritus of past conflicts and contribute towards a new Europe based on trust and mutual understanding between different peoples. Individuals like Václav Havel and Adam Michnik had forcefully articulated this sentiment at the trilateral exchange of views in Bratislava in April 1990. Thus for many reform-minded writers and intellectuals, trilateral cooperation was regarded as a morally 'good thing', which could help resolve the region's ancient animosities.

The first summit meeting of East Central European leaders took place in early 1991. On 15 February 1991, Havel, Ántáll and Walesa met in the historic town of Visegrad in Hungary. In contrast to the Bratislava meeting, their deliberations at Visegrad had a much clearer focus. Their concern was to identify what forms of cooperation would facilitate their coordinated 'return to Europe'. The result was the signing of the 'Declaration of the Cooperation ... on the Road to European Integration'.[24] The Visegrad summit did not create a new organisation, and it certainly did not create a new military alliance. Indeed, President Havel stressed that 'I can see no reason for creating new military alliances', whilst Prime Minister Ántáll insisted that it would be wrong to create new 'blocs' out of cooperative initiatives.[25] Nonetheless, the Visegrad declaration did at least signify a new willingness to work more closely together in overcoming common problems. This led to efforts to coordinate policy through a series of joint ministerial and deputy ministerial meetings on issues such as transport, communications, energy and finance.

The Visegrad summit received a mixed reception from the international community. Whilst it was warmly welcomed in the West as evidence of a willingness to cooperate on a multilateral basis, the summit was viewed with suspicion in Moscow as well as in Bucharest and Sofia. Some influential Soviet commentators suggested that it was little more than a poorly disguised anti-Soviet bloc. Similar criticisms can still be heard from the more chauvinistic end of the Russian political spectrum today. On the other hand, Ukraine welcomed the summit, and expressed a desire to cooperate closely with the Visegrad countries, which Minsk saw as a possible bridge to the West. Ukraine subsequently asked to join the Visegrad group, and has become a keen collaborator with its western neighbours in other schemes for regional cooperation (as we have seen).

Whilst Ukraine responded warmly to the creation of the Visegrad group, the Romanians reacted with barely disguised hostility. They feared being excluded from the process of European integration, and were mistrustful of Hungarian policy towards Transylvania. Initially Bucharest asked to join the Visegrad triangle, but when this request was (not unexpectedly) rejected, they made clear their deep disquiet at what it they regarded as a potentially threatening development. The Romanian Foreign Minister, Adrian Nastase, later accused the West of trying 'to reshape Eastern Europe's map', whilst another Foreign Ministry official criticised the 'unacceptable, artificial differentiation' in Western policy towards the region.[26] The creation of the Visegrad group also stimulated a process of Romanian–Bulgarian foreign policy coordination. Both Bucharest and Sofia feared being relegated to the 'second division' as the Visegrad three 'elbowed' their way to the head of the queue to join the EU and NATO.

Despite the unease of some regional neighbours, the second summit of the three East Central European leaders took place in October 1991 in Cracow. It signalled a shift in the focus of the Visegrad triangle away from the dismantling of the Soviet bloc and towards full integration into Western economic, political and security structures.[27] This was evident from the Cracow declaration, in which the Visegrad three agreed to continue cooperation between their countries, and made explicit their aspiration 'to participate in

Europe's political, economic, and institutional systems as well as in its system of security'.[28] They also emphasised their desire for 'a close and institutionalized' cooperation with NATO. This followed an appeal issued the previous day by the three countries' foreign ministers in which they argued that 'in Europe there is no place for different levels and types of security – security must be identical for all'. They also argued that 'there is a need to create conditions for the direct inclusion of Poland, Czechoslovakia and Hungary in the activities of the [NATO] alliance'.[29] However, the three governments failed to reach agreement on the creation of a free trade zone within the triangle – an issue which was assuming ever-growing importance as a result of the disastrous collapse in intra-CMEA trade (a collapse precipitated by the switch to hard currency transactions).

The third summit of the Visegrad triangle took place in Prague in May 1992. Some have seen it as the most successful to date. The Prague communique grandly announced the emergence of 'a new pattern of relations in Central Europe', and went on to record a number of significant agreements and joint statements. First, the three stressed that a strong NATO and a sustained US presence were of the utmost importance for European security, and reiterated their desire to join the alliance at the earliest possible date. Second, they agreed to submit a joint application for membership to the European Community – a decision subsequently repudiated by Czech Prime Minister Klaus. Third, they issued a statement calling for the recognition of Macedonia. This was significant because it suggested the beginnings of a coordinated approach to at least some foreign policy questions.[30] Fourth, the three heads of government signed a declaration promoting cross-border cooperation. And, last but not least, they finally agreed to establish a free trade area.

The issue of a regional free trade zone had been on the agenda for some time. As we have seen, talks on this pressing concern broke down at the Cracow summit in October 1991. However, at a trilateral meeting in Budapest in April 1992 a 'Central European Cooperation Committee' was created in order to provide a multilateral forum for consulting on common economic and political concerns associated with their 'return to Europe'. The subsequent agreement to establish a free trade area in May 1992 led to intensive negotiations which dragged on throughout the summer and autumn. Finally, in December 1992, an agreement was signed creating the Central European Free Trade Area (CEFTA).

126 The international politics of East Central Europe

The CEFTA agreement provided for the phased removal of barriers to trade and the creation of a free trade zone of 65 million consumers. This required the elimination of most barriers to trade over what was initially proposed to be an eight-year period (later reduced to five). In stage one, which was to last from December 1992 until March 1993, some goods were to be exempted from import duties. In stage two, which was to last three or four years, duties on 'ordinary' goods were to be dismantled. Finally, in stage three, which was to last from three to eight years, duties on 'sensitive' commodities (such as steel, textiles and agricultural products) would be removed. The Visegrad countries hoped that the CEFTA agreement would accelerate regional economic recovery through a revival of multilateral trade. They also hoped to send a signal to the EU that they were able to cooperate together on a multilateral basis, and that they were willing to act in the spirit of the times by liberalising trade.[31]

The creation of CEFTA reflected a significant broadening of the Visegrad group's rationale, away from political consultation and foreign policy coordination towards practical economic cooperation. This was widely welcomed as a positive and long-overdue step forward for the East Central Europeans. The creation of a more liberal multilateral trading regime will, it is hoped, facilitate economic growth in the region. However, the CEFTA agreement is modest in its scope and aims, and will not actually create a completely free trade zone. First, a system of quotas will remain for agricultural goods, even though tariffs will be removed. Second, it fails to address non-tariff barriers, of which (as the Poles have found out much to their irritation) the Hungarians and Czechs have developed a formidable array. Finally, it allows for exemptions on the grounds of public morality, public policy, security, protection of fledgling industries, environmental protection and similarly nebulous concepts equally open to tendentious interpretation. Moreover, the CEFTA treaty has not been accompanied by any agreement on a common exchange rate policy or cooperation in financial matters (such as the creation of a central bank). Thus the successful implementation of the CEFTA agreement will require considerable political will and a positive commitment to the process of building a regional market. This may be difficult to achieve, particularly at a time of economic hardship and recession. Experience suggests that economic downturn usually leads to protectionist measures, as governments seek to protect their industries from foreign competition.

The Visegrad group thus faces an uncertain future. The form of multilateral cooperation that the Visegrad framework has promoted remains a largely informal process with a minimal institutional structure. Although President Walesa has spoken of turning the Visegrad group into an 'EC-2', there is little support for this elsewhere in the region (even in Poland). The initial impetus towards greater regional cooperation that was evident in 1991–92 has been weakened by the break-up of Czechoslovakia and by continuing bilateral disputes – particularly between Hungary and Slovakia. Moreover, the early development of the Visegrad group was very much bound up with the perceived threat to the region from the USSR. The collapse of the Soviet state has therefore weakened this external incentive to cooperation, even though the domestic travails of Russia continue to cast a long geostrategic shadow over the region.

There are also mixed feelings in Budapest, Bratislava, Prague and Warsaw about the utility of the Visegrad framework. Whilst the Poles tend to be very committed to this process of regional cooperation, arguing that it could provide tangible economic and political benefits, and that it contributes to the broader process of European integration, others are more sceptical. In particular the Czech Prime Minister Václav Klaus has emerged as a trenchant critic of multilateral cooperation in East Central Europe. He has argued that Visegrad is an artificial construct largely imposed on the original three by the West, and believes that the Czech Republic can best achieve integration into the EU and NATO if it acts unilaterally. He therefore opposes any further institutional 'deepening' of the Visegrad group, and is not adverse to its 'widening' to include Slovenia, and perhaps Croatia, Ukraine and Romania. The Hungarians take a more pragmatic view than either the Poles or the Czechs: they see Visegrad as a process rather than an institution, and are keen to see it develop into a loose framework for economic and political cooperation. Finally, the Slovaks increasingly view Visegrad as an essential link to their more developed Western neighbours. They recognise that it provides them with a privileged access to Western organisations that they would not necessarily enjoy if they negotiated with the West on their own.

Thus as J. F. Brown has argued, 'In perspective, 1992 might well be seen as the high point of Visegrad ... it was precisely during 1992 that shadows and complications appeared which increasingly made Visegrad – in its original form, at any rate – irrelevant'.[32] The process of regional cooperation was subsequently weakened by Poland's domestic political turmoil, the break-up of Czechoslovakia, bilateral disputes (particularly between Hungary and Slovakia) and asymmetries between the Visegrad partners (Poland's population is seven times larger than that of Slovakia). Moreover, the changing geopolitics of the post-communist East, with the break-up of the USSR and Yugoslavia, and the growing differentiation within Central and Eastern Europe, meant that a 'regional concept of three states – or even four with Slovakia – now seemed provincial and obsolete'. In conditions of dynamic and unpredictable change, 'a *firm*, institutionalised alliance, between Poland, the Czech Republic, and Hungary, forming a single entity in relation to the principal regional issues, could have been advantageous to its members and a stabilizing force. But there was never much hope, intention, or chance of Visegrad ever being that'.[33]

The underlying problem with Visegrad has been twofold. First, there is disagreement as to the extent to which – if at all – East Central Europe possesses a distinct sense of regional *identity*. This is a fundamental issue, for as many commentators have argued, no robust international organisation can survive unless it is sustained by a shared sense of identity and common purpose.[34] The second fundamental question is whether the Visegrad process rests on a secure bedrock of mutual *interests*.

The political significance of the Visegrad countries' regional identity is hard to measure. Certainly, many intellectuals in East Central Europe define their regional identity in terms of a distinctive Central European heritage – *Mitteleuropa*. However, the association of this with the Danubian lands of the Austro-Hungarian Empire tends to marginalise the Poles, who were never fully incorporated within the Habsburg state. Moreover, as we have seen, the concept of *Mitteleuropa* has always been a rather amorphous one. It is defined not so much by a specific geography or even by defined socio-political characteristics as much as by a mood, an attitude of mind.[35] Building a cohesive political and economic structure on the basis of such an amorphous cultural identity will therefore be difficult. If the Visegrad states are to develop a more politically significant regional identity, this will require careful and sustained nurturing over many years – or a pressing security threat.

As regards the common interests of the Visegrad countries, these must be weighed against their competing or conflicting interests. The Visegrad four share common interests arising from their mutual experience of communist authoritarianism. They share broadly similar goals in terms of economic and political reform. They also share a common aspiration to rejoin Europe. But on the other hand they are economic competitors, with industrial and financial structures which are not compatible. Their political elites are divided on many issues pertaining to the European integration process, even though they share the common strategic goal of 'returning to Europe'. Finally, individual countries – primarily Hungary and Slovakia – are divided by bilateral disputes. It is therefore debatable whether or not the Visegrad countries share enough common interests to sustain a dynamic process of quadrilateral cooperation.

The external environment has also become less propitious for multilateral cooperation between the Visegrad countries. In the beginning, Western countries were keen supporters of the Visegrad process. They treated it as test of the East Central Europeans' ability to cooperate constructively in multilateral fora, and implied that this was a prerequisite to their future participation in the EU. The EU thus sought to bolster the Visegrad process by dealing with its members collectively whenever possible. To this end, they conducted their political consultations with East Central Europeans as a group rather than individually. The first such meeting between leaders of the Visegrad states and EU representatives (which took place at foreign ministerial level) occurred in October 1992 in Luxembourg. This was followed shortly afterwards in London by the first summit of heads of government of the Visegrad triangle with the President of the European Council and the President of the European Commission.[36]

Yet by mid-1994 it was apparent that the EU's earlier privileging of the Visegrad group was waning. This occurred as a result of a strategic reassessment by leading EU states of developments in Central and Eastern Europe. By mid-1994, the lack of cohesion within the Visegrad group was becoming ever more apparent. There was also growing recognition of the political and economic importance of Bulgaria and Romania, and a feeling that there was little justification for treating a country like Slovakia more favourably than either of these two countries or, for that matter, Slovenia. The US was also increasingly aware of Romania's strategic importance given the presence of the Russian Fourteenth Army in Transdienstr and the unstable military situation around the Black Sea. Washington therefore encouraged the West Europeans to deal with Bucharest in a more sympathetic manner. By the time of the Essen European Council meeting in December 1994, the shift in Western policy towards Central and Eastern Europe was apparent. At the Essen summit it was announced that, in future, annual summits of EU heads of government would be held with their counterparts in all six countries of Central and Eastern Europe (rather than just the four Visegrad states). Similarly, foreign and interior ministers would meet twice a year, whilst other ministers were to meet annually.[37]

The prospects facing the Visegrad group are thus at best uncertain. It does seem as if the zenith of quadrilateral regional cooperation has passed, and that the degree of policy coordination between them will remain limited. The Visegrad group's distinctive identity and common interests do not appear to be strong enough to overcome the bilateral disputes, power asymmetries and differing foreign policy perspectives which divide the four countries. Nor is the EU as enthusiastic about quadrilateral cooperation as it was in 1991–93. On the other hand, there are some policy sectors where regional cooperation can offer obvious benefits – the fight against transnational crime being one. There is also:

> another, grass-roots Visegrad at work in cross-border trade between Poland, Slovakia and the Czech Republic, between the Euroregions (cross-border development zones) of the Dreilanderck and Brandenburg-Pologne as well as Carpathia. Although hindered by the absence of sufficient border crossings, this activity nonetheless provides an essential impetus to the more sluggish governmental-sponsored initiatives.[38]

Moreover, cooperation and consultation within the Visegrad framework has created a momentum of its own, despite the absence of a formal organisational structure.[39] For example, the implementation of the CEFTA agreement has required the creation of a number of permanent standing committees. Thus although there is little or no chance that it will develop into an 'EC-2' (as President Walesa suggested at one stage), the Visegrad group is likely to survive as a forum for multilateral consultation and limited policy coordination amongst countries which 'still have more in common with each other than with their western neighbours'.[40]

The costs and benefits of regional cooperation

In a region of Europe deeply scarred by past conflicts, multilateral cooperation can offer many benefits. It can provide a stimulus to regional economic activity, giving a fillip to cross-border trade and investment. It can improve transport and communication links in geographically contiguous areas divided by state borders. It can reduce misunderstanding and mistrust between neighbouring communities by increasing transnational communication. It can render borders more permeable, thus contributing to the transcendence of a Europe based on rivalrous nation states. This in turn will tend to transform people's perception of their identity, creating a more developed sense of regional or sub-regional identity (particularly if – as in the case of the Danubian lands of Central Europe or the old Hansa cities of the Baltic – it is based on past cultural or trading communities).

Closer regional interaction can, however, have negative effects too, particularly in the short term. Open borders can allow cross-border criminal activity to flourish: this has proved a severe problem in much of Eastern Europe, given the rise of black market activities and associated mafiosa-style gangsterism. A more liberal trading regime between neighbouring countries can also exacerbate economic rivalry and competition, especially if there is a substantial disparity in economic structures either side of the border. Again, this has proved to be a problem on the borders of, *inter alia*, Poland and Germany, and Hungary and Ukraine. Finally, as we have seen in the case of Poland, more permeable borders can generate fears about a loss of national identity and possible future challenges to the territorial integrity of the state. This is particularly the case when the state-building process is still at a relatively early stage (as it is, for example, in Slovakia).

Despite the short-term costs associated with closer regional cooperation, experience from Western Europe still suggests that the benefits outweigh the costs. Regional cooperation is one of the essential building blocks of a Europe 'whole and free'. In Central and Eastern Europe, a series of regional organisations have been created, with overlapping membership and shared competencies. This network of regional organisations stretches from the Council of Baltic Sea States in the north, through the Visegrad group and the Carpathian Euroregion, down to Alpe Adria and the Central European Initiative in the south. More substantive and institutionalised multilateral cooperation in East Central Europe would serve the interests of the peoples of this region and would contribute to European integration.

However, even if the benefits of regional cooperation do outweigh the costs, there are a number of major difficulties involved in developing multilateral forms of cooperation in East Central Europe. First, the divisions and antagonisms in Central and Eastern Europe cannot simply be wished away. There are some intractable ethno-national cleavages in the region, and some thorny bilateral disputes. Cooperation in the Visegrad forum has been impeded by Slovak–Hungarian controversies, and by the difficulties generated by the break-up of Czechoslovakia. Regional cooperation in fora such as the Council of Baltic Sea States or the Central European Initiative has also been handicapped by bilateral tensions – some of them involving the East Central Europeans. One example is lingering tensions between Warsaw and Vilnius over the treatment of the Polish minority in western Lithuania (a problem we will consider in the following chapter).

Second, the development of regional cooperation is complicated by the emergence of multipolarity and power politics in contemporary Eastern Europe. The focus of this is Russia, the region's potential hegemon. Russia's importance is apparent from the evolution of the Visegrad group, whose development has been directly influenced by the course of Soviet, then Russian, foreign policy. For example, the Soviet use of force in Lithuania in January 1991, the attempted coup of August 1991, and the Russian elections of December 1993 have all have provided a spur for cooperation between the East Central Europeans in the Visegrad framework. Ukraine's concern with Russia's external policy has also led it to develop close relations with its western neighbours – hence the enthusiasm with which it has approached multilateral organisations such as the Visegrad group, the Carpathian Euroregion and the Central European Initiative.

Hungary's relations with its neighbours also reflect the continuing significance of balance-of-power considerations in this region.

Hungary is concerned about the formation of a tacit 'Little Entente' between Romania, Slovakia and Serbia.[41] As with the 'Little Entente' of the inter-war years, these three countries all benefited at Hungary's expense from the Treaty of Trianon, and all three are concerned about Hungary's policy towards the Magyar diaspora. Given its concern about the emergence of a new Little Entente, Budapest has sought to foster good relations with Ukraine, a country that is also concerned about Romanian irredentism.[42] Romania's concern with Budapest's foreign policy is evident from the open hostility it displayed towards the Visegrad group, and its refusal to participate in the Carpathian Euroregion. Cooperation within the Visegrad framework also acted as a spur for closer cooperation between Bucharest and Sofia. Thus the emergence of a multipolar balance of power in Eastern Europe is having a direct effect on the developing patterns of regional cooperation in this part of Europe.

Finally, regional cooperation in Central and Eastern Europe is highly sensitive to domestic political developments. As the temporary loss of office by Meciar in Slovakia in the spring of 1994 demonstrated, leadership changes in East Central Europe can have significant implications for external relations. In this case, it led to an improvement in bilateral relations with Hungary, which helped improve the atmosphere for multilateral cooperation within the Visegrad group. Domestic political changes can also lead to a shift in the focus of external relations. For example, the socialist government in Hungary that came to power in the summer of 1994 attached greater significance to improving relations with its neighbours than did its conservative predecessor. It thus seems that in states which have only recently regained their sovereignty, external relations are much more susceptible to domestic political changes than established nation states like Britain and France.

Conclusion: regional organisations and international relations in East Central Europe

The final question to consider is the significance of multilateral cooperation in East Central Europe for the nature of international relations in the region. To what extent – if at all – do multilateral organisations modify state behaviour and perceptions of the 'national interest'? This is one of the most hotly contested questions in international relations theory today, raising as it does issues which are fundamental to our understanding of the essential nature of contemporary international relations.[43]

The extent to which international organisations can affect the behaviour of states depends on the nature of the organisation considered. One can place international organisations on a spectrum, depending on the capacity and will of member states to surrender sovereignty on various issues.[44] At the lower end of the continuum is inter-governmental cooperation and policy harmonisation; at the higher end is supranational integration. Most forms of regional cooperation in East Central Europe are of the former type. Organisations such as the Visegrad group, the Central European Initiative, the Council of Baltic Sea States and the Carpathian and Neisse Euroregions primarily entail policy cooperation and harmonisation, with some elements of functional cooperation (one example of this being the creation of CEFTA). Regional cooperation in East Central Europe does not yet entail any significant pooling of state sovereignty, despite the fears of some nationalist groups. This is particularly apparent in the case of the Euroregions. One analyst has argued that:

> All Euroregions have been established in accordance with the domestic policies of the central governments of the countries involved and with the existing system of international agreements. The Euroregions thus have no legal status of their own in the international community; they do not affect existing state borders and their activities are regulated by domestic legal and administrative systems.[45]

Nevertheless, Euroregions may influence the implementation of domestic policies in their local areas and can have an impact on central government decision-making. Euroregions can also help strengthen integrative trends between neighbouring countries.

In the case of other regional organisations in East Central Europe, none of them involve a significant pooling of state sovereignty on the part of their members either. Instead, they tend to serve as fora for limited inter-governmental consultation and policy coordination.[46] The states involved also tend to regard them as a means to limited and specific ends, not as an end in themselves. This is evident from the Visegrad group (and, to a lesser extent, the Central European Initiative), which is regarded by most of its members as a transitional instrument for preparing the way for membership of the EU.

Nonetheless, regional organisations are significant in two important respects. First, they are a manifestation of a process of geo-economic regionalisation which has become more apparent since the end of the Cold War. Their existence thus provides fuel to the debate on an emerging Europe of the regions. They also reflect the multidimensionality of the integration process in Europe, which is occurring on a formal and informal basis at a regional as well as transnational level. Second, regional organisations are another manifestation of an 'international society of states' in East Central Europe. Although such regional bodies do not involve a significant pooling of state sovereignty, they do change the context within which states act and define their interests. They can help build consensus and identify areas of common interest between states, and also facilitate a process of socialisation for elite groups.[47] Regional organisations are thus a prime example of what has been termed 'international regimes', that is, 'sets of explicit or implicit principles, norms, rules and decision-making procedures around which actor expectations converge'.[48] The development of such regimes in East Central Europe will therefore contribute to the gradual reshaping of international relations in the region, facilitating a growth in the forms of international governance and the consolidation of an international society in the wider Europe.[49]

Regional relations in East Central Europe are thus diverse and multifaceted, and may have important long-term consequences for the nature of international relations in Europe. Yet as we have seen, the prospects for future regional cooperation are bound up with developments in the wider Europe – in both the West and the East. It is thus to East Central Europe's relations with the wider Europe that we now turn, beginning with the countries to the East: Lithuania, Ukraine, Belarus and, last but certainly not least, Russia.

Endnotes

1   The text of the Visegrad 'Declaration of the Cooperation of the Republic of Hungary, the Czech and Slovak Federal Republic and the Republic of Poland on the Road to European Integration' is reprinted in *Report on Eastern Europe*, 2, no. 9, 1 March 1991, pp. 31–2.

2   One of the first attempts to ameliorate the impact of the Cold War on Central Europe was the establishment in 1955 of the *Forschungsinstitut für den Donauraum*. This was a research institute established by the Austrians with the objective of identifying areas of common interest between the Danube's

riparian states. For further details see Lincoln Gordon, *Eroding Empire: Western Relations with Eastern Europe*, Washington, DC, Brookings Institution, 1987, pp. 277–8.

3   For a beautifully written and informative study of the culture and traditions of the Danubian lands see Claudio Magris, *Danube: A Sentimental Journey From the Source to the Black Sea*, London, Collins Harvill, 1990.

4   Misha Glenny, *The Rebirth of History: Eastern Europe in the Age of Democracy*, London, Penguin, 1990, p. 219.

5   Paolo Perulli, 'The political economy of a "mid-European region", the Alpe Adria Community', in Colin Crouch and David Marquand, eds, *Towards Greater Europe: A Continent Without An Iron Curtain*, Oxford, Blackwell, 1992, pp. 154–69 (p. 158).

6   'Tension between hybrid members set to influence leadership struggle', *The Guardian*, 7 March 1994.

7   Alice Landau, 'Regional cooperation in Central and Eastern European countries: a spring-board for the European Community or a path to autonomy'. A paper presented to the European Consortium for Political Research Joint Workshops, Madrid, 17–22 April 1994.

8   Alfred Reisch, 'The Central European Initiative: to be or not to be?', *RFE/RL Research Report*, 2, no. 34, 27 August 1993, pp. 30–7 (p. 36).

9   The Committee of the Regions (COR) was established by the Maastricht Treaty, and met for the first time in March 1994. The COR will have 189 members (93 representatives of regions and 96 of local communities) and will be entitled to be consulted on EU proposals involving 'economic and social cohesion', trans-European networks, public health, education and culture. 'Devolved power redraws map', *The Guardian*, 7 March 1994.

10   To this end the CEI has sought to cooperate with other, more longstanding regional groups such as the *Comunità Alpe Adria*, *Comunità Arge Alp* (Community of the Central Alps, established in 1972) and *Cotra* (*Comunità di Lavoro della Alpi Occidentali*, the working community of the western border regions of the Alpine arc, i.e., France, Italy and Switzerland). These three organisations themselves held a conference establishing official collaboration in 1978.

11   David Kirby, *The Baltic World 1772–1993. Europe's Northern Periphery in an Age of Change*, London, Longman, 1995, p. 406.

12   J. Fitzmaurice, *The Baltic: A Regional Future*, London, Macmillan, 1992, pp. 138–53.

13   Dzintra Bungs, 'Seeking solutions to Baltic–Russian border issues', *RFE/RL Research Report*, 3, no. 13, 1 April 1994, pp. 25–32 (p. 31).

14   As Mark Galeotti writes, 'Russian organised crime is becoming an international issue. Russian criminals are opening up new drug smuggling routes from Central Asia to Europe, and Russia's overstretched and under-supervised airports represent an ideal transit point for couriers from Latin America and the Far East alike. Russian "mafias" also have developed a powerful presence in East/Central Europe, notably Bulgaria, Hungary and Poland. Thus, they also pose a threat to the emerging democracies and free markets of the region.' Galeotti, *The Age of Anxiety. Security and Politics in Soviet and Post-Soviet Russia*, London, Longman, 1995, p. 186. See also Stephan Handelman,

Comrade Criminal: The Theft of the Second Russian Revolution, London, Michael Joseph, 1994; James Sherr, 'Russia, geopolitics and crime', *The World Today*, February 1995, pp. 32–6; Frank Gregory, 'Unprecedented partnerships in crime control, law enforcement issues and linkages between Eastern and Western Europe since 1989', in Malcolm Anderson and Monica den Boer, eds, *Policing Across National Boundaries*, London, Pinter, 1994, pp. 85–105; Phil Williams, 'Transnational criminal organisations and international security', *Survival*, 36, no. 1, spring 1994, pp. 96–113; and Kjell Engelbrekt, 'Sharp rise in drug trafficking and abuse in former East bloc', *RFE/RL Research Report*, 3, no. 9, 4 March 1994, pp. 48–51.

15 Christopher Ulrich, 'The growth of crime in Russia and the Baltic Region', *RFE/RL Research Report*, 3, no. 23, 10 June 1994.

16 Alfred A. Reisch, 'Transcarpathia and its neighbours', *RFE/RL Research Report*, 1, no. 7, 14 February 1992, pp. 55–7.

17 Alfred A. Reisch, 'Hungarian–Ukrainian relations continue to develop', *RFE/RL Research Report*, 2, no. 16, 16 April 1993, pp. 22–7 (p. 27).

18 The Carpathian Euroregion embraces two southern Polish voivodships, four Hungarian counties and Ukraine's Transcarpathian *oblast* (Zakarpattya); six eastern Slovak counties opted for associate membership, while neighbouring Romanian counties declined the invitation to participate. Alfred A. Reisch, 'Hungary's foreign policy toward the East', *RFE/RL Research Report*, 2, no. 15, 9 April 1993, p. 41.

19 Daniel Tarschys, 'The Council of Europe: towards a vast area of democratic security', *NATO Review*, December 1994/January 1995, pp. 8–12 (especially pp. 10–11).

20 Jan B. de Weydenthal, 'Controversy in Poland over "Euroregions"', *RFE/RL Research Report*, 2, no. 16, 16 April 1993, pp. 6–9.

21 Jan B. de Weydenthal, 'German plan for border region stirs interest in Poland', *RFE/RL Research Report*, 1, no. 7, 14 February 1992, pp. 39–42.

22 Weydenthal, 'Controversy in Poland over "Euroregions"', p. 9.

23 Rudolf Tokes, 'From Visegrad to Cracow: cooperation, competition and coexistence in Central Europe', *Problems of Communism*, XL, no. 6, p. 113.

24 For details see Joshu Spero, 'The Budapest–Prague–Warsaw triangle, Central European security after the Visegrad Summit', *European Security*, 1, no. 1, spring 1992, pp. 58–83.

25 For the text of the Visegrad summit declaration and an analysis by Jan B. de Weydenthal see 'The Visegrad Summit', *Report on Eastern Europe*, 1 March 1991, pp. 28–32.

26 Romania's sensitivity over Transylvania, and its suspicions over the foreign policy goals of the triangle, were further revealed in September 1991, when an article in a little-known Polish journal advocating the incorporation of Transylvania in a Central European economic region centred on the Trilateral led to a series of heated exchanges between Bucharest and Warsaw. For details see Dan Ionescu, 'Transylvania and Romanian–Polish relations', *Report on Eastern Europe*, October 11, 1991, pp. 24–7.

27 Pál Dunay, *Das Alte Ungarn im Neuen Europa? Ungarische Sicherheitspolitik nach dem Systemwandel*, HSFK Report 2/1993, Frankfurt am Main, Hessische Stiftung Friedens-und Konfliktforschung, 1993, pp. 60–7.

28   For the text of the Cracow declaration see *European Security*, 1, no. 1, spring 1992, pp. 104–8.
29   Jan B. de Weydenthal, 'The Cracow Summit', *Report on Eastern Europe*, 25 October 1991, pp. 27–9.
30   The Visegrad triangle's statement on Macedonia can be found in *East European Reporter*, May/June 1992, p. 35.
31   Pavel Zivalik, 'The Visegrad four: opportunity for Central European integration or leverage against EU closed doors?', paper presented to the European Consortium for Political Research Joint Workshops, Madrid, 17–22 April 1994.
32   J. F. Brown, *Hopes and Shadows: Eastern Europe After Communism*, London, Longman, 1994 p. 215.
33   *Ibid.*, pp. 216–17.
34   This point is made in Soledad Garcia, ed., *European Identity and the Search for Legitimacy*, London, Pinter, 1993, p. 101.
35   Glenny, *op. cit.*, pp. 186–7.
36   For details see 'Weekly review', *RFE/RL Research Report*, 1, no. 45, 13 November 1992, p. 70.
37   'EU decides on Eastern Europe's favoured few for early entry', *The Guardian*, 5 October 1994.
38   George Kolankiewicz, 'Consensus and competition in the Eastern enlargement of the European Union', *International Affairs*, 70, no. 3, 1994, pp. 477–95 (p. 489).
39   Milada Anna Vachudova, 'The Visegrad four: no alternative to cooperation?', *RFE/RL Research Report*, 2, no. 34, 27 August 1993, pp. 38–47 (p. 46).
40   Kolankiewicz, *op. cit.*, p. 480.
41   See Paul Lendvai, 'Central Europe 1: what about the Hungarian minorities?', *World Today*, December 1992, p. 216; and 'Hungary fears for its future', *Foreign Report*, 26 November 1992, p. 1.
42   Romania is the only country to have made official territorial claims on Ukraine. See Roman Solchanyk, 'The politics of state-building, centre–periphery relations in post-Soviet Ukraine', *Europe-Asia Studies*, 46, no. 1, 1994, pp. 47–68 (p. 63).
43   For a useful survey of the main issues in this debate see Friedrich Kratochwil and Edward Mansfield, *International Organisation: A Reader*, New York, Harper Collins, 1994.
44   See for example Paul Taylor, 'A conceptual typology of international organisation', in A. Groom and P. Taylor, eds, *Frameworks for International Cooperation*, London, Pinter, 1990, pp. 13–17. See also Taylor's book, *International Organization in the Modern World. The Regional and the Global Process*, London, Pinter, 1993.
45   Weydenthal, 'Controversy in Poland', p. 7.
46   One particularly sceptical view of the role of multilateral regional organisations is that of A. Leroy Bennett, *International Organisations: Principles and Issues*, 5th edn, New Jersey, Prentice-Hall, 1991, who argues that regionalism (i.e., regional organisations) 'possesses limited dynamics of its own. Regionalism exerts little magnetic force that tends to pull states away from the poles of national power and purposes. Regional organizations are

formed not for their own sake but to promote the enhancement of national interests. If functionalism ever results in a surrender of national sovereignty, the current evidence suggests that the period of time in which this will generally occur is not imminent' (p. 249).

47 On this point see Robert O. Keohane, *After Hegemony: Co-operation and Discord in the World Political Economy*, Princeton, Princeton University Press, 1984, p. 26. For an analysis of the impact of international institutions on post-Cold War Europe, see R. Keohane, J. Nye and S. Hoffmann, eds, *After the Cold War. International Institutions and State Strategies in Europe, 1989–1991*, Cambridge, Harvard University Press, 1993.

48 Stephen Krasner, *International Regimes*, Ithaca, Cornell University Press, 1983.

49 A number of authors have drawn attention to the resemblance between regime theory and the 'English School' of international relations (of which Hedley Bull was a leading exponent). For an analysis of the similarities and differences, see Tony Evans and Peter Wilson, 'Regime theory and the English School of international relations: a comparison', *Millennium: Journal of International Studies*, 21, no. 3, 1992, pp. 329–51.

Chapter Six

Relations with the East

Some East Europeans had illusions after 1989. None was more common, and more quickly dispelled, than the one they harboured about their neighbour to the East. Their enthusiasm for things Western, their determination to join (or rejoin) the 'European mainstream', led them to hope they could firmly turn their backs on the Soviet Union now that Soviet domination had been broken. But other East Europeans, more realistic or more fatalistic, realized that this could never be the case: geography, economics, and history, both recent and more distant, dictated a continuing connection – different from before, but close and complex. (J. F. Brown[1])

The most dramatic manifestation of the collapse of the Cold War in Europe has been the reorientation of the Visegrad countries' foreign policy priorities from East to West. After the Iron Curtain descended across the heart of *Mitteleuropa* in the late 1940s, Poland, Czechoslovakia and Hungary found themselves locked into the Soviet-dominated structures of the 'socialist community'. The geostrategic earthquake of 1989–90 fundamentally and irrevocably changed this. The Warsaw Pact and the CMEA were abolished; Soviet troops were withdrawn from Central Europe; and the Visegrad states began their return to Europe. The geopolitical topology of the region has been further altered by the disintegration of the once mighty 'Land of Lenin'. These changes, along with the disruption caused by the transition from central planning to market economies, resulted in the virtual collapse of trading ties between former CMEA member states. A radically new pattern of international relations has thus emerged in Central and Eastern Europe.

Yet as they themselves have realised, the East Central Europeans cannot simply turn their backs on their Eastern neighbours. Geography, economics and history mean that the destinies of the

Visegrad countries cannot be insulated from developments in Russia and the other Soviet successor states. These new East European states – particularly Russia – will continue to exert an inescapable influence on the East Central Europeans in three main ways: first, their political instability, economic difficulties and powerful armed forces pose a potential threat to regional security; second, there are national diasporas throughout Eastern Europe, creating potential sources of tension in bilateral relations; and third, the Visegrad countries remain largely dependent on the former Soviet Union for supplies of energy and other raw materials.[2]

From the perspective of Russia, Ukraine, Belarus and the Baltic republics, the East Central Europeans are important because they provide a potential gateway to Western Europe. All the Soviet successor states fear the creation of a new Europe 'from Brest to Brest', which will effectively isolate them from the European mainstream. This fear is particularly acute in Russia, which worries that it will be cut off from Europe, and regarded not as part of Eastern Europe, but rather as 'Western Asia'.

The aim of this chapter is thus to examine the changing dynamics of relations between the Visegrad countries and their Eastern neighbours. It begins by briefly considering the historical evolution of relations in this region, before concentrating on developments since 1989. As we shall see, despite the creation of countries like Belarus or Ukraine which have not previously existed as modern states (in the Westphalian sense of the term), international relations in the region are still very much coloured by the legacy of the past. Once again, therefore, external relations in Central and Eastern Europe exhibit elements of both historical continuity and change.

Between Russia and Germany

Any analysis of relations between East Central Europe and the countries to the east must consider the geopolitical context within which this relationship takes place. The pattern of international relations in the region has been decisively shaped by one inescapable geopolitical fact of life. For much of their history, the East Central Europeans have found themselves being treated as pawns in a broader struggle for dominance between Europe's great powers. This has been a perennial source of suffering and trauma. In the

seventeenth and early eighteenth century, Sweden sought to pursue its
great-power ambitions at the expense of the Poles, whilst the
Habsburgs pursued their imperial dreams at the expense of the
Hungarians, Czechs and Slovaks. By the nineteenth and twentieth
centuries, however, it was Germany and Russia that had emerged as
the decisive great-power influences on the region. As the influence of
one or the other has risen, that of their rival has declined. Moreover,
the East Central Europeans have suffered both from Russo-German
conflict, and from Russo-German collusion – as the four divisions of
Poland demonstrate all too tragically.

In the late nineteenth century, Russian influence in East Central
Europe declined in the face of the rising power of the Wilhelmine
Reich. Imperial Germany's economic prowess and military muscle
gave it a growing political influence in Eastern Europe and the
Balkans, much to the annoyance of the Tsar. Russian influence in the
region declined even more in the early twentieth century, until it
effectively collapsed in 1917–18 amidst revolution and military
defeat. With the defeat of the Red Army before the gates of Warsaw
(the 'miracle on the Vistula' as the Poles subsequently dubbed it[3]), the
Bolsheviks' fleeting dream of exporting revolution by military means
evaporated. Moreover, as the post-war revolutionary wave subsided,
and pro-Bolshevik insurrections in Hungary and elsewhere were
suppressed, the newly created USSR found itself facing an Eastern
Europe largely dominated by virulently anti-Russian and
anticommunist White dictatorships.

In the inter-war years, therefore, Soviet influence in Eastern
Europe was minimal. Throughout the twenties and thirties,
Moscow's policy objectives in the region were primarily defensive,
focusing on the need to contain the rising power of Germany. When
this proved impossible to do with the cooperation of France and
Britain, Stalin adopted the more devious policy of signing a non-
aggression pact with the Hitler.[4] Although this was undoubtedly
unpalatable for many ardent communists, from Stalin's point of view
it had the added advantage of giving the USSR territorial gains in
Eastern Europe.[5]

The 'Socialist Commonwealth' and East Central Europe

By late 1944 Hitler's great gamble – 'Operation Barbarossa' – had
failed, and the victorious Red Army was pushing the ragged

remnants of the Wehrmacht back towards the frontiers of the Reich. For the peoples of East Central Europe, this was a mixed blessing. 'Liberation' from Nazi oppression was accomplished only at the cost of Moscow acquiring a decisive voice in the domestic affairs of Eastern Europe. This was a prospect many in the region viewed with horror. In Poland, for example, traditional Russophobia was reinforced by the 1943 Katyn massacres,[6] and by the Red Army's failure to support the Warsaw Uprising. The exiled Polish Communist Party had earlier been decimated by Stalin's purges. Once placed in power it enjoyed very limited popular support in this largely conservative, rural and Catholic country. In the case of Hungary, which had been a former Axis supporter, it was treated by the Soviets as occupied enemy country. Here again, the indigenous Communist Party enjoyed very little public support, and consolidated its tenuous grip on the political system only by a judicious mixture of 'salami tactics' and naked force. Only in Czechoslovakia was the Red Army popularly perceived as a liberating force. Indeed, it was with Czechoslovakia that the Soviets had the one real chance of developing an 'organic' relationship in the post-war period. The Czechoslovaks shared cultural and linguistic ties with the Slavs of the USSR; the Munich betrayal had alienated many from the Western powers; and the Communist Party was the strongest and most influential political force in the country, winning approximately 38% of the vote in free elections in 1946.[7]

However, the Soviet Union quickly lost whatever political capital it enjoyed in Czechoslovakia, and ultimately failed to develop an organic relationship with any of its East European neighbours.[8] Instead, as the harsh bipolar logic of the Cold War imposed its suffocating grip on Europe, the Soviet political and economic system was foisted upon Eastern Europe. The consequence of this was that from the very start these new communist regimes lacked both national and democratic legitimacy. Although local communist parties consolidated their grip on power throughout the early 1950s, the region remained a zone of instability and turbulence. Soviet and communist control over Eastern Europe was repeatedly challenged: in East Germany in 1953; in Poland and Hungary in 1956; in Czechoslovakia in 1968; and again in Poland in 1970, 1976 and 1980–81.[9]

Soviet policy towards Eastern Europe was motivated by two key concerns. The first was strategic: East Central Europe 'has historically constituted an invasion funnel from the West into Russia. Similarly, it has constituted an invasion funnel from Russia into Central and Eastern Europe'.[10] From the very inception of the USSR, its leaders had perceived the wider international community – dominated, as they saw it, by imperialist countries – to be irredeemably hostile to the very existence of their state. War, they believed, was inevitable, given the militaristic nature of finance capital. Hence Eastern Europe was regarded as a vital buffer zone: both to provide a defensive glacis against invading forces, and to provide a forward deployment area for offensive operations against the West.[11] The second key concern was political and ideological: Eastern Europe represented the first step in the universalisation of the Soviet system. The USSR did not consider itself to be merely another state: rather, it conceived of itself as the representative and pioneer of a new form of societal organisation that had universal validity and application. Communism in Eastern Europe thus provided 'proof' of the historical inevitability of the victory of Marxist–Leninist ideas on a global scale, and constituted an important means of ideological legitimacy for the Soviet system.

In order to consolidate the cohesion of the new commonwealth of 'fraternal socialist allies', the USSR created two international organisations – the Warsaw Pact and the CMEA. At the same time, in order to bind countries like Poland and Czechoslovakia more closely to the 'socialist community', Moscow played the 'German card' and invoked – with some success – the demon of 'German revanchism'. Throughout the Cold War, Soviet policy towards Eastern Europe was more keenly focused on the so-called 'Iron Triangle' countries of the Warsaw Pact's northern tier: Poland, Czechoslovakia, and the GDR. These three countries were of greatest geostrategic importance to Soviet military planners, and the latter two were also the most economically developed of the CMEA states. For this reason, Moscow was more concerned about signs of instability or ideological heresy in these countries than it was in Hungary, Romania or Bulgaria.

Soviet efforts to consolidate a stable network of friendly allied countries in its East European buffer zone enjoyed only limited success. Throughout this period, Soviet policy towards the region had to confront an inescapable dilemma: either to emphasise ideological orthodoxy and political cohesion, or to encourage the development of more viable, legitimate and therefore stable regimes in Eastern Europe by tolerating a process of economic and political reform. Such reform, however, would inevitably lead to a more polycentric Soviet bloc. This dilemma – orthodoxy and cohesion versus viability and polycentrism[12] – was never adequately resolved in the pre-Gorbachev years. Indeed, it could never be resolved whilst Moscow continued to regard the West as irredeemably hostile, and Eastern Europe as a vital buffer for the defence of the Soviet *Rodina*.

Gorbachev and Eastern Europe: from the 'Brezhnev doctrine' to the 'Sinatra doctrine'

It was only in the second half of the 1980s that the dilemma of cohesion or viability in Soviet–East European relations was adequately resolved.[13] When Mikhail Gorbachev became General-Secretary of the CPSU in March 1985, he instigated a programme of far-reaching domestic reform. This programme of domestic restructuring necessitated a benign international environment, characterised by East–West cooperation rather than Cold War confrontation. Proponents of this 'new political thinking' (as the foreign policy corollary of *perestroika* and *glasnost* was called) argued that cooperation with the West was now a realistic possibility, and that the West was not irredeemably hostile to the Soviet state. This fundamental reassessment of the international security environment, coupled with the domestic imperatives of *perestroika*, had profound implications for Eastern Europe.[14]

Two of Gorbachev's most important foreign policy objectives were cooperation with the West and the reintegration of the USSR into the global economy. These goals had an explicitly European dimension, which was embodied in the concept of a 'Common European House'.[15] Such a 'common house' was not feasible, however, whilst the 'Brezhnev doctrine' was still in place.[16] Thus Gorbachev and Shevardnadze were increasingly pressed by the West to make a clear commitment to the principles of the non-use of force and respect for national sovereignty in dealings with their East European allies. This Gorbachev did most explicitly in his July 1989 speech to the Council of Europe. Yet the most memorable expression of the change in Soviet policy towards Eastern Europe came from Gorbachev's foreign policy spokesman, Gennady Gerassimov: in early 1989 he declared that the 'Brezhnev doctrine' had been replaced by the 'Sinatra doctrine' (a reference to Frank Sinatra's song 'My Way').

The renunciation of the Brezhnev doctrine thus reflected the radically changed policy priorities of the Soviet Union in the age of *perestroika* and 'new thinking'. As a consequence of the dramatic re-evaluation of Soviet security and military doctrine which the Gorbachev leadership encouraged, Eastern Europe was no longer regarded as being an irreplaceable buffer zone. Gorbachev was also more interested in the viability of the political and economic systems in Eastern Europe than in the ideological orthodoxy and cohesion of the Soviet bloc. Although the Soviet leadership was not willing to intervene openly in the domestic power struggles of the East European communist parties, Gorbachev undoubtedly favoured the advent to power of reform-minded communists committed to political liberalisation and economic modernisation. He and Shevardnadze also hoped that the CMEA would develop into a more effective forum for multilateral cooperation and integration, with a more decentralised decision-making structure and quasi-market mechanisms.[17]

Alas, given the steadily deteriorating economic situation in the CMEA countries and the degree of political disillusionment which was widespread in Eastern Europe, such reformist hopes proved as utopian as 'fried snowballs'. By 1988, the Soviet Union had lost control over developments in Eastern Europe. Once the Soviets had ruled out the use of force to maintain the system, the days of *real existierender Sozialismus* were numbered. The formation of the Mazowiecki government in Poland on 19 August 1989 – the first non-communist government in the region for over four decades – thus became the prelude to a radical transformation of both politics and international relations throughout Soviet bloc.

Post-communist Eastern Europe and the USSR

Within the space of a relatively few months, communist power structures crumbled away throughout Eastern Europe. This precipitated a radical geopolitical restructuring of international relations throughout the region. Four events were central to the transformation of Soviet–East European relations after the disintegration of communism. First was the disbanding of the Warsaw Pact, and the start of an irreversible process of Soviet military disengagement from East Central Europe. Second was the dissolution of the CMEA and the sharp decline in transnational economic exchanges in the region. These two events consummated the demise of the 'socialist community'. Third was German unification on Western terms (i.e., continued membership by the *Bundesrepublik* of NATO and the European Community). Fourth was the declaration by the post-communist countries of East Central Europe of their intention to rejoin Europe.

These four developments had profound consequences for Soviet–East European relations. Politically, they meant that bilateral relations between the USSR and its former communist allies had to be placed on a new legal and diplomatic footing – hence the importance attached to negotiating new bilateral treaties. Militarily, they led to the emergence of a dramatically new strategic topology on the continent, and created a widely perceived 'security vacuum' in Central and Eastern Europe.[18] Economically, the break-up of the Soviet bloc compounded the deepening economic and social crisis that was spreading across the area. This in turn undermined the stability of the fragile new democracies in Central and Eastern Europe, creating an atmosphere of uncertainty and greater insecurity.

In this new strategic context, Soviet policy towards its new post-communist neighbours was 'a study in making a virtue out of necessity'.[19] Gorbachev and Shevardnadze, whilst publicly welcoming the advent of democracy in the region, engaged in a damage-limitation exercise.[20] Nonetheless, all mainstream political forces in the USSR recognised that Eastern Europe had been irretrievably 'lost', and Soviet foreign policy consequently focused on relations with the US, the EU, the G7 and the 'near abroad'. Indeed, from 1990 until mid-1993, Eastern Europe largely disappeared from Moscow's international agenda.[21] During this period, Moscow's policy towards Eastern Europe was limited to untangling the webs of economic and military policy that had bound the 'socialist community' together, and establishing new, treaty-based diplomatic relations. Its positive, long-term aims in the region were less clear. As one commentator wrote at the time,

> Moscow requires only two things of East Europe:
> 1. Don't join NATO.
> 2. Pay in dollars.
> These are the gut national interests that Moscow has in East Europe. In terms of their economies and the move towards democracy, East Europe can do what it pleases.[22]

The break-up of the USSR and the changing geopolitics of Eastern Europe

The problems of re-establishing a new, cooperative relationship between the post-communist regimes of East Central Europe and the USSR were compounded by the growing fragmentation of the Soviet Union along republican lines. This was most pronounced in the three Baltic republics, which by mid-1990 were striving openly and energetically for full independence from Moscow. But they were not alone, for in the course of 1990 most of the Soviet Union's constituent republics began asserting their sovereignty and behaving like autonomous international actors. Thus for example Lithuania asserted its independence in March 1990, whilst Russia declared its sovereignty (within the USSR) in June. Ukraine and Belarus followed suit in July.

For neighbouring countries in East Central Europe, this presented a new set of foreign policy dilemmas. With the 'republicanisation' of the USSR, diplomacy in Eastern and Central Europe became a more complex multi-level game. On the one hand, the Visegrad states wanted good relations with the All-Union authorities in Moscow. On the other, they were aware that the power of the central authorities was steadily weakening, and recognised that they could not afford to snub their immediate neighbours (like the Ukraine, Belarus and Lithuania) by failing to develop diplomatic relations with them. However, cultivating closer links with individual republics could have alienated Moscow, which in turn might have generated new security problems (especially if Moscow had decided not to honour its agreements on troop withdrawals or the supply of much-needed energy resources).

The solution to this dilemma was the 'dual-track' policy, an approach which the Poles claimed to have pioneered. It involved developing relations in parallel with both the Soviet government and individual republics, depending on their degree of independence from Moscow. As more and more Soviet republics proclaimed their sovereignty in the course of 1990–91, the debate within the Visegrad countries over *Ostpolitik* intensified.[23] The key issue was the extent to which the East Central Europeans should develop relations with individual Soviet republics, especially the three Baltic republics, which were openly striving for full independence from Moscow.

The disintegration of the USSR following the abortive August coup of 1991 transformed the geopolitical situation in Eastern

Europe and obviated the need for the Visegrad states to continue with the careful diplomatic juggling of their twin-track policy. It did not, however, resolve the dilemmas of their *Ostpolitik*. On the contrary, the break-up of the Soviet Union led to the political pluralisation of the whole territory between the Baltic and the Black Sea, creating a new strategic landscape, with new international actors, more volatile relationships and unique patterns of regional interaction.[24] This more fluid and unstable international environment in the East placed even heavier demands on the foreign ministries of the Visegrad countries.

Since the collapse of communism and the break-up of the USSR, the *Ostpolitik* of the East Central Europeans has had to respond to four major developments in East European geopolitics. The first is the virtual absence of effective international structures for multilateral cooperation and integration. The disintegration of the USSR, on top of the break-up of the Warsaw Pact and the CMEA, has created a host of new states but a dearth of multilateral structures. The institutions and practices of international society are consequently weak and underdeveloped. Inter-state relations are dominated by realpolitik calculations and the search for a stable regional balance of power.[25] In this situation, contemporary international relations in Eastern Europe and the former Soviet Union are characterised by the existence of international anarchy in its rawest and most primordial form.[26] This contrasts sharply with Western Europe, where NATO, the Council of Europe and the EU provide well tried fora for inter-governmental consensus-building and supranational integration.[27]

The second is the emergence of an independent and sovereign Ukraine. This constitutes 'the most significant geostrategic development in Europe since the end of the Second World War'.[28] With a population of 51,707,000, rich agricultural land, significant industrial potential, nuclear weapons and an army which might eventually number between 150,000 and 200,000,[29] Ukraine will inevitably be a major power in the region. Moreover, the immediate eastern neighbour of Poland, Hungary and Slovakia is now Ukraine, not Russia. Given Ukraine's size and potential, this will have a profound impact on international relations in the region. Ukraine already possessed a quasi-international status before the disintegration of the Soviet Union, being a member of the UN and its affiliated and associated international organisations. Hence its independence could be built upon an already existing international juridical base.[30] Nevertheless, the political scene inside Ukraine has proven to be somewhat volatile, which has created some uncertainty about the direction of the new republic's foreign and security policies.

The third new feature of regional relations is that, with the partial exception of Poland, none of the East Central European states share a border with Russia. Russia's borders are now back to where they were three centuries ago, before the 1654 Treaty of Union between Russia and Ukraine signed by Tsar Alexis and Hetman Bohdan Khmelnytsky. Poland's only border with Russia is Kaliningrad, a thin slither of territory cut off the rest of the RSFSR by Lithuania and Belarus. The Russian Federation remains the regional great power, by virtue of its size, population and resource potential, but the fact that it is now largely non-contiguous with East Central Europe is of tremendous political and military importance. At the very least, it distances Russia even further from the heartlands of Europe, and reinforces the RSFSR's Eurasian character.[31]

The final distinctive feature of the geopolitical landscape of Eastern Europe is the prevalence of national minorities and arbitrarily drawn borders. Across the region, there are potential conflicts over minority rights and unresolved irredenta.[32] On the peripheries of East Central Europe, in former Yugoslavia and Moldova, this has led to vicious fighting. Elsewhere in this area (notably in the Baltic republics) it is the cause of inter-communal tension, political controversy and diplomatic wrangling. Since 1990, issues of ethnicity have assumed a growing importance on the international agenda. The question of rights for national minorities, for example, is increasingly regarded as a matter of international concern, rather than being simply an internal domestic issue.

The political pluralisation of the lands between the Baltic and the Black Sea has placed new demands on the *Ostpolitik* of the Visegrad countries. The geopolitical diversity of the region has given the East Central Europeans much greater scope for diplomatic and political manoeuvring. They now have a better chance of avoiding being sandwiched between the two regional great powers, Germany and Russia. Yet the Visegrad countries also face new challenges and dilemmas. In particular, they must avoid becoming embroiled in an unstable multipolar balance of power, with a shifting pattern of draughtboard alliances, rival nationalisms and unresolved irredenta.[33] In the next section, we will consider how the East Central Europeans have responded to the changed geopolitics of Eastern Europe, and how successful they have been in balancing the conflicting demands of foreign and security policies.

Poland's *Ostpolitik*

Poland's Eastern policy must be seen in the context of its broader foreign and security policy objectives. Since the first Solidarity government, Polish foreign policy has had two broad goals. The first is to develop close and cooperative relations with its immediate neighbours. This is seen as vital in order to defuse questions of national minorities and historically disputed borders; to facilitate trade and economic links; and to foster a benign external security environment. The second broad goal is the integration of Poland into West European economic, political and security structures, and into a broader international network of multilateral organisations. Warsaw has attached primary importance to the EU and NATO, but has also been a keen supporter of regional groupings such as the Visegrad forum, the Council of Baltic Sea States, and the Central European Initiative.[34]

Although the emphasis of Poland's foreign policy since 1989 has been on rejoining Europe, Warsaw has recognised the importance of developing good relations with its Eastern neighbours. This has not been unproblematical, given the historical legacy of mutual suspicion and mistrust between Poles and the Russians, Lithuanians, Belarussians and Ukrainians to their East. However, the foundations of a new approach to Poland's Eastern neighbours were laid by the Polish dissident movement in the post-war period. During the Cold War, many Polish émigrés, Catholic intellectuals and human rights activists – dreaming of the time when Poland would be free of communist and Soviet domination – began thinking of how to build new relations with their Eastern neighbours. A pivotal role in this debate was played by the Paris-based journal *Kultura*. One particularly influential writer was Juliusz Mieroszewski, who advocated reconciliation with Lithuania, Belarus and Ukraine, along with a clear recognition of the permanence of existing borders and a renunciation of claims to Vilnius and L'viv. This school of thought was influential amongst Solidarity activists and leaders in the 1980s, and shaped the thinking of individuals like Adam Michnik and the former Foreign Minister Skubiszewski. Contemporary Polish *Ostpolitik* has thus been greatly influenced by debates which took place in dissident and émigré circles in previous decades.

From 1990–91, in the face of the growing republicanisation of the USSR, Warsaw pursued its dual-track policy towards the All-Union authorities in Moscow and the increasingly assertive Soviet republics. Thus, for example, in October 1990, Foreign Minister Skubiszewski travelled to the USSR, where he met both Soviet officials and the leaders of Russia, Ukraine and Belarus. As a result, declarations of friendship and cooperation were signed with both Russia and Ukraine (although not with Belarus or Lithuania). From late 1990 onwards, the emphasis of this dual-track policy shifted as greater attention was paid to the constituent republics of the Soviet Union, rather than to the All-Union authorities in Moscow. This reflected both the declining power of Moscow vis-à-vis the republics, and the election on 9 December 1990 of Lech Walesa as the Polish President. He was keen to improve relations with Russia, Ukraine and Belarus, and had long been sympathetic to Lithuanian aspirations for independence.[35]

Throughout this time, policy towards the USSR and individual Soviet republics remained a contentious issue. A number of trenchant criticisms were made of the early policy of the Polish government towards the East. To start with, it was argued that seeking to play the 'Soviet card' when negotiating with the Germans at the time of the 'Two plus Four' talks on unification was both counterproductive and ill-considered. Second, the government was criticised for failing to agree a timetable for the early withdrawal of Soviet troops from Polish territory – in part because of a heavy-handed attempt to play the Soviet card with the Germans.[36] By the time the Poles had decided they wanted Soviet troops withdrawn, the Soviets were finding it hard to relocate troops withdrawn from Hungary and Czechoslovakia, and so were in no hurry to add to their housing difficulties by an early withdrawal of troops from Poland. Third, the Polish government was criticised for underestimating the importance of Russia within Soviet politics and for failing to recognise the consequences of Russia's drive for independence and sovereignty. Thus Boris Yeltsin was not invited to visit Warsaw in the spring of 1991, even though this would have helped cement relations with the Russian Federation. Fourth, it was argued that Polish suspicions of Soviet–German *rapprochement* in 1990 and 1991 were all too evident: this merely served to irritate both Bonn and Moscow, and did not improve Warsaw's diplomatic room for manoeuvre.[37] Finally, the dual-track policy was criticised by some as being far too cautious. Such critics argued that Poland should have been a much more active supporter of the independence of Ukraine, Belarus and the Baltic states.

These debates over Poland's *Ostpolitik* reflected the geopolitical dilemmas and uncertainties of the post-Cold War period. The slow but ineluctable disintegration of the USSR necessitated a careful balancing act between the All-Union authorities in Moscow and individual Soviet republics. When the Soviet Union finally fell apart at the end of 1991, Polish foreign policy faced a new problem: how to balance relations with Russia and relations with its more immediate Eastern neighbours – Lithuania, Belarus and Ukraine. As we shall see, Warsaw has experienced both successes and failures in its attempt to manage this new set of geopolitical dilemmas.

Polish–Russian relations

The shadows of the past continue to haunt relations between Warsaw and Moscow. For cultural, political and religious reasons, relations between these two Slavic peoples have seldom been good. Imperial Russia participated in the divisions of Poland in the eighteenth century, and suppressed Polish liberation struggles throughout the nineteenth century. In the twentieth century, Polish relations with the Soviet state were from the beginning poor. The reborn Polish state was immediately embroiled in war with the Red Army. On the eve of World War Two, Stalin colluded with Hitler in the fourth partition of Poland. In 1940, the Soviets massacred several thousand Polish officers in the Katyn forest. In 1944, the Red Army failed to support the Warsaw Uprising. And in 1981, the Soviet Union supported the suppression of Solidarity.

Polish resentment over past Soviet outrages lingered on after the break-up of the USSR, and threatened to poison Polish–Russian relations. Some influential Poles, including Leszek Moczulski (the leader of the Confederation for an Independent Poland) and Jaroslaw Kaczynski (the head of the Centre Alliance) argued that Russia should be held responsible for past Soviet crimes such as the Katyn massacre. On the other hand, Adam Michnik and many of the leaders of Poland's democratic movement have argued that to saddle Russia alone with the responsibility for the crimes of the Stalinist system would adversely affect Polish–Russian relations for years ahead with no obvious advantage to Poland. They have therefore encouraged a more conciliatory and constructive approach to Polish–Russian relations. This more conciliatory approach has won growing acceptance within Poland because of President Yeltsin's emphasis on shared democratic values and his willingness to lay to rest some of the ghosts of the past.[38]

A landmark in the development of Polish–Russian relations was the Treaty of Friendship and Good-Neighbourly Relations, signed in Moscow on 22 May 1992 by Presidents Yeltsin and Walesa. The treaty signalled a long-awaited breakthrough in bilateral relations, and was widely regarded as opening a new era in relations between Warsaw and Moscow. The two Presidents also signed a special declaration which condemned 'the Stalinist regime [for] having inflicted great and irrevocable damage on the Polish and Russian nations'. Walesa and Yeltsin pledged to do the utmost 'to overcome the negative legacy of the past and to create qualitatively new bilateral relations for the future on the basis of ... international law, democracy and human rights'. Finally, this summit meeting witnessed the signing of ten further bilateral agreements, the most important of which was one finalising a timetable for the withdrawal of Russian troops from Poland.[39]

Given the symbolic importance attached by Warsaw to historical controversies, the willingness of President Yeltsin to clarify the Soviet role in past events has helped dissipate some the Poles' traditional Russophobia. For example, in October 1992, the *Sejm* adopted a resolution welcoming Yeltsin's release of the Soviet documents dealing with the Katyn massacre. The resolution declared that 'the release of the documents creates a new moral situation in Polish–Russian relations. The whole truth must be revealed, the crimes punished, and justice done.' President Walesa also stated that Poland would remember Yeltsin for having made such a 'courageous decision'.[40] The Poles later welcomed the release of six secret protocols to the Molotov–Rippentrop Pact, and requested access to secret archives in Moscow in order to investigate a number of unresolved issues in Polish–Soviet relations. These included: collaboration between the Gestapo and the NKVD in persecuting Polish prisoners; the death of Poland's wartime commander General Wladyslaw Sikorski in a plane crash in 1943; the Red Army's failure to aid the Warsaw Uprising; the role of Soviet Marshal Konstanty Rokossowski, who served as the Polish Minister of Defence from

1949 to 1956; and the preparations for a Soviet military intervention in 1980–81.[41]

A further fillip to Polish–Russian relations was given by the withdrawal of Russian troops from Poland. On 28 October 1992 – eighteen days ahead of schedule – the last Russian combat troops left Polish soil. Some Russian logistical forces remained until September 1993, but their role was simply to facilitate the continued withdrawal of Russian troops from eastern Germany. The withdrawal of Russian combat troops was symbolically important because, as President Walesa said, it 'finally confirmed Polish sovereignty.... the permanent presence of foreign troops on our territory constantly brought to mind the violence inflicted on Poland [during and after World War Two], recalled the trampling on international law and human freedom'.[42]

Polish–Russian relations, however, continue to face other difficulties. One thorny problem is Kaliningrad, which once formed part of East Prussia (when it was known as Königsberg). Kaliningrad is important not only for Polish–Russian relations, but also for Russo-German relations.[43] The territory contains an important Russian naval base, at Baltiisk, which has long housed the headquarters of the Soviet Baltic Fleet, and which will now become home to the bulk of the Russian Baltic Fleet (currently stationed in Liepaja).[44] The Polish government has become increasingly concerned about the substantial build-up of Russian military forces in the Kaliningrad *oblast*, as President Walesa made clear in February 1994. But Kaliningrad is also of growing importance as a possible zone of special economic development. The Polish attitude towards these proposals has been ambivalent: although they recognise it would help stabilise this part of Russia, they also fear that it would attract German investment that might otherwise go to Gdansk or other Polish cities. Nonetheless, at the May 1992 Walesa–Yeltsin summit, an agreement was reached on developing cross-border contacts between the northern Polish local government councils, or voivodships, and Kaliningrad.[45]

Polish–Russian economic relations are another area where problems – and opportunities – are much in evidence. The switch to hard currency transactions in Polish–Russian trade led to a dramatic slump in the overall volume of both exports and imports, given the shortage of hard currency in both countries. Poland currently runs a trade deficit with Russia, from which it imports the bulk of its oil and gas. The virtual collapse of bilateral trade has deepened the economic recession in both countries. The recognition by the international community of the desirability of stimulating intra-East European trade led to an agreement in October 1993 whereby the EBRD and the World Bank would provide credits to Polish and Russian banks to finance Polish–Russian trade. Although this plan remains in its early stages, it represents a practical step towards improving bilateral relations. If it is successful, it could serve as a model for expanding inter-regional trade throughout Eastern Europe and the former Soviet Union.

The period of steady improvement in Polish–Russian relations initiated by the May 1992 Walesa–Yeltsin summit ran into difficulties in the summer of 1993. It was from this time onwards that Russian foreign policy began showing signs of a new assertiveness. Moscow started more actively defending its interests in the 'near abroad' and became a more forceful proponent of closer integration within the CIS. At the same time, after a hiatus of three years, Russia once again began to speak of its 'vital interests' in Eastern Europe. In September 1993, for example, Russian Foreign Minister Kozyrev insisted that 'East Central Europe has never ceased to be an area of interest for Russia'.[46] This renewed interest in Eastern Europe was highlighted by Moscow's strenuous diplomatic efforts in late 1993 to prevent the East Central Europeans gaining membership of NATO.[47]

A more ominous note was struck by Sergei Stankevich, one of Yeltsin's political advisors. During a visit to Warsaw in February 1993, he argued that Ukraine fell within Russia's sphere of influence and that Poland should therefore avoid developing close political and military relations with Kiev.[48] One Western diplomat in Ukraine subsequently reported that Russian officials were warning East European countries 'not to bother building large embassies in Kiev because within eighteen months they will be downgraded to consular sections'. The Russian Ambassador to Kiev, Leonid Smoliakov, is also reported to have described Ukraine's independence as a 'transitional' phenomenon.[49]

These developments demonstrate the difficulties Warsaw faces in developing a new *Ostpolitik* in conditions of an unstable regional balance of power, compounded by domestic instabilities in Russia and the other Soviet successor states. Foreign-policy making in a multipolar context is never straightforward, but in Central and Eastern Europe today, domestic political uncertainties, nationalist passions and economic difficulties have made it even more complicated. The changed geopolitics of post-Cold War Eastern Europe presents new dilemmas for Poland. The break-up of the Soviet Union; the emergence of Russia as a regional great power; and the independence of Ukraine, Belarus and the Baltic republics – these developments have created a new pattern of international relations in the region. Russia itself is striving for great-power status, and is seeking to forge a more cohesive CIS. Russia is thus wary of external involvement in CIS affairs, which it fears may be designed to encourage a more independent stance by countries like Ukraine and Belarus.[50] Russia is also highly suspicious of any moves to expand NATO eastwards. Warsaw must therefore tread carefully if it is to avoid being entangled in the multipolar instability which characterises international relations in Eastern Europe and the former Soviet Union.

At the moment, Polish policy towards Russia is proceeding on a pragmatic and multi-track basis. Four key themes can be identified. First, Warsaw is striving to build a strong partnership with a democratic Russia sharing common market-orientated economic goals. This involves a series of practical steps to facilitate, for example, bilateral trade and military cooperation. Second, the Polish government is seeking to develop close cultural and political relations with all Soviet successor states, in order to support their national identities and give recognition to their political independence. Third, Poland is seeking to 'Europeanise' its Eastern policy, in order to avoid having to choose between East and West. Warsaw therefore sees its *Ostpolitik* as part of a more ambitious European task of creating a new Europe 'whole and free'. To this end, Poland has sought to enlist the support of Western governments, the EU and international economic organisations (such as the EBRD, World Bank and IMF) for its policy of developing good relations with its Eastern neighbours. Finally, Poland has made it clear that whatever the outcome of political struggles to its east (in other words, even if democracy in Russia collapses), it intends to remain on the side of Europe and the West – hopefully as members of Western organisations such as the EU and NATO.

Polish–Ukrainian relations

Historically, the lands between Germany and Russia have constituted a buffer zone of weak and quarrelsome states. Divisions in the region have allowed the two neighbouring great powers to pursue their hegemonic aspirations in Eastern Europe. Seen in this light, the relationship between Poland and Ukraine could have important geopolitical implications. In the changed strategic landscape of post-Cold War Europe, the emerging 'strategic partnership' between Warsaw and Kiev could provide a significant element of regional stability. With a combined population of 91 million, a Warsaw–Kiev axis would be an influential factor in the international politics of Central and Eastern Europe.

Yet Polish–Ukrainian relations have historically been troubled by territorial disputes, ethnic tensions and religious antagonism. They have long fought for control of Galicia, whilst disputes between the Polish Catholic Church and the Ukrainian Orthodox Church stretch back through the past millenium. Simmering resentments led to a string of reciprocal atrocities in World War Two, the memory of which still lingers amongst the older generation. Relations were also damaged by the Ukrainian annexation of L'viv (once a bastion of Polish culture and regional influence), and by the post-war 'ethnic cleansing' indulged in by both sides.[51]

The need to confront and transcend this dark historical legacy was recognised by both Polish and Ukrainian dissidents in the 1970s and 1980s. Discussions between the two sides began in the early 1970s, and blossomed into more practical forms of cooperation with the emergence of Solidarity in 1980. This cooperation continued throughout the period of martial law in Poland, and bore fruit after the collapse of the Soviet bloc when Solidarity and *Rukh* (the Ukrainian Popular Movement) established formal political contacts and began laying the foundations for a new era in bilateral relations.

The emergence of an independent and sovereign Ukraine was thus publicly welcomed by the Polish authorities, whatever private doubts they might have entertained in the light of their past history. In October 1990 (as part of Poland's dual-track policy), the two sides signed a declaration of friendship and cooperation.[52] When on 24 August 1991 Ukraine announced its independence from the USSR, the Polish government and the *Sejm* immediately expressed their full support. Indeed, Poland was the very first state to recognise Ukrainian independence – a fact which provided a very positive start to their bilateral relationship. President Kravchuk subsequently declared that the development of close ties with Warsaw was to be one of Ukraine's primary foreign policy objectives.

Bilateral relations were placed on a formal, legal basis in May 1993, when Presidents Kravchuk and Walesa signed a treaty of friendship and cooperation.[53] A treaty of defence cooperation has also been signed, which could provide the basis for a bilateral strategic axis.[54] At the same time, whilst a good working relationship has been cultivated at the inter-governmental level, relations at the local level have grown rapidly. Cross-border contacts have mushroomed over the last few years, as local authorities, individual enterprises, civic organisations and trading groups have established links – largely for economic purposes. Some attempt has been made to regulate these informal cross-border contacts (for example the October 1992 agreement on cross-border commercial, transport and telecommunication links), but much of it has remained spontaneous and unlicensed.

Both Warsaw and Kiev have become aware of the geostrategic significance of their bilateral relations. Since their May 1993 summit in Kiev, both Presidents Walesa and Kravchuk have referred to their relationship as a 'strategic partnership'.[55] Close cooperation would be mutually beneficial, and could contribute to the stability of the wider Europe. For Kiev, Poland represents the 'gateway to the West': Poland straddles Ukraine's main trade routes to the West, and good relations with Poland are seen in Kiev as being a prerequisite for establishing closer links with the EU and West European governments.[56] Ukraine also wants to establish good political and military relations with Poland in the light of its difficult relations with two of its other neighbours, Russia and Romania. For Warsaw, Ukraine offers a potentially attractive market and a trade conduit to the even more promising markets of Russia. Poland also has a strong security interest in a stable and independent Ukraine: political and economic failure in Ukraine would not only unleash a flood of refugees heading westwards, it might also precipitate the re-incorporation of Ukraine into Russia, bringing a neo-imperialist Russia once again up to Poland's borders.

Yet despite the benefits a 'strategic partnership' could offer to both states, a number of intractable bilateral problems remain. The first is economic: trade between the two sides remains low, largely because of a lack of hard currency. This means that nearly 50% of trade is conducted through barter arrangements. At the same time, Poland and Ukraine are competitive in similar products – agricultural goods, metals, chemicals and fuels – and might well find themselves competing for the same markets in the West.[57] Second, some influential Russians have voiced their displeasure at the developing relationship between Kiev and Warsaw, and have warned the Poles against building too warm a relationship with Ukraine. As we have already seen, this has heightened the dilemmas facing Poland's *Ostpolitik*, and led many Poles to advocate a more cautious approach to relations with Ukraine.[58] Third, Ukrainian foreign and security policy has proved ambiguous if not contradictory over recent years. Whilst professing its neutrality and non-nuclear status, the Ukrainian government has also suggested the creation of a new security bloc in Eastern Europe (excluding the Russians), and for a long while blew hot and cold on the question of giving up its nuclear weapons.[59] This somewhat mercurial approach to security policy reinforced the Polish government's sense of caution when dealing with its Ukrainian counterpart. Finally, there are a number of simmering disputes over property between the Polish Catholic Church and the Ukrainian Uniate (Orthodox-rite) Church, most notably that in Przemysl.[60]

If these potential problems can be successfully managed, the gains to both sides of a close relationship could be considerable. Both states share a common geostrategic problem: they live in the perpetual shadow of powerful neighbours – in Poland's case Germany, in Ukraine's case Russia. By establishing a close bond, these two medium-sized countries could create a bastion of stability in the region. Indeed,

> If Poland and Ukraine could cooperate closely, they would not only help overcome their isolation but could eventually form a powerful alliance with real European influence. Before this could happen, however, they would have to exorcise their past as decisively as the French and Germans did theirs after World War II. The interests of both countries demand this. It will be a sign of their maturity if they realize it, and it will secure their future if they achieve it.[61]

Polish–Belarussian relations

As with so many states in this turbulent and heterogenous part of Europe, history has bequeathed Polish–Belarussian relations a difficult legacy. Belarus has all too frequently provided the battleground for bloody conflicts between its more powerful neighbours – Poland in the West, and Russia in the East. The early twentieth century witnessed a nationalist revival in Belarus, but this was brutally interrupted by the outbreak of the Great War. During this titanic struggle, the front line ran through the heart of Belarus. With the coming of revolution and civil war, Belarus was once again a major battleground – this time between Reds and Whites. Similarly, when war broke out between Poland and Russia in 1920, Belarus provided the battlefield for the two armies. To cap it all, the end of this war resulted in a national tragedy – the division of the country. Belarus was only reunited as a result of the infamous Nazi–Soviet pact of 1939, which simultaneously resulted in the fourth partition of Poland.[62] It is therefore of little surprise that Poland and Belarus have a radically different perspective on twentieth century history. As a consequence of these historical differences, the emergence of an independent Belarus was viewed with some unease by Warsaw.

These early tensions were apparent from the initial failure to agree a declaration of friendship and cooperation. Poland had responded to Russian and Ukrainian declarations of sovereignty in July 1990 by signing declarations of friendship and cooperation with them in the following October. However, no such declaration was signed with Belarus, despite Minsk's declaration of sovereignty. The reasons for this initially frosty relationship between Warsaw and Minsk were threefold. First, Belarus said that it could not accept the finality of the Polish–Belarussian border because it had not been a party to the August 1945 Polish–Soviet treaty. Second, Minsk argued that Poland did not respect the rights of the Belarussian minority, pointing out that Warsaw refused to recognise the Bialystok region of north-west Poland as ethnically Belarussian territory. Third, Warsaw was suspicious of Belarus because of its apparent lack of real independence from the All-Union authorities in Moscow.

Yet Polish–Belarussian relations experienced an unexpected turn-around as a consequence of the August 1991 coup in Moscow. The failure of the putsch led to a declaration of independence from the USSR by Belarus, a decision 'greeted by joy' by the Polish Senate on 30 August. The following day the *Sejm* added its voice of approval to the Belarussian declaration of independence. Polish thinking towards Belarus was explained by Zdzislaw Najder (an advisor to President Walesa) in the following way: 'for Belarus, Poland is the only window to Europe, and if we do not help the Belarussians to find themselves a place in the new Europe, who will?'[63]

Over subsequent months, a series of high-level meetings took place which gave further momentum to the growing thaw in Polish–Belarussian relations. In October 1991, Belarussian Prime Minister Kebich visited Warsaw to sign both an 'Accord on Trade and Economic Cooperation' and a 'Declaration of Good-Neighbourliness, Mutual Understanding and Cooperation'.[64] Poland formally recognised Belarussian independence on 27 December 1991. This was followed by a series of agreements on transport and cross-border communications;[65] bilateral trade, banking and investment; and agricultural cooperation. More importantly, a consular convention and an agreement to establish diplomatic relations were signed in March 1992, whilst the long-awaited Treaty on Good-Neighbourly Relations and Friendly Cooperation was signed in June 1992 during a visit of Belarussian President Stanislaw Shushkevich to Warsaw.[66] The importance of Poland to Belarus was underlined during this visit when President Shushkevich opened the Belarussian Embassy in Warsaw – the first ever Belarussian embassy abroad.[67]

Thus, as Stephen Burant has noted, 'Poland's relations with Belarus represent a success for its foreign policy-makers, who since the summer of 1990 have been attempting to effect a rapprochement'.[68] A key element in this *rapprochement* has been the more sympathetic approach by both sides to the concerns of their national minorities. The Polish minority in Belarus numbers some 418,000 (out of a population of 10 million). Poles in Belarus – unlike Poles in Lithuania – have tended to support Belarussian independence, and have had good links with the Belarus Popular Front. Opportunities to study the Polish language have also improved in Belarus over the last two years. One source of tension, however, is religion. Polish priests travelling to Belarus to look after the interests of the Roman Catholic Church there tend to speak only Polish, even though there are three times as many Belarussian-speaking Catholics than Polish Catholics in Belarus. This means that Belarussian Catholics are often forced to pray in Polish – a cause of much resentment.

The Belarussian minority in Poland numbers between 200,000 and 400,000. They mostly live in the Bialystok region, which is one of the poorest and most underdeveloped in Poland. In the past, they have tended to be the victims of Polish prejudice, largely because many Poles do not accept that they live in what is still an ethnically mixed state. This minority is also becoming more assertive, and given that they are concentrated in an area along the Polish–Belarussian border, the potential exists for a territorial conflict over the right to secession.[69] This is an issue which therefore requires careful handling by the Polish and Belarussian governments if it is not to generate renewed bilateral tensions.

Poland's relations with Belarus epitomise the dilemmas facing its *Ostpolitik*. Efforts to cement a closer political relationship with Minsk have generated sharp criticism from Moscow. This was highlighted in November 1992 when the then Polish Prime Minister, Hanna Suchocka, visited Minsk and called on the Belarussian government to exercise greater independence. This appeal was widely denounced in Russia, and aggravated the suspicions of Poland harboured by some of Belarus's more pro-Russian politicians.[70] Since mid-1993, the weakening economic position of Belarus has made Minsk far more amenable to Russian calls for a more integrated CIS. Belarus has also strengthened its bilateral ties with Russia economically, politically and militarily.[71] Given these developments, Polish policy needs to be carefully calibrated in order to cultivate good relations with Minsk without unduly antagonising Russia.

Polish–Lithuanian relations

Relations between these two Catholic countries, both of which produced large anticommunist and anti-Soviet popular movements, have been burdened with the legacy of the past and with the problems of national minorities. For 400 years, Poles and Lithuanians were part of the same state – the *Rzeczpospolita Obojga Narodow* – with a single elected ruler and one parliament. This intimate relationship began with the marriage of the Lithuanian Grand Duke Jagiello to the Polish Queen Jadwiga in 1386, and was cemented by the Polish–Lithuania victory over the Teutonic knights at the Battle of Grunwald in 1410. The *Rzeczpospolita* was formally established by the 1569 Treaty of Lublin and existed until the third partition of Poland, in 1795.

In 1830, and again in 1863, Poles and Lithuanians fought side by side for independence against their Russian oppressors. However, in the late nineteenth century, Polish and Lithuanian paths began to diverge. The Lithuanian nationalist movement defined itself in opposition to both Russian political domination and Polish cultural hegemony. With the collapse of the tsarist empire towards the end of

World War One, Lithuanian nationalists made their bid for an
independent nation state. This led to fierce fighting with Poland,
particularly for the ancient Lithuanian capital of Vilnius (Wilno).
Their defeat in this war and the loss of Vilnius in 1922 led to a bitter
feeling of humiliation in Lithuania, and in the inter-war years both
countries used all means short of war to harm each other.[72] Lithuania
waged a virulent campaign to rid the language, culture and literature
of Polish influences, and regaining Vilnius became a national
obsession. This was finally achieved in 1939, as a consequence of the
fourth division of Poland.

The Poles and the Lithuanians therefore have different perceptions
of their shared history. For the Poles, the union with Lithuania is
associated with the golden age of Polish history, the Jagiellonian
period. There is also considerable popular empathy with their
smaller Catholic neighbour. For the Lithuanians, on the other hand,
the *Rzeczpospolita* is seen as a time when the Lithuanian national
identity was submerged under the cultural and political hegemony of
Poland. The Lithuanians also harbour bitter memories of the loss of
Vilnius and the humiliation of the war with Poland.[73]

With the establishment of communist regimes in both countries,
visible signs of national animosity were suppressed. Indeed, by the
1970s and 1980s, the Lithuanians were beginning to appreciate the
advantages of their historic links with Poland. Knowledge of the
Polish language gave Lithuanians access to Polish publications and
Polish television, which were much more entertaining and
informative than their Soviet equivalents. As the chains of communist
orthodoxy began loosening in the late 1980s, anticommunist
nationalists in both countries started exploring the prospects for a
new, more cooperative relationship between Warsaw and Vilnius. In
November 1989, for example, Lithuanian nationalist leaders wrote a
letter 'To Our Friends the Poles'. This letter promised that 'a free and
democratic Lithuania will cooperate in a friendly manner with a free
and democratic Poland'.[74] Thus when Lithuania declared its
independence on 11 March 1990, *Sajūdis* leaders hoped that Poland
would give them full support in their struggle against the Soviet
Union.

For their part, Poland's leaders perceived a close political affinity
between Solidarity and *Sajūdis*, both of which embodied national
revolutions against communist regimes imposed on their peoples by
Stalin. The Polish public was also fully in sympathy with the

aspirations for independence of their neighbours. Consequently, the Lithuanian declaration of independence was warmly welcomed by the Polish government, *Sejm*, political parties and public, and Warsaw gave considerable diplomatic support to the Lithuanians. A high-point in this regard was the 'working visit' of the Lithuanian Prime Minister Prunskiene to Warsaw on 21 June 1990, when she met Prime Minister Mazowiecki, Foreign Minister Skubiszewski and parliamentary leaders.

Nonetheless, Poland did not offer full diplomatic recognition to Lithuania. The excuse for this was that Poland had not recognised the Soviet takeover of the Baltic republics in the first place. The real reason, however, was that the Polish government did not want to antagonise Moscow. Stephen Burant wrote at the time,

> The Polish heart might plead for support for Lithuania's aspirations to independent statehood, perhaps even for formal diplomatic recognition of Lithuania. But the Polish head would caution that because Moscow remains the dominant military and political power in Eastern and Central Europe and because several important issues remain to be resolved between Poland and the Soviet Union, Poland must exercise restraint on the issue of Lithuanian independence.[75]

The August 1991 coup fiasco obviated the need for such caution, and Poland subsequently moved rapidly to establish full relations with Lithuania. Yet following this, bilateral relations deteriorated sharply. The reasons for this had to do with lingering tensions over national minorities. First, there is a Polish community of approximately 258,000 in Lithuania, constituting 7% of the country's population, and concentrated in the countryside around Vilnius. In the late 1980s, they began to feel uneasy about the rise of Lithuanian nationalism. As usual, the key disputes concerned the access to economic and social resources. Poles in Lithuania complained that they were six times less likely to enter higher-education institutions than their Lithuanian compatriots; that ethnically Polish areas received 50% less funding from the central government; and that Polish areas had the lowest per capita number of doctors, hospitals, schools and telephones in the country. They also resented the November 1988 Lithuanian language law, and the follow-up legislation of January 1989. This resentment led Polish local government bodies from Vilnius, Salcininkai, Trakai and Svencionys to proclaim the formation of a Polish National-Territorial

District within the Republic of Lithuania. The central government in Vilnius – concerned about possible secessionist moves – responded by dissolving these elected local government bodies and appointing commissioners in their place. The Polish government in turn expressed its concern about minority rights, although without endorsing the actions of the Polish community in Lithuania (much to the annoyance of that community).

Secondly, there is also a small Lithuanian community in Poland. This numbers between 10,000 and 30,000, and claimed they that they enjoyed even fewer rights than Poles in Lithuania. Traditionally, few resources have been given to this community, and no Lithuanian-language books were published in Poland. This began to change in the early 1990s, largely because the Polish government hoped that better conditions for the Lithuanian minority would encourage the Lithuanian government to treat its Polish minority more sympathetically.

Questions of minority rights remain a sensitive issue in Polish–Lithuanian relations. Serious problems have also arisen at the Lazdijai/Ogrodniki customs post, where travellers frequently have to wait several days, unless they bribe officials. Nonetheless, signs of a *rapprochement* between Warsaw and Vilnius have begun to appear. After four years of negotiations, a bilateral treaty of friendship and cooperation was signed in April 1994. This treaty has subsequently been ratified by both parliaments, despite some domestic unease in Poland. It has also been reported that Lithuania 'is considering exploiting its historical ties with Poland to develop a special relationship with the Visegrad countries as a means of pressing its case for EU membership'.[76] It may therefore be that a new period in Polish–Lithuanian relations is beginning, in which past links and geopolitical affinities might be exploited for mutual benefit.

The *Ostpolitik* of the Czech and Slovak Republics

Soviet–Czechoslovak relations

Following the velvet revolution, Prague's post-communist leadership was determined to replace the hated 1970 Friendship and Cooperation Treaty. This treaty was seen as the diplomatic expression of the Brezhnev doctrine, and it was widely felt that bilateral relations should be based on a new legal and more equitable basis. Negotiations on such a treaty proved difficult, however, and dragged on inconclusively throughout 1990 and most of 1991. The two key stumbling blocks were the question of Czechoslovakia's freedom to join existing alliances (namely NATO), and the issue of compensation for environmental damage caused by Soviet military forces.

The diplomatic log jam was broken only after the abortive August coup. Within five weeks, the text of a new bilateral treaty had been agreed. The CSFR–USSR Treaty of Good-Neighbourliness, Friendly Relations and Cooperation was initialled by the two foreign ministers in October 1991, and a formal signing ceremony was planned for December 1991 in Moscow.[77] This, however, was prevented by the break-up of the Soviet Union.

CSFR–Russian relations

With the collapse of the USSR, Czechoslovak leaders moved quickly to develop diplomatic relations with the Soviet successor states – first and foremost, Russia. Negotiations for a bilateral treaty took place on the basis of the October 1991 CSFR–USSR Treaty, and made rapid progress. In April 1992 the CSFR–Russia Treaty was signed in the Kremlin by Presidents Havel and Yeltsin. It was regarded by both sides as a model of its kind – both for Russia's relations with the ex-Warsaw Pact countries, and for Czechoslovakia's relations with the Soviet successor states.

The CSFR–Russian treaty was interesting in a number of respects. First, it contained a strong condemnation of the 1968 invasion of Czechoslovakia – apparently at the insistence of the Russian side.[78] Second, the treaty referred to the 'traditional friendship between the peoples of the two states', a phrase not found in the CSFR–German treaty. Third, reference was made in the treaty to the need for 'good-neighbourliness and partnership', even though the two sides were not, strictly speaking, neighbours (Dienstbier indirectly admitted that this was a mistake apparently overlooked by experts on both sides!). Finally, the treaty stressed the 'significance of uncompromising adherence to human rights and basic freedoms and to the principles of democracy, humanitarianism, and the rule of law'.[79]

In the course of 1992, therefore, relations between the CSFR and the Russian Federation improved considerably. Soviet troops were withdrawn, and a new bilateral state treaty signed. The thorny issue of compensation for damages caused by Soviet troops in Czechoslovakia after 1968 was also amicably resolved.[80] The only other outstanding issue was the debt of the former Soviet Union, which had proven difficult to resolve due to the parlous state of the Russian economy and the breakdown in trading links between former CMEA partners. Despite this, CSFR–Russian relations developed positively throughout 1992. One encouraging factor was that the CSFR–Russian friendship treaty did not become a controversial domestic political issue (in the way the CSFR–German Treaty did).

However, the break-up of the Czechoslovak Federation on 1 January 1993 meant that Prague and Bratislava had to re-establish diplomatic relations with their Eastern neighbours in the light of their changed geopolitical situation. The break-up of the CSFR also raised questions concerning the validity of international treaties and agreements entered into by the CSFR, and complicated even further the pattern of ethno-national relations in Eastern Europe.

The Czech Republic's *Ostpolitik*

Czech–Russian relations

The break-up of the CSFR reinforced the *Mitteleuropäische* identity of the Czech Republic by shifting its geopolitical centre of gravity westwards. It also left Slovakia as a 'buffer' between the Czech lands and the instability of the CIS. Yet Russia remains an important economic partner for the Czech Republic, both because of imports of Russian oil and natural gas, and because of Russia's huge market potential. Prague also has a strong interest in the consolidation of democracy and market prosperity in the East, and regards itself as having 'a certain responsibility' for encouraging good relations between the West and Russia, given its central geographical location and its Slavic culture.[81]

Czech–Russian relations were placed on a formal legal basis by the Treaty of Friendship and Cooperation signed in Prague in August 1993 during President Yeltsin's state visit. At this summit, the controversial issue of Prague's future membership of the EU and NATO was raised. At this stage, Yeltsin's position was that 'Russia does not have the right to prevent a sovereign state from joining a European organisation'. Since then, however, the Russian position has hardened, and disagreements over the question of future NATO membership for the East Central Europeans have cast a renewed shadow over relations between Prague and Moscow. Foreign Minister Kozyrev's comments to the effect that the Czech Republic was in Russia's sphere of interest also elicited a rebuke from President Havel in February 1994. Havel said that such talk caused anxiety in the Czech Republic, and reiterated his country's desire to become a 'normal European country', which included joining NATO and the EU. For his part, Kozyrev promised he would stop using such a formulation if it reminded the Czechs of their recent past, but insisted that any extension of NATO would estrange Russia and discriminate against it. He also argued that the issue of NATO enlargement was no longer topical given the Partnership for Peace proposal, and maintained that Russia had the right to express its opinion about 'how European security can be most favourably ensured'.[82] This issue of NATO membership is likely to remain a bone of contention between Prague and Moscow for some time to come.

Czech–Ukrainian relations

Although the Czech Republic does not share a border with Ukraine, Czech–Ukrainian relations are important for both economic and security reasons. Ukraine is the Czech Republic's second biggest economic partner in the CIS after Russia, and all of Prague's vital oil and gas imports from Russia pass through Ukraine. Prague is also aware that 'Ukraine is a major neighbour for two of its Visegrad partners, and this must not be overlooked. Stability in this part of Europe is immensely important for the stability of the entire European continent, especially in its Central region.'[83]

Slovakia's *Ostpolitik*

Whereas the break-up of the CSFR reinforced the Czech Republic's Western orientation, it accentuated the importance of Bratislava's economic and geostrategic relations with its Eastern neighbours. Economically, Slovakia has long been more dependent on the Soviet market than Bohemia or Moravia, given its substantial armaments industries and heavy industrial sector. Slovakia has been affected much more severely than the Czech lands by the collapse of the Eastern market, and many Slovaks have consequently placed much faith on a revival of trade with Russia and Ukraine. These hopes were fuelled by Meciar's call for the construction of a new railway from Bratislava to the Ukrainian border using the broader gauge of the former Soviet rail network. This, he claimed, would provide a major fillip for Slovakia's Eastern trade. Bratislava is also more sensitive to developments in the CIS than is Prague (given its geographical proximity), and its relations with Ukraine are complicated by trans-border national minorities.

Slovak–Russian relations

Relations between Bratislava and Moscow were formalised in a bilateral state treaty signed during Yeltsin's visit to Slovakia in August 1993. A five-year military cooperation agreement was also signed by the respective defence ministers. This provided for closer defence and security consultation, along with the delivery of Russian military spare parts to the Slovak army.

Slovakia's economic and political relations with the East have raised more fundamental questions concerning its foreign policy orientation. In contrast to the enthusiastically pro-Western approach of the Czech Republic, Slovakia has appeared to favour a more 'balanced' approach to its Eastern and Western neighbours. This was apparent from the negotiations over the state treaty. One controversial paragraph stipulated that neither side would assist in a military attack by a third party by allowing the attacking troops on to its territory. This would have rendered Slovakia neutral in any future conflict involving NATO and Russia, and would therefore have been incompatible with any future alliance commitments. For this reason the offending paragraph was withdrawn at the last moment, and Slovakia's desire to return to Europe reiterated. Nonetheless, the commitment of Bratislava to Western integration has been questioned, and it does appear as if Slovakia will remain more sympathetic than the other Visegrad states to the security interests of Moscow.[84]

Slovak–Ukrainian relations

Ukraine is an important regional partner for Slovakia. Not only are closer economic relations potentially advantageous to both sides, but good political relations are also important given the inter-ethnic bonds which link them. Some 10,000 Slovaks live in the western-most *oblast* of Zakarpattya (or Transcarpathia), whilst approximately 21,000 Ukrainians reside in Slovakia. There is also a small Ruthenian community (the *Rusyn*) which straddles the Slovak–Ukrainian border. From 1919 to 1945, Zakarpattya belonged to the CSFR (prior to that it had been part of the Austro-Hungarian Empire). In a referendum held in the *oblast* on 1 December 1991, 78% voted for Zakarpattya to become a 'special self-governing administrative territory' within an independent Ukraine. Some extremist and ultra-nationalist political groups amongst the Ruthenians have called for either independence for Zakarpattya or unification with Slovakia.[85] However, these remain minority views, and Bratislava has underlined that it has no territorial demands on Ukraine.[86] The status of Zakarpattya thus remains a sensitive political issue, although not one which has prevented the development of cooperative relations between Slovakia and Ukraine (both bilaterally and on a multilateral, regional basis).

Hungary's *Ostpolitik*

Budapest's overriding foreign policy goal is integration with the West. But it cannot ignore its powerful Eastern neighbours, nor its central geopolitical location. Hungary has also been very much affected by the violent break-up of Yugoslavia, which has produced three new states along its southern border, and which has led to violations of Hungarian airspace and territory by the Serbian military.

Given Hungary's simmering disputes with Serbia and Romania, and lingering tensions with Slovakia and Croatia, Hungary's policy towards Russia and Ukraine is very much tied up with its aim of creating a stable regional balance of power. Linked to this is Budapest's concern to safeguard the rights of the Magyar diaspora. Relations with its Eastern neighbours are therefore a vital but delicate area of Hungary's wider foreign policy goals.

Hungarian–Soviet relations

The sharp westward reorientation of Hungarian external relations after the March 1990 elections was evident from two developments:

the withdrawal of Soviet troops in June 1990, and the replacement of the USSR by Germany as Hungary's main trading partner by the end of the year. Nevertheless, Hungary remained heavily dependent on energy supplies from the Soviet Union, particularly after the escalating civil war in Yugoslavia forced the closure in September 1991 of the Adria pipeline (which delivered oil from the Middle East).

Throughout 1990 and 1991, Budapest conducted a dual-track policy towards the Soviet authorities in Moscow and the individual republics. For example, in December 1991 Prime Minister Ántáll visited Moscow to sign a new treaty of friendship and cooperation with the Soviet government.[87] At the same time, bilateral treaties were signed with the Russian Federation and Ukraine. The Hungarians also became firm supporters of the independence of the Baltic republics, even though they granted them full recognition only after the abortive coup of August 1991. Relations with the Baltic states were subsequently further developed in August 1992, when Foreign Minister Jeszenszky visited the Baltic region and signed bilateral state treaties with all three republics.

Hungarian–Ukrainian relations

Of all the new bilateral relationships in Eastern Europe, relations between Hungary and Ukraine are perhaps the warmest. Budapest and Kiev have worked hard to develop close and cooperative relations, with encouraging results. In September 1990 President Arpad Goncz became the first head of state to visit Ukraine after the republic had declared its sovereignty that summer. Then, in December 1991, Hungary became the first country to establish diplomatic relations with Ukraine and to open an embassy in Kiev. The same month saw the signing of a bilateral state treaty, which included a clause ruling out all border changes and mutually renouncing once and for all any territorial claims. Later, in March 1992, Ukraine opened an embassy in Budapest – Kiev's first bilateral embassy for seventy-three years. The Ukrainian Deputy Foreign Minister Boris Tarasyuk called the opening of the embassy a 'special event' which testified to the two countries' 'exemplary relations'. He also recalled that Hungary played a 'pioneering' role in establishing a link between his country and the outside world. This warm bilateral relationship was further reinforced in February 1993, when

President Kravchuk visited Budapest and signed a number of bilateral agreements.

The exceptionally good relations enjoyed by Hungary and Ukraine can be attributed to four factors.[88] First, Hungary quickly recognised the importance and potential of Ukraine, and made a determined effort to build good relations with its large Eastern neighbour. Moreover, for Budapest, good relations with Ukraine are vital in order to offset the danger of a new 'Little Entente' between Romania, Serbia and Slovakia. Second, Ukraine perceived Hungary as its window on the West, and hoped that by building good relations with Budapest, it would open a gateway to *Mitteleuropa* and, beyond that, to the EU. This is also the rationale behind Kiev's keen interest in participating in regional cooperation schemes such as the Carpathian Euroregion, the Central European Initiative and the Visegrad forum. Third, both sides hoped to develop mutually beneficial economic and trading relations, despite the short-term problems arising from the collapse of the CMEA and the turmoil of economic transformation. Finally, Ukraine has adopted a far-sighted policy on minority rights, which includes a recognition of the notion of collective rights. This policy has been much praised within Hungary, and promoted by Budapest as a model for other countries with Magyar minorities to emulate.[89]

This last point is particularly important given the tensions generated by ethnicity and minority nationalism in the region. Ukraine is the only country with a substantial Hungarian minority that accepts that national minorities have collective rights. It has also demonstrated a willingness to consider territorial autonomy for its national minorities. Budapest also believes that the Magyar minority in Ukraine is treated better there than anywhere else in the region. The Hungarian government has particularly welcomed the expansion of the network of Hungarian-language elementary and middle schools, and the willingness to teach Hungarian history in all schools in ethnic Magyar areas where the language of instruction is Hungarian (this is not something that other countries with substantial Hungarian minorities have been willing to do).[90]

One potentially complicating factor in Hungarian–Ukrainian relations is the question of Zakarpattya, which is home to some 160,000 Magyars (12.5% of the total population of the *oblast*). The Joint Declaration on Minority Rights created a much better environment for the Magyar minority, as did the liberal nationality law passed by the Ukrainian parliament in 1992. But – with the experience of the Crimea fresh in its mind – the Ukrainian parliament reacted cooly to the vote by Hungarians in the Beregszasz *raion* of the Zakarpattya   *oblast* in December 1991 to form a Magyar 'national district', a vote taken at the same time as the *oblast* voted to adopt a 'special self-governing administrative status'.[91] This vote has still not been accepted by the parliament (which has promised to take up the matter in separate legislation), but the issue has not been pressed by the Hungarian government. On a more positive note, both governments have worked closely together with Slovakia and Poland to establish a Carpathian Euroregion, designed to stimulate cross-border exchanges on a local basis (see chapter 5).

Hungarian–Russian relations

Whilst Hungary enjoyed increasingly warm relations with Ukraine after the break-up of the Soviet Union, relations with Russia remained lukewarm for most of 1991 and early 1992. One reason for this was economic: Russia's parlous economic condition meant that Moscow was an increasingly unreliable trading partner. It was even unable to abide by its barter agreements. Thus although Hungary remained among Russia's top ten most important trading partners, Russia itself was running a trade deficit with Hungary of $1.7 billion at the start of 1992.[92]

Economic problems were not the only reason for the initial coolness in Hungarian–Russian relations. Another important factor was the changed geopolitics of Eastern Europe. 'One should keep in mind', Jan Zielonka has argued, 'that Central European relations with Russia are of a different strategic nature than their relations with the USSR. Although Russia remains the most powerful state in Eastern Europe, it was the independent Ukraine, Byelarus and Lithuania which became the immediate neighbours of the [Visegrad states] following the collapse of the USSR'.[93] Hungary therefore placed much greater emphasis on relations with its immediate Eastern neighbour – Ukraine – than it did with Russia.

Yet Hungary shares one important factor in common with Russia: a concern with minority rights. 'Hungary's diaspora is second in size only to Russia's among European nations.... As a result, the Hungarian leadership has empathetic feelings for the problems of divided nations and seeks to promote the rights of ethnic minorities'.[94] Their common concern with problems of minority rights led to the issuing of a joint declaration on the issue. It stated their intention to promote the international codification of minority rights and to coordinate their actions in fora such as the UN and the CSCE.[95] Russia also emerged as an important ally for Hungary during its stint on the UN Security Council.[96]

This joint declaration was issued at a summit meeting in Budapest between Presidents Goncz and Yeltsin in November 1992. This was the first visit by any high-ranking Russian in the post-Soviet period, and led to a tangible improvement in bilateral relations. During the summit, President Goncz stressed that Russia was a major factor in the region's stability, and expressed his hopes that Yeltsin's visit would put relations between their two countries on a new and improved footing. As is usual on such occasions, the summit contained a mixture of symbolic gestures and substantive agreements. In terms of political symbolism, Yeltsin laid a wreath at the Soviet war memorial in Budapest, and visited the grave of Imre Nagy. More substantively, agreement was reached on the outstanding financial issues arising from the stationing of the Southern Group of Soviet Forces (SGSF) in Hungary during the Cold War, and on the repayment of the former Soviet Union's debt to Hungary.[97]

The Yeltsin–Goncz summit of November 1992 thus ushered in a more cooperative phase in Hungarian–Russian relations. Bilateral trade has also shown signs of recovery since 1992, partly recouping some of the dramatic fall-off which occurred in 1989–91. Unfortunately, a number of clouds have since cast a shadow over the newly improved relationship between Budapest and Moscow. In January 1993, for example, the Russian parliament delayed the ratification of the bilateral state treaty because of the inclusion of a condemnation of the 1956 Soviet invasion. Hungary and Russia have also backed different sides in the war in former Yugoslavia: Hungary has traditionally been sympathetic towards Croatia, whilst Russia has long empathised with its fellow Slavs in Serbia. Finally, Moscow has become increasingly vociferous in its opposition to the Eastern expansion of NATO, a stance which has brought it into conflict with Budapest. Nonetheless, bilateral relations remain broadly amicable and businesslike, with a potential for further bilateral cooperation (particularly in the area of minority rights for national diasporas).

Conclusion

The context within which the countries of East Central Europe have conducted their *Ostpolitik* has profoundly and irrevocably changed since 1989–91. The collapse of communism and the break-up of the Soviet Union has produced a radically new topology of power relations in Central and Eastern Europe. A much more complex pattern of international relations has emerged in the region, with new states, new webs of bilateral relations and a more polycentric system. A key feature of international relations in this region is the prevalence of ethno-national fissures which criss-cross state boundaries. This is one of the main features distinguishing Eastern Europe from Western Europe. Another is the dearth of established and robust institutions for multilateral cooperation. Ethno-national tensions and an institutional vacuum, coupled with severe economic difficulties and political fluidity, have thus left international politics in Eastern Europe unstable and unpredictable.

Faced with this unsettling turbulence to their East, the Visegrad countries have pinned their hopes on a return to Europe. Yet they now recognise that they cannot ignore their Eastern neighbours. Eastern Europe offers opportunities for trade, investment, cultural enrichment and political cooperation. However, it also presents potential dangers. In the past, the East has all too often been a source of threats to the security of the Visegrad countries. With worsening instability in the former Soviet Union and the Balkans, there are growing concerns that instability in the East may generate problems of economic dislocation, mass migration, trans-national crime and military conflict.

The Visegrad countries' main worry is the uncertainty of the reform process in Russia. Following the break-up of the USSR, only Poland shares a border with Russia (and then only with Kaliningrad). Nonetheless, Russia remains the regional great power, with a formidable military machine and vital interests in its 'near abroad'. Russia today is struggling to complete its transition to a market economy and to consolidate its fragile democratic institutions.[98] If the reform process succeeds, and Russia develops into a stable, democratic and pacific power, a potential security threat to East Central Europe will have been removed. But if the reform process stalls, and Russia embarks on a more aggressive defence of its interests in its 'near abroad', then the Visegrad states will find themselves once again in the ominous shadow of their former hegemon. The East Central Europeans are thus keenly interested in developments in both Russia and the CIS (particularly as they affect Ukraine and Belarus).

The uncertainty surrounding Russian foreign and security policies has created a major dilemma for the Visegrad states: should they seek to develop close relations with Kiev and Minsk and attempt to bolster these states' sovereignty? Or should they acknowledge Russia's hegemony in its 'near abroad', pursue a low-key approach towards their Eastern neighbours, and concentrate their energies on integration with the West? This is a major foreign policy dilemma for the Visegrad countries, to which there is no easy answer.

This dilemma in turn raises even more profound questions concerning the contours of the new Europe. In the past, East Central Europe has acted as a bulwark of Latin Christendom against the Orthodox East. The *Mitteleuropa* debate of the 1980s echoed these past notions by defining East Central Europe in terms of an opposition to Russia and the Asiatic East. The danger today is that the Visegrad states may concentrate on integrating into Western structures to such an extent that they simply turn their back on their neighbours in the East.

This option undoubtedly appeals to some in East Central Europe given the turmoil in the CIS. Trying to insulate themselves from the instabilities to their east must seem attractive to many in the region. Yet such a development would not only spell the end of hopes for a Europe 'whole and free', it would also generate new divisions in a continent only recently freed from the nightmare of the Cold War. This could have worrying consequences for European security. Samuel Huntington has argued that in the post-Cold War world, the 'great divisions among humankind and the dominant source of conflict' will not be ideological or economic, but cultural. 'Nation states will remain the most powerful actors in world affairs, but the principal conflicts of global politics will occur between nations and groups of different civilisations. The clash of civilisations will dominate global politics. The fault lines of civilisations will be the battle lines of the future'.[99] One of these civilisational fault lines listed by Huntington is that between the 'Western' and the 'Slavic–Orthodox'. The fault line between them runs through Central and Eastern Europe. Thus if Huntington is correct, a major danger facing Europe is the emergence of a new East–West conflict, this time pitting the countries of Western and Central Europe against the Slavic–Orthodox countries to their east.

There is, however, a more optimistic and constructive scenario for the future. As we have already noted in chapter three, historically the Visegrad countries have not simply acted as the eastern bulwark of Latin Christendom. They have also been the conduit for peaceful cultural and economic exchanges between East and West. It is thus not inconceivable that instead of constituting a defensive glacis for Western and Central Europe against the Orthodox East, East Central Europe could function as a buckle uniting East and West. As Saul Cohen has suggested (see p. 49), the Visegrad countries could act as 'hinge states' within a 'gateway region', thus facilitating 'the boundaries of accommodation' between the CIS and the EU. Russia, Ukraine and Belarus all see the Visegrad countries as a 'bridge' to the West. Whilst providing a gateway to the West for the East Europeans, the Visegrad states could also provide a conduit to the East for 'European' values of democracy and human rights. In this way, the stability of the transatlantic security community could be gradually expanded into the post-communist East.

Relations between the Visegrad countries and the Soviet successor states are therefore of considerable significance for the future political, economic and strategic topology of Europe. As Richard Staar has written,

> The future of what used to be called Soviet–East European political relations will ... be determined by whether Warsaw, Prague and Budapest can build bridges linking Moscow with Brussels.[100]

Endnotes

1   J. F. Brown, 'Relief without relaxation: Eastern Europe ponders the CIS', *RFE/RL Research Report*, 1, no. 8, 21 February 1992, pp. 17–20.

2   'In Central Europe, too, there are signs that what Yeltsin has called the "stepping up of foreign policy" is acquiring more economic content. In the view of several former Ministers of the defeated centre-right in Poland and Hungary, there is real risk that the energy sectors in these two countries could be exposed to very high levels of Russian influence. On several occasions, straw men have emerged in privatisations fronting for *Gazprom* and other Russian firms, and whilst Russian pressure over energy remains discreet, it is now being felt.' James Sherr, 'Russia: geopolitics and money', *The World Today*, February 1995, pp. 32–36 (p. 35).

3   On 30 July, 1992, the *Sejm* voted 15 August 'official Army Day', to coincide
     with this 1920 'miracle on the Vistula'.
4   C. J. Bartlett, *The Global Conflict. The International Rivalry of the Great
     Powers, 1880–1990*, 2nd edn, London, Longman, 1994, pp. 212–17.
5   'The ten-year Non-Aggression Pact which resulted from Ribbentrop's visit [to
     Moscow in August 1939] came as a great shock to the west, although not to
     western governments. It also came as a shock to the communist parties of the
     west; once more they were to damage their own prospects by supporting
     Soviet foreign policy. Probably it came as a shock to the Russian people too,
     but they accepted the view that only thus could the German threat be diverted
     from Russia. The shock might have been shattered had they known of the
     secret protocol of the Pact. This divided Poland into Russian and German
     sectors, and allowed the USSR to regard Finland, Estonia, Latvia, and
     Bessarabia as her own sphere (Lithuania was later added).' J. N. Westwood,
     Endurance and Endeavour. Russian History 1812–1992, Oxford, Oxford
     University Press, 1993, p. 340.
6   In April 1943 the Nazis announced the discovery in Katyn forest of a mass
     grave containing some 14,000 Polish soldiers who had been interned by the
     Soviets shortly after the invasion of 1939. The Germans accused the Soviets
     of the massacres, whilst Moscow responded by denying any responsibility and
     denouncing the German claims as Nazi propaganda. Against the advice of the
     British government, who felt that it was better to leave the matter to rest until
     after the war, the Polish government in exile in London asked the
     International Red Cross to mount an investigation. Moscow then broke off
     diplomatic relations with the Polish government in London, and increased
     their support to the rival exile Polish political forces in the USSR. Only later
     did the Russians admit the Soviet authorities' role in the Katyn massacre. For
     details see Philip Longworth, *The Making of Eastern Europe*, London,
     Macmillan, 1992, p. 45.
7   For details see Martin Myant, *Socialism and Democracy in Czechoslovakia,
     1945–48*, Cambridge, Cambridge University Press, 1981; Frantisek August
     and David Rees, *Red Star Over Prague*, London, The Sherwood Press, 1984;
     and Jon Bloomfield, *Passive Revolution: Politics and the Czechoslovak
     Working Class, 1945–48*, London, Allison and Busby, 1979.
8   Sarah Meiklejohn Terry, ed., *Soviet Policy in Eastern Europe*, New Haven,
     Yale University Press, 1984, p. 5. Jonathan Steele has described the way in
     which the Soviets' 'Eastern Europe empire was felt and seen differently in
     Russia from the way the population of Western powers viewed their colonies.
     For one thing Russian civilians did not settle in Eastern Europe, except for a
     handful married to local people. The Soviet presence in East Germany,
     Hungary, Czechoslovakia and Poland consisted of an embassy, military
     garrisons, the KGB, and a few state-owned trading concerns.... Second,
     Eastern Europe was largely out of bounds for Russian tourists. Occasional
     groups travelled there, again under tightly supervised conditions. Eastern
     Europe, although in theory part of the Soviet "camp", was considered alien
     territory. The traveller, crossing by train from the Soviet Union to Poland,
     would find barbed wire and watch-towers on the Soviet side of the frontier.
     It was as though Poland was already part of "the West", a threatening culture

from which Russians must defend themselves'. J. Steele, *Eternal Russia*, London, Faber and Faber, 1995, p. 152.

9   Karen Dawisha and Philip Hanson, eds, *Soviet–East European Dilemmas: Coercion, Competition and Consent*, London, Heinemann for the RIIA, 1981; and L. P. Morris, *Eastern Europe Since 1945*, London, Heineman, 1984.

10   Vernon Aspaturin, 'Has Eastern Europe become a liability to the Soviet Union? (1) The political-ideological aspects', in Charles Gati, ed., *The International Politics of Eastern Europe*, New York, Praeger, 1975, pp. 17–36 (p. 23).

11   See Gerard Holden, *The Warsaw Pact: Soviet Security and Bloc Politics*, Oxford, Blackwell, 1988; Raymond Garthoff, *Deterence and the Revolution in Soviet Military Doctrine*, Washington, DC, Brookings Institution, 1990; and Derek Leebaert and Timothy Dickinson, eds, *Soviet Strategy and New Military Thinking*, Cambridge, Cambridge University Press, 1992.

12   For a discussion of this dilemma, see J. F. Brown, *Eastern Europe and Communist Rule*, Durham, Duke University Press, 1988, ch. 2.

13   See Karen Dawisha, *Eastern Europe, Gorbachev and Reform*, Cambridge, Cambridge University Press, 1988; and Alex Pravda, *The End of the Outer Empire: Soviet–East European Relations in Transition, 1985–90*, London, Sage for the RIIA, 1992.

14   Robin Alison Remington, 'Changes in Soviet security policy toward Eastern Europe and the Warsaw Pact', in George E. Hudson, ed., *Soviet National Security Policy Under Perestroika*, Boston, Unwin Hyman, 1990, pp. 221–45.

15   For details see Neil Malcolm, 'The "Common European House" and Soviet European Policy', *International Affairs*, 65, no. 4, autumn 1989, pp. 659–76; Hannes Adomeit, 'Gorbatchows Westpolitik (I): "Gemeinsames europäisches Haus" oder "Atlantische "Orientierung?"', *Osteuropa*, no. 6, 1988, pp. 419–34; and Hannes Adomeit, 'Gorbatchows Westpolitik (II): Die Beziehungen im "Gemeinsames Haus"', *Osteuropa*, no. 9, 1988, pp. 815–34.

16   The 'Brezhnev doctrine' – the doctrine of limited sovereignty for communist states within the Soviet bloc – was formulated in the wake of the Warsaw Pact crushing of the 'Prague spring'. The classic statement of the 'Brezhnev doctrine' is S. Kovalev, 'Suverenitet i internatsional'nye obyazannosti sotsialisticheskikh Stran', *Pravda*, 26 September 1968, p. 4.

17   Richard F. Staar, *East-Central Europe and the USSR*, London, Macmillan, 1991, p. 26.

18   A. G. V. Hyde-Price, 'After the Pact: East European security in the 1990s', *Arms Control*, XII, no. 2, September 1991, pp. 279–302.

19   Staar, *op. cit.*, p. 1.

20   Libor Roucek, 'USSR/Eastern Europe: a wary damage-limitation', *The World Today*, June 1991, pp. 95–8.

21   In January 1991, at a time when Gorbachev had allied himself more closely to conservative elements in the security forces, the International Department of the CPSU Central Committee Secretariat issued a document advocating the use of economic and political leverage to protect Soviet interests in Eastern Europe. Although Mark Galeotti has described this as 'a post-Warsaw Pact "Brezhnev Doctrine" of sorts', it did not result in any significant shift in actual Soviet policy towards the region. See Galeotti, *The Age of Anxiety:*

Security and Politics in Soviet and Post-Soviet Russia, London, Longman, 1995, p. 129.

22   Michael G. Roskin, *The Rebirth of East Europe*, Englewood Cliffs, Prentice-Hall, 1991, pp. 194–5.

23   Anna Sabbat-Swidlicka, 'Senate calls for changes in Eastern policy', *Report on Eastern Europe*, no. 39, September 1990.

24   'Struggling to define their nations' interests, to build new institutions out of a contested past, in an environment where effective regional security structures do not exist, the leaders of the new states [of the former Soviet Union] face almost insurmountable difficulties. They have often been forced to make foreign-policy decisions before a clear consensus on national priorities has been reached. These decisions, in turn, have had an impact on the political elites in neighbouring states, who also have been taking only the first tentative steps on the international stage. For any state making the transition to independence, there are enormous pressures on its new leaders, groups, and institutions. When not just one but fifteen states are simultaneously making choices that will affect the region's total decision-making environment, the potential for a downward spiral of misperception, misinformation, and mistrust is considerable.' Karen Dawisha and Bruce Parrott, *The New States of Eurasia. The Politics of Upheaval*, Cambridge, Cambridge University Press, 1994, p. 195.

25   As Hugh Miall notes, 'a traditional anarchic state system' exists in Eastern Europe and the former Soviet Union in which 'the issue of the use of force is still on the agenda in relations between states' in the region. See his thoughtful Chatham House paper, *Shaping the New Europe*, London, Pinter for the RIIA, 1993, p. 22.

26   For a discussion of the much-contested notion of 'anarchy', see Helen Milner, 'The assumption of anarchy in international relations theory: a critique', *Review of International Studies*, 17, no. 1, January 1991, pp. 67–85.

27   See for example William Wallace, *The Transformation of Western Europe*, London, Pinter, 1990; and Mathias Jopp, *et al.*, *Integration and Security in Western Europe: Inside the European Pillar*, Boulder, Westview, 1990.

28   Roy Allison, *Military Forces in the Soviet Successor States*, Adelphi Paper 280, London, Brassey's for the IISS, October 1993, p. 36.

29   On 21 February 1992, President Kravchuk stated that the future size of the Ukrainian army would be 200,000–220,000. Then, in July 1992, after Ukraine had ratified the CFE Treaty, Deputy Foreign Minister Tarassuk suggested that the army would in future be in the region of 400,000, not the 220,000 mentioned earlier (*Research Report*, 26 June 1992, p. 57, and 17 July 1992, p. 56). However, as Roy Allison notes, 'Until at least summer 1992, the projections of Ukrainian leaders for the size of their future armed forces were shrouded with unreality. They appeared to take little account of the real defence burden the country was likely to labour under, nor was there much appreciation of the true economic plight of the state, especially if the economic rift with Russia were to deepen.' Since mid-1992, a more hard-headed and realistic attitude has emerged. Current reform plans now envisage armed forces of 200,000–220,000 by the year 2000, although as Allison observes, '[if] resource constraints are fully taken into account, the optimal

size for the Ukrainian armed forces in their final form could be in the range
of 100–150,000 men', Allison, *op. cit.*, p. 42.

30   Vernon V. Aspaturian, 'Farewell to Soviet foreign policy', *Problems of Communism*, XL, no. 6, November–December 1991, pp. 53–62 (p. 61).

31   Peter Ferdinand, 'Russia and Russians after communism: Western or Eurasian?', *The World Today*, November 1991, pp. 225–9.

32   For details see Dennis Hupchick, *Conflict and Chaos in Eastern Europe*, London, Macmillan, 1994.

33   For a discussion of the logic of alliance patterns in a multipolar system, see Thomas J. Christensen and Jack Snyder, 'Chain gangs and passed bucks: predicting alliance patterns in multipolarity', *International Organization*, 44, no. 2, spring 1990, pp. 137–68.

34   Jan B. de Weydenthal, 'Finding a place in Europe', *Report on Eastern Europe*, no. 52, 28 December 1990; and Jan B. de Weydenthal, 'Rapprochement with West continues', *Report on Eastern Europe*, nos 51/52, 20 December 1991.

35   In his inauguration speech, Walesa declared that 'we want to be a good neighbour. We are linked to Ukraine, Belarus, and Lithuania by centuries of common history.' He was subsequently criticised in *Izvestiya* for having 'apparently forgotten about the Soviet Union – the Soviet Union of which Ukraine, Belarus, and, for the time being, even Lithuania are parts.' Stanislav Kondrashov, 'Coachman, do not drive the horses too fast', *Izvestiya*, 3 January 1991.

36   At a meeting of the Committee for the Defence of the Country on 13 March 1990 chaired by President Jaruzelski, but with the participation of Prime Minister Mazowiecki and several other high-ranking officials, it was decided that 'the withdrawal of the Soviet troops should be made dependent on the developments in the international situation' – in other words, on 'the evolution of the German problem' and on progress in the CFE negotiations. See Maria Wagrowska, *Rzeczpospolita*, 8 May 1990.

37   Jerzy Marek Nowakowski, 'Germany, Russia and the Polish question', *Przeglad Polityczny*, no. 3, 1992.

38   Richard Sakwa, *Russian Politics and Society*, London, Routledge, 1993, p. 304.

39   The Treaty of Friendship and Good-Neighbourly Relations was based on the draft of the Polish–Soviet treaty agreed in October 1991, and consisted of 21 articles. The most important articles of the treaty, which is to last fifteen years, are a recognition of each other's territorial integrity; a rejection of the use of force in their mutual dealings; a promise to resolve any conflicts through peaceful means; a pledge of non-interference in each other's internal affairs; agreement on holding political consultation and to expand economic and cultural cooperation; and respect for civil and religious rights of ethnic minorities. For details see Jan B. de Weydenthal, 'Poland and Russia open a new chapter in their relations', *RFE/RL Research Report*, 1, no. 25, 19 June 1992, pp. 46–8.

40   Vera Tolz, 'The Katyn documents and the CPSU hearings', *RFE/RL Research Report*, 1, no. 44, 6 November 1992, pp. 27–33.

41   'Weekly report', *RFE/RL Research Report*, 1, no. 43, 13 November 1992, p. 71.

42   Jan B. de Weydenthal, 'Poland free of Russian combat troops', *RFE/RL Research Report*, 1, no. 45, 13 November 1992, pp. 32–5.

43   See Timothy Garton Ash, *In Europe's Name. Germany and the Divided Continent*, London, Vintage, 1993, pp. 405–6.

44   'Military and security notes', *RFE Research Report*, 1, no. 44, 6 November 1992, p. 58.

45   Alfred A. Reisch, 'Central Europe's disappointments and hopes', *RFE/RL Research Report*, 3, no. 12, 25 March 1994, p. 34.

46   Quoted by Allen Lynch, 'After Empire: Russia and its Western neighbours', *RFE/RL Research Report*, 3, no. 12, 25 March 1994, p. 14. Kozyrev defined the 'particular interests of Russia in this part of Europe' in terms of a 'common border with Kaliningrad', 'a common sea' (the Baltic), a common history and cultural and economic ties.

47   Renée de Nevers, *Russia's Strategic Renovation*, Adelphi Paper 289, London, Brassey's for the IISS, July 1994, pp. 66–7.

48   'Russia trying to isolate Ukraine', *Financial Times*, 12 March 1993, p. 48.

49   Chrystia Freeland, 'Russia trying to isolate us, say Ukrainians', *Financial Times*, 17 March 1993.

50   Sidney Bearman, ed., *Strategic Survey 1992–93*, London, Brassey's for the IISS, 1993, p. 106.

51   On the often conflictual relationship of the early Polish and Ukrainian nationalist movements, see Jerzy Tomaszewski, 'The national question in Poland in the twentieth century', in Mikuláš Teich and Roy Porter, eds, *The National Question in Europe in Historical Perspective*, Cambridge, Cambridge University Press, 1993, pp. 293–316 (pp. 298–308).

52   The signing of this declaration was followed in January 1991 by an agreement expanding economic contacts, and in March 1991 by the establishment of a joint commission on Polish and Ukrainian minorities. See Jan B. de Weydenthal, 'Economic issues dominate Poland's Eastern policy', *RFE/RL Research Report*, 2, no. 10, 5 March 1993, pp. 23–6.

53   This treaty was formally ratified in June 1993 on the occasion of the then Polish Prime Minister Suchocka's visit to Kiev, when an additional six agreements were signed. Two bodies have also been created in order to facilitate the further development of bilateral relations: the Polish–Ukrainian Commission on Trade and Economic Cooperation, and the Presidents' Committee on Polish–Ukrainian Relations.

54   Allison, *op. cit.*, p. 37.

55   The expression 'strategic partnership' was first used by Ukraine's Deputy Foreign Minister Boris Tarasiuk, who used it to describe his vision of a continent-wide geopolitical architecture based on two principal axes: the Franco-German alliance and the Polish–Ukrainian 'strategic partnership'. See Ian J. Brzezinski, 'Polish–Ukrainian relations: Europe's neglected strategic axis', *Survival*, 35, no. 3, autumn 1993, pp. 26–37 (p. 28).

56   As J. F. Brown has argued, for Ukraine, 'it is ... relations with Poland that will really count. These will decide whether Ukraine gravitates West or East.' Good relations with Poland will facilitate Ukraine's integration into Central Europe, whilst poor relations with both Poland and Russia will leave Ukraine what it once was: 'a marchland [*sic*] separating Europe from God knows

what.' J. F. Brown, 'Present hopes and past shadows', *RFE/RL Research Report*, 1, no. 1, 3 January 1992, pp. 1–4 (p. 2).

57   Jan B. de Weydenthal, 'Polish–Ukrainian rapprochement', *RFE/RL Research Report*, 1, no. 9, 28 February 1992, pp. 25–7.

58   Despite talk of a Ukrainian–Polish 'strategic partnership' and the need for military cooperation, 'Warsaw has also sought to maximise its role in eastern and central Europe through bilateral ties with Russia – a policy that precludes a hard and fast commitment to Ukraine. Polish president Lech Walesa, for example, called for "a Warsaw–Moscow axis" in the region and emphasized that "I would like Poland and Russia to be the pillars in eastern Europe".' Karen Dawisha and Bruce Parrott, *op. cit.*, p. 212.

59   These issues will be discussed further in chapter eight, 'The search for security'.

60   Jan Zielonka, *Security in Central Europe*, Adelphi Paper 272, London, Brassey's for the IISS, autumn 1992, p. 23.

61   Brown, 'Relief without relaxation: Eastern Europe ponders the CIS', p. 20.

62   The new borders of the Soviet Republic of Belarus closely followed the Polish–Soviet demarcation line proposed by the British Foreign Minister, Lord Curzon, in 1920. See Keith Sword, ed., *The Times Guide to Eastern Europe: The Changing Face of the Warsaw Pact*, London, Times Books, 1990, pp. 214–23.

63   *Rzeczpospolita*, 30 August 1991.

64   This declaration covered a range of topics, but most importantly it underlined that neither side had territorial claims on the other; declared that both sides respected the ethnic, cultural and linguistic identity of their national minorities; called for an expansion of cultural, economic, environmental and policing cooperation; and established diplomatic and consular relations.

65   As a result of this agreement, a new railway from Minsk to Paris via Brest and Warsaw is to be built; Belarus was given access to the Polish port of Gdynia; and ten existing but disused border crossing points are to be reopened.

66   This state treaty created a legal framework for the development of close political, economic and cultural exchanges, and emphasised both sides' commitment to peaceful relations and bilateral cooperation. Its most important clauses include those dealing with the inviolability of borders; a renunciation of territorial claims; respect for minority rights; and cooperation in political, security and economic matters.

67   Stephen R. Burant, 'Polish–Belarussian relations', *RFE/RL Research Report*, 1, no. 37, 18 September 1992, p. 41.

68   *Ibid.*, p. 41.

69   Zielonka, *op. cit.*, p. 24.

70   For example, Sergey Shatokhin, Chairman of the Committee on Volga Salvation, has urged Minsk to reject not only proposals for a Baltic-to-Black Sea Federation (which he said was part of the West's 'geostrategic plans') but also improved ties with Poland, which was alleged to have come 'under the wing of the German eagle'. He also underlined Belarus's geopolitical importance by insisting that 'the key to the fulfilment or failure of the West's

geostrategic plans and the key to Slavic unity is today in the hands of Belarus.' Quoted in Dawisha and Parrott, *op. cit.*, p. 215.

71 See for example Vera Rich, 'Why Belarus matters', *The World Today*, March 1994, pp. 43–4; Ustina Markus, 'The Russian–Belarussian monetary union', *RFE/RL Research Report*, 3, no. 20, 20 May 1994, pp. 28–32; and Kathleen Mihalisko, 'Belarus: neutrality gives way to "collective security"', *RFE/RL Research Report*, 2, no. 17, 23 April 1993, pp. 24–31. In February 1995, Belarus signed an agreement with Russia allowing Russia to patrol Belarus's three 'external borders' (with Poland, Latvia and Lithuania). As the head of Russia's border guards, Colonel-General Andrei Nikolayev proudly announced that, as a result of this agreement, Russia had pushed its military border 384 miles to the west of its 'administrative border'. 'Ghosts of Bolshevik past march again', *The Guardian*, 28 February 1995.

72 David Kirby, *The Baltic World 1771–1993. Europe's Northern Periphery in an Age of Change*, London, Longman, 1995, pp. 282–85, 336.

73 Stephen R. Burant, 'Polish–Lithuanian relations: past, present, and future', *Problems of Communism*, XL, no. 3, May–June 1991, pp. 67–84.

74 *Gazeta Wyborcza*, Warsaw, 16 November 1989.

75 Burant, *op. cit.*, p. 72.

76 Saulius Girnius, 'Reaching West while eyeing Russia', *Transition. Issues and Developments in the Former Soviet Union and East-Central and Southeastern Europe*, 1, no. 1, 1994, pp. 14–18 (p. 17).

77 For details see Jan Obrman, 'Treaty signed with the Soviet Union', *Report on Eastern Europe*, 1 November 1991, pp. 1–4.

78 Two of the distinctive features of Russian foreign policy which emerged before the break-up of the Soviet Union were the emphasis placed on common democratic values and the willingness to address sensitive historical issues. Thus for example when Yeltsin visited Czechoslovakia in May 1991 (his first official visit to the East Central Europe) he went far beyond Gorbachev's expression of 'regret' over the 1968 invasion and instead called it a 'gross mistake and interference in Czechoslovakia's international affairs'. See Libor Roucek, *After the Bloc: The New International Relations in Eastern Europe*, RIIA Discussion Paper No. 40, London, Chatham House, 1992, p. 11.

79 The treaty also called for regular meetings between the two sides; broadening cooperation in the spheres of economics, science, culture, education, health care, crime fighting, the law and environmental protection; a common commitment to nuclear, conventional, chemical and biological disarmament in Europe; and for neither side to allow its territory to be used for aggression or other violent acts against one of the signatories. For details see Jan Obrman, 'Russia and Czechoslovakia sign friendship treaty', *RFE/RL Research Report*, 1, no. 19, 8 May 1992, pp. 17–21.

80 The agreement on this issue was signed by the two environmental ministers, Josef Vavrousek and Viktor Danilov-Danil'yants, in April 1992. In a nutshell, it was agreed that all damages caused by Soviet forces would be paid by awarding to the CSFR the installations and buildings left behind by the Soviet military. In addition, Russia agreed to transfer to the CSFR all proceeds already collected from the sale of former Soviet property in Czechoslovakia.

81 Miloslav Had and Jirí Valenta, eds, *Czech National Interests: Contribution to a Discussion*, Prague, Institute for International Relations, 1993, p. 27.

82 Reisch, *op. cit.*, p. 36.

83 Had and Valenta, *op. cit.*, p. 28.

84 The coalition government created by Meciar in December 1994 has reiterated its desire in principle to join NATO and the EU. However, the new defence minister is Jan Sikat of the Slovak National Party, which is pan-Slavic, pro-Russian and anti-Western. The minister responsible for negotiating with the EU is Jozef Kalman, who speaks Russian but not English, and who belongs to the Workers' Party, which is suspicious of the West and hostile to the IMF. Meciar has also agreed to demands from the Workers' Party that the question of Slovakia's NATO membership would have to be put to a referendum. Thus as one Western diplomat in Bratislava commented, 'There are still plenty of general statements on wanting to join the EU and NATO, but a lack of detail and a lack of the institutional machinery needed to progress towards membership'. Quoted in 'Western aims on the wane', *The Guardian*, 26 January 1995.

85 Roman Solchanyk, 'The politics of state-building: centre-periphery relations in post-Soviet Ukraine', *Europe-Asia Studies*, 46, no. 1, 1994, pp. 47–68 (pp. 61–4).

86 As Misha Glenny suggests, this could lead to the 'cutest border conundrum in Eastern Europe', in which 'an area demands to be attached to a country that refuses to accept it'. See his book *The Rebirth of History*, London, Penguin, 1990, p. 210–11.

87 Both sides stressed that this bilateral treaty was one signed between equals, and therefore qualitatively different from those signed in the communist years. The treaty also explicitly described the Soviet invasion of Hungary in 1956 as unacceptable and unlawful. *Keesing's Record of World Events*, 37, no. 12, December 1991, p. 386–7.

88 'Frontiers and minorities', an interview with Ivan Baba, *East European Reporter*, IX, no. 4, July/August 1992, pp. 55–7.

89 The philosophy underpinning Ukraine's policy towards its Hungarian community was spelt out in the joint declaration on the basic principles guaranteeing the rights of national minorities, signed in May 1991. Hungary regards this joint declaration as a model for its negotiations with other countries, and has signed a similar one with Croatia. In it, both sides agreed that national minorities should have guaranteed rights as individuals and 'together with other members of their groups' – the first time that any country bordering Hungary had formally recognised the concept of collective rights. The agreement stated that both sides would respect the right of their citizens to decide which nationality they belong to and are to help ensure that the minorities' ethnic, cultural, linguistic and religious identities are preserved. Education is to be made available to minority nationalities in their own tongue, and arrangements for this are to be made by a joint Hungarian–Ukrainian committee. This committee met for the first time in Budapest on 29 July 1992. The main results were an agreement to open more border control points, and an agreement on the preparation of material for textbooks on history and geography. A. Reisch, 'Agreements signed in Ukraine to upgrade

bilateral relations', *Report on Eastern Europe*, II, no. 25, 21 June 1991, pp. 14–17.

90   Edith Oltay, 'Minorities as stumbling block in relations with neighbours', *RFE/RL Research Report*, 1, no. 19, 8 May 1992, pp. 26–33 (p. 31).

91   Alfred A. Reisch, 'Transcarpathia's Hungarian minority and the autonomy issue', *RFE/RL Research Report*, 1, no. 6, 7 February 1992, pp. 17–23.

92   One consequence of this huge trading deficit was the agreement in June 1992 on the largest arms transaction in Eastern Europe since the collapse of communism. By this contract Russia agreed to supply Hungary with twenty-eight MiG-29 interceptors, off-setting the $800 million cost against Russia's $1.7 billion debt to Hungary. 'Hungary in $800m Russian Mig deal', *Financial Times*, 19/20 June 1993.

93   Zielonka, *op. cit.*, p. 39.

94   Nikolai Travkin, 'Russia, Ukraine and Eastern Europe', in Stephen Sestanovich, ed., *Rethinking Russia's National Interests*, Washington, DC, The Center for Strategic and International Studies, 1994, pp. 33–41 (p. 40).

95   Alfred A. Reisch, 'Hungary's foreign policy toward the East', *RFE Research Report*, 9 April 1993, pp. 39–48 (p. 41).

96   Sakwa, *op. cit.*, p. 305.

97   The agreement on the SCSF involved a so-called 'zero option', whereby the Hungarians gave up their 60-million forint claim for environmental damage and Russia gave up its 50-million forint claim for installations left in Hungary. At the same time, Hungary agreed to provide $10 million 'humanitarian aid' to the Russian army in the form of medical supplies and to consider the feasibility of helping to build housing for the families of Russian soldiers. As regards the repayment of the former Soviet Union's debt to Hungary (which amounted to nearly $1.7 billion), it was agreed that some of this would be repaid in the form of Soviet-made military technology and spare parts, badly needed by the Hungarian armed forces. 'Military and security notes', *RFE/RL Research Report*, 1, no. 47, 27 November 1992, pp. 59, 63.

98   See for example Douglas W. Blum, ed., *Russia's Future. Consolidation or Disintegration?*, Oxford, Westview Press, 1994; and David Lane, ed., *Russia in Flux. The Political and Social Consequences of Reform*, Aldershot, Edward Elgar, 1992.

99   Samuel P. Huntington, 'The clash of civilisations?', *Foreign Affairs*, summer 1993, pp. 22–49 (p. 22).

100 Staar, *op. cit.*, p. 19.

Chapter Seven

Relations with the West

> For decades the West resisted the communist threat and supported
> our struggle for human rights, but it had also grown accustomed
> to the status quo. It is hardly surprising that the collapse of
> communism leaves it somewhat bewildered. For us, however, it is an
> historical turning point comparable in scale to the fall of the Roman
> Empire. This crisis will perhaps not last for two centuries, but it is
> going to continue for a good many years. Faced with this situation,
> what the West lacks is not good will, but, I repeat, courage and
> political imagination. (Václav Havel[1])

The central and overriding foreign policy objective of the new
democracies of East Central Europe is to return to Europe. This
notion has acquired almost mythical and spiritual connotations; its
practical meaning is somewhat hazy. It implies four things: rejoining
the cultural, normative and religious mainstream of Europe; joining
European institutions such as the Council of Europe and the EU;
integrating into the European economy; and participating in the
transatlantic and West European security community. As we have
seen in chapter three, in the long-running debate on *Mitteleuropa*,
dissident intellectuals from the region stressed that East Central
Europe's past links with the West had been artificially severed by the
Soviet Union during the Cold War. The return to Europe is an
attempt to restore these links, and to position the region firmly
within the orbit of the West.

This chapter explores some of the most salient dimensions of East
Central Europe's relations with the West. There are currently a whole
host of international actors playing a role in political and economic
developments in the region. These include multilateral economic
organisations, such as the OECD, the IMF, the World Bank, GATT
(now renamed the World Trade Organisation), CoCom, the EIB
(European Investment Bank), the UN ECE (United Nations'

Economic Commission for Europe) and the Paris Club; countless non-governmental organisations; and non-European countries such as the USA, Japan, China and some of the 'four little Dragons' (notably South Korea). However, this chapter focuses on the most important international organisations and Western countries. It begins by assessing the Visegrad countries' relations with the Council of Europe. It then considers the role of the EBRD – the only international economic organisation created as a result of the end of the Cold War. This is followed by a more extensive analysis of developing relations with the European Union – the organisation which, more than any others, the East Central Europeans long to join. The chapter also assesses the central role of Germany in the region. Germany has long been the most influential Western state in the region, and its future relations with the new democracies on its eastern border will be decisive for the wider stability of Central and Eastern Europe. The chapter concludes with a brief evaluation the significance for the wider Europe of relations between the Visegrad countries and the West.

The Council of Europe

Democratisation is the central domestic political task facing the Visegrad countries. It is widely seen as a precondition for overcoming the legacy of communism and for achieving integration into European institutions. As the countries of East Central Europe seek to build and consolidate stable liberal democracies, they are looking to the West for advice and practical help.[2] The most important Western organisation in this respect is the Council of Europe.

The Council was established in May 1949, making it the very first organisation for European cooperation established in the post-war period. It was founded on three pillars: pluralist democracy, human rights, and the rule of law. In 1949, many Europeans hoped that the Council would pioneer a new form of integration on the continent, embracing political union, social progress and the protection of human rights. Although these early aspirations proved too ambitious, the Council of Europe has nonetheless developed a substantial system of cooperation amongst its members. This covers areas as diverse as culture, education, scientific and technological research, harm-onisation of legal standards and documents, communication and information, social questions and environmental protection. Many of these activities have been overshadowed by the work of the EU, with its programmes such as EUREKA and ESPRIT, and its new bodies such as the European Environmental Agency. Nevertheless, the Council's central and indispensable role in the field of human rights, European parliamentarianism and the codification and standard-isation of European law has remained unchallenged.[3] This was formally recognised at the CSCE Copenhagen conference in June 1990. This meeting recorded the 'important expertise' of the Council of Europe in the field of human rights and agreed to consider further ways and means to enable the Council to make a contribution to the Human Dimension of the CSCE.

The structure and organisation of the Council of Europe makes it eminently suitable to play a central role in encouraging the democratisation process in Eastern Europe. As Catherine Lalumière, the organisation's former Secretary-General, has argued, the Council of Europe enjoys the advantage of already possessing 'a solid structure for multilateral governmental and parliamentary co-operation in the field of human rights and has the experience and potential to expand its activities in this field'.[4] The Council consists of a small secretariat; a Parliamentary Assembly; three legal instruments (the European Convention on Human Rights (1950), the European Social Charter (1965) and the European Convention for the Prevention of Torture and Inhuman and Degrading Treatment or Punishment (1989)); and a court of appeal – the European Court of Human Rights (ECHR) at Strasbourg. It thus operates with legally binding agreements, and has a mechanism for supervision and control.[5] The jurisdiction of the ECHR, for example, supersedes that of national courts, and is potentially a significant guardian of human rights and personal freedoms.

The fact that the Council of Europe embodied the liberal democratic values which communism rejected meant that for four decades the organisation was anathema to the Soviet Union and its East European allies. Yet the Council of Europe was one of the first European organisations to extend a welcome to the countries of Central and Eastern Europe following the collapse of communism. Indeed, the events of 1989 have given the Council of Europe new purpose and a new lease of life. Contacts with the countries of East Central Europe began on a tentative basis in June 1987, when the then Secretary-General of the Council of Europe, Mr Oreja, paid a semi-official visit to Hungary. This was followed by a visit to Poland in March 1988. However, the turning point was the speech by Gorbachev to the Parliamentary Assembly of the Council of Europe on 6 July 1989. As well as signalling the formal abandonment of the Brezhnev doctrine, this speech also cleared the way for closer contacts between Soviet bloc states and the Council of Europe.

The Council responded promptly to the changes in Central and Eastern Europe by inventing a new category for involvement in its work. This was 'special guest status', and was accorded to Hungary, Poland, Yugoslavia and the Soviet Union in June 1989; to Czechoslovakia in May 1990; to Bulgaria in July 1990; and to Romania in February 1991. Full membership was granted only once fully free elections had been held. This meant that Hungary became a member in November 1990, Czechoslovakia in February 1991, Poland in November 1991 and Bulgaria in May 1992.[6] Following the break-up of the CSFR, the Czech and Slovak Republics were admitted to the Council of Europe in June 1993 (Slovakia's admittance was controversial, given Slovakia's treatment of its ethnic Hungarian minority, and Budapest accepted Slovakia's application only after vigorous lobbying by its Visegrad partners – see pp. 95–6).

In seeking to facilitate the transition to democracy in Eastern Europe, the Council of Europe has been able to draw upon its experience in helping with the construction of legal systems and pluralist democracies in Spain and Portugal during their transitions from dictatorship to democracy. The Council decided to provide assistance to the new democracies of Eastern Europe at three different levels: first, consciousness raising, information and dialogue (on the major principles of democracy and human rights); second, 'assistance and cooperation' (in order to strengthen the democratic changes under way and to train new leaders); and third, integration (bringing the East Europeans into the programmes and activities of the Council of Europe, and opening the way to their possible accession to the organisation as full members).[7]

A major new initiative towards Central and Eastern Europe was launched at the Council of Europe's special ministerial meeting in Lisbon (March 1990), in which all East European states except Romania participated. At this meeting, the Council approved the 'Demosthenes programme'. This programme was designed with two broad aims in mind: first, 'to strengthen the reform movement towards genuine democracy'; and second, 'to facilitate their smooth and progressive integration in the circles and institutions of European cooperation'.[8] The content of the programme draws heavily from the three traditional pillars of the Council of Europe – pluralist democracy, human rights and the rule of law – and primarily takes the form of short meetings such as seminars and workshops. All initiatives under the rubric of the programme must come from the democratising state and not from the Council, both to avoid charges that the Council of Europe is forcing its concept of democracy on the post-communist states, and to minimise the risks of duplication.

One interesting area of work under the Demosthenes scheme is the Demo-Droit programme, which is concerned with legislation and the transformation of the legal systems of states participating in Council of Europe activities. Help is provided in the drafting of new constitutions and in the framing of other important laws which influence the character of the political system. To facilitate the Demo-Droit programme, a special commission was organised in 1990 specifically to assist countries in drafting new constitutions. This is the European Commission for Democracy through Law (referred to more frequently as the Venice Commission). It is composed of experts on constitutional, administrative and international law, and has already provided assistance to Romania, Bulgaria, Albania, Estonia, Latvia and Russia. The Venice Commission also assisted Hungary in drafting its law on minorities, and has taken an initiative to draw up its own 'Draft Proposals for a European Convention for the Protection of Minorities'.[9]

As we have seen (pp. 98, 162, 173), the protection of national minorities is rapidly becoming a key issue in Central and Eastern Europe. It has been a recurrent theme at high-level international conferences, seminars and workshops.[10] In addition to the Venice Commission's proposals, the Parliamentary Assembly of the Council of Europe adopted an Additional Protocol to the European Convention on Human Rights 'Concerning National Minorities and Their Members' in February 1993. This initiative has been given strong backing by both the German Chancellor Helmut Kohl and the Austrian Chancellor Frantz Vranitsky. The CSCE (now the OSCE) has also established a post of High Commissioner for National Minorities, and has devoted considerable time and energy to the thorny issue of minority rights. There is therefore a growing consensus in Europe today that effective legal protection of minorities' rights is 'one of the paths that must be followed in order to try to defuse ethnic conflicts and lay lasting foundations for peace on the European continent'.[11]

The Council of Europe is widely regarded in Eastern Europe (particularly in the Visegrad states) as an important international organisation which can play a key role in strengthening the process of political democratisation in the post-communist world. 'The Council of Europe', it has been argued, 'has become the "conscience of Europe".'[12] It might lack the economic clout which other organisations wield, but it is held in high esteem throughout East Central Europe. The Hungarians, for example, agreed after discussions with the Council to change their whole legal system and reform their Code of Criminal Procedure to accommodate the standards laid down in the European Convention on Human Rights. More importantly perhaps, they also agreed to make provision for its operating mechanism.

The importance of the Council has been underlined by Gabor Kardos, a specialist in international law at Budapest University. He has suggested that 'The Council of Europe, which has served to reinforce parliamentary democracy internationally for decades, could definitely contribute to the protection of the new [democratic] institutions, especially through its legal regime to protect human rights in Europe'. He has also stressed the important role the Council can play in the 'transmission of political culture', and has suggested that it can 'provide a kind of "maturity test" for these newly democratized states' before they are admitted to the EU.[13]

Membership of the Council of Europe is therefore widely seen as signifying the acceptance of a country as a democratic member of the European comity of nations. Consequently it provides a valuable safeguard against subsequent backsliding on human rights and democratic practices. It also has a powerful symbolic value which should not be underestimated.[14] Membership of the Council offers to the new democracies a badge of political maturity, tolerance and respect for human rights. For this reason, the Visegrad countries hope that their membership will prove their credentials as stable democracies when they apply to join the EU – which is the real prize to which they all aspire.

In facilitating the consolidation of stable democracies in Central and Eastern Europe, the Council of Europe is making a valuable contribution towards European peace and security. As Catherine

Lalumière has argued, 'Security, peace and stability are not solely the fruit of military action or economic development. They also stem from the nature of political systems and the values on which they are based.' By fostering a commitment to pluralist democracy, human rights and the rule of law in Central and Eastern Europe, the Council of Europe can help generate what she has termed 'democratic security'. This is 'based on a commitment to pluralistic democracy, human rights and the rule of law', as well as 'tolerance, respect for others, respect for foreigners, respect for multi-cultural, multi-ethnic or multi-religious societies'.[15] The Council's current Secretary-General, Daniel Tarschys, has also championed the organisation's role as a promoter of 'democratic security', arguing that by 'strengthening the democratic institutions and respect for human rights and the rule of law in all parts of our Continent, the Council of Europe can also make an important contribution to European security'.[16]

President Havel has argued that the Council of Europe should become 'the political, legislative and ideological centre' of the new Europe.[17] If this is to come about, the Council will need to make major changes to its structure and functioning. The European Court of Human Rights in Strasbourg – which, with a massive backlog of cases, has become a victim of its own success – urgently needs new decision-making procedures. The Council of Europe also needs to develop new mechanisms to deal with issues such as the legal protection of minorities. Thus if the Council is to fulfil its task of supporting and facilitating the transition to democracy in Central and Eastern Europe, it will need 'more resources and greater political clout. It must be reshaped to meet the challenge of the twenty-first century'.[18]

The European Bank for Reconstruction and Development

The prospects for consolidating stable democracies and ensuring peaceful international relations in East Central Europe hinge on successful economic restructuring. Developing efficient and productive social market economies in the region is thus of decisive importance. Although the sacrifices and travails that this task entails will inevitably have to be borne by the East Central Europeans themselves, the West cannot stand idly by looking on, as Václav

Havel has put it, 'as though it were a mere visitor at a zoo or the audience at a horror movie, on edge to know how it will turn out'.[19]

It was in recognition of this that the EBRD was created. Inaugurated on 15 April 1991, largely on the initiative of President Mitterrand, the EBRD was 'the first pan-European institution of the post Cold War era'.[20] This is significant because it reflects the importance attached to economic factors in the process of building a more united and secure continent. The EBRD is also particularly interesting because it was not conceived as simply another International Economic Organisation (IEO) on the Bretton Woods model. Rather, the EBRD was unique in that it had an explicit political mandate to use its funds in order to foster democratic polities and pluralist civil societies, in which respect for minority rights would be guaranteed.[21] As Jacques Attali, the first President of the EBRD, put it (in characteristically grandiose terms), 'The Bank is not just building market economies for goods and services but is also helping to reconstruct nations in which people will have a freer and fuller future'.[22]

The EBRD was also novel and interesting in two other respects. To begin with, it was the first international organisation to combine the roles of merchant and development bank: at least 60% of its funds were earmarked for the private sector, whilst 40% were to be used for restructuring state-owned enterprises and other public sector infrastructure projects. Second, Jacques Attali argued that the Bank's main job was to 'influence the West' to open up markets for East European products. As we shall see later in this chapter, the reluctance of the EU to open its markets up to competition from the East is a major bone of contention in East Central Europe and a reflection of the West's short-sighted selfishness.

The EBRD was in many ways one of the most imaginative initiatives taken by Western nations in response to the turmoil and opportunities that have flowed from the events of 1989.[23] Sadly, the ambitious, not to say visionary, mandate of the EBRD – which was in large part the creation of the Bank's first President – was not matched by concrete achievements.[24] The gulf between the Bank's magnificent vision and its subsequently disappointing results mirrors the switch from the euphoria of 1989–90 to the later mood of pessimism and self-doubt. The turning point for the EBRD came in April 1993, when reports were published about the extravagant spending on decorations at the Bank's lavish new headquarters on

Exchange Square, London.[25] This contrasted sharply with the relatively low disbursements of loans to projects in Central and Eastern Europe. Indeed, by the end of 1992, the EBRD had spent more on fitting out its own offices, paying salaries and meeting other overheads (£128 million) than it had disbursed in loans and investments in Eastern Europe and the former Soviet Union (£101 million).[26]

As hostile press criticism mounted, Jacques Attali was forced to resign in June 1993.[27] The new President was Jacques De Larosière. He immediately began reorganising the Bank, breaking up the President's Cabinet and the Political Department, and scrapping the initial division between merchant and development banking in favour of a 'country by country' approach.[28]

After the upheavals and controversies of recent years, the Bank is still grappling with fundamental questions of responsibilities, management and leadership.[29] With the departure of Attali, the EBRD lost an able and visionary President who – whatever his personal foibles – succeeded in placing Eastern Europe high on the international agenda.[30] In future the EBRD is likely to adopt a more pragmatic and low-key approach. It needs to streamline its bureaucratic decision-making procedures to facilitate a more effective disbursement of funds – and to avoid charges of corruption and sleaze.[31] It will also have to decide on the balance to be struck between investing in private sector projects and in supporting public sector infrastructure projects. This is a sensitive and controversial question, and one that raises fundamental issues about the EBRD's very *raison d'être*.

As the countries of Central and Eastern Europe struggle to overcome the problems arising from radical economic restructuring, the EBRD can play a constructive – albeit modest – role. The Visegrad countries have in actual fact done rather well from the Bank. Out of 95 projects approved from April 1991 to June 1993, over 51% of them were in East Central Europe – with the largest share going to Poland.[32] Yet for most East Central Europeans, their primary concern is not the EBRD but the EU. Market access is much more crucial for the economic recovery of the Visegrad countries than the disbursement of relatively meagre EBRD funds. As one Czech official pointed out at the time when controversy over the Bank's lavish expenditure on its own headquarters was at its height, 'We are trying to get much closer to the Community. The EBRD is not what you call top of the agenda'.[33]

The European Union: from cooperation to membership?

Membership of the EU is the ultimate foreign policy goal to which
the Visegrad countries aspire. Membership would represent the
culmination of dreams of a return to Europe. Throughout the region,
it is widely believed that membership of the Union would not only
symbolise their entry into the European family of democratic states,
but it would also stabilise their tender democracies, provide the
environment for achievement of prosperous social market economies
and – above all – ensure their security. However, membership of the
Union will entail not only substantial changes to the legal and
economic structures in East Central Europe, it will also require
radical changes to the institutions, policies and decision-making
processes of the EU itself. It will also raise new questions concerning
the future shape of European international relations and the nature
of its institutional structures.

Relations between the Union and East European states are a
relatively recent development. In 1974, the EEC offered to conclude
bilateral agreements with East European countries, but – given Soviet
hostility towards the Community at this time – only Romania
accepted.[34] It was only in June 1988 that a joint declaration was
signed in Luxembourg establishing official relations between the EEC
and the CMEA. This paved the way for the establishment of
diplomatic relations between the Community and individual Central
and East European countries. This in turn resulted in the signing of
a series of commercial and economic cooperation agreements. The
Hungarians led the way here, signing a ten-year trade and
commercial and economic cooperation agreement with the EC in
September 1988. This was followed by a four-year agreement
(limited to trade in industrial products) between the EC and
Czechoslovakia, signed in December 1988; and a five-year trade and
cooperation agreement between Poland and the EC, signed in
September 1989.[35]

The evolution of East–West relations in the late eighties from
detente to cooperation provided the context for a qualitative change
in the nature of EC relations with the East European countries. In
July 1989 at the Paris meeting of the Group of Seven (G7) and the
European Commission, two historic decisions were taken: first, that
any East European country embarking on the path of democratic
and market-orientated reform would receive Western aid; and

second, that this aid would be coordinated by the European Commission.

The G7 and the Commission were supported by the OECD group of 24, who agreed to contribute to a substantial aid programme for East European countries committed to reform – which in mid-1989 meant Poland and Hungary. Thus was born the PHARE ('Poland/ Hungary: Aid for Restructuring of Economies') operation, which the Commission has been coordinating.[36] Coordinating the provision of Western aid to Eastern Europe was essential given the large number of governments and agencies involved.[37] The Commission was given this important responsibility because of the EC's economic weight in Europe, its geographical proximity to the region and because it was seen as 'neutral' in security terms.

As a result of the historic decisions reached at the July 1989 Paris summit, the EC became the leading Western organisation involved in the unfolding reform process in Eastern Europe. With the revolutionary upheavals of November and December 1989, the Community found itself facing a rapidly changing East–West relationship in Europe – a process which was destined to affect the whole course and direction of the integration process in Europe. When the Council of Ministers met in Strasbourg in December 1989, it was clear that the Community would now have to respond to the rising expectations and new demands from the post-communist regimes to its east.

Following the Strasbourg summit, the debate on EC–East European relations switched to the issue of negotiating 'Association Agreements' (now called 'European Agreements') with individual East European countries, which would replace the more limited series of trade and economic cooperation agreements mentioned above. These would be based on Article 238 of the Treaty of Rome, and would include institutionalised political dialogue and regular consultations as well as more substantial forms of economic, industrial and commercial cooperation. Their main objective was trade liberalisation, which was to be followed later by measures facilitating the free movement of people, services and capital. However, they would not automatically lead to full Community membership.[38]

One significant feature of the Community's evolving relationship with the countries of Eastern Europe was that from early on it was made clear that the granting of associate status to East European countries would be conditional not only on market-orientated economic reform, but also on steady progress towards political democratisation.[39] Thus, as with the EBRD, closer economic ties with the EC were to be conditional upon steady progress in respect for human rights and the rule of law. As the new democracies struggled to free themselves from their communist past, the PHARE programme was extended to cover most of Central and Eastern Europe. By February 1993, therefore, the number of countries covered by the PHARE programme had grown from two to ten and the volume of finance tripled. Moreover, in July 1992 the European Commission, following an initiative taken by the European Parliament, launched a pilot project called the PHARE Democracy Programme. This was designed to support non-partisan, cross-party projects aimed at facilitating the consolidation of stable parliamentary systems and pluralist civil societies.[40]

The much trumpeted Europe Agreements were finally initialled with Czechoslovakia, Hungary and Poland on 16 December 1991 (after months of often bad-tempered negotiations). New Europe Agreements with the Czech and Slovak Republics were agreed in September 1993 following the break-up of the CSFR.[41] The Agreements with Poland and Hungary came into force on 1 February 1994, whilst those with Slovakia and the Czech Republic (along with Bulgaria and Romania) came into force on 1 February 1995.[42] Their declared aim was threefold: to improve the opportunities for access by the East Central Europeans to EU markets; to prepare the associated countries for eventual EU membership; and to create a preferential system of trade with the signatories. The Agreements also established a framework for regular political dialogue, consultation and joint decision making between the EU and the associated countries. These Agreements did not promise full membership, nor did they rule it out: rather, they shrouded this crucial question in ambiguity and left it open.

More controversially, after fierce protectionist pressures from a number of individual member states, they left in place substantial non-tariff barriers on the access of agricultural goods, steel and textiles to EU markets.[43] The agreements therefore disappointed the expectations of the Central Europeans for a rapid movement to free market access and early membership. A particular grievance was that they provided only a partial opening up of EU markets in the areas of agricultural products, textiles and steel – all of which were crucial export goods for the Visegrad states. As EBRD President Attali said in 1992, the Europe Agreements appeared to be designed to 'restrict their access to key western markets rather than to integrate them'.[44] Despite this, the agreements will have a significant impact on the economic sovereignty of the associated countries: Jacques Delors, for example, has estimated that, as a result of these agreements, 50% of economic decisions concerning Poland will be made in Brussels by 1995.

The Visegrad states continued to pressurise the Community for an explicit list of conditions for membership, as well as a timetable for negotiations leading to union. In September 1992 they presented a memorandum to this effect to the Community. In response to such persistent requests, the European Council meeting in Edinburgh in December 1992 issued a document entitled 'Towards a Closer Association with the Countries of Central and Eastern Europe'.[45] Depressingly, this failed either to specify any such conditions for membership or to affirm clearly the prospect of future member-ship.[46] It was only at the Copenhagen summit in June 1993 that the European Council issued a clear statement that the Visegrad four, along with Bulgaria and Romania, could become members once they met certain conditions. The EU also announced further limited trade concessions at Copenhagen, and provided for a structured relation-ship between the Central and East Europeans and the institutions of the EU in all its three 'pillars'.

Following the Corfu summit (June 1994), the Commission drew up a 'pre-accession' strategy designed to prepare the way for eventual membership of the Union. This was approved at the Essen summit (December 1994), and it was at Essen that the opening to Central and Eastern Europe finally became irreversible.[47] At the summit it was agreed to further limited market access and to boost economic aid to Central and Eastern Europe. More significantly, a new mechanism for involving ministers from the region in EU meetings was agreed. The Central and East European six[48] will now meet annually with EU heads of government; foreign and interior ministers will meet together twice a year; and other ministers (such as those for finance, the environment, research, telecommunications and justice) will meet annually.[49] Although no timetable or detailed strategy was fixed, it now seems likely that negotiations on membership will begin after the 1996 inter-governmental conference, and will take place in 1997–98. Membership may then be possible in 1999–2000. It is also likely that negotiations on membership will be conducted bilaterally, rather than as a group. This might mean early entry by the Czech Republic and possibly Slovenia, followed by Hungary and Poland, then Slovakia, Bulgaria, Romania and the three Baltic republics.[50]

Thus in a remarkably brief period of time, a striking transformation in relations between the EU and the countries of the former Soviet bloc has taken place. Limited cooperation agreements have been superseded by Europe Agreements, and now the prospect of an Eastern expansion of the Union is firmly on the agenda.[51] No one doubts the difficulties entailed in opening up the EU to membership by the post-communist democracies in the East. As President Mitterrand commented at the Essen summit, fully integrating the economies and societies of Central and Eastern Europe could take ten to fifteen years, even after formal membership has been granted.[52] On the other hand, there is enormous political will and determination in East Central Europe to achieve membership at the earliest possible opportunity. The Hungarians established a European Affairs Scrutiny Committee in parliament in 1993 in order to ensure all new legislation was compatible with that of the EU. They have also joined the Poles and Czechs in making such compatibility a legal requirement. Similarly, the former Slovak Prime Minister Jozef Moravcik claimed that when a new law crossed his desk, his first thought was 'Is this compatible with the laws of the European Union?'. In Poland, a white paper is due to be published in 1995 specifying what changes are required to bring the Polish legal system up to EU standards. This work is expected to last five or six years.[53]

Sadly, the enthusiasm and commitment in the Visegrad countries has not been matched by the West Europeans. On the contrary, the EU member states have responded to the historic challenge of reuniting a divided continent with a lack of imagination and a meanness in spirit which beggars belief.[54] The EU has consistently failed to open its markets up in the areas where the East Central Europeans are most competitive: agricultural products, steel, and textiles. Quite understandably, this has caused tremendous resentment in the Visegrad countries, who point out that they have largely eliminated trade barriers against Western goods, but are not only being denied free access to the markets they could best compete in, but are also being asked to open their service and financial sectors to competition from stronger Western firms.[55] The result has been a growth in the EU's trade surplus with the former Warsaw Pact countries, from £2.5 billion in 1989 to around £4 billion at the end of 1993.[56] As the Vienna Institute for Comparative Economics has noted, 'The widening trade and current account deficits are widely regarded as the major obstacles to sustained economic recovery for the east Europeans'.[57]

This could have dire consequences for the political stability and economic prosperity of the Visegrad four. The macroeconomic policies of these countries are designed to combat inflation by a combination of restrictive monetary policies and tight fiscal policies.[58] Given the associated need to reduce the government deficit, any reduction of unemployment and improvement in economic growth cannot be achieved by domestic reflation, but only by an expansion of foreign trade. Hence export-led growth may be the only way to prevent long-term structural unemployment and continued domestic recession. If the economic situation in the region remains bleak, the prospects for a strengthening of democratic institutions and political practices in East Central Europe will be greatly reduced. As the experience of Europe in the inter-war years demonstrates, in conditions of deep-seated recession and acute social tensions, support for authoritarian and demagogic political leaders may well grow to alarming proportions.[59]

The EU therefore faces a real test of commitment: is it prepared to support the reform process in Eastern Europe with more than rhetoric and statements of good intention? If so, it must practice what it preaches – that is, free trade and market liberalisation – and open its markets to Eastern Europe. As an EBRD report of October 1994 commented, 'The main threat to eastern European exports and investment comes from actual, threatened and "latent" trade remedy action employed for purposes of managing trade to support industrial policy objectives in the EU.... Anything other than liberal trade exposes western governments to charges of hypocrisy and stifles their own growth potential as well as that of the transition economies'.[60]

West European failure to liberalise trade reflects the impact of powerful sectional interests within EU member states. It also illustrates the dilemmas that opening up the EU to new members from the East will pose. The end of the bipolar division of Europe and the collapse of communism has removed the political and strategic obstacles to membership of the EU by the East Central

Europeans. But it has also radically changed the external context within which the West European integration process has unfolded in the post-war period.[61] The Maastricht Treaty on European Union was – in part – the initial response of the twelve to the changed European environment, but failed to resolve the underlying tension at the heart of the European Community between inter-governmentalism and supranationalism. The EU will indubitably continue to evolve as it adapts to the changing dynamics of post-Cold War European international relations. On 1 January 1995, the EU expanded from twelve to fifteen members with the accession of Sweden, Finland and Austria, and in 1996 an inter-governmental conference will be held to decide the future structure and functioning of the Union. However, enlargement to the East will necessitate further far-reaching changes in the Union – with inevitable consequences for international politics in Europe in the twenty-first century.

Enlargement to the East will force major changes to the institutions, decision-making procedures and policies of the EU. Difficult decisions will have to be made regarding the number of European commissioners and the size of the European Parliament. The number of official languages may have to be reduced if translation and interpretation costs are not to spiral out of control. The question of what constitutes a 'qualified majority vote' in the Council of Ministers, and when majority voting procedures should be adopted, will generate heated disputes. Debates in the Council of Ministers will have to become less formal and more parliamentary in style. Expansion to the East will also shift the geopolitical centre of the EU eastwards, thereby significantly altering the process of cross-national coalition building within the European Council. Not only will it alter the traditional pattern of bargaining between the poorer south and the wealthier north of the EU, it may well disrupt the Franco-German alliance: as one economist has suggested, 'A mighty country – such as a united Germany surrounded by East European satellites – cannot for long pretend to be the political and economic equal of France'.[62]

Some have suggested that without a further 'deepening' of the integration process, 'widening' to perhaps twenty or more members will result in institutional paralysis. This, it is feared, would spell the end of the cohesion of the EU and result in the emergence of a debilitating power struggle within a loose inter-governmental framework. To avoid this danger, they have called for a greater use of majority voting in the Council of Ministers, a strengthening of the powers of the European Parliament, a delegation of powers to the Commission, and other steps to strengthen supranational mechanisms for collective decision making and policy implementation.[63] Others, hostile to the whole project of European political and economic union, are enthusiastic supporters of 'widening' precisely because they believe it will spell the end of 'Euro-federalist' dreams.[64]

The implications of enlargement for the policies and budgetary arrangements of the Union are no less profound. Eighty per cent of the EU budget is accounted for by two policies: the Common Agricultural Policy (CAP) and the structural funds (the European Regional Development Fund and the Social Fund).[65] It is doubtful whether the CAP could survive an Eastern enlargement. The Visegrad countries are two-and-a-half times more agricultural than the EU average, and specialise in dairy farming – the area most protected by CAP. On present policies, the cost of CAP would therefore have to increase from ECU 30 billion to ECU 45 billion.[66] The structural funds (designed to promote economic convergence within the Union) would have to increase from ECU 25 billion to ECU 60 billion. Admitting the Visegrad four would therefore require a 60% rise in incumbent contributions, or – more likely – major cuts in spending.[67] Moreover, poorer states like Portugal and Greece could end up as net contributors to the EU budget – a prospect that would generate enormous tensions within the EU.

Enlargement of the EU to the East will therefore precipitate major changes in both the EU and East Central Europe. As William Wallace has argued, the task facing the EU is 'managing the transformation of the West European Community into a European "System" without producing a structure as unwieldy as the eighteenth century Polish Constitution or an economy so inadequately managed that it cannot bear the burdens of adjustment which have to be faced'.[68] Achieving this transformation may well alter the EU beyond recognition over the coming years. In a nutshell, the options facing the EU are a disintegration of the integration project from overstretch and institutional paralysis; the emergence of a more cohesive and federated Union; or – and this is the outcome which seems most likely at present – some form of 'variable geometry' in a Europe of concentric circles and different speeds. Whatever the outcome, the EU faces major challenges as a result of opening up to the East. The Visegrad countries will also have to make further changes to their economies and societies, and come to terms with the fact that rejoining Europe will require them to surrender some of their hard-won sovereignty and independence to a Union which is less than a federal state but more than an international organisation. This will in turn have profound implications for the pattern of international relations in the region, as the Visegrad states find themselves embedded in a European system characterised increasingly by institutional complexity, multiple identities and overlapping authorities.[69] European integration is therefore the single most important issue on the policy agenda of the Visegrad countries. It is also an issue of central importance for Europe's post-Cold War security. As the European Commissioner Hans van den Broek has noted, 'Enlargement to the east is in the very first place a political issue relating to security and stability on our continent'.[70]

Germany and East Central Europe

So far we have analysed the Visegrad countries 'return to Europe' in terms of their deepening relations with Western Europe's multilateral organisations. But Warsaw, Budapest, Prague and Bratislava are also busy building up new bilateral links with individual Western states. Austria, given its geographical proximity, its longstanding cultural influence and the legacy of the Habsburg Empire, has emerged as an important economic and political actor in the region. It enjoys a 'special relationship' with Hungary, and is active in a number of regional fora, including Alpe Adria, the CEI and – since 1 January 1995 – the EU. France, given its longstanding geopolitical preoccupation with German preponderance in Central Europe, has traditional strategic and cultural interests in Eastern Europe. The Visegrad states also attach considerable importance to their bilateral relations with Washington, and are keen to see a continuing strong and assertive US presence in Europe.[71] However, one country more than any other plays a crucial role in the region – Germany. 'The new Germany', Misha Glenny has written, 'will have an enormous, even a decisive, influence on the structure and prospects of the new Eastern Europe'.[72]

Relations between the Teutons and eastern Slav and Magyar neighbours defy easy categorisation. They have been marked by elements of conflict and cooperation, antagonism and symbiosis, oppression and assistance.[73] Throughout virtually all of its history, whether in the form of the Holy Roman Empire, Brandenburg-Prussia or the Third Reich, Germany has posed a threat to the security of East Central European states – especially Poland and the Czech lands. This has left a legacy of profound mistrust between the *Bundesrepublik Deutschland* and its eastern neighbours. An old Polish adage asserts that 'for as long as the world exists the German and the Pole will never be brothers'.[74] On the other hand, the lands of *Mitteleuropa* have been greatly enriched by German communities, culture, trade and technology. This complex and ambiguous legacy led František Palacký, the great nineteenth century Czech historian, to sum up Czech history in terms of ten centuries of continuous struggle between Germans and Slavs. This struggle, he wrote, was 'a contest as well as an emulation, a rejection as well as an acceptance of German customs and laws by the Czechs', and led 'not only to victory or subjection but also to reconciliation'. Thus, he concluded, 'Even today history and geography pose the same task to the Czech nation: to serve as a bridge between Germandom and Slavdom, between the West and East in Europe in general'.[75]

In one thousand years of contest and emulation, the nadir of German relations with its eastern neighbours was undoubtedly the Nazi era. Armed with all the technology, industry and Enlightenment rationality the modern world could offer, the Nazi state set about its search for *Lebensraum* in the east with unbridled ruthlessness and determination. 'Nazism', Claudio Magris has written, 'is the unforgettable lesson of the perversion of the German presence in Europe'.[76] The legacy of those dark years has lasted – albeit with diminishing intensity – down to the present. With the unification of Germany, and its assumption of full sovereignty, some in Eastern Europe (primarily amongst the older generation) have wondered whether the nightmare of yesteryear is about to begin anew.

Yet the Bundesrepublik today is not comparable with the Hitler regime – nor indeed with any previous German state. Germany today is democratic, pluralist and stable. Its social market economy has – on the whole – provided a judicious mixture of productive dynamism, prosperity and social justice. Its foreign policy is characterised by a commitment to multilateralism, European integration and international cooperation. And the greatest concern regarding German security and defence policies today is not resurgent militarism but the lingering tendency towards pacifism and a failure to participate actively in UN peacekeeping and peace-enforcing missions.[77] Germany remains a large and economically powerful country, occupying a pivotal position at the very heart of the new Europe. But as a stable modern democracy, it is no longer a security threat to its neighbours – east or west.[78] As President Havel commented in Berlin in January 1990, 'Germany can be as large as she wants to, as long as she stays democratic'.[79]

Germany's contemporary role in East Central Europe remains that of a hegemon, but of a *benign* hegemon – rather like the USA's role in Western Europe in the early post-war years. Germany's interests in the region are fourfold: it has growing economic interests in the Visegrad countries; it has strategic interests in creating a buffer zone of stable and secure states around its eastern borders;[80] it has political interests in developing good relations with the East Central Europeans, both to secure international allies and to guarantee the interests of German minorities in the region; and it has longstanding cultural affinities with *Mitteleuropa*. Since the watershed years of 1989–90, the importance of East Central Europe within the BRD's foreign policy has steadily grown. In the past, Germany's *Ostpolitik* has focused primarily on Moscow. In the 1990s, however, instability in Russia and the growing economic importance of East Central Europe have increased the relative importance of the Visegrad countries for Bonn.[81]

Within the space of a few years following the disintegration of the CMEA, Germany resumed its dominant economic role in East Central Europe, both in terms of trade and foreign direct investment.[82] German capital will inevitably play a decisive economic role throughout the region during and after the transition to a market economy.[83] Germany's economic preponderance is based not only on the sheer size of its economy, but on 'the quality of its products, the trade surplus, the savings rate, and the reputation of the currency built up over forty years'.[84] Poland, Hungary, the Czech Republic and Slovakia are therefore destined to become economic fiefdoms of Europe's industrial giant – Germany. This prospect is viewed with mixed feelings in the region. As the Czechs are fond of saying, 'the only thing worse than being dominated by the German economy is not being dominated by it'.[85] There are some concerns that the Visegrad countries may be exploited for their cheap labour or used as a dumping-ground for toxic waste. There are also worries that Germany may be tempted to use its economic leverage for political purposes: this worry has led the Visegrad countries to seek to diversify their external economic relations in order to reduce their dependency on the German economy.[86] But on the whole, German investment is welcomed as a means of developing a modern industrial infrastructure, creating jobs and acquiring managerial 'know-how'.

Deepening economic ties between the Visegrad countries and Germany have been accompanied by more intensive political relations, relations which have been characterised by growing warmth and cooperation. Naturally, there have been some sources of friction. For example, Kohl's inept handling of the Oder–Neisse border issue in 1989–90 rekindled Polish suspicions of Germany's long-term intentions.[87] The border issue was finally settled by the 'two-plus-four' negotiations in July 1990,[88] but four problems remain: the German minority in Silesia and Pomerania (Poland);[89] the issue of compensation for the estimated three million *Sudetendeutsch* expelled from Czechoslovakia after 1946;[90] attacks on visiting Poles by racist skin-heads and neo-Nazi thugs in eastern Germany; and Bonn's desire to use its Eastern neighbours as a *cordon sanitaire* for seekers of asylum in Germany.[91]

However, none of these problems has irrevocably damaged relations between the East Central Europeans and Germany. New bilateral treaties of friendship and cooperation have been signed, and Bonn has emerged as the tribune for the Visegrad countries within the EU, NATO and the WEU. Germany is the region's main supplier of economic aid, investment and training, and has provided substantial practical support for democratisation and the development of vibrant civil societies.[92] More recently, the Germans have admitted Polish officers to the Bundeswehr Academy in Hamburg for training. These intensive exchanges mean that the German model of political, economic and social organisation exerts a powerful influence over the new democracies in the East. Consequently, the Visegrad countries have emulated a number of legal and constitutional features of the BRD. The German social market economy is also 'by far the most influential model for the post-communist regimes'.[93] German society, culture and way of life thus all contribute to the magnetism of the modern-day Bundesrepublik for the new democracies of East Central Europe.[94]

These developments highlight how strikingly different relations between the Visegrad countries and Germany are today compared

with what they were before 1945. The spread of democracy, literacy
and prosperity, along with the deepening of complex interdependence
and globalisation, have transformed Germany – and Germany's
relations with the Visegrad countries – at the same time as they have
transformed the wider pattern of international relations in Europe.
Germany is inevitably the hegemonic power in East Central Europe,
but its influence today is generally positive and constructive.
Suspicions about long-term German policy remain, particularly in
Poland. Yet even in Poland, there is no doubt that the 'internal and
international conditions for a permanent Polish–German reconciliation are now better than at any other time in recent history', even
though this process 'will take a long time and is likely to suffer many
tactical setbacks'.[95]

Ambivalent feelings and deeply rooted stereotypes continue to
influence Czech and Slovak attitudes towards Germany,[96] but both
Prague and Bratislava have consciously pursued a policy of close
alignment with Bonn.[97] The Hungarians are the most relaxed about
the German presence in *Mitteleuropa*. The reasons for this are that
they do not border on Germany, and therefore have no border
disputes; there are no problems with minority national communities;
and they have been one-time allies. Hungary also won an enormous
debt of gratitude from the Bonn government for taking the
courageous decision to allow East Germans to cross its border into
Austria on 10 September 1989 – the event which precipitated the
collapse of the East German regime and the unravelling of
communist power in Europe.[98]

One crucial reason why the pervasive German presence in
Mitteleuropa today is less feared or resented than in the past is that
the BRD is firmly anchored in robust multilateral institutions such as
NATO and the EU. Vladimir Handl, a leading Czech analyst of
German policy, has argued that 'thanks to its membership in Western
structures, Germany could affect the Czech Republic adversely only
by agreement with its partners'.[99] Another study of Czech national
interests has argued that a 'democratic and prosperous federalized
Germany, integrated internationally and gradually also on a supranational level, – a "European" Germany – represents a great chance
for the Czech Republic. It can do a great deal to assist the transformation of the Czech state and its incorporation in western structures.'[100]

Germany's integration into the EU and NATO is thus an essential
feature of the contemporary European security system. It provides

reassurance to Germany's neighbours that the Bundesrepublik will not revert to the old Bismarckian role of *Wanderer zwischen den Welten* ('wanderer between the worlds'), playing off East and West in order to build a new German order in Europe. It also makes Germany's strong presence in *Mitteleuropa* more palatable to the Visegrad countries. The success of Germany's future *Ostpolitik* is therefore closely bound up with its continued *Westbindung* – its continued anchorage in, and identification with, European multilateral organisations (first and foremost, the EU). As Dirk Verheyen has observed,

> For historical, geopolitical, and cultural reasons, it is inevitable that the united Germany will in the coming years and decades once again occupy its Janus-like position as a multifaceted 'bridge' between the West and East, with all the opportunities and liabilities that this entails, including pressures from an economically troubled Eastern Europe and USSR for economic and financial assistance....
>
> Whether the reunited Germans will manage their power responsibly and play their new global as well as Central European roles effectively, with a solidly anchored Western identity, that is clearly the essence of an enduring German Question.[101]

Conclusion

Since the dismantling of the Iron Curtain, relations with the West have become the centrepiece of the foreign and security policies of the Visegrad countries. The East Central Europeans regard close relations with Western organisations and governments as vital for the success of their economic restructuring and for the consolidation of their young democracies.[102] Indeed, their return to Europe is not only crucial for their external relations, it also has important implications for their domestic policies. By aligning themselves closely with West European structures and norms, the Visegrad countries are increasingly being permeated by 'European' values such as human rights, democracy and pluralism. In this way, the political cultures and national identities of the Visegrad countries are being gradually transformed into a more 'European' pattern.

The West thus exerts a pervasive influence on developments in the lands to its immediate east – an influence which has been enhanced by the revolution in information technology that occurred in the 1970s and 1980s.[103] As Timothy Garton Ash has argued, if the revolutions of 1989 were inspired by anything, it was by the 'ideology' of liberal democracy and the 'model' of Western Europe.[104] Western Europe has presented an attractive political model defined by limited government, the rule of law, competitive elections and a culture of political tolerance. It is seen as an area of economic prosperity, dynamic technological innovation and consumerism, based on a social market economy. Its vibrant culture – from its avante-garde artists to its television soaps – has also been much admired.

The Visegrad countries' desire for Western economic aid and political support offers the West a useful set of policy tools for influencing political developments in the region. Closer economic links between East and West can be made contingent on steady progress towards democratisation and respect for human rights. In this way, Western economic aid and support can provide a positive inducement for democratic change in the countries of post-communist Europe.[105] The desire to join the EU has already played a significant role in moderating the Hungarian–Slovak bilateral dispute over the Danubian dams (see pp. 95–9), and has helped ameliorate nationalist tensions throughout the region. As Gabriel Munuera has argued, the interest of the Visegrad countries 'in joining the European Union has also indirectly enhanced the position of the CSCE and the [Council of Europe], whose approval and membership of which are perceived as prerequisites for the highly coveted adhesion to the Union'.[106]

The EU thus has an historic opportunity to influence domestic politics and international relations in post-communist Central and Eastern Europe. In doing so, it can make a major contribution to European peace and security. Instability in Central and Eastern Europe would have dire consequences for the security of Western Europe. Even if some EU countries – such as Britain, with its historical identity as an island nation – believe they can insulate themselves from turbulence in the East, countries like Germany and Italy recognise their vulnerability. Moreover, if the EU fails to take action to support the reform process in East Central Europe, Germany may be tempted to act alone – conjuring up the very demons that post-war European integration was designed to exorcise.

Thus given the threats to European security that instability in the post-communist East would generate, the aim of Western policies towards Central and Eastern Europe must be to enmesh the region in an ever-deepening network of political, economic and social interdependencies. Western governments and multilateral organisations can provide positive economic and financial incentives for democratic reform in the East. By raising the costs of political recidivism, a significant disincentive can be created which might help deter East European elites from reverting to pre-war patterns of authoritarian populism. More importantly, expanding the existing networks of multilateral cooperation and supranational integration through the gradual incorporation of the new Eastern democracies will help diffuse common normative values throughout Central and Eastern Europe. It will also help socialise the new post-communist elites into habits of compromise and consensus, without which modern liberal democracies cannot survive.[107] Thus by providing positive incentives for democratic reform and developing an even more extensive institutionalised framework for multilateral cooperation, it will be possible to give practical encouragement to liberal and reforming coalitions in the East, and to impede the emergence of autarkic, repressive and nationalist policies in these fragile polities.[108]

However, integrating the new democracies into Western organisations involves a whole host of problems and dilemmas. One of the more naive illusions in Europe today is that organisations like the EU, NATO or the Council of Europe can expand their membership to the East without undergoing major changes in their structure and functioning. This is simply not possible. Both the EU and the Council of Europe will have to revise their decision-making procedures significantly if they are to cope with the additional demands of new members from the East. Yet expansion to the East has now become politically unstoppable for nearly all Western organisations. It is a question of *when* and *how*, not *if*. The key issue facing most Western organisations in the mid-1990s, therefore, is how their Eastern expansion can be effected in ways which strengthen security in Europe, without at the same time undermining the viability of these multilateral organisations themselves.

It is also important to recognise that the responsibility for supporting the reform process in East Central Europe will fall primarily on the shoulders of the West Europeans, rather than the

Americans (in contrast to the late 1940s, when the USA played the decisive role in aiding the reconstruction of Western Europe). Above all, it is the EU which will be called upon to develop a much closer and more supportive relationship with the new democracies to its east. The EU – in collaboration with the Council of Europe and the EBRD – must therefore face up to the new demands and responsibilities placed on it by history, and recognise the need to play a more constructive role in Central and Eastern Europe.

Unfortunately, most of the political and economic elites in Western Europe have yet to grasp the nettle and commit themselves to a more proactive role in supporting restructuring in the East. President Havel is not the only Central European to bemoan the West's lack of imagination, and its failure to develop a policy which is anything other than short term or defensive.[109] Following the traumatic process of ratifying the Maastricht Treaty, and faced with the apparently insurmountable problems of ethno-national conflict in Russia and the Balkans, the EU has become increasingly self-absorbed. Growing doubts about monetary and political union have not been conducive to the generation of creative approaches towards Eastern enlargement. The EU has thus become too wrapped up with internal considerations, and too sensitive to narrow sectional interests. The plethora of restrictions on market access epitomises the small-mindedness and lack of vision of Western Europe when faced with the historic responsibility of building a continent 'whole and free'.

Of course, the main burdens of democratic transition and economic reform will have to be borne by the peoples of East Central Europe themselves. This is only to be expected: reform in the region 'has been a boot-strap operation, self-generated and self-supported as far as it has come'.[110] The benefits of successful reform, however, will be experienced by Europeans in both East and West, in the form of a more stable, secure and democratic continent. It is therefore in the enlightened self-interest of the West to nourish the reform process in the East. If short-sighted concerns and vested national interests prevent this, then the consequences for the future stability and order of Europe could be dire:

> If reform fails because of a lack of financial support, or through a lack of openness to Central European exports to Western Europe, or because of excessive reticence toward membership in the European Community system, then we will all pay in security terms.[111]

Endnotes

1   Václav Havel, 'A call for sacrifice: the co-responsibility of the West', *Foreign Affairs*, March/April 1994, pp. 2–7.

2   Adrian Hyde-Price, 'Democratization in Eastern Europe: the external dimension', in Geoffrey Pridham and Tatu Vanhanen, eds, *Democratization in Eastern Europe: Domestic and International Perspectives*, London, Routledge, 1994, pp. 220–254. See also Geoffrey Pridham, Eric Herring and George Sandford, eds, *Building Democracy? Democratisation in Eastern Europe*, London, Leicester University Press, 1994.

3   Eva Nowotny, 'The role of the CSCE and the Council of Europe in facilitating a stable transition toward new political structures in Europe', in P. Volten, ed., *Uncertain Futures: Eastern Europe and Democracy*, New York, IEWS, 1990, pp. 51–61 (p. 60).

4   *The Secretary General's Contribution to the Informal Ministerial Conference on Human Rights*, Rome, 5 November 1990, Strasbourg, Council of Europe, CIM-DH (90)3.

5   The Council of Europe has concluded 132 conventions and agreements covering different aspects of European cooperation. This has effectively created a *European legal space* which would otherwise require more than 25,000 bilateral treaties. *Frankfurter Allgemeine Zeitung*, 10 July 1989.

6   *State of Relations Between the Council of Europe and the Countries of Central and Eastern Europe*, Strasbourg, Council of Europe, May 1991; and *Council of Europe Co-operation and Assistance Programmes for Countries of Central and Eastern Europe*, Strasbourg, Council of Europe, SG/INF (91)2.

7   *The Council of Europe and Human Rights*, Strasbourg, Council of Europe, September 1990, CIM-DH (90)4, p. 27.

8   *Council of Europe Cooperation and Assistance Programmes for Countries of Central and Eastern Europe*, Strasbourg, Council of Europe, SG/INF (91)2,3.

9   'The proposal contains elaborate norms and principles to protect minorities against threats to their existence such as expulsion or forced assimilation. The draft also sets limits to the unrestricted exercise of minority rights and stipulates certain obligations such as respect for national legislation and the rights of others. It thus tries to strike a balance between security at the level of the group and the individual and considerations of state security and stability. In addition, the draft proposes to set up a European Committee for the Protection of Minorities which may transfer a case to the highest body of the Council of Europe, the Committee of Ministers (ie, the foreign ministers of the member states). In the assessment of Kux, this proposal provides "the most far-reaching, comprehensive approach to minority problems, both by stipulating broad minority rights and obligations and by designing effective legal mechanisms of implementation".' Michael Andersen and Mette Skak, 'The new Western Ostpolitik: challenges, current state and issues', paper presented to the ECPR Joint Sessions of Workshops, Leiden, 2–8 April 1993, in the workshop 'Responses of Western European Institutions to Changes in the Former Soviet Union and Central and Eastern Europe'.

10   See for example 'Parliaments and the protection of minorities', *Democracy*, Newsletter of the Strasbourg Conference on Parliamentary Democracy, no. 16, October 1994.

11   Klaus Schumann, 'The role of the Council of Europe', in Hugh Miall, ed., *Minority Rights in Europe. The Scope for a Transnational Regime*, London, Pinter for the RIIA, 1994, pp. 87–98 (p. 91).

12   Ralph Beddard (Rapporteur), 'The Council of Europe', in Ralph Beddard and Dilys M. Hill, eds, *Emerging Rights Within the New Europe*, Southampton Papers in International Policy, no. 2, Southampton, Mountbatten Centre for International Studies, 1992, pp. 2–8 (p. 5).

13   G. Kardos, 'A Hungarian view on the All-European Protection of Human Rights', *All-European Human Rights Yearbook*, 1, 1991, pp. 151–5 (p. 152).

14   See for example the speech by the organisation's Secretary-General, Catherine Lalumière, 'The Council of Europe in the construction of a wider Europe', given at the Royal Institute of International Affairs, London, 28 February 1990.

15   Catherine Lalumière, 'The Council of Europe: a pan-European organisation for democratic security'. Lecture given at St Anthony's College, Oxford, 11 March 1993.

16   Daniel Tarschys, 'The Council of Europe: towards a vast area of democratic security', *NATO Review*, December 1994/January 1995, pp. 8–12 (p. 12).

17   Quoted by Catherine Lalumière in 'The Council of Europe's place in the new European architecture', *NATO Review*, 40, no. 5, October 1992, pp. 8–12 (p. 12).

18   *Ibid.*, p. 9.

19   Havel, *op. cit.* (p. 5).

20   'The spirit of eastern promise', *Financial Times*, 29 March 1993.

21   *Political Aspects for the Mandate of the European Bank in Relation to Ethnic Minorities*, London, EBRD, 1993. See also Karoly Okoliscsanyi, 'The EBRD's first year', *RFE/RL Research Report*, 1, no. 23, 5 June 1992, pp. 41–6.

22   For details of the EBRD's rationale and operation see Andrew Williams, 'The multilateral economic institutions and the new Europe', in Andrew Williams, ed., *Reorganising Eastern Europe: European Institutions and the Refashioning of Europe's Security Architecture*, Aldershot, Dartmouth, 1994, pp. 73–90.

23   This assessment is not universally accepted. Some have argued that the EBRD was little more than a power play by President Mitterrand with the active involvement of Jacques Attali, and that the EIB could have done much the same with far less pomp and far less expenditure on overheads.

24   Hannes Androsch's judgement on the EBRD ('Transformation in Central and Eastern Europe', *The World Today*, October 1994, pp. 194–7) is damning: 'Set up with great fanfares three years ago, it has quite dramatically failed to be a decisive factor and its impact upon the economies in transition has been negligible' (p. 196).

25   'EBRD to tighten budget process', *Financial Times*, 20 April 1993.

26   'The bank that likes to say yes – to itself', *Financial Times*, 13 April 1994.

27   His letter of resignation was reprinted in the *Financial Times*, 26/27 June 1993, p. 2.

28   'de Larosière unveils plan to give EBRD a sharper focus', *Independent*, 9 November 1993.

29   'Next steps at the EBRD', *Financial Times*, 28 June 1993.

30   'No European public figure has been more assiduous in calling for a new spirit
      of economic cooperation to unite east and west', *Financial Times*, 26/27 June
      1993.
31   In March 1995 allegations surfaced that the EBRD's biggest project to date
      (funding a nuclear power station at Mochovce in Slovakia) had been decided
      by a small group of Frenchmen within the Bank (including the EBRD's French
      President, de Larosière), and subsequently awarded to a French company. An
      Englishman responsible for East European energy projects, Martin Blaiklock,
      who was leading a valuation of the Mochovce plant, was also removed and
      replaced by – yet another Frenchman. For details see 'European bank in
      nuclear split', *Independent on Sunday*, 19 March 1995, and 'EBRD fends off
      nuclear attack on Slovakian loan', *The European*, 24–30 March 1995.
32   'Bank faces uphill fight to define way forward', *Financial Times*, 26/27 June
      1993, p. 2.
33   'Eastern Europe looks askance at bank', *Financial Times*, 16 April 1993. See
      also Karoly Okolicsanyi, 'Eastern views of the EBRD', *RFE/RL Research
      Report*, 2, no. 23, 4 June 1993, pp. 50–2.
34   A limited trade agreement was signed between the EC and Romania in 1980,
      and in 1987 negotiations began to enlarge its provisions to include agriculture
      and cooperation. However, these were suspended, together with diplomatic
      relations, on 24 April 1989, because of both the deteriorating human rights
      situation, and Romania's failure to meet its obligations under the 1980
      agreement. On 20 December 1989, the day of the Timisoara uprising, the
      Commission finally decided to freeze the 1980 agreement.
35   For details, see John Pinder, *The European Community and Eastern Europe*,
      London, Pinter for the RIIA, 1991; *EC–Eastern European Relations*, ICC
      Background Brief, Strasbourg, Commission of the European Communities, 7
      November 1990; and Richard Davy, 'The Central European dimension', in
      William Wallace, ed., *The Dynamics of European Integration*, London, Pinter
      for the RIIA, 1990, pp. 141–54.
36   In 1990, the Community provided ECU 500 million (£350 million) to
      Eastern Europe under the PHARE scheme; in 1991, the figure was ECU 850
      million.
37   'Twenty-four governments, countless non-governmental institutions, up to
      seven multilateral agencies, combined with some 30 policy categories and up
      to eight target countries (including the Balkans and the USSR), all suggests a
      major problem of ensuring coherence and effectiveness for the West'. J. M. C.
      Rollo with J. Batt, B. Granville and N. Malcolm, *The New Eastern Europe:
      Western Responses*, London, Pinter for the RIIA, 1990, p. 128.
38   Jan B. Weydenthal, 'Czechoslovakia, Hungary and Poland gain Associate
      Membership in the EC', *Report on Eastern Europe*, 7 February 1992; and
      David Kennedy and David Webb, 'The limits of integration: Eastern Europe
      and the European Communities, *Common Market Law Review*, 30, no. 6,
      December 1993.
39   Jackie Gower, 'EC relations with Central and Eastern Europe', in Juliet
      Lodge, ed., *The European Community and the Challenge of the Future*, 2nd
      edn, London, Pinter, 1993, pp. 283–99 (p. 290).
40   Details in *Democracy: Newsletter of the Strasbourg Conference on*

Parliamentary Democracy, no. 13, May 1993, p. 4 (published by the International Institute for Democracy, Strasbourg).

41 The Agreement with the Czechoslovak Federation lapsed on 1 January 1993 when the Federation broke up. Subsequently new Association Agreements were negotiated with the two republics, and these were eventually initialled on 23 June 1993.

42 'Eastern four in first steps to join EU', *The Guardian*, 2 February 1995.

43 Major reductions in quotas for agricultural products were opposed by the French government (with the tacit support of Ireland and Belgium), which was sensitive to the domestic political pressures of French farmers. This French move generated considerable controversy at the talks, and led to a temporary withdrawal of the Poles from the negotiations on 19 September 1991. A major reduction in quotas for textiles was opposed by the less developed members of the Community such as Portugal, whilst the Spanish, along with the French, Italians and Portuguese, opposed significant reductions in quotas on steel.

44 'Eastern vision', *Financial Times*, 29 October 1992.

45 Report by the Commission to the European Council, SEC/92/2301, Edinburgh, 11–12 December 1992.

46 See Gabriella Izik Hedri, 'The EC and the "Visegrad Triangle" states', *Osteuropa*, February 1993, pp. 154–66; Joseph C. Kun, *Hungarian Foreign Policy. The Experience of a New Democracy*, Westport, Praeger, 1993, pp. 75–6, 93–6, 108–11; and Jan B. de Weydenthal, 'EC keeps Central Europe at arm's length', *RFE/RL Research Report*, 2, no. 5, 29 January 1993, pp. 29–31.

47 'Heads of government back new links for the 21st century', *The Guardian*, 10 December 1994.

48 The Visegrad four along with Bulgaria and Romania.

49 'EU decides on Eastern Europe's favoured few for early entry', *The Guardian*, 5 October 1994.

50 'Slovenes and Czechs head long line to join EU', *The Guardian*, 24 September 1994. Slovenia, it may be surprising to learn, already has a higher per capita income than Greece or Portugal. See also 'Six ex-communist states take big step towards EU', *The Guardian*, 1 November 1994.

51 Hungary formally applied for EU membership on 1 April 1994, Poland following shortly afterwards, on 8 April.

52 Jacques Attali has also stated that the East Europeans 'will need at least 20 years to get out of the mire and sufficient resources from Western institutions'. In his characteristically challenging manner, he went on to argue that if such Western help is not given, 'the desperate populations of these countries will start to think a return to military dictatorship is a small price to pay for a return to employment, social protection and accessible consumer goods. Western Europe has no global vision of a continental Europe. Everybody is fixated with their own national problems. We really need a new generation of visionary statesmen.' See his interview in *Globe Hebdo*, reprinted in *The Guardian*, 26 January 1994.

53 'Eastern Europe and the EU: laying down the law', *The Economist*, 10 December 1994, pp. 40–3; and David Dyker, 'Free trade and fair trade with

Eastern Europe', *RFE/RL Research Report*, 2, no. 26, 25 June 1993, pp. 39–42.

54   'Welcome Eastern Europe', *The Economist*, 10 December 1994, pp. 15–16.
55   Josef C. Brada, 'The European Community and Czechoslovakia, Hungary and Poland', *Report on Eastern Europe*, 6 December 1991, pp. 27–32 (p. 31); and 'Fortress Europe keeps eastern neighbours out', *Financial Times*, 19 October 1992.
56   'Eastern dismay as EU exploits the post-communist markets', *The Guardian*, 1 January 1994.
57   'When the East's dreams evaporate', *The Guardian*, 19 November 1994.
58   See Heinz Kramer, 'The EC and the stabilisation of Eastern Europe', *Aussenpolitik*, 43, no. 1, 1992, pp. 12–21; and Alexis Galinos, 'Central Europe and the EU: Prospects for closer integration', *RFE/RL Research Report*, 3, no. 29, 22 July 1994, pp. 19–25.
59   The danger posed by demagogic nationalists is illustrated by Istvan Csurka. Whilst serving as an MP and Vice-President of the ruling Hungarian Democratic Forum (MDF), Csurka published an eight-page article in which he depicted the Hungarian nation being choked by 'contacts in New York, Paris and Tel Aviv'. He also argued that 'The West seems to have totally lost its former ability to serve as a model of social organisation ...; the leaders of the West are preoccupied with their own survival, and the only message they are still able to convey to the world is that of an article of fashion: the "consumer".' His outspoken anti-Semitic and anti-liberal views led to his subsequent expulsion from the MDF. See *RFE/RL Research Report*, 1, no. 40, 9 October 1992, p. 28; and *East European Reporter*, 5, no. 5, October 1992, pp. 47–48.
60   Quoted in 'EU protectionism threatens progress of old Eastern Bloc', *The Guardian*, 20 October 1994.
61   Desmond Dinan, *Ever Closer Union. An Introduction to the European Community*, London, Macmillan, 1994, p. 475.
62   'Europe's hard core', *The Economist*, 21 November 1992, p. 109. See also Christian Deubner, 'Deutschland, Frankreich und die Europäische Union: Die Interessen laufen auseinander', *Internationale Politik und Gesellschaft*, no. 3, 1994, pp. 211–22.
63   See for example Jan Q. Th. Rood, 'The EC and Eastern Europe over the longer term', in *The Community and the Emerging European Democracies. A Joint Policy Report*, by Gianni Bonvicini, *et al.*, London, Chatham House, June 1991, pp. 13–27 (pp. 23–4).
64   Margaret Thatcher is a prime exponent of this view. See her autobiography, *The Downing Street Years*, London, Harper Collins, 1993, pp. 769–70.
65   For details see Stephen George, *Politics and Policy in the European Community*, 2nd edn, Oxford, Oxford University Press, 1991, chapter 11, pp. 190–202.
66   'Dilemma over Eastern approaches', *The Guardian*, 9 May 1994.
67   'EU's outstretched hand to the East begins to waver', *Financial Times*, 23 November 1994.
68   William Wallace, 'From twelve to twenty four? The challenges to the EC posed by the revolutions in Eastern Europe', in Colin Crouch and David Marquand, eds, *Towards a Greater Europe: A Continent Without an Iron Curtain*, London, Blackwell, 1992, pp. 34–51 (p. 38).

69   Adrian Hyde-Price, *European Security Beyond the Cold War: Four Scenarios for the Year 2010*, London, Sage for the RIIA, 1991, pp. 249–52.

70   'Six must wait for EU date', *The Guardian*, 5 November 1994.

71   President Havel has declared that 'I think the American presence in Europe is still vital. In the twentieth century, it was not just Europe that paid for American isolationism; America itself paid a price. The less it committed itself at the beginning of European conflagration, the greater the sacrifices it had to make at the end'. 'Why NATO must not say no to the Czechs', *The Guardian*, 19 October 1993. J. F. Brown has also written that, 'The American role [in Eastern Europe] could be a special one. Nowhere in the world was the prestige of the United States so high. The East Europeans ... wanted an American presence. In just what form they were not sure: economic, if possible, but also culturally and educationally in the broadest sense possible.' *Surge to Freedom: The End of Communist Rule in Eastern Europe*, Twickenham, Adamantine Press, 1991, p. 264.

72   Misha Glenny, *The Rebirth of History. Eastern Europe in the Age of Democracy*, London, Penguin, 1990, p. 226.

73   Piotr Wandycz, *The Price of Freedom: A History of East Central Europe From the Middle Ages to the Present*, London, Routledge, 1992, p. 9.

74   Quoted in 'A historic reconciliation', *Newsweek*, 24 June 1991, p. 18.

75   Quoted in Milan Hauner, 'The Czechs and the Germans: a one thousand-year relationship', in Dirk Verheyen and Christian Soe, eds, *The Germans and Their Neighbours*, Boulder, Westview, 1993, pp. 251–78 (p. 259).

76   Claudio Magris, *Danube*, London, Collins Harvell, 1990, p. 32

77   Adrian Hyde-Price, 'Uncertainties of security policy', in W. Paterson, P. Merkl and S. Padgett, eds, *Developments in German Politics*, London, Macmillan, 1992, pp. 153–71.

78   'The West European nationalisms that caused the greatest recent troubles, those of Germany and Italy, are now clearly benign, and the conditions for a return to aggressive nationalism are absent in both countries. Outsiders sometimes fear that outbreaks of anti-immigrant extremism in Germany signal the return of German fascism, but the forces of tolerance and decency are overwhelmingly dominant in Germany, and the robust health of German democracy and of German academic and press institutions ensures they will remain dominant.' Stephen van Evera, 'Hypotheses on nationalism and war', *International Security*, 18, no. 4, spring 1994, pp. 5–39 (p. 34).

79   Quoted in Hauner, *op. cit.*, p. 252.

80   Wolfgang F. Schlör, *German Security Policy*, Adelphi Paper 277, London, Brassey's for the IISS, 1993, pp. 27–9. See Timothy Garton Ash, 'Germany's choices', *Foreign Affairs*, July/August 1994, pp. 65–81.

81   The Central and East European share of German trade exceeds that of Russia by three or four times. German interests in Russia are therefore primarily concerned with strategic and security issues. Vladimir Handl, 'Germany in Central Europe: Czech perceptions', Paper presented to the International Political Studies Association Conference in Chicago, February 1995.

82   'German business looks east for the long term', *Financial Times*, 9 December 1991.

83   András Inotai, 'Economic implications of German unification for Central and Eastern Europe', in Paul B. Stares, ed., *The New Germany and the New Europe*, Washington, DC, Brookings Institution, 1992, pp. 279–304.

84   Timothy Garton Ash, *In Europe's Name. Germany and the Divided Continent*, London, Vintage, 1994, p. 382.

85   Quoted by Robert Gerald Livingston, 'United Germany: bigger and better', *Foreign Policy*, no. 87, summer 1992, p. 168.

86   Inotai, *op. cit.*, pp. 294, 296.

87   For details see Jan B. de Weydenthal, 'The politics of the Oder–Neisse line', *Radio Free Europe Background Report*, 217, 15 December 1989.

88   Renata Fritsch-Bournazel, *Europe and German Unification*, New York, Berg, 1992, pp. 102–3.

89   Arthur R. Rachwald, 'Poland and Germany: from foes to friends?', in Dirk Verheyen and Christian Soe, eds, *The Germans and Their Neighbours*, Boulder, Westview, 1993, pp. 231–50 (pp. 242–6)

90   In one of his first – and most controversial – acts, President Havel apologised to the Germans for what he described as 'a deeply immoral act'. This encouraged the *Sudetendeutsche Landsmannschaften* (the associations of expellees from the Sudetenlands) to press for compensation from the Prague government. Prague has refused to negotiate on this, but did at one stage offer to hold discussions with the *Landsmannschaften* at the non-governmental level. Although the Federal German government refuses to take up the issue, the Czech government has been pressed on the question of compensation by the Bavarian *Land* government, which has been supported by the Slovak government. For details see Hauner, *op. cit.*, pp. 242–53, 256–7; 'Meddling in Eastern Europe', Foreign Report, *The Economist*, 30 January 1992; Jan Obrman, 'Sudeten Germans controversy in the Czech Republic' and Paulina Bren, 'Czech restitution laws rekindle Sudeten Germans' grievances', both in *RFE/RL Research Report*, 3, no. 3, 14 January 1994, pp. 9–16 and 17–22.

91   Following unification, the Bonn government offered Poland, the Czech Republic and Hungary substantial financial inducement to finance transit camps and onward deportation for asylum-seekers from Germany ('Germany urges migrant controls', *Financial Times*, 16 February 1993). The Czech government argued for a regional approach to this problem, but in the end Warsaw, Budapest and Prague reached their own individual agreements with Bonn. In the Polish case, this involved payments of DM120 million to finance the operation.

92   Former Prime Minister Jan Krzysztof Bielecki declared Germany to be 'Poland's most important partner in all areas'. Quoted in Jan B. Weydenthal, 'The Polish–German reconciliation', *RFE/RL Research Report*, 2, no. 29, 5 July 1991, p. 19.

93   John Gray, 'From post-communism to civil society: the reemergence of history and the decline of the Western model', *Social Philosophy and Policy*, 10, no. 2, summer 1993, pp. 26–50 (p. 36). He argues that the influence of the German social market economy is in part due to the fact that 'much of the institutional and cultural inheritance of the Eastern European peoples is German in origin' and that 'For Eastern Europeans, it is self-evident that

Germany has become the dominant economic power in Europe, and it is likely that this dominance will be increased, rather than diminished, over the coming decades.... The German model, then, is perceived in Eastern Europe, and even in Russia, as the real success story of the postwar period. By contrast, Anglo-American capitalism is perceived to be in steep and inexorable decline – its banks and governments broke and its culture in disrepute and disarray; nothing is expected of it in terms of a contribution to the transition process, and it is nowhere adopted as a model' (p. 36).

94 Timothy Garton Ash, *op. cit.*, p. 383. See also William E. Paterson, 'Gulliver unbound: the changing context of foreign policy', in W. Paterson, P. Merkl and S. Padgett, eds, *Developments in German Politics*, London, Macmillan, 1992, pp. 137–52 (pp. 148–9).

95 Rachwald, *op. cit.*, pp. 247–8.

96 Ferdinand Seibt, 'Unbelebte Nachbarschaften, Versäumte Gelegenheiten. Teschen, Deutsche und Slowaken', *Merkur Deutsche Zeitschrift für Europäisches Denken*, no. 549, 1994, pp. 1074–5.

97 Václav Havel's decision after becoming President to visit Germany before Poland was widely criticised in Poland, but reflected the consciously pro-German approach of the new post-communist elite. Paul G. Lewis, 'Poland and the other Europe', in Jonathan Story, ed., *The New Europe. Politics, Government and Economy Since 1945*, Oxford, Blackwell, 1993, pp. 358–77 (p. 370).

98 Adrian Hyde-Price, 'GDR–Soviet relations', in Alex Pravda, ed., *The End of the Outer Empire. Soviet–East European Relations in Transition, 1985–90*, London, Sage, 1992, pp. 151–67 (p. 164); and Gwyn Prins, ed., *Spring in Winter. The 1989 Revolutions*, Manchester, Manchester University Press, 1990.

99 Vladimir Handl, 'Developments in Germany and Czech–German relations', *Perspectives*, no. 2, winter 1993–94, pp. 39–46 (p. 44).

100 *Czech National Interests. Contribution to a Discussion*, Prague, Institute for International Relations, 1993, p. 24

101 Dirk Verheyen, *The German Question. A Cultural, Historical, and Geopolitical Exploration*, Boulder, Westview, 1991, p. 204.

102 The former Hungarian Foreign Minister has argued that '[f]ull membership in institutions that provide political, economic and military security – organisations like the Council of Europe, the European Community and NATO – is essential for consolidating Central and Eastern Europe'. *International Herald Tribune*, 22 October 1992.

103 Ernest Kux, 'Revolution in Eastern Europe – revolution in the West?', *Problems of Communism*, XL, no. 3, May/June 1991, pp. 1–14 (p. 8).

104 Timothy Garton Ash, 'Eastern Europe: the year of truth', *New York Review of Books*, 15 February 1990, pp. 17–22; and 'Revolution: the springtime of two nations', *New York Review of Books*, 15 June 1989, pp. 3–10.

105 For the view that Western economic diplomacy in Eastern Europe is a malign attempt to impose capitalism on the region and prevent the development of an indigenous 'Third Way', see Peter Gowan, 'Western economic diplomacy and the new Eastern Europe', *New Left Review*, no. 182, July/August 1990, pp. 63–84.

106   Gabriel Munuera, *Preventing Armed Conflict in Europe: Lessons From Recent Experience*, Chaillot Paper 15/16, Paris, WEU Institute for Security Studies, June 1994, p. 22.

107   On the role of multilateral bodies in fostering socialisation and common norms, see Clive Archer, *International Organisations*, London, Unwin Hyman, 1983, pp. 156–63.

108   Jack Snyder, 'Averting anarchy in the new Europe', *International Security*, 14, no. 4, spring 1990, pp. 5–41.

109   Quoted in Glenny, *op. cit.*, p. 235.

110   Thomas Simons, *Eastern Europe in the Postwar World*, 2nd edn, London, Macmillan, 1993, p. 234.

111   *International Herald Tribune*, 30 May 1991.

Chapter Eight

The search for security

the siege continues for so long a time the enemies have to change
they have nothing in common but the desire to annihilate us
when some hordes depart others immediately appear
Goths Tatars Swedes imperial legions...

(Zbigniew Herbert, 1982[1])

Mars, the god of war, has cast a long and terrible shadow over East
Central Europe. For over two thousand years, an almost endless
succession of invading armies has swept over the lands between the
Baltic Sea and the Danube. The peoples of this geographically
exposed region have had to fight constantly to preserve their
independence and cultural identity against predatory neighbours. At
the same time, conflicts in East Central Europe have often been the
trigger for wider international disputes. In the twentieth century,
Eastern Europe has twice been the catalyst for global conflagration.
In the watershed years of 1947–49, it was again conflicts in – or
rather over – Eastern Europe that precipitated the bipolar division of
Europe. Subsequently it was in Central and Eastern Europe that the
flashpoints of the Cold War occurred – Berlin 1948–49 and 1961,
Budapest 1956, Prague 1968, Warsaw 1980–81. Eastern Europe has
thus been a crucial fulcrum of modern international politics. As
Henry Kissinger has observed, 'The principal cause of European
conflicts in the past 150 years has been the existence of a no-man's
land between the German and Russian peoples'.[2]

The search for security in East Central Europe is thus of great
consequence for the stability of the European society of states. The
collapse of communism freed the peoples of Eastern Europe from
Soviet domination. But it also created a security vacuum in the region
and unleashed long-suppressed national animosities. Since 1989,
therefore, the Visegrad countries have been striving to consolidate

and preserve their national independence, territorial integrity and societal cohesion. The return to Europe – which has been the leitmotiv of their post-1989 foreign policy – has increasingly been seen as including the goal of joining Western security and defence structures, particularly NATO.

This chapter will explore the nature of the security problems facing the Visegrad countries, and assess the efficacy of existing policy responses to them. It begins by evaluating the nature of the changed security agenda in the region. This is followed by a review of the changes in both the security environment in Eastern Europe and the defence policies of the Visegrad states since 1989. Consideration is also given to what role – if any – the West should play in fostering security and order in the lands to its immediate east. The chapter concludes by assessing the nature of the emerging security system in East Central Central on the eve of the twenty-first century.

The changing security agenda in East Central Europe

Security is pre-eminently an example of what W. B. Gallie has termed an 'essentially contested concept'.[3] Innumerable tomes have been written defining, analysing, disputing and – more recently – deconstructing its meaning and implications. Hedley Bull provides a definition which is no worse than others, and better than many. 'Security in international politics', he writes, 'means no more than safety: either objective safety, safety which actually exists, or subjective safety, that which is felt or experienced'.[4] Security has traditionally been defined in terms of military threats to states: increasingly, this narrow and state-centric definition is regarded as ontologically and methodologically flawed.[5] More recently – and particularly since the end of the Cold War – the concept of security has been expanded to include economic, political, social and environmental challenges, not only to states, but – more importantly – to societies and individuals.[6] Security is thus increasingly conceived of today as a multidimensional and multilevel concept.

This broadening of the concept of security reflects not only the dictates of changing intellectual fashion, but – more importantly – the changing nature of the security agenda in the modern world. This is nowhere more apparent than in the lands between the Baltic and the

Danube. Historically, security threats to East Central Europe have derived from the region's unfavourable geostrategic location between more powerful and expansionist neighbours: Sweden in the north; Russia in the east; Turkey in the south; and Austria and Prussia in the west. In the early twentieth century, this geopolitical equation was simplified as Germany and the Soviet Union became the two main contenders for influence in the lands between them.

East Central Europe's vulnerability to external aggression was exacerbated both by the physical typology of this part of Europe (with its broad plains and absence of natural barriers to invasion), and by the nationalist rivalries which bedevil this heterogenous region. Having stood at the confluence of four mighty multinational empires (the Habsburg, Ottoman, tsarist and Wilhelmine empires), Eastern Europe has been left with a kaleidoscopic profusion of ethnic, national, linguistic and religious cleavages. The territorial irredenta and nationalist diasporas that this produced after 1919 gave rise to intractable international conflicts. These were aggravated by the region's pervasive economic backwardness, social inequalities and 'parochial-subject' political culture. These problems were all too painfully evident in the inter-war years, when common borders inevitably meant hostile relations, further weakening the security of the region. 'Thus', as Joseph Rothschild has written, 'the "blame" for the demise of the region's independence must be charged to its own fundamental weaknesses, the instability of its institutions, and its irresponsible governments, as well as to the active and passive faults of the Great Powers.'[7]

Given East Central Europe's internal weaknesses and exposed geostrategic location, it has traditionally been a classic example of what Martin Wight called a 'buffer zone'. 'A buffer zone', he argued, 'is a region occupied by one or more weaker powers between two or more stronger powers; it is sometimes described as a "power vacuum"'. The stronger powers surrounding this buffer zone will strive to ensure that their rivals do not gain control over the weaker states on their borders. Thus, as Wight suggests, 'Fluctuations of power make most buffer zones unstable and ambiguous. A policy adopted by one great power to preserve the neutrality of a buffer state may be seen by its rival as reducing the buffer state to a satellite; and a buffer state may be regarded by the same statesman, in different circumstances, as either a defensive bulwark or a springboard for further expansion.'[8]

The realist assumptions which underpin this notion of a 'buffer zone' may no longer hold true today, but they were apposite to the inter-war years. At this time, European international relations were characterised by great-power rivalry, realpolitik calculations and a balance-of-power arrangement. In this context, the security options of the East European 'buffer states' were severely limited:

> It is broadly true that politics, like nature, abhors a vacuum; and a buffer state cannot achieve security on its own. The first condition of its stability is an equivalence of political pressure from the surrounding great powers; the second is a readiness on the part of more distant great powers to go to war in its defence; only the third is its own strength. This is illustrated by the history of Eastern Europe between 1919 and 1941.[9]

The contemporary security agenda in East Central Europe

The historical record does not offer much comfort to the Visegrad countries when they consider how best to guarantee the security of their peoples. The traditional mechanisms and institutions of 'international society' – the balance of power, international law, diplomacy, war and management role of the great powers[10] – have not served the Poles, Hungarians, Czechs or Slovaks particularly well in the past three hundred years. Within the context of great-power rivalry and multipolar instability, the precarious geostrategic situation of the East Central Europeans left them with few security options. The stability of the adversarial bipolar era offered 'security' of a sort, but only at the cost of domestic freedom and national independence. With the disintegration of the East–West divide, some security analysts have warned of the likely return of multipolar instability to Europe. John Mearsheimer, for example, expects West European states to begin 'viewing each other with greater fear and suspicion, as they did for centuries before the onset of the Cold War'.[11] However, these fears have not materialised. Instead, a new security agenda has emerged which reflects a profound change in the nature of contemporary international relations.

The end of the Cold War has not been followed by a reversion to fluid patterns of multipolarity characterised by traditional balance-of-power politics. Instead, a new 'concert of Europe' has emerged, with the main European powers adopting a largely consensual and collaborative approach to the problems of maintaining peace and stability on the continent.[12] This new European concert is not without its fault lines – particularly between Russia and the West – but, by and large, it has facilitated a broad pan-European consensus on issues as diverse as German unification, the Gulf War, the institutionalisation of the OSCE and the war in former Yugoslavia. For the Visegrad countries, this European concert has resulted in a much more benign external environment. For the first time in many centuries, the region is no longer viewed by its neighbours through the perspective of realpolitik and great-power rivalry. Although the East Central Europeans continue to harbour some lingering concerns regarding Russia – and, to a much lesser extent, Germany – the region is no longer used by the great powers as a 'strategic-diplomatic chessboard' in a 'tournament of distinctive knights'.[13]

The reasons for this are complex and varied, and have to do with the changing character of European international relations in an era of interdependence, globalisation, institutional integration and democratisation. These issues – and their implications for East Central Europe – will be more thoroughly explored in the concluding chapter. Suffice it to say, the changed nature of European international relations has altered the security agenda in Europe. Today the main threat to peace and security comes not from inter-state war but from conflicts internal to states. These indigenous security risks arise from two associated processes in Eastern Europe: a resurgence of nationalism, and the upheavals generated by the process of post-communist transition. With the end of the Cold War, ethnic and other related forms of intercommunal strife have emerged as the single most pressing security concern in the new Europe.[14] As far as East Central Europe is concerned, there are four main nationalities problems with potential security implications: first, and most seriously, the Hungarian diaspora in Transylvania, Slovakia, Voijovdina and Ukraine; second, the German community in Silesia; third, the Polish minorities in Lithuania, Belarus and Ukraine; and finally, the possibility of a future breakdown in relations between Czechs and Slovaks.[15]

These latent ethno-national tensions may assume a more acute form given the severe socio-economic strains in East Central Europe generated by the process of transition from communist autocracy to capitalist democracy. The economic costs of the transition have proved much higher than many initially expected, although there have been encouraging signs of economic recovery in some parts of East Central Europe in 1994–95. Nonetheless, the continuing recession in many parts of Western Europe, coupled with the protectionist practices of the EU, do not bode well for the Visegrad countries. If economic conditions fail to improve, or if they deteriorate further, then forms of chauvinistic nationalism and authoritarian populism may well find fertile soil. Such unsavoury political forces would encourage a search for scapegoats amongst minority communities, along with a witch-hunt against 'enemies' within and without – a development which would not augur well for the peace of Europe. As Václav Havel warned in his speech to the European Parliament in February 1991, Eastern Europe is in danger of becoming a 'zone of chaos and hopelessness'. In this situation, 'demagogic, nationalist, totalitarian messiahs' might come to power who could threaten the security of Europe as a whole.[16]

The prominence of domestic considerations on the security agenda of East Central Europe illustrates the extent to which the nature of contemporary European security has changed. In contrast to the inter-war years, the directly military aspects of security have declined in saliency. Military issues are still of concern to the Visegrad countries, but the non-military aspects of security have grown in importance. The contemporary security agenda is increasingly concerned with the economic, political, societal and environmental causes of insecurity – for example, economically motivated migration from the East;[17] drug smuggling and transnational crime; and cross-border pollution and environmental degradation. This has stretched the traditional notion of security, and led to an increasingly multidimensional understanding of the nature of international security. As in Western Europe, the security agenda is increasingly dominated by rather nebulous risks and challenges, rather than by specific threats. In other words, East Central Europe is no longer threatened by a 'clear and present danger', in the shape of an identifiable *enemy*.[18]

The nearest the Visegrad countries come to having an identifiable enemy is Russia. Yet portraying Russia as a 'clear and present danger' is not unproblematic. First, with the partial exception of Poland (which borders on the enclave of Kaliningrad), the East Central Europeans no longer share a common border with Russia. This has greatly improved their strategic situation, and makes the prospect of a Russian military invasion far less likely. Second, post-communist Russia remains committed to creating an open market economy and pluralist liberal democracy. Third, under Yeltsin and Kozyrev, Russia has aimed at developing more cooperative relations with the Visegrad countries. Although Russian foreign and security policies have displayed signs of an increasing assertiveness since mid-1993, this has not been aimed at restoring its 'outer empire' in East Central Europe. Rather, it has had two concerns: to defend what it regards – with some justification – as its vital interests in its 'near abroad'; and to prevent Russia from being isolated from the wider European integration process.

Nonetheless, instability in Russia has caused unease in East Central Europe. This unease has been fuelled by a series of disturbing developments in Russian politics: the Soviet coup of August 1991; the electoral successes of Vladimir Zhirinovsky in December 1993; the growing influence of the military and political hardliners following the crushing of the Duma in October 1993; and the assault on the Chechen capital, Grozny, in the winter of 1994–95. The weakening of Belarussian neutrality since early 1993 has also rekindled fears of Russia's military and strategic influence spreading westwards.[19] The fear of Russian revanchism thus constitutes a major source of perceived (or subjective) insecurity in East Central Europe, even though it does not as yet amount to an objective security threat.[20]

One other regional security concern is the civil war in former Yugoslavia. This has had a direct impact on Hungary. Hungary has been drawn into the politics of the civil war by its arms sales to Croatia and the presence of a small Hungarian community in the province of Vojvodina, now part of Serbia. Hungary has also had its airspace violated by the Serbian airforce on over twenty occasions, and, more seriously, Hungarian villages near the border town of Barcs were attacked by Serbian bombers in October 1991.[21] Furthermore, Hungary has suffered economically by enforcing UN sanctions against Serbia and Montenegro (the former Yugoslavia having been one of Hungary's most important trading partners), and through the cost of coping with the influx of refugees escaping the fighting.[22] Hungary has made much of its vulnerability to the conflict in former Yugoslavia, and has used this to develop further its relationship with NATO and the WEU. Thus, for example, the October 1992 decision by Budapest to allow NATO AWACS surveillance aircraft to fly over Hungarian airspace and monitor the non-fly embargo in Bosnia-Herzegovina led to a new stage in Hungarian security collaboration with the West.

The end of the Cold War has therefore generated very different security concerns in East Central Europe from those which previously existed. In contrast to the inter-war years, the main cause of insecurity comes not from foreign states, but from problems internal to the region – primarily nationalist animosities and societal dislocation. The sense of insecurity is heightened by the lack of firmly established regional mechanisms for collective security and conflict prevention. It is this which has given rise to a perceived security vacuum in the region.[23] As Václav Havel told his NATO audience in March 1991, 'our countries are dangerously sliding into an uncertain political, economic and security vacuum'. The old, imposed structures had collapsed, he warned, but new ones were developing only 'slowly and with difficulty, if at all'. Thus, 'it is becoming evident that without appropriate external relations the very being of our young democracies is in jeopardy'.[24]

A 'grey zone' of uncertain security status has thus appeared in East Central Europe, which the Visegrad four find deeply unsettling. Before considering their attempts to fill this security vacuum, let us first assess the significance of the changed strategic environment in the region.

Strategic realignment, military reform and regional security

Since 1989, far-reaching changes have taken place in the security environment of East Central Europe. They have occurred largely because of one development: the decline and subsequent disintegration of the USSR. The rapid decay of Soviet communism led first to the collapse of communist power in Eastern Europe, then to the dissolution of the Warsaw Pact, and finally to the withdrawal of Soviet forces stationed in Germany, Eastern Europe and the Baltic republics. By 1995, this process of Russian military disengagement from Central and Eastern Europe had profoundly altered Europe's strategic topology.

The Russian military withdrawal from the region has fundamentally changed the strategic situation facing East Central Europe. Since 1990, the Visegrad countries have been developing their own national military doctrines and restructuring their armed forces. At the same time, they have sought to strengthen their national sovereignty by forging a web of bi- and multilateral relations with each other and with their neighbours in East and West. In this section, the main developments in regional security will be outlined, and an assessment made of their implications for the defence and security policies of the Visegrad countries.

The withdrawal of Soviet/Russian troops from Central and Eastern Europe

The catalyst for Soviet military and political disengagement from Eastern Europe was the Kremlin's dramatic reappraisal of its external security environment. In short, the Gorbachev leadership realised that the West was 'neither *consistently* hostile, militarily aggressive, nor politically belligerent towards the Soviet Union'.[25] Eastern Europe was therefore no longer essential as a military *cordon sanitaire*. Indeed, the 'new political thinking' emphasised the need for a cooperative relationship with the West and the building of a common security arrangement in Europe. This inevitably entailed a new political relationship with the East Europeans and a reduction in offensively postured Soviet armed forces in the region.[26]

This process of strategic restructuring began in December 1988, with Gorbachev's announcement (at the UN General Assembly) that 50,000 Soviet troops would be withdrawn from Eastern Europe by the end of 1991, as part of a unilateral reduction of 500,000 in the overall strength of the Soviet Army. However, this modest but positive step was quickly overtaken by events. The 'people's revolutions' of 1989 radically altered the nature of Soviet–East European relations. The implosion of communist power was followed by calls for the withdrawal of Soviet stationed forces from the region. The unification of Germany also made the continued presence of 380,000 Soviet troops in East Germany politically untenable. Thus in July 1990, an agreement was reached between Gorbachev and Kohl which included a pledge that all Soviet troops in Germany would be withdrawn by 1994.

In the case of Hungary, the newly elected democratic government finally reached agreement with the USSR in March 1990 on the withdrawal of the 65,000 Soviet combat forces in the 'Southern Group of Forces' (which had been in the country since 'Liberation' in 1944). This withdrawal was completed ahead of schedule, in June

1991.[27] The new non-communist government in Czechoslovakia was also able to negotiate an agreement on relatively swift troop withdrawals with the USSR. The withdrawal of the 73,500 Soviet troops from Czechoslovakia was formally agreed in February 1991, during President Havel's visit to Moscow. Soviet forces had been stationed in Czechoslovakia following the crushing of the 'Prague Spring', and their withdrawal (also completed by June 1991) was seen by many Czechoslovaks as intrinsic to the restoration of their country's full sovereignty.

It was only in the case of Poland that no early agreement was reached on a Soviet military withdrawal. There were a number of reasons for this. For the Soviets, a military presence in Poland was useful in order to protect their lines of communication with Soviet forces in Germany; the Soviet military was also in no hurry to withdraw from its barracks in Poland, because of a dearth of housing for Soviet military personnel in the USSR. On the Polish side, the government's failure to secure an early agreement reflected its ambivalent attitude to the Soviet military presence: for much of 1990, it seemed as if Warsaw was interested in maintaining a Soviet military presence in Poland as a counterweight to German influence, and as a possible bargaining chip in their negotiations with Bonn on a new bilateral treaty.[28] By the time the Polish government had decided that they would prefer the Soviet military to leave (in the autumn of 1990), a conservative retrenchment was gathering momentum in Moscow, and the Poles' interlocutors were in no mood to make concessions. It was only after the failure of the abortive coup in Moscow in August 1991 that an agreement on the withdrawal of Soviet forces was finalised.[29] In October 1991, an 'agreement in principle' on the withdrawal of the 59,000 Soviet forces was concluded (5,000 of them were withdrawn during the negotiations). By late October 1992, all Russian combat troops had been withdrawn from Poland. Some 6,000 support troops remained to facilitate the withdrawal of Russian troops from Germany, but they finally left in September 1993.

The demise of the Warsaw Pact

With communism's collapse in East Central Europe, it was clear that the Warsaw Pact could not continue in its existing form, for three main reasons. First, the Warsaw Pact had never been an effective instrument of multilateral security cooperation, but from the start was dominated by the USSR, in a way that bore no resemblance to the USA's role in NATO.[30] Second, the Warsaw Pact was responsible for the invasion of Czechoslovakia in 1968, and had prepared operational plans for a possible invasion of Poland in 1981. Finally, the Pact was built on the ideological principles of Marxist–Leninism, which assumed that party-to-party relations would form the essential core of relations between 'socialist states'. For these reasons, the continued existence of the Pact became deeply problematical after 1989.

Nonetheless, for much of 1990 it seemed as if a *modus vivendi* between Moscow and their East European 'allies' had been reached. In return for a partial demilitarisation of the Pact, and a commitment to phase it out when a CSCE-based system of pan-European collective security had been created, the East Europeans agreed to preserve the Pact as a framework for limited multilateral security cooperation (especially in terms of arms control negotiations and verification) and political dialogue. This was codified at the important June 1990 Moscow meeting of the Political Consultative Committee (PCC) of the Warsaw Treaty Organization (WTO).[31] It also seemed as if the Poles, and perhaps the Czechoslovaks too, were interested in preserving some sort of security cooperation with the USSR in order to provide a counterweight to growing German influence in the region. Thus as late as November 1990, the then Polish Deputy Defence Minister Janusz Onyszkiewicz said that the Pact might still enjoy 'a brief second life' as a consultative body that 'can fill a certain political void that otherwise would be created in Central Europe'.[32]

However, by the winter of 1990–91, the mood in East Central Europe had hardened. Poland and Czechoslovakia came to share Hungary's view that the Warsaw Pact no longer made a positive contribution to the security of the region. Yet, when faced with calls for the abolition of the Pact's remaining military structures, Moscow began to procrastinate. Nevertheless, following the Soviet use of force in Vilnius and Riga in January 1991, the leaders of the three Visegrad states met in Budapest to agree a timetable for the dissolution of the Warsaw Pact. Shortly afterwards, Gorbachev sent a letter to the Soviet Union's five Pact allies in which he proposed that a meeting of the PCC be held with a view to closing down the organisation's remaining military mechanisms. In the end, a meeting of foreign and defence ministers from the Pact's six members was convened in Budapest, at which it was agreed that the military structures of the Pact (including the joint command, its committees, general staff and precepts for joint war games) would be terminated at the end of March 1991. A further meeting of the PCC in Prague was held in July 1991 in order to wind up the Pact's remaining political functions. Thus after thirty-six years, the WTO formally ceased to exist.

The 'renationalisation' of defence policy

One of the central objectives of Soviet policy within the Warsaw Pact had been to subordinate East European military policy to the requirements of the Soviet Army, and thus to prevent the emergence of national military doctrines. This was especially so for the Pact's so-called 'iron triangle' – the GDR, Poland and Czechoslovakia.[33] Consequently one of the first tasks of the new post-communist governments in East Central Europe was to develop authentically *national* defence doctrines. As the Visegrad countries develop their own military doctrines, and begin the task of restructuring and redeploying their forces, a common theme is that they do not see any other state or alliance as their enemy, and do not wish to threaten anyone else.[34] They also emphasise the defensive nature of their armed forces; their desire to cultivate good relations with their neighbours; and their strategic goal of integration into West European organisations, including NATO, the EU and the WEU.[35]

Three features define the evolving military strategies and defence policies of the Visegrad countries. First is a redeployment of their forces in a *tout azimous* fashion. Previously, the bulk of their troops (particularly their armoured divisions and those at a higher category of preparedness) had been deployed in the western half of their countries, to counter – or threaten – NATO forces in Central Europe.[36] Now the Visegrad countries are beginning to redeploy their forces more evenly throughout their national territories in order to be able to counteract security threats from whatever direction.

Second, all the Visegrad countries have made substantial reductions in their defence budgets. Some estimates suggest that the level of military expenditure in the region has fallen by approximately 50% since 1989. These cuts have been concentrated on military procurement programmes, and have had serious consequences for certain industries (such as machine building and metallurgy) and regions – most notably Slovakia, where 70,000 workers are dependent on the defence industry for employment.[37] Whilst cutting back on their defence expenditure and reducing the size of their armed forces, the East Central Europeans have also committed themselves to creating smaller but more professional, better-trained and well equipped armies. Hungary, the Czech Republic and Slovakia are keen to move towards all-volunteer forces eventually, whilst Poland favours retaining a system of national military service. Even so, Poland has reduced military service from eighteen to twelve months, and some 10,000 conscripts annually have been encouraged to serve in the police, rather than the army.[38]

Third, the armed forces of the region are being restructured in ways which seek to reinforce national defence without threatening their neighbours. Hungary, for example, took a decision early on to scrap its SCUD and FROG short-range ballistic missiles, in order to remove this particular threat to its neighbours.[39] In a similar vein, large offensively orientated armoured units have been reorganised into smaller units; territorial defence forces have been created, along with more mobile, rapid-deployment forces; and airforces are being restructured for national territorial defence.[40]

One problem facing all the East Central European countries is that they want to restructure and improve the quality of their military forces, whilst at the same time making substantial savings in defence expenditure. These two objectives will prove extremely difficult to combine, because well equipped all-volunteer armed forces are a lot more expensive than the conscript armies favoured by the old Warsaw Pact. Indeed, the deep cuts in defence expenditure throughout the region have greatly undermined the morale and operational ability of the armed forces, casting serious doubts on their ability to maintain national security.[41] Moreover, it is evident that none of the East Central European states can hope to preserve their national independence and territorial integrity by relying solely on their own national military forces.[42] For this reason, the East Europeans have been busy constructing a network of ties with other countries and with multilateral organisations, in order to try to forge a web of diplomatic relationships across Europe which will make the actual deployment of their limited military forces politically unnecessary.

Bilateral military relations

One important dimension of the new security policies of the Visegrad states has been bilateral cooperation with their immediate neighbours. During the Cold War, these bilateral relations were often very formalised and of limited significance, given the more rigid bipolar structure of European politics at that time. Today, however, in the context of a more polycentric Europe with a perceived security vacuum in East Central Europe, cordial bilateral relations are a vital factor in regional stability. One important aspect of these new bilateral arrangements has been military cooperation agreements. These have provided for practical military cooperation in a number of areas, and have also promoted an atmosphere of trust and mutually beneficial cooperation between armies. In this way, they have acted as an important confidence- and security-building measure.

After the break-up of the Warsaw Pact and the USSR, the Visegrad countries were keen to negotiate military cooperation agreements with the Soviet successor states – especially Russia. This was important given the prohibitive price of Western military equipment and their continuing dependence on Russia for most of their military supplies and spare parts – an unfortunate legacy of the Warsaw Pact days. It also provided a way for Russia to repay some of its outstanding foreign trade debts with the Visegrad states. Thus in November 1992 Hungary and Russia signed a military cooperation agreement which provided for continuing supplies of Russian-produced military equipment to the Hungarian army. An even more important deal was reached in June 1993, when Russia agreed to supply Hungary with twenty-eight MiG-29 fighters in partial repayment of unpaid foreign trade debts. This represents 'the biggest arms deal in the region since the demise of the Warsaw Pact in 1991'.[43] Hungary has also signed a bilateral military cooperation agreement with Ukraine; Slovakia one with Ukraine; and Poland has concluded similar agreements with Lithuanian, Belarus and Ukraine.

At the same time, a large number of bilateral military cooperation agreements have been signed with Western countries. Poland signed defence cooperation agreements with France and Greece in 1992, and with Belgium and the Netherlands in 1993. Polish–German relations have steadily deepened, with arrangements for Polish officers to train at the Bundeswehr academy in Hamburg, and joint

Polish–German training manoeuvres. Poland's bilateral defence cooperation arrangements with France and Germany have also been supplemented by trilateral cooperation, following the meeting of the three defence ministers in Paris in March 1994. Germany has also agreed to supply Hungary with free spare parts and equipment from the stocks of the former east German *Nationale Volksarmee* – an arrangement later expanded to include Poland and the Czech Republic. The USA has provided considerable financial assistance for military training and seminars in the region. Agreements on bilateral military cooperation have also been signed with neutral countries. Hungary, for example, has concluded agreements with Austria, Switzerland and Sweden. Sweden in particular has shown a willingness to develop military cooperation (for both political and commercial reasons), offering training for limited numbers of Hungarian officers and providing some arms deliveries. Sweden and Finland, along with the Netherlands, have been very active in training future peacekeeping forces.

Finally, a network of bilateral military treaties has been constructed amongst former Warsaw Pact members.[44] Hungary has concluded one with Romania (December 1990); with Czechoslovakia (January 1991); with Poland (March 1991); with Bulgaria (1991); and with Slovakia (October 1993). In February 1991, Poland and Czechoslovakia also signed a military cooperation agreement. None of these military accords include mutual defence commitments, or supranational military cooperation. Rather, they are 'cooperation and exchange of experience' agreements, which provide for collaboration in defence doctrine; training of commanding officers and technical personnel; the lending of training grounds; and arms production and arms purchases.[45] Similarly, the Polish–Hungarian agreement on military cooperation covers scientific work, training and the exploration of markets and joint sources of supplies, without specifying any mutual defence commitments.[46]

The Hungarian–Romanian military cooperation agreement is particularly interesting. Although there are serious political tensions between the two governments, there is considerable evidence to suggest that relations between the armed forces of the two countries are genuinely cordial. Moreover, Hungary has also concluded a unique bilateral 'open skies treaty' with Romania (allowing mutual aerial inspection). Such military cooperation contributes significantly towards regional security.

Political tensions between Hungary and Slovakia have also not prevented bilateral military cooperation. Although the Hungarian proposal to negotiate an 'open skies' treaty and 'open barracks' inspection scheme was turned down by Slovak Prime Minister Meciar in April 1993, a five-year military cooperation agreement was signed in October 1993. This provided for an exchange of information on large troop movements, the exchange of military observers, and the coordination of air defence and aviation activity in border areas.[47]

Hungary has also attempted to defuse the military tension along its border with Serbia. Following the bombing of a Hungarian village in October 1991, the two countries have agreed to create a neutral airspace corridor along their shared border, and to install a hotline between their air defence commands.

Regional security initiatives

The emergence of a security vacuum in Central and Eastern Europe has led to a number of proposals for new multilateral security structures. Many of these initiatives have been prompted, or accompanied, by regional schemes for closer political and economic cooperation. However, few of these proposals have appealed to the Visegrad states, primarily because their security policies have been increasingly focused on one central aim – becoming full members of NATO.

The East Central Europeans' own regional cooperation arrangements within the Visegrad framework have included some agreements on low-level military cooperation (including logistical support, exchange of information, troop movements, exercises, etc.) but have consciously eschewed creating a multilateral military alliance (see p. 123). Instead the Visegrad countries have argued that 'there is a need to create conditions for the direct inclusion of Poland, Czechoslovakia and Hungary in the activities of the [NATO] alliance'.[48] The Central European Initiative has also avoided discussion of military or security issues. Hungary did at one stage propose the creation of a 'zone of confidence' between the original four founding members of the CEI, in which offensive weapons would be withdrawn from a zone of 50 kilometres (initially along the Austrian–Hungarian–Yugoslav borders), but this received a very cool reaction from its partners.[49] Since then, neither the CEI nor its predecessors (the 'Pentagonale' and the 'Hexagonale') have formally discussed security issues on a multilateral basis.

One confusing – and confused – proposal for filling the regional security vacuum came from President Walesa. In March 1992, at a time when NATO countries were sending very unclear signals to Eastern Europe about the prospects for closer ties with the alliance, Walesa proposed creating an alternative to NATO – a 'NATO-bis'. NATO-bis, he suggested, would embrace the states of Central and Eastern Europe – including Poland, Czechoslovakia, Hungary, Ukraine, Belarus and Russia – and would prepare them for eventual NATO membership. Meanwhile, its members would renounce all territorial claims, and it would function as a partner for NATO.[50] When asked by a female journalist to explain further his conception of NATO-bis, Walesa's reply was 'NATO-bis is as lovely as you madam'. Walesa's chief security advisor, Jerzy Milewski, was subsequently forced to explain that NATO-bis was 'an idea and not a project existing in real life'.[51] This proposal generated a lively debate in Poland in the summer of 1992, but did not find its way into Poland's new defence doctrine (adopted on 2 November 1992).

A similar initiative was put forward by Belarussian President Stanislau Shushkevich in April 1993. In the face of growing calls (led by his chief political rival, Prime Minister Vyacheslau Kebich) for Belarus to join the CIS collective security pact signed in May 1992, Shushkevich proposed the creation of a 'belt of neutral states' in Europe. This neutral belt would include Poland, Hungary, Romania and Moldova, and possibly the three Baltic states. Such an arrangement would be, he declared, 'a security guarantee for member-states and serve as a model for the world'.[52] This plan received a cool response in East Central Europe, and little support within Belarus (which decided to join the CIS collective security pact on 9 April 1993).

Another initiative, similar to both those of Walesa and Shushkevich, was proposed by Ukrainian President Leonid Kravchuk in May 1993. In a document entitled *Strengthening Regional Stability and Security in Central-Eastern Europe*, he outlined the vision of a security zone encompassing the Baltic states, Belarus, the Czech Republic, Slovakia, Hungary, Bulgaria, Romania and Austria – but pointedly excluding Russia.[53] Once again, the Visegrad countries moved quickly to distance themselves from this scheme – both to avoid unnecessarily antagonising Russia, and because they did not want to do anything that might detract from their goal of joining NATO.[54]

The absence of effective regional cooperation structures which could fill the security vacuum in Central and Eastern Europe has led the Visegrad countries to explore pan-European, transatlantic or West European solutions to their security concerns. In the immediate wake of the 1989 revolutions, the idealistic new elites of East Central Europe tended to look to the CSCE to provide a pan-European collective security system. Since 1990–91, they have looked to NATO for firm security guarantees and full membership. In the future, they might look more to the EU and its defence arm, the WEU. In the following section, we will consider East Central Europe's changing approach to Europe's evolving security architecture: the OSCE (formerly the CSCE), NATO and the WEU.

Collective security through the OSCE?

For about twelve months after the democratic revolutions of 1989, the new post-communist governments of East Central Europe (including that of the GDR until October 1990) were leading advocates of the creation of a pan-European system of collective security. To provide the institutional foundation of this new collective security system, they looked to the CSCE – the Conference on Security and Cooperation in Europe.

The CSCE process began in 1972 as a means of peacefully managing the East–West conflict. These discussions culminated in the Helsinki summit of heads of state and government in 1975, an event which marked the high point of détente. The summit agreed the CSCE Final Act – a political not a legal document – containing three sections, or 'baskets': the first dealt with security matters; the second with economic, scientific, environmental and technological issues; and the third with humanitarian concerns, which included human rights and cultural contacts. The Helsinki declaration also launched a series of follow-up meetings and review conferences, designed to monitor implementation of CSCE decisions and promote pan-European dialogue and cooperation. It is important to recognise that the CSCE was only a 'process', and lacked any firm organisational structure. Moreover, its agreements – which had to be adopted on a unanimous basis – were only political statements 'of intent and commitment', rather than legally binding international treaties.

Despite these apparent limitations, the CSCE has been one of the great success stories of modern European diplomacy. It not only helped sustain East–West dialogue through the 'Second Cold War'[55] of the early 1980s, but also kept the issue of human rights high on the international agenda. Moreover, it provided an important forum for negotiations on confidence- and security-building measures.[56] This helps explain its attraction to the cohort of former dissidents who came to power in East Central Europe in 1989. They wanted the CSCE to subsume the organisational structures of the Cold War – both the Warsaw Pact and NATO – and become the institutional foundation of a new pan-European collective security regime.[57] To this end, they proposed a series of initiatives throughout 1990 designed to lay the foundations of a more robust and effective CSCE organisation.

Although most Western countries were sceptical about schemes for collective security and unwilling to countenance the dissolution of NATO, there was a broad consensus throughout Europe for reinforcing the role of the CSCE in post-Cold War European security. To this end, the CSCE summit of 19–21 November 1990 adopted the *The Charter of Paris for a New Europe*. This codified the new pan-European consensus on human rights, liberal democracy and market economics, and provided for the formal institutionalisation of the CSCE. The Charter created two key decision-making bodies, the Council of Foreign Ministers and the Committee of Senior Officials (now called the Ministerial Council and the Senior Council respectively), and three new permanent institutions: the Secretariat, based in Prague; the Conflict Prevention Centre, based in Vienna (now superseded by the Forum on Security Cooperation); and the Office for Free Elections, based in Warsaw (subsequently renamed the Office for Democratic Institutions and Human Rights (ODIHR)).[58] The Paris summit also witnessed the signing of the CFE (Conventional Forces in Europe) Treaty; the 'Declaration of Twenty-Two States', which formally announced the end of the East–West conflict; and international endorsement for the 'Two-Plus-Four' Treaty on German unification.

The CSCE was further developed in 1991 with the adoption in June of the Berlin Emergency Mechanism.[59] However, the CSCE's apparent powerlessness in the face of both the Soviet crackdown in the Baltic republics in January 1991[60] and the gathering civil war in Yugoslavia fuelled the East Central Europeans' growing awareness of the limitations of the CSCE. These limitations derived from three

242   *The international politics of East Central Europe*

fundamental features of the CSCE: the principle of unanimous decision making (partially modified in 1992 to allow for 'consensus minus one'[61]); its lack of effective enforcement mechanisms against 'rogue' states; and its legally non-binding character.

By mid-1991, therefore, the early optimistic aspirations for a collective security system based on the CSCE had largely dissipated. President Havel, a particularly eloquent exponent of a CSCE-based collective security system in 1990, commented as early as March 1991 that although he still had the same long-term vision of such a system, he now recognised that 'the way to it is likely to be longer and more complicated than we originally supposed'.[62] The Visegrad countries continued to support the further institutionalisation and consolidation of the CSCE,[63] but increasingly their security aspirations centred on NATO. Only a collective defence alliance like NATO, they came to believe, could provide them with the security guarantees they so earnestly desired.

Nevertheless, the East Central Europeans remained firm supporters of the CSCE, arguing that it could provide a multilateral context within which to address the increasingly pressing issues of inter-communal strife and ethnic animosity. The 'Helsinki II' review conference of March–July 1992 was important in this respect because it significantly strengthened the CSCE's mechanisms in the area of preventive diplomacy, conflict prevention and crisis management.[64] The concluding document, aptly entitled 'The Challenges of Change', signalled an enhanced role for the Committee of Senior Officials in the area of conflict prevention; established an innovative new post of High Commissioner for National Minorities (HCNM);[65] and agreed in principle to the possibility of future CSCE peacekeeping operations. It also created a permanent CSCE Forum for Security Cooperation, and established a number of CSCE missions to areas of actual or potential conflict.[66] By 1994, the CSCE had become, in its own words, 'the primary instrument for early warning, conflict prevention and crisis management in the region'.[67] This role was further codified and enhanced at the CSCE summit in Budapest in December 1994 – at which the decision was also taken to change the name of the CSCE to the OSCE (Organization for Security and Cooperation in Europe) in recognition of its permanent institutionalised presence in Europe's security architecture.

The OSCE's increasingly important role in preventive diplomacy and conflict prevention accords closely with the current security concerns of the East Central Europeans. By seeking to identify and peacefully resolve ethno-national conflicts, the organisation is responding to some of the most pressing issues on the changing European security agenda.[68] The importance attached to the OSCE was underlined in September 1994 by László Kovác, the Hungarian Foreign Minister and OSCE Chairman-in-Office in 1995, who declared that Hungary had a 'special interest' and 'a firm conviction that the CSCE has, and will surely have in the long run too, an indispensable role to play in bringing about increased security and stability in this region'.[69]

The Visegrad countries thus have much more limited expectations of the OSCE than they did in the months of optimism following the 1989 revolutions. Nonetheless, they continue to value its unique contribution to European security. Both Hungary and Slovakia, for example, have welcomed the efforts of the HCNM to mediate in their bilateral disputes over minority rights.[70] The OSCE today thus fulfils five vital functions: first, it provides a forum for promoting and codifying common standards, values and norms of behaviour, particularly in the sphere of human rights and the peaceful resolution of conflicts; second, it offers a series of mechanisms for the continuous monitoring of human rights, both for individuals and for national minorities;[71] third, it acts as a forum for promoting military transparency, arms controls, and confidence- and security-building measures, thereby 'reducing dangers of armed conflict and of misunderstanding or miscalculation of military activities which could give rise to apprehension';[72] fourth, it provides a framework for pan-European multilateral diplomacy across a comprehensive range of issues; and finally, it is developing instruments for preventive diplomacy, conflict avoidance and crisis management.[73]

East Central Europe and NATO

As the conviction grew in East Central Europe that the CSCE could not provide the basis for a robust pan-European collective security system, attention focused increasingly on NATO. No longer regarding it as the illegitimate offspring of the Cold War, the Visegrad countries increasingly began to praise its contribution to the overall security of the continent. Hungary led the way in seeking to develop a closer and more cooperative relationship with NATO,[74] but by early 1991 all the Visegrad governments had arrived at a more positive assessment of the alliance. NATO was not only seen as a vital element of stability in an otherwise turbulent continent, it was also increasingly regarded as the only organisation which could provide East Central Europe with the security guarantees it so pressingly sought.[75]

The questions of security guarantees from NATO and future membership of the alliance were raised by President Havel in March 1991 during his visit to NATO headquarters in Brussels – the first visit by a head of state from the Warsaw Pact. He argued that although he recognised that 'for a number of different reasons, our country cannot become a regular member of NATO for the time being', nonetheless, 'we believe that an alliance of countries united by the ideals of freedom and democracy should not be forever closed to neighbouring countries that are pursuing the same goals'. Jiří Dienstbier's call for a security guarantee was phrased even more bluntly: 'From NATO we want to know that, if we were threatened, we'd be treated at least as Kuwait, if necessary'.[76] The desire for closer institutional cooperation with NATO, along with some form of security guarantee from the sixteen member states and a commitment that the alliance would not permanently close the door on its democratic neighbours in the East, was clearly expressed by all the Visegrad states at their summit in Cracow in October 1991. Since then, joining NATO has remained the focus of the Visegrad countries' security policy.

The response of NATO to this persistent wooing has been cautious but sympathetic. Whilst flattered to hear that its former adversaries now regard it has having an irreplaceable role in post-Cold War Europe, the alliance has resisted calls to expand its membership or extend its security guarantees into East Central Europe. Nonetheless, it has been actively developing a closer and more institutionalised relationship with Europe's new democracies. In July 1990, NATO issued the London declaration, which extended 'the hand of friendship' to its former adversaries in the Warsaw Pact, and called for the creation of a process of regular diplomatic liaison between NATO and the post-communist countries to its east.[77] The North Atlantic Assembly – NATO's parliamentary body – also played an active role in strengthening political contacts between the sixteen and the former Warsaw Pact countries. The Assembly's offer of accepting 'associate delegates' from Central and Eastern Europe was warmly welcomed by the Visegrad states – with Hungary being the first to accept. These 'associate delegates' have since been involved in the work of the Assembly's committees, whilst the Assembly itself has provided a forum for multilateral discussions on European security.[78]

June 1991 witnessed further efforts by NATO to codify and define its evolving relationship with its former Warsaw Pact adversaries. At the Copenhagen meeting of NATO's North Atlantic Council, a long-awaited statement was issued, 'Partnership with the Countries of Central and Eastern Europe'.[79] It praised the contribution made by regular diplomatic liaison to 'fostering new patterns of constructive dialogue and bonds of friendship', and stated that the NATO countries saw the development of their relations with the countries of Central and Eastern Europe as 'a process over time, designed to promote both mutual reassurance and increasingly close ties'.[80]

The Copenhagen statement was welcomed by the Central and East Europeans, but with reservation: on the two substantial issues which concerned them most – namely formal security guarantees and the promise of future membership – NATO had made no significant concessions. Manfred Wörner, the late NATO Secretary-General, argued that 'we are not indifferent' to the security of Eastern Europe. Nevertheless, he spoke of NATO having only an indirect role in Eastern Europe: 'Our [NATO] security spills over and contributes to deterring the idea that use of force, directly or indirectly, might lead to results'.[81] Later, at the Prague Conference on European Security in April 1991, he argued that 'formal guarantees, formal membership relations are not on the cards', primarily because 'NATO does not seek a shift of balance, or an extension of military borders to the East'. Nonetheless, he suggested that closer security relations with the new democracies of Central and Eastern Europe would develop over time. 'These states neither want to be neutral nor components of a buffer zone, and nor do we. We want them to be constructive partners with an important contribution to make to a more cooperatively conceived security equation in Europe'. He went on to argue that what NATO could currently offer was 'a multiple and intensive web of relations which does not exclude the Soviet Union', and which would 'provide reassurance, as much as a steady, incremental improvement in the objective security situation'.[82]

A decisive step in the development of new relations with former Warsaw Pact countries was the establishment of the North Atlantic

Cooperation Council (NACC) in November 1991. The creation of the NACC marked the culmination of a series of initiatives taken since the London declaration of July 1990, and represented a significant new departure for the NATO alliance. Manfred Wörner wrote that 'The creation of the North Atlantic Cooperation Council (NACC) in late 1991 has affected NATO more than any other decision reached during my tenure as Secretary General'.[83] The NACC originated with a US–German initiative first broached in October 1991.[84] The plan was enthusiastically welcomed by Visegrad foreign ministers meeting in Cracow, and formally adopted by NATO at the Rome Council in November 1991.[85]

The inaugural meeting of the NACC was held on 20 December 1991. During this meeting, it was announced that the USSR had formally ceased to exist. With the subsequent creation of the Commonwealth of Independent States (CIS), membership of the NACC expanded to include all former Warsaw Pact members and the Soviet successor states, along with Albania. Finland also participated as an observer. By the spring of 1992, therefore, membership of the NACC had risen from the original 25 to 37 states.

The NACC was conceived as a framework for consultations and cooperation on security and related issues where alliance members could offer experience and expertise. These issues include defence planning, democratic concepts of civil–military relations, scientific and environmental affairs, civil–military coordination of air traffic management and defence conversion. The NACC operates on the basis of a *Work Plan for Dialogue, Partnership and Cooperation*, which gives direction to its deliberations. The NACC has also created a number of other bodies: the High Level Working Group (HLWG), which consults on CFE-related matters;[86] the Group on Defence Matters (GDM), which promotes cooperation on defence-related issues; and the Ad Hoc Group on Cooperation in Peacekeeping (AHG).[87] Although the NACC has not provided the Visegrad countries with the security guarantees they have been seeking, it has promoted consultation and multilateral security cooperation. This, in the opinion of Secretary-General Wörner, has 'helped to prevent the formation of competing alliances in Central and Eastern Europe. The NACC has given the countries of Central and Eastern Europe an instrument for addressing their security concerns and for identifying multilateral solutions'.[88]

Worthy and useful though the work of the NACC undoubtedly was at this time, it still did not meet the perceived security requirements of the Visegrad countries. The East Central Europeans therefore continued to press NATO for a promise of future membership. In the spring of 1993, they found a powerful tribune in the shape – yet again – of Germany. Both the Foreign Minister, Klaus Kinkel, and the Defence Minister, Völker Rühe, began quietly putting the case for a selective expansion of the alliance. However, in the face of strong doubts about the wisdom of such a move within NATO, and the vocal opposition to any selective expansion of NATO on the part of the Russians,[89] the issue of expansion was postponed in favour of a new initiative: the 'Partnership for Peace' scheme.[90]

The Partnership for Peace (PFP) initiative was originally proposed by US Secretary of Defence Les Aspin at the NATO defence ministers' meeting in Travemünde in October 1993, and formally adopted by NATO at the Brussels summit in January 1994. Whilst the PFP programme neither entails NATO membership nor involves security guarantees to individual partners, it does envisage a future 'NATO expansion that would reach to democratic states to our East, as part of an evolutionary process, taking into account political and security developments in the whole of Europe'. It also allows a partner state to consult NATO in the event of 'a direct threat to its territorial integrity, political independence, or security'.[91] In effect, by offering a menu from which various forms of cooperation can be chosen (joint training exercises, technical assistance, peacekeeping operations, etc.), the PFP programme allows participating states to set their own pace towards closer military integration and compatibility with NATO countries.[92] In this way the Visegrad states can place themselves in a good position for early membership of NATO when the alliance finally commits itself to an Eastern expansion.[93]

The issue of NATO's expansion is now firmly on the agenda. Indeed, President Clinton has declared that the question now is not 'whether NATO will take on new members, but when and how'.[94] Yet there are strong arguments both for and against a selective and early expansion of NATO eastwards. Let us begin by summarising the main arguments in favour. These focus on the issues of Russian policy, the changing European security agenda, and intra-alliance concerns.

Arguments in favour of selective expansion of NATO eastwards

(1) Expansion would provide a defence against an aggressive and revanchist Russia. Russia, it is argued, is politically unstable, economically weak and militarily powerful. This is a dangerous cocktail, which understandably generates security fears in East Central Europe. Accepting new members from the East now, when there is no major crisis, it is argued, would also be more sensible than waiting until Russia presents a direct and immediate threat to the region (when NATO expansion would be seen as an aggressive and escalatory action).

(2) Bringing the Visegrad countries into NATO would promote stability in the East, thereby providing assurance for domestic entrepreneurs and foreign investors. This would in turn help generate economic recovery and democratic consolidation, which is very much in the security interests of the West.

(3) Failing to open up NATO to the new democracies in the East would amount to a major loss of political will and international credibility on the part of the West. 'Betraying the hopes of East-Central Europe', one writer has suggested, 'would be another stage in the West's own tragic deconstruction'.[95] At best it would reflect Cold War inertia, at worst appeasement.[96]

(4) Membership of the alliance, and participation in its political and military structures, would help consolidate the process of democratic restructuring of civil–military relations in East Central Europe. This would in turn help stabilise the new democracies in the region, thereby contributing to peaceful relations between states.

(5) Failing to open up NATO to new members on a selective basis undermines the incentive for the post-communist democracies to develop mature, responsible and stabilising foreign and security policies. If membership were to be offered to states which demonstrated their commitment to democracy and the peaceful resolution of conflicts, this would encourage other states in the region to reform their foreign and security policies in similarly peaceful and democratic ways.[97]

(6) NATO, it is argued, must remain relevant to Europe's security needs or it will die.[98] The threat to the transatlantic area for which NATO was originally configured has gone. The most pressing security concerns for the West Europeans are on NATO's eastern and southern flanks. NATO must therefore respond to the needs of the

Visegrad countries by providing them with security guarantees and full membership of the alliance. If NATO fails to do this, 'Germany – or any other country in the same position, will find it necessary to take unilateral action to restrain the conflict. The West should therefore adopt an active political and military attitude'.[99]

(7) Finally, it is suggested that for the Visegrad states, membership of NATO could take a variety of forms. It need not follow the British or German model, with full military and political integration into alliance structures: it could be modelled on the Spanish or French example, with political participation but no military integration; or it could follow the Danish or Norwegian model, with no foreign troops or nuclear weapons being stationed on their territory in peacetime. In this way, it is argued, NATO membership could be offered to the East Central Europeans on a more flexible and adaptable basis.[100] More importantly, such an arrangement may also be more acceptable to the Russians.[101]

Arguments against a selective expansion of NATO eastwards

A growing body of opinion within NATO is coming round to the view that the alliance should open up to new members from the East.[102] Nonetheless, there remain powerful arguments against a selective expansion of NATO. Once again, they focus on Russia, the nature of the security agenda and intra-alliance concerns.

(1) Expanding NATO into East Central Europe would, it is argued, antagonise Russia and provide ammunition for chauvinist forces opposed to domestic reform and cooperative relations with the West. At the Budapest CSCE summit in December 1994, President Yeltsin warned that NATO expansion would create 'new poles of opposition' and engender a 'cold peace' in Europe. Similarly, Foreign Minister Kozyrev argued that NATO enlargement would provoke 'a return to the destructive logic of blocks and counterblocks'.[103] As Owen Harries has argued, 'to attempt to incorporate Eastern Europe into NATO's sphere of influence, at a time when Russia is in dangerous turmoil and when that nation's prestige and self-confidence are badly damaged, would surely be an act of outstanding folly.[104]

(2) Expanding NATO in Central and Eastern Europe could entangle the alliance in some of the ethno-national conflicts which bedevil this historically disputatious region. One worst-case scenario,

for example, is that of a future Hungarian nationalist government, facing domestic pressures at home, and emboldened by its membership of NATO, threatening to use military action to protect its ethnic kin in Romania, Serbia or Slovakia.

(3) Some argue that NATO's expansion would not in fact improve the climate of European security, but could well worsen it.[105] This is because improved security for one state may generate perceptions of insecurity in neighbouring states, thereby fostering a regional arms race and draughtboard alliance systems. NATO is thus faced with a classic 'security dilemma'.[106] For example, if Poland were to become a member of NATO, Russia might well respond by strengthening its already substantial military garrison in Kaliningrad. A strengthened Russian military presence in this area would in turn heighten security concerns in the Baltic republics and the Scandinavian countries.[107]

(4) There is a belief that NATO is not well suited to tackling many of the security challenges that the Visegrad countries are currently concerned about – an influx of refugees, economic dislocation, political unrest, nationalist agitation, and so on. As an organisation designed – in the words of NATO's first Secretary-General, Lord Ismay – to 'keep the Russians out, the Americans in and the Germans down', NATO is ill-suited to tackling many of the risks and challenges on the contemporary European security agenda.[108] 'NATO', it has been argued, 'cannot address the political and economic roots of ethnic conflicts, nor does it have the political and economic levers to contain intra-regional conflicts. The EU is better positioned in both respects'.[109]

(5) Providing credible security guarantees to East Central European countries would be costly for NATO countries, thereby further eroding the elusive 'peace dividend'. North American and West European electorates are expecting significant defence savings following the end of the Cold War, and it would be politically difficult to justify the additional expenditure that an expansion of NATO membership would entail.

(6) Although the Americans now favour the early expansion of NATO, many other alliance countries are less convinced. Some fear that, rather than enhancing their own security, expansion would weaken it (both because of the risks of 'entrapment' in nationalist conflicts and because of the dynamics of the 'security dilemma'). The Danish Prime Minister, for example, warned in October 1993 that enlargement could jeopardise 'our own security'.[110] It is therefore

essential to ensure that expansion enhances rather than weakens the overall security and effectiveness of the alliance.

(7) There are a number of military difficulties in providing security guarantees to the Visegrad countries. What would this mean in terms of SACEUR's operational planning? Would not NATO troops have to be forward deployed in Poland or Hungary, if the security guarantees were to be credible? This, however, could well be illegal under the terms of the CFE Treaty.[111] If US and West European forces were not forward deployed, would not NATO have to develop a substantial power-projection capability, above and beyond that already envisaged for NATO's new Rapid Reaction Force?[112] Moreover, extending NATO's nuclear umbrella over these new members could generate enormous political controversies in Western Europe (particularly in Germany), especially if this involved significant changes in nuclear strategy, doctrines, deployments or hardware.

(8) Once the process of enlargement begins, it may be politically difficult to halt – and this would fundamentally challenge the very nature and effectiveness of the alliance. For example, if Poland joined, why not Lithuania; or if Slovakia, why not Slovenia? The process of selective widening of NATO could rekindle memories of inter-war 'spheres of influence', and may also be potentially destabilising for those excluded, increasing regional suspicions and undermining reform.[113] On the other hand, the large-scale expansion of NATO would transform it from a collective defence alliance into a collective security organisation. This would not be welcomed by many of NATO's existing members, given the mixed record of previous collective security arrangements.

Resolving NATO's Eastern dilemmas

The question of opening up NATO to new members from the East presents the alliance with a real dilemma. NATO is currently conducting a study into the modalities of opening up to new members.[114] However, it is increasingly apparent that although expanding the alliance may solve some problems, it would generate many others. There are no easy fixes to the security concerns of the Visegrad countries. Moreover, given that many contemporary security problems in the region are *internal* to states rather than *external*, and are *economic* and *political* rather than *military*, it is not clear whether NATO can effectively address them.

In the immediate future, therefore, the wisest counsel would be to continue with the broad thrust of current NATO policies. The NACC could be upgraded as a forum for multilateral security consultation and cooperation, and military cooperation schemes (for training, military exercises and joint peacekeeping operations) could be intensified. The PFP programmes could also be made more effective in order to allow states to move closer to NATO on a 'self-selecting' basis.[115] However, an early expansion of NATO would probably be counterproductive, given the problem of the 'security dilemma' in Central and Eastern Europe.

In the long-term, the issue of NATO enlargement can best be resolved through the process of European integration. When the Visegrad four join the EU, they will participate in the Union's Common Foreign and Security Policy, which allows for, in the words of the Maastricht Treaty on European union, 'the eventual framing of a common defence policy, which might in time lead to a common defence'. They will also be eligible for membership of the WEU, an organisation which formally provides firm security guarantees for its members. However, it is only NATO that possesses the military wherewithal to give such security guarantees any credibility. Once the East Central Europeans join the EU and the WEU, therefore, NATO membership will have to follow if the WEU's security guarantees are to be more than paper promises.[116]

This still leaves the West with the thorny problem of how to avoid antagonising Russia. NATO officials have been keen to assure Yeltsin that NATO wants to build a new Europe 'not against, not without, but with Russia'.[117] Chancellor Kohl has also stressed that any expansion of the alliance must be accompanied by an 'intensive partnership' with Russia and Ukraine.[118] NATO officials now talk of pursuing a 'twin-track policy' involving the cultivation of a 'strategic partnership' with Russia on the one hand, and expansion of NATO into East Central Europe on the other. This may well take the form of a formal treaty with Russia, including greater rights of consultation and some form of non-aggression pact. Yet finessing this will require much more in the way of diplomatic skills and political vision than the West has demonstrated in recent years.[119]

One final point to note is that the issue of NATO enlargement is bound up with even more fundamental questions concerning the alliance's place and function in Europe's post-Cold War institutional architecture. Membership of NATO by the Visegrad states will undoubtedly change the character of the alliance, and may lead to a greater emphasis being placed on Article 4 commitments to collective security than to Article 5 commitments to collective defence. However, NATO is already in a process of change and adaptation. Since the end of the East–West conflict, NATO has radically revised its strategy, force structure and configuration. NATO's future is very much bound up with debates in Washington on America's role in Europe, and with debates in Europe on the nature and scope of the EU integration process. NATO's Eastern enlargement – as in the case of the EU – will therefore accelerate a process of change and restructuring within the alliance which is already well under way.[120]

East Central Europe, the EU and the WEU

Although the EU remains primarily a 'civilian power', it does have an impact on European security. Since the 1969 Hague summit, EC members have sought to coordinate some aspects of their foreign policies in the framework of European Political Cooperation (EPC). Article III of the 1987 Single European Act indicated the Community's interest in discussing the 'economic and political' aspects of security in the EPC context. More significantly, the Maastricht Treaty announced the formation of a 'Common Foreign and Security Policy' (CFSP), which, as we have seen, may in time include defence. The Treaty also recognised the WEU as 'an integral part of the development of the European Union', which may ask the WEU 'to elaborate and implement [the Union's] decisions and actions ... which have defence implications'. A declaration on the WEU attached to the Treaty also noted the member states' intention to 'build up WEU in stages as the defence component of the Union'.[121]

The growing importance of the EU's role in European security reflects the Union's role as the key forum for multilateral political and economic cooperation in Europe. The EU is not – and perhaps never will become – a multinational federal state, but it is already more than an international organisation. It is a hybrid body, combining elements of supranationalism and inter-governmentalism: as such, it has helped transform the pattern of European international relations by institutionalising multilateral consultation, cooperation and integration. The EU can therefore play an important part in addressing many of the non-military aspects of security which figure so prominently on the contemporary security agenda of East Central Europe. This has been widely recognised. Hans van den Broek, the Commissioner responsible for relations with Central and Eastern Europe, has for example stated that 'enlargement to the east is in the very first place a political issue relating to security and stability in our continent'.[122]

One major initiative launched by the EU has been the 'European Stability Pact' (also known as the 'Balladur Plan' or the 'Pact for Stability'). The idea for such a pact originated with French Prime Minister Edouard Balladur in the spring of 1993, and was adopted by the twelve member states as a joint action of the CFSP. An inaugural conference was held in Paris in May 1994 involving the six Central and East European associates, the three Baltic states and Slovenia, along with the US, Russia and representatives of relevant international organisations. This was followed by a series of round-table meetings at two regional 'tables' – one for Central Europe, the other for the Baltic area. These regional negotiations culminated in a two-day conference in Paris where the 'Stability Pact' was signed. Attached to it were no fewer than ninety-two 'good-neighbourliness and cooperation agreements and arrangements'. This, a French diplomat grandly announced, enshrined 'the most comprehensive mutual guarantees of international borders since the First World War'. The Stability Pact – which will be guaranteed by the OSCE – represented a major exercise in preventive diplomacy, whereby ethno-national conflicts would be pre-empted by agreements on borders and minority issues. The EU saw its role as being no more than a catalyst for the Stability Pact, although there was indubitably an implicit link between these bilateral agreements and future accession to the EU.[123]

The Stability Pact has been viewed with some scepticism in both Western and Eastern Europe. Nonetheless, it does reflect a growing awareness within the EU that the Union cannot remain indifferent to the security concerns of the new democracies to the east. This awareness is also apparent from the WEU's initiatives towards Central and Eastern Europe. In June 1992, the WEU Council meeting in Petersberg (near Bonn) issued a declaration which included the foundation of the Forum of Consultation.[124] This Forum is analogous to the NACC and meets at least twice a year. However, it is smaller than the NACC and more regionally focused, embracing only the nine countries of Central and Eastern Europe which have signed, or are negotiating, association agreements with the EU.[125]

More significantly the WEU decided at its Council meeting in Luxembourg on 9 May 1994 to create the status of 'Associate Partners' for the nine Central and East European members of the Forum of Consultation. This signified a qualitative deepening of relations between the WEU and the new democracies, allowing them to 'take part directly in collective European policy-making in the specific field of defence'.[126] The Associate Partners will be able to attend WEU Council meetings on a bi-weekly basis; will be able to associate themselves with WEU operations; and will be encouraged to participate in relevant exercises and planning for such operations. The Associate Partners will still not receive formal security guarantees from the WEU. Nonetheless, this move has been widely welcomed in East Central Europe as a 'qualitative and quantitative leap forward' in security links with the West.[127] It is also hoped that by becoming more closely acquainted with Western defence structures and procedures, the nine Associate Partners will be able to contribute more effectively to stability in the region. 'Through firmer institutional links with the West', Rudolf Joó has suggested, 'these countries might become not only "consumers" of security, requesting Western resources and guarantees, but increasingly security "providers", offering their capabilities in the pursuit of common objectives'. This could include contributing to crisis management, cooperation in European military equipment projects, coordination of pan-European (OSCE) issues, including verification of CFE agreements, and eventual participation in multinational formations answerable to the WEU, such as the European Corps.[128]

The Visegrad countries are therefore very keen to participate in WEU activities, particularly so given that this provides an indirect means of achieving integration in Western security structures. As the Polish defence minister Kolodziejczyk has observed,

> Our chances for integration with the WEU are much greater than chances for entry into NATO. All the more so as the WEU is a component of NATO and therefore this is a means of entering into the European defence system if not by the front door then by the kitchen entrance. This represents a very tempting proposal which we will certainly take up one hundred per cent.[129]

Conclusion: weaving a security 'web' in East Central Europe

The end of the East–West conflict in Europe created a security vacuum in East Central Europe. It also radically changed the nature of the security agenda in the region. Today, many of the security problems facing the Visegrad states – particularly those associated with ethno-national identity – are internal to states rather than inter-state in nature. Moreover, many of these security concerns are of an economic, political, societal or environmental character, and are not amenable to straightforward military or diplomatic solutions.

There are therefore no simple solutions to the new security concerns of East Central Europe. Restructured armed forces and new national defence doctrines cannot by themselves ensure national security; the OSCE cannot easily be transformed into an effective collective security organisation; expanding NATO generates as many problems as it solves; and the WEU is in no position to offer credible security guarantees to its Associate Partners. There are 'no easy answers or quick fixes to security issues in Central Europe. The West should be aiming to diminish steadily rather than abolish overnight the security concerns of Poland, the CSFR and Hungary'.[130]

To this end, a multifaceted and comprehensive security 'web' must be woven in the wider region. It should consist of a series of criss-crossing and overlapping relationships and structures, embracing Germany and Russia, and stretching from the Baltic area to South-Eastern Europe. This security web will have many strands: new, defensively orientated armed forces and military doctrines; bilateral treaties guaranteeing minority rights and territorial borders; regional organisations for multilateral cooperation (such as the Visegrad group, the CEI, the Baltic Council and Alpe Adria); European legal conventions with provision for minority rights (within the framework of the Council of Europe); functional military cooperation (NATO's PFP); pan-European structures for preventive diplomacy, conflict prevention and crisis management (OSCE); and participation in West European defence and security decision making (WEU Associate Partner status). Above all, in weaving this security web, it is essential to remember that security in East Central Europe cannot simply be provided by military security guarantees, alliance commitments or balance-of-power arrangements. Even more important is the task of promoting reconciliation between different communities and ethno-national groups; consolidating democratic institutions and practices;

nurturing economic recovery and social justice; and encouraging multilateral cooperation and supra-national integration.[131]

Such a complex and multidimensional security web cannot provide a cast-iron solution to the diverse security problems facing the Visegrad four. Nonetheless, it does at least offer a feasible approach for developing a framework capable of addressing the multifaceted security challenges facing the region on the eve of the twenty-first century. Weaving such a security web in East Central Europe also provides a means to extend eastwards the transatlantic 'security community' – a community of states in which war, or the threat of war, no longer plays any part in relations between states. Extending this security community eastwards offers the best hope of building the type of 'pacific union' envisaged by Kant in his classic, *Perpetual Peace: A Philosophical Sketch*.[132] Building such a pacific union will be a long and difficult task. Much will depend on the political maturity and self-restraint of the peoples of Central and Eastern Europe. But it also requires that, in the words of Václav Havel,

> the West come to understand that the great task of self-defense against the communist menace has been supplanted today by an even more difficult task: to assume courageously, in its own interests and in the general interest, its share of the responsibility for the new organization of things in the entire northern hemisphere.[133]

Endnotes

1 'Report from a town under siege', quoted in *Eastern Europe*, Amsterdam, Time-Life Books, 1986, p. 39.

2 Quoted by the Minister for Foreign Affairs of Romania, Mr Nastase, in 'A new security order in Europe', *Symposium of the Assembly of the Western European Union*, Berlin, 31 March–2 April 1992, official record, Paris, Assembly of the WEU, 1992, p. 27.

3 W. B. Gallie, 'Essentially contested concepts', in Max Black, ed., *The Importance of Language*, Englewood Cliffs, Prentice Hall, 1962, pp. 121–46.

4 Hedley Bull, *The Anarchical Society*, London, Macmillan, 1977, p. 18.

5 J. Ann Tickner, 'Re-visioning security', in Ken Booth and Steve Smith, eds, *International Relations Theory Today*, Cambridge, Polity, 1995, pp. 175–97.

6 We have already noted the concept of 'democratic security' advocated by the Council of Europe (see p. 194). For an analysis of the wider dimensions of security see Barry Buzan's influential book *People, States and Fear: An Agenda for International Security in the Post-Cold War Europe*, 2nd edn, Hemel Hempstead, Wheatsheaf, 1991.

7   Joseph Rothschild, *Return to Diversity: A Political History of East Central Europe Since World War II*, Oxford, Oxford University Press, 1989, p. 8.

8   Martin Wight, *Power Politics*, London, Penguin for the RIIA, 1979, pp. 160–1.

9   *Ibid.*, p. 166.

10   See Hedley Bull, *op. cit.*

11   John Mearsheimer, 'Back to the future: instability in Europe after the Cold War', *International Security*, 15, no. 1, summer 1990, pp. 5–56 (p. 47). See also John Gray, 'From post-communism to civil society: the reemergence of history and the decline of the Western model', *Social Philosophy and Policy*, 10, no. 2, summer 1993, pp. 26–50 (especially p. 48).

12   Philip Zelikow, 'The new concert of Europe', *Survival*, 34, no. 2, summer 1992, pp. 12–30.

13   Nick Rengger took this 'felicitous phrase' from Stanley Hoffman. See Rengger's thoughtful article, 'No longer "a tournament of distinctive knights"? Systemic transition and the priority of international order', in Mike Bowker and Robin Brown, eds, *From Cold War to Collapse: Theory and World Politics in the 1980s*, Cambridge, Cambridge University Press, 1993, pp. 145–74 (p. 149).

14   For a discussion of the relationship between nationalism and war see Stephan Van Evera, 'Hypotheses on nationalism and war', *International Security*, 18, no. 4, spring 1994, pp. 5–39.

15   See Michael Watson, *Contemporary Minority Nationalism*, London, Routledge, 1990; Istvan Deak, 'Uncovering Eastern Europe's dark history', *Orbis*, 34, no. 1, winter 1989, pp. 51–65; and Neil Ascherson, 'Old conflicts in the new Europe', *Independent on Sunday*, 18 February 1990, pp. 3–5.

16   *The Guardian*, 21 February 1991, p. 4.

17   Gil Loescher, *Refugee Movements and International Security*, Adelphi Paper 268, London, Brassey's for the IISS, 1992; and Michael Shafir, 'Immigrants, refugees, and postcommunism', *RFE/RL Research Report*, 3, no. 23, 10 June 1994, pp. 33–5.

18   'We are no longer confronted with an enemy, but with dangers; and it was easier to see the enemy, but it is not so easy to see the dangers. What exactly are the dangers?
       – Religious and ethnic conflicts, putting in doubt existing political borders.
       – Mass migration on a new scale of the High Middle Ages, ie., mass migration of peoples.
       – Political destabilization in Eastern and Central Europe and first of all in the former Soviet Union.
       – Dangers created by the international economy. That means, dangers created by competition and also by a tendency to economic protectionism.
       – Temptation of hegemony. This temptation concerns not only the United States, but also Germany in Europe and Russia in Eastern and Central Europe.
       – Totalitarian temptation. That means lack of confidence on the domestic and international scene when the legitimacy of power seems to be weak.
       – The feeling of insecurity, which is extremely important in my sense, in the definition of the present situation.'

Bronislaw Geremek, 'Post-communist challenges', in Armand Clesse, Richard Cooper and Yoshikazu Sakamoto, eds, *The International System After the Collapse of the East–West Order*, Dordrecht, Martinus Nijhoff, 1994, pp. 356–61 (p. 360).

19 Kathleen Mihalisko, 'Belarus: neutrality gives way to "collective security"', *RFE/RL Research Report*, 2, no. 17, 23 April 1993, pp. 24–31.

20 Even a defence 'hawk' like Brzezinski acknowledges that 'neither the alliance nor its prospective new members [from East Central Europe] are facing any imminent threat' and that talk of a Russian military threat 'is not justified, either by actual circumstances or even by worst-case scenarios for the near future'. Quoted in Michael E. Brown, 'The flawed logic of NATO expansion', *Survival*, 37, no. 1, spring 1995, pp. 34–52 (p. 36).

21 See Alfred A. Reisch, 'Hungary: foreign policy reorientation a success', *Report on Eastern Europe*, nos 51/52, 20 December 1991.

22 For details see *The Yugoslav Crisis and its Impact on Hungary*, Tamas Wachsler (Special Rapporteur), Report by the Defence and Security Committee of the North Atlantic Assembly, November 1992 (AJ 247 DSC(92)8), Brussels, North Atlantic Assembly, 1992.

23 Howard Frost has argued that this security vacuum derives from the 'region's lack of international structure, uncertain democracy, weak economies, ethnic strife, and potentially troublesome neighbours to the East'. H. Frost, 'Eastern Europe's search for security', *Orbis*, 37, no. 1, winter 1993, pp. 37–53 (p. 37).

24 'President Havel visits NATO', *NATO Review*, 39, no. 2, April 1991, pp. 29–35.

25 Raymond Taras and Marshal Zeringue, 'Grand strategy in a post-bipolar world: interpreting the final Soviet response', *Review of International Studies*, 18, no. 4, October 1992, pp. 355–75 (p. 366).

26 On Soviet 'new thinking' in the military and security sphere, see Michael McGuire, *Perestroika and Soviet National Security*, Washington, DC, Brookings Institution, 1991; Christoph Bluth, *New Thinking in Soviet Military Policy*, London, Pinter, 1990; R. I. Garthoff, *Deterrence and the Revolution in Soviet Military Doctrine*, Washington, DC, Brookings Institution, 1990; Derek Leebaert and Timothy Dickinson, eds, *Soviet Strategy and New Military Thinking*, Cambridge, Cambridge University Press, 1992; and Stephen Shenfield, *The Nuclear Predicament: Explorations in Soviet Ideology*, London, Pinter for the RIIA, 1987.

27 A. Kazerznev, 'The last parade of the southern group of forces', *Komsomolskaya Pravda*, 6 June 1991.

28 Jonathan Eyal, 'Central and Eastern Europe', in Alex Pravda, ed., *Yearbook of Soviet Foreign Relations: 1991 Edition*, London, I. B. Tauris, 1991, p. 98.

29 Jan B. de Weydenthal, 'Prospects for Polish–Soviet relations', *Report on Eastern Europe*, 2, no. 38, September 20, 1991, pp. 11–14.

30 For example the still unpublished Statute of the Joint Armed Forces and Agencies in Command of Them in Wartime, which dates back to 1979–80. This Statute, it is believed, regulated the full transfer of national decision-making powers to Soviet commanders in the event of war. See Douglas Clarke, 'The military institutions of the Warsaw Pact', *Report on Eastern Europe*, no. 49, 7 December 1990.

31   Douglas Clarke, 'Warsaw Pact: the transformation begins', *Report on Eastern Europe*, no. 25, 22 June 1990.

32   Vladimir V. Kusin, 'Security concerns in Central Europe', *Report on Eastern Europe*, 2, no. 10, 8 March 1991, p. 25–40.

33   Gerard Holden, *The Warsaw Pact: Soviet Security and Bloc Politics*, Oxford, Basil Blackwell, 1989; and Jonathan Eyal, ed., *The Warsaw Pact and the Balkans*, London, Macmillan for the RUSI, 1989.

34   The Polish military doctrine of February 1990 was very explicit on this point: 'The armed forces of the Republic of Poland will not undertake any actions that could cause other states to have concern for their own security'. Quoted in Michael Sadykiewicz and Douglas Clarke, 'The New Polish defense doctrine: a further step toward sovereignty', *Report on Eastern Europe*, no. 18, 4 May 1990.

35   Poland adopted two documents which constitute the basis of a new national defence doctrine in November 1992. Hungary's current national security doctrine was adopted in the spring of 1993. See Jan B. de Weydenthal, 'Poland's security policy', *RFE/RL Research Report*, 2, no. 14, 2 April 1993, pp. 31–3; Alfred A. Reisch, 'The Hungarian army in transition', *RFE/RL Research Report*, 2, no. 10, 5 March 1993, pp. 38–52; and Jan Obrman, 'Military reform in the Czech Republic', *RFE/RL Research Report*, 2, no. 41, 15 October 1993, pp. 37–42.

36   See Douglas Clarke, 'A realignment of military forces in Central Europe', *Report on Eastern Europe*, 2, no. 10, 8 March 1991, pp. 41–5.

37   Sharon Fisher, 'The Slovak arms industry', *RFE/RL Research Report*, 2, no. 38, 24 September 1993, pp. 26–30. For the wider picture see Douglas L. Clarke, 'Eastern Europe's troubled arms industries', Parts 1 and 2, *RFE/RL Research Report*, 3, nos 14 and 21, 8 April and 27 May 1994 respectively, pp. 35–43 and 28–39.

38   Louisa Vinton, 'The Walesa Presidency takes shape', *Report on Eastern Europe*, 2, no. 7, 15 February 1991, pp. 10–16.

39   Reisch, *op. cit.*, p. 48.

40   On the Hungarian case see for example Istvan Gyarmati, 'A Hungarian security policy for the 1990s', *Defense and Disarmament Alternatives*, 3, no. 4, April 1990, pp. 3–4.

41   In Hungary for example, almost one-third of professional soldiers live near or below the poverty line. Moreover, Hungarian Army Commander Colonel General Kalman Lorincz has argued that cuts in the defence budget will negatively affect the training of air force pilots, the development of airborne and UN peacekeeping units, military education and the training of reservists. For a comprehensive review of the present condition of the Hungarian armed forces see Reisch, *op. cit.*, pp. 38–52.

42   The purely military element in Czechoslovakia's security policy is relatively small. As Jiří Dienstbier once noted: 'Military doctrine? It makes sense for the United States. But for Czechoslovakia?' Quoted in *The Economist*, 30 March 1991, p. 47.

43   Alfred A. Reisch, 'Hungary acquire's MiG-29s from Russia', *RFE/RL Research Report*, 2, no. 33, 20 August 1993, pp. 49–56 (p. 55).

44   For full details see Frost, *op. cit.* pp. 50–3; Alfred A. Reisch, 'New bilateral

agreements', *Report on Eastern Europe*, no. 45, 8 November 1991; and Joshu Spero, 'The Budapest–Prague–Warsaw triangle: Central European security after the Visegrad summit', *European Security*, no. 1, 1992, pp. 58–83.

45 Vladimir Kusin, 'Security concerns in Central Europe', *Report on Eastern Europe*, 8 March 1991, p. 35. See also *Financial Times*, 28 February 1991, p. 6.

46 *BBC Summary of World Broadcasts*, International Affairs: USSR and East European Relations, EE/1029 A2/1, 25 March 1991, London, BBC.

47 Gabriel Munuera, *Preventing Armed Conflict in Europe: Lessons From Recent Experience*, Chaillot Paper 15/16, Paris, WEU Institute for Security Studies, June 1994, p. 19.

48 Jan B. de Weydenthal, 'The Cracow summit', *Report on Eastern Europe*, 2, no. 43, 25 October 1991, pp. 27–9.

49 For details see Douglas Clarke, 'Hungary proposes border security zone', RAD Background Report/181, Hungary, *Radio Free Europe Research*, 27 September 1989.

50 For details see 'Military and security notes on Poland', *RFE/RL Research Report*, 1, no. 44, 6 November 1992, p. 61.

51 Paul Latawski, 'NATO and East Central Europe: the case of Poland', in Andrew Williams, ed., *Reorganising Eastern Europe: European Institutions and the Refashioning of Europe's Security Architecture*, Aldershot, Dartmouth, 1994, pp. 41–56.

52 Mihalisko, *op. cit.*, p. 31. See also Karen Dawisha and Bruce Parrott, *Russia and the New States of Eurasia. The Politics of Upheaval*, London, Macmillan, 1994, pp. 213–15.

53 Ian J. Brzezinski, 'Polish–Ukrainian relations: Europe's neglected strategic axis', *Survival*, 35, no. 3, autumn 1993, pp. 26–37 (p. 31). Sergey Stepashin, the chairman of the Russian Duma's Defence and Security Committee, described this proposal as a blatant attempt to impose a *cordon sanitaire* around Russia. See Dawisha and Parrott, *op. cit.*, p. 212.

54 'The fact that similarly extensive contractual institutionalisation of multi-layered cooperation has failed to materialise is not only connected with the special reservations of individual states. It is also linked with the sincere declarations on all sides that a new military alliance or even a separate bloc is not the desired goal. This serves to calm down some of the more mistrustful neighbours, such as Romania and Serbia, and signal to the West that these countries definitely want membership in the European Union and NATO. For this reason, Kiev's proposal to create a kind of special zone in the territory between NATO and Russia was unanimously rejected.' M. Hatschukjan, 'Foreign policy reorientations in East Central Europe', *Aussenpolitik*, 45, no. 1, 1994, p. 57.

55 The phrase is taken from Fred Halliday's influential book, *The Making of the Second Cold War*, London, Verso, 1983.

56 At Stockholm in 1986 a document on confidence- and security-building measures was adopted. This was subsequently expanded and improved in the Vienna 1990 and 1992 documents.

57 For an analysis of proposals to create such a collective security regime, and an assessment of their strengths and weaknesses, see Adrian Hyde-Price,

European Security Beyond the Cold War: Four Scenarios for the Year 2010, London, Sage, 1991, pp. 214–25.

58   For details and analysis see A. Hyde-Price, 'CSCE in 1991', in Alan J. Day, ed., *The Annual Register 1992*, London, Longman, 1992.

59   The Emergency Mechanism provides for a meeting of the Committee of Senior Officials to be convened at short notice if at least 13 states agree. It was subsequently invoked in July, August, September and October 1991 in order to discuss the deteriorating situation in Yugoslavia.

60   The violent actions by OMON security forces in Lithuania caused 22 CSCE states to invoke the Conference on the Human Dimension (CDH) mechanism agreed at the third follow-up meeting in Vienna. This mechanism allows other states to raise suspected human rights abuses at any time. The Soviet Union vetoed the calling of a special CSCE meeting to discuss the events in the Baltic republics, but the mechanism did at least provide a chance for the international community to register its disapproval.

61   Walter Kemp, 'Giving teeth to the CSCE', *The World Today*, October 1994, pp. 183–5.

62   Speech at NATO's headquarters on 21 March 1991.

63   The continuing commitment of the East Central Europeans to the further institutionalisation of the CSCE was apparent from the Czechoslovakia Memorandum on European Security of 9 April 1991. The Czechoslovak Memorandum called for the adoption of an Emergency Mechanism (subsequently achieved at the Berlin CSCE meeting in June 1991); the further development of the Conflict Prevention Centre; the strengthening of the CSCE procedures for the peaceful settlement of disputes; and the eventual building of 'multinational armed forces of the CSCE member states by way of bilateral and multilateral cooperation'. For details see 'Text' of Memorandum on European Security, in *FBIS-EEU-91-069*, 10 April 1991, Washington, DC, Foreign Broadcasting Information Service, pp. 8–9. The 'Prague Thesis' subsequently agreed upon by the Foreign Ministers of Czechoslovakia and Germany on 11 April 1991 stated that 'The Czechoslovak memorandum on security in Europe represents a significant contribution to the continuation of such developments in Europe'; *FBIS-EEU-91-071*, 12 April 1991, p. 9. Furthermore, at the bilateral meeting on 27 September 1991 (at which they discussed, inter alia, the Yugoslav crisis), Presidents Walesa and Havel called for the creation of peacekeeping forces under the auspices of the CSCE or another international organisation. See *Report on Eastern Europe*, 2, no. 39, 27 September 1991, p. 42.

64   A. Heraclides, *Helsinki-II and its Aftermath: The Making of the CSCE into an International Organization*, London, Pinter, 1993.

65   'The task of the High Commissioner for National Minorities is to provide '"early warning" and, as appropriate, "early action" at the earliest possible stage in regard to tensions involving national minority issues that have the potential to develop into a conflict affecting peace, stability, or relations between participating states.' Document of the 1992 Helsinki follow-up meeting, *The Challenges of Change*, 'Decisions', Chapter 1, para. 23. The full mandate of the HCNM is contained in Chapter 11, Helsinki, CSCE, 1992. For analysis and commentary see K. Huber and R. Zaagman, 'Towards the

prevention of ethnic conflict in the CSCE: the High Commissioner on National Minorities and other developments', *International Journal on Group Rights*, 1, no. 1, 1993, pp. 51–68; and D. Chigas, 'Bridging the gap between theory and practice: The CSCE High Commissioner on National Minorities', *Helsinki Monitor*, 5, no. 3, 1994, pp. 27–41.

66 See A. Hyde-Price, 'The CSCE in 1992', in Alan J. Day, ed., *The Annual Register 1993*, London, Longman, 1993, pp. 412–13.

67 'Towards a genuine partnership in a new era', CSCE summit of heads of state and government, Budapest, CSCE, December 1994, paragraph 8.

68 M. Lucas, ed., *The CSCE in the 1990s: Constructing European Security and Cooperation*, Baden-Baden, Nomos Verlagsgesellschaft, 1993.

69 *CSCE Newsletter*, 1, no. 9, 7 October 1994, p. 1.

70 For details see the two CSCE documents *Letter From the HCNM Concerning the Hungarian National Minority in the Slovak Republic and Comments Thereto*, Rome, Secretariat of the Conference on Security and Cooperation in Europe, Prague, 29 September 1993, and *Visit of the CSCE High Commissioner on National Minorities to Slovakia and Hungary*, Secretariat of the Conference on Security and Cooperation in Europe, Prague, CSCE communication no. 122, Prague, 23 April 1993.

71 See Richard Dalton, 'The role of the CSCE', in Hugh Miall, ed., *Minority Rights in Europe. The Scope for a Transnational Regime*, London, Pinter for the RIIA, 1994, pp. 99–111; and Konrad J. Huber, 'The CSCE and ethnic conflict in the East', *RFE/RL Research Report*, 2, no. 31, 27 August 1993, pp. 30–6.

72 Fourth paragraph of the Document on CBM and Certain Aspects of Security and Disarmament included in the 1975 Helsinki Final Act.

73 See Konrad J. Huber, 'The CSCE's new role in the East: conflict prevention', *RFE/RL Research Report*, 3, no. 31, 12 August 1994, pp. 23–30; and Wilhelm Höynck, 'CSCE works to develop its conflict prevention potential', *NATO Review*, 42, no. 2, August 1994, pp. 16–22.

74 In mid-1990, the new Hungarian Foreign Minister, Geza Jeszenszky, declared 'Above all, we want to reorientate Hungary's foreign policy towards the West, to move as close as possible to Western Europe, economically, culturally, and politically, ... and the Cold War is over ... it no longer makes sense to declare oneself neutral.' Alfred Reisch, 'Hungary: interview with Foreign Minister Geza Jeszensky', *Report on Eastern Europe*, 1, no. 30, 27 July 1990, pp. 17–18.

75 Václav Havel called the alliance 'the only functioning, democratic security structure on the continent today', whilst his foreign minister, Jiří Dienstbier, when asked what he thought about NATO replied, 'I have only one objection. We are not a member'. Quoted by Mient Jan Faber, 'Good morning Europe!', in Mary Kaldor, ed., *Europe From Below: An East–West Dialogue*, London, Verso, 1991, p. 146.

76 'Those who live in the grey area look for a gleam in the West', *The Economist*, 30 March 1991, p. 48.

77 The arrangements for this diplomatic liaison are that former WTO states would not have missions inside the NATO complex, but that they would designate senior people in their embassies in Belgium to undertake this

function. They could liaise with NATO members' national missions and with specified senior people on the NATO International Staff. Much of this liaison takes place through the office of the Assistant Secretary-General for Political Affairs, Henning Wegener.

78   For further details, see Simon Lunn, 'Alliance parliamentarians develop contacts with the East: 35th annual session of the North Atlantic Assembly', *NATO Review*, 37, no. 6, December 1989, pp. 19–23.

79   'Partnership with the Countries of Central and Eastern Europe', statement issued by the NAC meeting in Ministerial Session in Copenhagen on 6 and 7 June 1991, published in *NATO Review*, 39, no. 3, June 1991, pp. 28–9.

80   The Copenhagen NAC committed NATO to: regular meetings of officials and experts to exchange views and information on a wide range of security issues; intensified military contacts between senior NATO military authorities and their counterparts in the East; participation of Central and East Europe in NATO's 'Third Dimension' activities (i.e., scientific and environmental programmes); an expansion of NATO's information programmes in the region; and the encouragement of greater contacts between the North Atlantic Assembly and parliamentarians in the East.

81   'Havel secures little but fine words from Nato', *Financial Times*, 23 March 1991. NATO Secretary-General Wörner also told the Grand National Assembly of Bulgaria on 13 June 1991 that 'NATO's very existence makes you, our neighbours to the East more secure, in the sense that there is a spill-over effect of the stability which NATO generates'.

82   Speech by Secretary-General Manfred Wörner, at the conference jointly sponsored by NATO and the government of the CSFR on the future of European security held at the Cernin Palace, Ministry of Foreign Affairs, Prague, 25–26 April 1991.

83   Manfred Wörner, 'Shaping the alliance for the future', *NATO Review*, 42, no. 1, February 1994, pp. 3–6 (p. 5)

84   'US–German call for closer Nato ties to the East', *Financial Times*, 4 October 1991.

85   'Alliance gets down to practicalities with former foes', *Financial Times*, 7 November, 1991.

86   For details see Amedeo de Franchis, 'The CFE Treaty – the role of the High Level Working Group', *NATO Review*, 40, no. 5, October 1992, pp. 12–16.

87   The Ad Hoc Group's report for the NACC ministerial meeting in June 1993 was published in *NATO Review*, 41, no. 4, August 1993, pp. 30–5.

88   Manfred Wörner, 'A vigorous alliance – a motor for peaceful change in Europe', *NATO Review*, 40, no. 6, December 1992, pp. 3–9 (p. 6).

89   See Suzanne Crow, 'Russian views on an eastwards expansion of NATO', *RFE/RL Research Report*, 2, no. 41, 15 October 1993, pp. 21–4.

90   For the background to this initiative see Michael Mihalka, 'Squaring the circle: NATO's offer to the East', *RFE/RL Research Report*, 3, no. 12, 25 March 1994, pp. 1–9.

91   'Partnership For Peace: Invitation', issued by the heads of state and government participating in the meeting of the North Atlantic Council held at NATO headquarters, Brussels, on 10–11 January 1994, press communique M-1 (94)2. The PFP invitation also invites participating states to send

permanent liaison officers to NATO headquarters and a separate partnership coordination cell at Mons (Belgium), to carry out, under the authority of the North Atlantic Council, 'the military planning necessary to implement the Partnership programmes'.

92 US Secretary of Defence William Perry has made it clear to the House National Security Committee that 'Many members of Partnership for Peace will never qualify for NATO membership'. Whereas for the Visegrad countries the PFP was 'clearly a path toward full membership', the Central Asian and Caucasian republics were 'places where I think it is virtually unthinkable that they would become full members of NATO'. 'US limits NATO's expansion East', *The Guardian*, 9 February 1995.

93 The former Polish Minister of Defence, Piotr Kolodziejczyk, has made it clear that the Poles 'treat our participation in the Partnership for Peace initiative as the path towards NATO'. See his article 'Poland – a future NATO ally', *NATO Review*, 42, no. 5, October 1994, pp. 7–10 (p. 9). Similarly, the Chief of the Foreign Affairs Directorate in the Czech Ministry of Defence, Jaromir Novotný, has stated that 'We see the PFP as a kind of test of maturity for the novices seeking eventual NATO membership'. See 'The Czech Republic – an active partner with NATO', *NATO Review*, 42, no. 3, June 1994, pp. 12–15 (p. 12).

94 President Clinton made this comment during his address to the *Sejm* in Warsaw, 7 July 1994.

95 Dana H. Allin, 'Can containment work again?', *Survival*, 37, no. 1, spring 1995, pp. 53–65 (p. 63).

96 President Havel has argued that 'democratic forces' in Russia would recognise that 'NATO is not Russia's enemy but its partner, that the expansion of NATO would bring Russia closer to democracy and prosperity'. Russia would protest at the expansion of NATO only if 'chauvinistic, Great Russian, crypto-totalitarian forces' gained power there. If the West were to yield to such protests, 'It would would mean the collapse of all the values the West stands for. It would mean encouraging imperial ambitions. It would mean selling out the nations that have invested so much in the struggle for their own freedom, and selling out the West's own freedom as well.' Václav Havel, 'Why NATO must not say no to the Czechs', *The Guardian*, 19 October 1993.

97 Grzegorz Kostrzewa-Zorbas has argued that 'NATO (and the WEU's) policy of nondifferentiation among the members of the former Warsaw Treaty Organization is broadly seen in the countries of Central Europe as proof of a lasting Yalta-like, Western-supported division of Europe. Failure to differentiate means failure to encourage change, especially among those who, like the Russian people, still have to make their final choice, a choice of geostrategic importance'. See his article 'Security for the East Europeans', *Problems of Communism*, XLI, nos 1–2, January 1992, pp. 148–9 (p. 148).

98 In the words of US Republican senator Richard Lugar, 'NATO will either expand or go out of business'. Quoted in Alfred A. Reisch, 'Central and Eastern Europe's quest for NATO membership', *RFE/RL Research Report*, 2, no. 28, 9 July 1993, pp. 33–47 (p. 46).

99   Theop van den Doel, *Central Europe: The New Allies? The Road From Visegrad to Brussels*, Boulder, Westview, 1994, p. 8.

100 Hungarian Foreign Minister Jeszenszky has proposed the conclusion of political treaties between NATO and the East Central European countries based on the French model, i.e., without belonging to the alliance's military command. This has been criticised by some in NATO as precisely the sort of step which would undermine the credibility of the alliance's mutual defence commitments and lead to the unravelling of NATO itself. See Alfred A. Reisch, 'Central Europe's disappointments and hopes', *RFE/RL Research Report*, 3, no. 12, 25 March 1994, pp. 18–37 (p. 27).

101 One leading Polish foreign policy analyst has recently suggested that in order to observe strictly Article 3, Point 2 in the May 1992 Polish–Russian State Treaty (which stipulates that 'neither side will allow that from her territory a third Power or Powers will make an act of aggression against the other Contracting Power'), 'it would be necessary to introduce in the treaty of Poland's access to NATO a clause concerning non-stationing of nuclear arms (the Norwegian precedent) and of the absence of foreign troops, bases and permanent infrastructures on her territory (the French precedent). This certainly would not exclude periodical exercises concordant with the rules of confidence-building measures agreed upon by the CSCE partners, nor facilities aiming at improving NATO forces' capability for peace-keeping or peace-making operations in Central-Eastern Europe.' Janusz Stefanowicz, 'Central Europe between Germany and Russia: a view from Poland', *Security Dialogue*, 26, no. 1, March 1995, pp. 55–64 (p. 63).

102 The shifting mood within NATO on this question was apparent in November 1992 when Dick Cheney, the former US Secretary of Defence, argued that offering membership to Poland, Czechoslovakia and Hungary was the best way of ensuring regional stability: 'I, for one, would advocate that eventually we will want to expand NATO and move it to the East'. *Research Report*, 13 November 1992, p. 63. The policy of the Clinton administration is summed up by the oft-repeated refrain, 'NATO is going to expand. It's not a question of whether – it's when and how'. See Michael Mihalka, 'Creeping toward the East', *Transition*, 1, no. 1, 30 January 1995, pp. 80–5.

103 'Russia rejects NATO status for the former East Bloc allies', *The Guardian*, 28 October 1993. It should be noted that – *pace* Václav Havel – that 'there is a solid consensus within Russia on the undesirability of Eastern Europe's joining NATO' which embraces the nationalists as well as liberal internationalists like Kozyrev. See Allen Lynch, 'After Empire: Russia and its Western neighbours', *RFE/RL Research Report*, 3, no. 12, 25 March 1994, pp. 10–17.

104 He continues, 'It could well provide a catalyst that would enable extreme chauvinistic elements in Russia to exploit frustrations, resentments and wounded national pride in ways that would have unpleasant consequences both internally and internationally'. Owen Harries, 'The collapse of "The West"', *Foreign Affairs*, 72, no. 4, September–October 1993, pp. 41–53 (p. 43).

105 This point was recognised by the former US Secretary of Defense Les Aspin, who argued that one of the advantages of PFP was that 'it avoids drawing

new security lines across the map of Europe that are liable to be destabilizing. Critics who wanted immediate NATO expansion have been allowed to ignore the issue of which countries should be admitted and in what sequence. It's not trivial. What would it have said about countries that were taken in right now? Would it signal to hardliners in Russia that it was OK to bully countries that were left out? Instead of drawing new lines that divide nations, the Partnership for Peace will establish new lines that connect nations.' Les Aspin, 'New Europe, new NATO', *NATO Review*, 42, no. 1, February 1994, pp. 12–14 (pp. 12–13).

106   For a thoughtful discussion of this influential concept, see Nicholas J. Wheeler and Ken Booth, 'The security dilemma', in John Baylis and N. J. Rengger, eds, *Dilemmas of World Politics. International Issues in a Changing World*, Oxford, Clarendon Press, 1992, pp. 29–60.

107   'A dream ticket for a disgruntled army', *The Guardian*, 15 December 1993.

108   This was acknowledged by Manfred Wörner when he addressed a conference in Bucharest on 4 July 1991: 'What NATO cannot offer is immediate membership, as the formal security guarantees do not provide a remedy to the specific ills of the region. If it is true that we have moved from the perspective of war to the difficulties of internal growth pains and intermittent problems of national crises, then the array of tools which we must jointly elaborate must go beyond the tools we used to employ to prevent Great Power conflagration'.

109   Michael E. Brown, *op. cit.*, p. 47.

110   'Back in the arms of Boris', *The Guardian*, 21 October 1993.

111   Article IV, paragraph 5 of the CFE Treaty seems to allow foreign troops to be deployed only in countries belonging to their pre-1990 military alliance: 'state forces belonging to the same group of state parties may locate battle tanks, armoured combat vehicles and artillery in active units in each of the areas described in this article...'.

112   For a discussion of the military implications of enlargement see Ronald D. Asmus, Richard L. Kugler and F. Stephen Larrabee, 'NATO expansion: the next steps', *Survival*, 37, no. 1, spring 1995, pp. 7–34 (pp. 14–20).

113   This fear has been articulated by, inter alia, Lithuanian President Brazauskas and Foreign Minister Gylys. On several occasions, they have argued that limited NATO expansion would increase tension and might lead to new divisions in Europe. Saulius Girnius, 'Reaching West whilst eyeing Russia', *Transition*, 1, no. 1, 1995, pp. 14–18 (p. 16).

114   'While it is premature to anticipate the results of this study, I can state with complete confidence that enlargement of the Alliance, when it occurs, will be done in a way that *preserves* the coherence and effectiveness of our decision-making, does *not* impair our core defence functions, and upholds the principles and objectives of the Washington Treaty'. Willy Claes, 'NATO and the evolving Euro-Atlantic security architecture', *NATO Review*, 42, no. 1, December 1994–January 1995, pp. 3–8 (pp. 4–5).

115   See for example Ole Diehl, 'Opening NATO to the East', *The World Today*, December 1993, pp. 222–3.

116   Willem Van Eekelen, the former Secretary-General of the WEU, has described this sequence as the 'Royal road'. In a speech to the Knokke Conference of

24 September 1993 entitled 'Transatlantic Relations in a New Context: A View from the WEU', he argued for 'first extending the EC, then WEU, and finally [considering] membership of NATO'. This 'Royal road' is not popular in the USA, where there is a broad consensus that 'the Alliance needs to avoid the trap of NATO expansion becoming hostage to the internal workings of the EU, over which Washington has little influence'. See Asmus, Kugler and Larrabee, *op. cit.*, p. 11.

117 'Yeltsin warns of war if Russia votes no', *The Guardian*, 10 December 1993.

118 'Europe's Post-Post-Cold-War defence wobbles into action', *The Economist*, 10 December 1994, p. 39. For the Russian view of elements of a future Russian–NATO partnership see Andrei Kozyrev, 'Russia and NATO: a partnership for a united and peaceful Europe', *NATO Review*, 42, no. 4, August 1994, pp. 3–6; and Alexei Pushkov, 'Russia and the West: an endangered relationship?', *NATO Review*, 42, no. 1, February 1994, pp. 19–23.

119 Hilmar Linnenkamp has pointed out that NATO's current policy towards Russia seems to be – ironically paraphrasing Lord Ismay's famous dictum about NATO's role in the 1950s – 'Keep the Russians in (in NACC, that is, or in a political and military coordination between Vancouver and Vladivostok), keep the Russians out (of NATO, at least in the near future), and keep the Russians down (as a future threat to her neighbours)'. H. Linnenkamp, 'The North Atlantic Cooperation Council – a stabilizing element of a new European order?', in Hans-Georg Ehrhart, Anna Kreikemeyer and Andrei Zagorski, eds, *The Former Soviet Union and European Security: Between Integration and Re-Nationalization*, Baden-Baden, Nomos Verlagsgesellschaft, 1993, pp. 219–28 (p. 225). See also Michael Mihalka, 'European–Russian security and NATO's partnership for peace', *RFE/RL Research Report*, 3, no. 33, 26 August 1994, pp. 34–45; and S. Neil MacFarlane, 'Russian, the West and European security', *Survival*, 35, no. 3, autumn 1993, pp. 3–25.

120 'The kind of NATO that could respond to Europe's new strategic challenges would bear little resemblance to the NATO of the Cold War. It would be based on a new political bargain between the United States and Europe, a different set of political and military understandings, as well as a new relationship with the East. This bargain would simultaneously expand the alliance's strategic horizon geographically and find new ways to share responsibilities and burdens. NATO's rationale and mission would be defined anew.' Ronald D. Asmus, Richard L. Kugler and F. Stephen Larrabee, 'Building a New NATO', *Foreign Affairs*, September–October 1993, pp. 28–40 (p. 31).

121 'Declaration on the Role of the Western European Union and its Relations with the European Union', issued by WEU members and noted by the 'Declaration on Western European Union' adopted by EC members along with the Treaty on European Union and its Protocols (all to be found in the 'Treaty on European Union', 7 February 1992, Cm 1934, European Communities, no. 3, 1992). See also Desmond Dinan, *Ever Closer Union? An Introduction to the European Union*, London, Macmillan, 1994, p. 472.

122 'Six must wait for EU date', *The Guardian*, 5 November 1994. Völker Rühe

has also noted that 'the EC is clearly now the reference point for the economic policies and political aspirations of nearly all European states.... This amounts to a "security function" in its own right, since it is not least economic crises that are likely to become the source of conflicts.' V. Rühe, 'NATO's evolving role in the new Europe', *European Security*, no. 1, 1992, p. 264. See also his article 'Adapting the alliance in the face of great challenges', *NATO Review*, 41, no. 3, 1993, pp. 3–5. Jirí Dienstbier, the Czechoslovak Foreign Minister, also emphasised the EC's security role as early as 1991. He argued that 'Talks now in progress about our association with the European Community strengthen our interest in questions about future security dimensions. We want the mechanism of political dialogue between Czechoslovakia and the European Community, which will be anchored in the association agreement, to include also questions concerning security'. See his article 'The future of European security. Prague conference confirms agreement on Basic ideas', *NATO Review*, 39, no. 3, June 1991, pp. 3–6 (p. 5).

123   *Le Pacte de Stabilité en Europe. Delcaration Finale*, Paris, French government paper, 21 March 1995. See also 'French confident new pact will end wars in Europe', *The Independent*, 20 March 1995; and 'Modest success for Balladur Pact', *The European*, 24–30 March 1995. Mathias Jopp, in *The Strategic Implications of European Integration*, Adelphi Paper 290, London, Brassey's for the IISS, 1994, notes that an attempt has been made to broaden the Pact to include 'questions of regional and functional cooperation, including problems of migration and relevant aspects of trans-European networks' (p. 53).

124   'Petersberg Declaration', issued by Western European Union Council of Ministers in Bonn on 19 June 1992.

125   The nine are the four Visegrad states, the three Baltic republics, Bulgaria and Romania.

126   David Heathcoa-Amory, 'The next step for Western European Union: A British view', *The World Today*, July 1994, pp. 133–6 (p. 134).

127   'EU offers nine Eastern nations a step to security link-up', *International Herald Tribune*, 7–8 May 1994, p. 2. Polish Foreign Minister Olechowski said that for the East Central Europeans the offer was 'symbolic but also concrete. We are going to be involved in the decision-making process and the security structures of the European Union.' See Jan B. de Weydenthal, 'East Central Europe and the EU: forging political ties', *RFE/RL Research Report*, 3, no. 29, 22 July 1994, pp. 16–18 (p. 17).

128   Rudolf Joó, 'Associate Partners: a new phase', *WEU Institute for Security Studies Newsletter*, no. 13, February 1995, p. 1.

129   Quoted in George Kolankiewicz, 'Consensus and competition in the Eastern enlargement of the European Union', *International Affairs*, 70, no. 3, 1994, pp. 477–95 (p. 495).

130   Trevor Taylor, 'NATO and Central Europe', *NATO Review*, 39, no. 5, October 1991, pp. 17–22 (p. 21).

131   'Security has, of course, never been limited to the protection of territorial integrity by military means. It also entails the notion of political sovereignty, including economic, legal, and cultural freedom of action. The internationalization, if not globalization, of these aspects of politics has

accentuated the nonmilitary dimensions of security in national decision-making.... The security of the fledgling democracies in Central Europe is first and foremost dependent on political, economic, and social developments, and in that respect, on access to the West.' Peter M. E. Volten, 'Security dimensions of imperial collapse', *Problems of Communism*, XLI, nos 1–2, January–April 1992, pp. 136–47 (p. 136).

132 Chris Brown, *International Relations Theory. New Normative Approaches*, Hemel Hempstead, Harvester Wheatsheaf, 1992, pp. 33–41.

133 Václav Havel, 'A call for sacrifice. The co-responsibility of the West', *Foreign Affairs*, March–April 1994, pp. 2–7 (p. 6).

Chapter Nine
Conclusion

Oh, East is East, and West is West,
and never the twain shall meet

(Rudyard Kipling[1])

The *annus mirabilis* of 1989 led many to hope that, at long last, Europe could become whole and free. In East Central Europe, where dreams of a return to Europe had been nurtured throughout the Cold War, it was widely believed that a new era of democracy, prosperity and national independence was about to dawn. National revival would be consummated by a process of rapid integration into European structures, which would in turn consolidate democratic government and facilitate prosperity.

But the 'euphoria of 1989, with its rejoicing over European unity, seems light-years away. Today in the West, Europessimism is back in fashion where Eastern Europe is concerned.'[2] In East Central Europe too, the mood of optimism and hope that characterised the heady days of late 1989 has gone. The spring of hope has become the winter of despair.[3] Throughout the region, a more sober realisation of the difficulties involved in building democratic polities and social market economies has emerged. The naively optimistic expectations surrounding early notions of the return to Europe have also dissipated. To some extent this was an inevitable, not wholly unexpected development. To begin with, the actual image of Europe held by most people in East Central Europe was not a realistic one. It was, in the words of Zarko Puhovski, 'an image composed of dreams, hope and television'.[4] Moreover, according to George Schöpflin,

'Entering Europe' was equated with membership of the European Community, with the arrival of large sums of investment capital and the opening of western markets to their products, with political integration and incorporation into the western security system. It all resembled a vague idea that entering Europe was rather like going into a bar, where the landlord would greet one with open arms and press a drink into one's hand.[5]

Unfortunately, life is not like this. The journey back to Europe has proved much more difficult to achieve than first thought. No adequate road maps exist, the way is littered with potholes, a series of checkpoints have been established by officious bureaucrats, and a traffic jam has developed. Indeed, the difficulties have sometimes appeared so daunting that some have wondered whether Kipling's lapidary epigram (which referred to Asia and Europe) might not also apply to East and West Europe. The experience of German unification has also been salutary. If reuniting the two halves of a divided nation has been difficult, some have reasoned, how much more difficult it will be integrating East Central Europe into Western structures.

The problems encountered in returning to Europe have engendered a mood of disenchantment in the Visegrad states. Some have even begun to question the wisdom of focusing so centrally on European integration.[6] Jozsef Szajer, the Vice-President of the Hungarian Young Democrats (FIDESZ), has observed that, 'the whole of the political class has been basing its legitimacy on joining the West'.[7] If this does not deliver discernible benefits, then the goal of rejoining Europe could lose its domestic appeal. This might well have adverse consequences for the development of democratic and peaceful politics in the region. This is because the European idea acts as 'an ideological shorthand for participatory democracy, the market economy, the rule of law, constitutional order and social citizenship for those nascent parties casting around for their own identities'.[8] The determination of the Visegrad countries to join the EU also means that 'they have a powerful incentive to treat ethnic minorities well, respect international borders and international norms, and conduct their internal and external affairs peacefully'.[9] The myth of belonging to Europe has thus imparted to national identity in the Visegrad countries a more benign and accommodating character. But if the social and economic costs of returning to Europe seem to outweigh the benefits, then the influence of outward-looking liberal reformers may wane, and political space could appear for nationalist demagogues like István Csurka (see p. 218). 'To this end it is imperative that the West maintains the dynamics of the European idea, making concessions where it can and signalling understanding where it cannot'.[10] The West has an historic opportunity to influence domestic developments in East Central Europe in ways which will be conducive to the emergence of a Kantian pacific union in Europe. Given the exceptional fluidity in political culture in the Visegrad countries in the early 1990s, a window of opportunity has opened – both for the West and, more importantly, for democratic reformers in the East. This window will not remain open for ever.

Towards a European pacific union

It should thus be clear that the strategic task facing the West at the *fin de siècle* is to engage proactively with the reform process in the East in order to lay the foundations for a Europe whole and free. This involves a series of political and economic measures to extend the transatlantic security community steadily eastwards. The first stage in this historic task will be the integration of the Visegrad countries into Western organisations – first and foremost, the EU. These countries have already demonstrated a commitment to embrace democratic values, and consequently deserve to be the first states admitted to Western multilateral organisations.

However, their incorporation into Western organisations must be seen as a first step along the way to building a European pacific union, not as a way of moving the borders of the 'West' eastwards. This is a very real danger. Given the turbulence and uncertainty of developments in Russia and the CIS, some in Western Europe may be tempted to bring the Visegrad states into European structures, and then to use them as a *cordon sanitaire* against the East. This temptation must be resisted in the interests of long-term stability in Europe. Pursuing such a policy would create new cleavages in Europe, and could ultimately generate destabilising tensions and conflicts with those excluded. In seeking to influence the shape of the new Europe, therefore, the West must take cognisance of the legitimate interests of all European states. The geopolitical location of the Visegrad countries means that they could function as a 'gateway' linking East and West. The Russian Foreign Minister Andrei Kozyrev has suggested that the 'future of Eastern Europe lies in its transformation – not into some kind of buffer zone, but into a bridge linking the East and West of the continent'.[11] Such a development would also be in the best interests of the Visegrad states. As Przemyslaw Grudzinski and Andrzej Karkoszka have argued,

> the East Central European states do not believe it in their interest – and certainly do not wish – to create a new division of Europe at their eastern frontiers. Rather, they perceive a clear need to help in the integration of their eastern neighbours with the rest of Europe. The East Central European states believe that they can play a unique role as the lynchpin between the West and Eastern Europe. Such a role will make them valuable partners to both sides and, at the same time, can guarantee their own most vital interest in security.[12]

Building a more integrated and cohesive Europe will not be without its complications, difficulties and setbacks. It may also force us to rethink many cherished assumptions about 'Europe' itself. As we have already noted, bodies like the Council of Europe, the EU, the WEU and NATO are all having to make fundamental changes to their organisational structures as they prepare to embrace new members from the East. One of the greatest fallacies in Europe today is that the Eastern expansion of Western organisations will simply mean the 'Westernisation' of the new members. This will most certainly not be the case.[13] The Visegrad countries' return to Europe is not only precipitating changes in the domestic politics of East Central Europe, it is also acting as a catalyst for the transformation of Western organisations. 'Eastern Europe today', it has been said, 'is a hinge of history, including ours'.[14] The return to Europe of the Visegrad countries therefore means that the structural dynamics of Europe in the twenty-first century will be significantly different from those which animated the continent during the years of Cold War bipolarity.

Political democratisation and international institutions

Given the uncertainties of both domestic and international politics, the process of nurturing a European pacific union will not be a smooth and linear process. It will proceed fitfully, through a process of disjointed incrementalism, punctuated by occasional qualitative leaps forward. A useful way of conceptualising this process of change towards a pacific union is to see it as a 'process utopia' rather than an 'end-point utopia'. Whereas end-point utopias focus on a specific set of final goals (for example, world government or universal disarmament), process utopias eschew visions of the final end-point in favour of modest, reformist steps which will reinforce benign or pacific trends. As Ken Booth has argued, 'history [is] an evolutionary process, not an eschatological story with a dénouement'. Therefore we cannot possibly know what a better world will look like. 'For the moment we can only identify sets of goals and attend to the major issues at hand'.[15]

A process utopian approach towards a Kantian pacific union should concentrate on reinforcing two benign trends: multilateral institutional integration, and political democratisation. Throughout this book, attention has been drawn to the importance of international organisations for peaceful and cooperative relations between different peoples and their states. Robust multilateral organisations can help mitigate the dangers of anarchy in European politics, and reinforce the foundations of international society. By providing fora and mechanisms for exchanges of information, they can help states identify their common interests and facilitate international agreements:

> Thus they constrain opportunistic behaviour, and they provide focal points for coordination. They make a difference not by imposing order 'above the nation-state' but by creating valued networks of ties between states. Among potential adversaries they may alleviate the security dilemma. In short, institutions provide a point of common reference for leaders trying to struggle with turmoil and uncertainty.[16]

The second benign trend in contemporary European politics is democratisation. Consolidating the process of political democratisation in the Visegrad countries, as well as in Russia and Eastern Europe, is one of the most important tasks facing Europe on the eve of the twenty-first century. There is a growing consensus in the academic and policy-making community that democracies do not fight wars with each other. Michael Doyle, for example, has argued that,

> Even though liberal states have become involved in numerous wars with nonliberal states, constitutionally secure liberal states have yet

to engage in war with one another. No one should argue that such wars are impossible; but preliminary evidence does appear to indicate that there exists a significant predisposition against warfare between liberal states.[17]

The proposition that 'democracies do not fight each other' is not universally accepted. Raymond Cohen, for one, has argued that 'the scope of the democracy–peace proposition is more circumscribed than usually claimed', given that as a phenomenon it 'is observably restricted in time, place and civilisation'. Nonetheless, he acknowledges that the argument 'does contain, incontestably, an historical core of truth. Since 1945 the North Atlantic/Western European states have enjoyed an uninterrupted period of peaceful relations'. This he ascribes to two key factors: democratisation and economic interdependence. He also suggests that the emergence of this transatlantic pacific union has been facilitated by 'ancient ties of civilization and culture'; diplomatic *linguae francae* (French and English); a common Christian legacy; governing elites with much in common; 'a strong sense of shared identity enshrined in communal organisations and legislation'; and a shared normative commitment to 'outlawing war as a legitimate instrument of statecraft within the community' along with 'mechanisms for the peaceful resolution of international conflict'.[18] These features increasingly permeate political, cultural and normative life in East Central Europe. Thus there are good reasons for believing that successful democratisation in the East will help lay the foundations for a European pacific union.

Supporting political democratisation in Central and Eastern Europe and further developing the network of multilateral institutions on the continent are the two key aspects of a process utopian strategy. These two processes are also closely connected in contemporary East Central Europe. For example, democracies are more likely than authoritarian regimes to adopt consensual decision-making procedures (based on negotiation and compromise). At the same time, international organisations (such as the EU and the Council of Europe) can play an important role in consolidating domestic democratisation. Thus 'a combination of economic and political incentives, an international presence and strong persuasion can serve to strengthen the effective creation and upholding of norms in the democratisation process'.[19]

The interconnectedness of democratisation and multilateral institutions reflects another significant feature of contemporary politics in East Central Europe. There exists, as we have already seen (pp. 68–9), a close linkage between domestic and international developments. Mainstream international relations theory has often been resistant to the idea that such an intimate relationship exists. Yet maintaining the fiction that a clear line of demarcation can be drawn between domestic and international politics is becoming increasingly absurd – particularly when one looks at contemporary East Central Europe. More than at any other time in recent history, 'developments in domestic East European politics stand in a close and highly complex relationship with changing international relations and create a situation of finely balanced interdependence'. The changing alignment of domestic political forces 'feeds back directly into international relations and the prospects for further economic integration and European cooperation. Both aspects are also related to changing relations between different groups and peoples within and across state boundaries'.[20]

The 'fragile nexus': democracy, economic reform and security

The interconnectedness of domestic politics and international relations is evident in another way. There is in East Central Europe today an intimate, but highly complex, set of reciprocal relations between democratisation, economic reform and security. Economic reform, including marketisation and privatisation, will facilitate the emergence of more vibrant civil societies, which alone can sustain pluralist democracies. On the other hand, economic reform (particularly of the shock-therapy type applied in Poland and elsewhere) involves considerable short-term economic dislocation. It also tends to deepen existing social inequalities. Economic reform can therefore place severe strains on societal cohesion and community spirit, thereby making it harder to achieve the consensus building and compromise which are the lifeblood of democratic politics.[21]

At the same time, democracy and market economies are security dependent, in the sense that neither will tend to last long in conditions of national insecurity. Yet national security is also very hard to achieve without stable polities based on functioning economies. As Martin Palous has argued,

Even as the countries of East Central Europe feel their way toward new multilateral security relationships, the fact remains that the surest guarantee of security in the region will be the success of their efforts to develop growing, well-functioning economies and stable democratic politics. This objective is a *conditio sine qua non*, and the highest priority of these countries. The observation that 'real' democracies do not wage wars against each other still gives reliable guidance to security thinking.[22]

Thus democratisation, markets and security are linked by a 'fragile nexus, but a vital one. External peril and internal demagoguery can both displace free markets and free governments unless security has been assured.'[23]

Security is also a prerequisite for tackling another problem which is closely linked to democratisation and the rule of law. This is the problem of nationalist diasporas and minority rights – a problem that faces most of Central and Eastern Europe, and significant corners of Western Europe too. Only if this problem is adequately resolved can a pacific union evolve in Europe.

Given diversity in the conditions and expectations of different ethno-national communities in East Central Europe, it is impossible to devise any single solution that is applicable to all countries and all minority groups. An essential starting point is to recognise that ethno-national diversity is one of the defining features of the Visegrad countries. It cannot be eliminated, only accommodated. Consequently the peoples of East Central Europe must learn to live with, and tolerate, the permanent presence of the 'other'. Given that ethnic diversity cannot be eliminated, a variety of approaches need to be employed to manage its consequences.[24] At the international level, these can be selected from a menu which includes the preventive diplomacy of the OSCE's High Commissioner for National Minorities, the Council of Europe's Protocol on National Minorities, and the more recent EU-sponsored 'Pact for Stability'. At the national level, forms of consociational democracy and territorial autonomy might be appropriate. At the societal level, dialogue between discrete communities should be promoted, and the problem of socially disadvantaged minority groups addressed. The most difficult issue to consider – both politically and ethically – is the question of individual versus collective rights.

Security, however, is a fundamental prerequisite for all these endeavours. If individuals, communities and states feel threatened, it will be extremely difficult to promote dialogue, tolerance and understanding. Only in conditions of security can an open and pluralist civil society develop in which individuals can acquire 'a number of crosscutting, politically relevant affiliations'.[25] Security is thus an essential precondition for the emergence of multiple identities. In conditions of insecurity, more narrowly focused and less tolerant forms of national identity will be encouraged:

> People basically live with multiple identities and these do not necessarily have a clear or permanent hierarchy in relation to each other. But in specific situations, especially the closer one comes to war in either literal or metaphorical forms, the more there will be a hierarchy. In these conditions national identity is usually able to organize other identities around itself. In more relaxed situations, other identities are certainly able to compete with the national one.[26]

Security is therefore a prerequisite for addressing the problems of national minorities in East Central Europe. Only then can multiple identities flourish, and the dangers associated with tribal loyalties and passions be avoided. This point has been eloquently articulated by Michael Walzer. He argues that what he calls 'tribalism' ('the commitment of individuals and groups to their own history, culture, and identity') is a 'permanent feature of human social life'. The parochialism which it breeds cannot be overcome, only accommodated. When this parochialism is threatened, then one becomes 'wholly radically parochial: a Serb, a Pole, a Jew and nothing else'. But, Walzer argues, 'this is an artificial situation in the modern world', because the self 'is more naturally divided: at least, it is capable of division and even thrives on it'. Thus, he concludes,

> Under conditions of security, I will acquire a more complex identity than the idea of tribalism suggests. I will identify myself with more than one tribe; I will be an American, a Jew, an easterner, an intellectual, a professor. Imagine a similar multiplication of identities around the world, and the world begins to look like a less dangerous place. When identities are multiplied, passions are divided.[27]

Globalisation and the future of the Visegrad states

The final issue to consider is the extent to which international politics in East Central Europe has been affected by developments in the wider global system. A constant theme running throughout this book has been that the domestic and foreign policies of the Visegrad countries cannot simply be understood by reference to past patterns of behaviour. Historical memories undoubtedly continue to influence the attitudes and assumptions of the peoples of these states – particularly so, given that the East Central Europeans are confronting once again many of their traditional concerns: completing the process of state building, overcoming their economic backwardness, integrating into the European mainstream. But traditional political and economic concerns have re-emerged in a very different domestic and international context. We have already noted the impact of democratisation and multilateral institutions on the region. In addition to these trends, the Visegrad countries have been transformed by modernisation, industrialisation and urbanisation, whilst the nature of international relations in the region has been significantly altered by globalisation and interdependence.

The Visegrad states have therefore regained their sovereignty in the context of an international system which has a very different set of structural dynamics from those of the international system in the early twentieth century. A defining feature of our era is 'the intense trend toward political fragmentation within the context of a globalizing economy'. We have already considered the impact of political fragmentation, as individuals search for a sense of community 'based on ethnicity, religion, language, and other primordial attributes'.[28] The other aspect of this new international dynamic that needs investigation is globalisation.

Globalisation is one of the most important features of late twentieth century international relations. It 'should be understood as the reordering of time and distance in our lives. Our lives, in other words, are increasingly influenced by activities and events happening well away from the social context in which we carry on our day-to-day activities'.[29] The accelerating pace of technological innovation and global economic activity over past decades has intensified trends towards informal integration and complex interdependence.[30] Improved communications and transport systems have facilitated the internationalisation of production, distribution and exchange, along with the globalisation of banking and financial services.[31] Consequently, major production and investment decisions are increasingly orientated towards international rather than domestic markets. 'Moreover', it has been argued, the revolution in communications and transport technologies has facilitated greatly the global interplay of cultures, values, ideas, knowledge, peoples, social networks, elites and social movements. That this is a highly uneven and differentiated process does not detract from the underlying message that societies can no longer be conceptualized as bounded systems, insulated from the outside world.... In the modern society the local and the global have become intimately related.[32]

There are two dimensions to this phenomenon that need to be considered: first, the impact of globalisation on East Central Europe itself; second, its impact on the wider international system, more specifically on the 'Europe' that the Visegrad countries aspire to join. As regards the impact of globalisation on the Visegrad countries themselves, this has been uneven. 'For much of the Cold War period', it has been said, 'globalization had a limited effect in eastern Europe. Communist regimes sought to maintain closed and autarkic societies, and actively resisted the diffusion of technologies such as the telephone and the computer which were essential elements of the "networked" industrial society of the West'.[33] Nonetheless, globalising pressures were increasingly experienced in Eastern Europe from the 1970s onwards, as détente encouraged a partial opening up to the world market and to the West. This was particularly the case for the countries of East Central Europe, given their geographical proximity, their cultural affinities and their expanding trade links. By the end of the 1980s, Western values, ideas and material goods had already begun to penetrate the Visegrad countries.

With the collapse of communism, East Central Europe has been opened up to the full force of globalisation and economic competition. Not only have a number of Western firms begun relocating production processes in the Visegrad countries, but substantial investment has gone into building modern systems of transport and communication. The region has also been opened up to 'the mass influx of western media, tourism, alternative lifestyles, secularism and other influences, all of which have had their resonances at the grass roots'.[34] The effects of globalisation on the region will undoubtedly be patchy. The Czech Republic has been more affected by changes in transport, communications, economic activity and tourism than Slovakia. Similarly, Budapest and its immediate environs already appear much more Westernised than more rural provinces in eastern Hungary. This is inevitable.[35] Nevertheless, globalisation has already had a significant effect on East Central Europe, and its impact is bound to increase as the Visegrad countries integrate into Western structures.

The impact of globalisation on the wider European international system which the Visegrad countries seek to join has been even more profound. The immediate effects of globalisation on Europe have been to intensify economic, social, political and cultural exchanges across the continent (particularly in Western and Central Europe); to stimulate further the proliferation of non-state actors and the volume of transnational interactions; and to increase the linkages between domestic and international affairs in both directions. In the longer term, global networks of production and finance, along with advances in transport and communications, will further erode the modern state's ability to act independently. Of course, no state has ever enjoyed complete autonomy. But in a globalised system, the constraints on the exercise of state power are even tighter. The modern state is thus becoming enmeshed within an extensive network of global interconnections, deeply permeated by trans-national forces and increasingly unable to fulfil its core domestic functions without recourse to international cooperation. Some commentators have even begun to speak of the 'crisis of the territorial nation-state in its traditional form'.[36] It has been suggested, for example, that globalisation 'is generating a more complex multi-level world political system.... Structures of authority comprise not only one but at least three levels: the macro-regional level, the old state (or Westphalian) level, and the micro-regional level. All three levels are limited in their possibilities by a global economy which has means of exerting its pressures without formally authoritative political structures.'[37]

The 'Europe' to which the East Central Europeans wish to return is therefore in a process of far-reaching change and adaptation. The nature of contemporary international relations is ineluctably evolving under the combined pressures of economic globalisation and political fragmentation. European states are no longer (if indeed they ever were) the unitary, monolithic, sovereign rational actors of some realist models: rather, they are fragmented institutional ensembles, composed of a number of different bureaucratic structures. This institutional ensemble oversees a wide range of policy areas, which are in turn deeply permeated by transnational forces. Europe's dense institutional network has also created new mechanisms for supranational governance. This is particularly true of the EU, which has pioneered a unique 'pooling' of sovereignty among its member states. A more complex and multilayered international system is thus emerging in Europe, comprised of fragmented interstate relations, transnational linkages, transgovernmental coalitions and cross-border exchanges.

The new democracies of East Central Europe are therefore rejoining a Europe that is gradually but ineluctably being transformed by globalisation, institutional integration and democratisation. A new and complex configuration of power relations is emerging in Western and Central Europe that is very different from the old Westphalian states system of the past three centuries (a system based on discrete, legally sovereign territorial states).[38] The sovereignty of the modern European state is being eroded from below by ethno-national groups and from above by both formal and informal processes of integration. This has created 'a new, supranational social formation' within which 'new concerns for a European division of labour appear to outweigh the old concerns for a Continental balance of power'. As Central and Western Europe simultaneously splinter into local units and consolidate into something bigger, an 'infinitely complex' product is emerging: 'an unprecedented three-layered confederation composed of the European Community (EC), several nation-states and a wide variety of regions. Thus the nation-state appears to survive but sovereignty, its old defining characteristic, is fading away.'[39]

The European states system of the twenty-first century – especially in Western and Central Europe – is therefore likely to be markedly different from the old Westphalian model. The Visegrad countries will find themselves having rejoined a Europe characterised by a variety of institutional authorities, actors, and identities. Conceptualising this increasingly complex, multidimensional and multilayered international system will be a major task of international relations theorists in the twenty-first century. A good starting point, however, is the model of a 'new medievalism' outlined by Hedley Bull in *The Anarchical Society*. This he described as 'a system of overlapping authority and multiple loyalty':

If modern states were to come to share their authority over their citizens, and their ability to command their loyalties, on the one hand with regional and world authorities, and on the other with sub-state or sub-national authorities, to such an extent that the concept of sovereignty ceased to be applicable, then a neo-mediaeval form of universal political order might be said to have emerged.[40]

As Bull and others have noted, such a system might prove less orderly than the states system of Westphalia.[41] Nonetheless, it does seem to accord with the underlying dynamics of contemporary international relations in Central and Western Europe. 'The interplay between globalisation and fragmentation', it has been suggested, 'points to a new century which may be more like the patchwork Middle Ages than the statist twentieth century, but with lessons learnt from both'.[42]

If it is indeed the case that the Europe to which the Visegrad countries are returning is increasingly exhibiting signs of a neo-medievalism, then we may have to reconsider many of our longstanding assumptions about international politics in East Central Europe. In a neo-medieval international system characterised by overlapping authorities and multiple identities, arrangements for democratic decision making and human rights may have to take different forms than in a more traditional Westphalian states system.[43] International security in such a neo-medieval order may also have to be organised differently from previous security systems. The emergence of something akin to a neo-medieval system will therefore force us to rethink many of the theoretical constructs and the political practices upon which European international society is based. It will also force us to think anew about how we can achieve a Kantian pacific union that provides both justice and order for all the tribes of Europe.

Endnotes

1   'The Ballad of East and West', 1889.

2   Gianni Bonvicini, *et al, The Community and the Emerging European Democracies: A Joint Policy Report*, London, Chatham House, June 1991, p. 7.

3   'It was the best of times, it was the worst of times, it was the age of wisdom, it was the age of foolishness, it was the epoch of belief, it was the epoch of incredulity, it was the season of light, it was the season of darkness, it was the spring of hope, it was the winter of despair...'. Charles Dickens, *A Tale of Two Cities*, 1859, p. 1.

4   Zarko Puhovski, 'The moral basis of political restructuring', in Chris Brown, ed., *Political Restructuring in Europe. Ethical Perspectives*, London, Routledge, 1994, pp. 201–22 (p. 218).

5   George Schöpflin, 'The rise of anti-democratic movements in post-communist societies', in Hugh Miall, ed., *Redefining Europe. New Patterns of Conflict and Cooperation*, London, Pinter for the RIIA, 1994, pp. 129–46 (p. 143).

6   Rudolf Andorka, 'Hungary: disenchantment after transition?', *The World Today*, December 1994, pp. 233–7; and Ian Traynor, 'Western aims on the wane', *The Guardian*, 26 January 1995. As early as 1991 a 'post-revolutionary hangover' could be detected in Poland, with a growing feeling that the return to Europe had 'brought less satisfaction than we had expected', *Polityka*, 27 April 1991. Quoted in Paul G. Lewis, 'History, Europe and the politics of the East', in Stephen White, Judy Batt and Paul Lewis, eds, *Developments in East European Politics*, London, Macmillan, 1993, pp. 262–79 (p. 271).

7   Quoted in Dana H. Allin, 'Can containment work again?', *Survival*, 37, no. 1, spring 1995, pp. 53–65 (p. 60).

8   George Kolankiewicz, 'Consensus and competition in the Eastern enlargement of the European Union', *International Affairs*, 70, no. 3, 1994, pp. 477–95 (p. 482).

9   Michael E. Brown, 'The flawed logic of NATO expansion', *Survival*, 37, no. 1, spring 1995, pp. 34–52 (p. 37).

10 Kolankiewicz, *op. cit.*, p. 482.

11 Andrei Kozyrev, 'The new Russia and the Atlantic alliance', *NATO Review*, 41, no. 1, February 1993, pp. 3–6 (p. 3).

12 Przemyslaw Grudzinski and Andrzej Karkoszka, 'East Central Europe in an uncertain world', in Jeffrey Laurenti, ed., *Searching for Moorings. East Central Europe in the International System*, New York, UN Association of the USA, 1994, pp. 10–38 (p. 16).

13 Wolfgang H. Reinicke, *Building a New Europe. The Challenge of System Transformation and Systemic Reform*, Washington, DC, Brookings Institution, 1993. Reinicke argues that the integration of the divided European political economy requires 'system transformation' in Central and Eastern Europe, and 'system reform' in Western Europe.

14 Thomas W. Simons, Jr, *Eastern Europe in the Postwar World*, 2nd edn, London, Macmillan, 1993, p. 260.

15 Ken Booth, 'Steps towards stable peace in Europe: a theory and practice of coexistence', *International Security*, 66, no. 1, January 1990, pp. 17–46 (p. 32).

16 Robert Keohane and Joseph Nye, 'Introduction: The end of the Cold War in Europe', in R. Keohane, J. Nye and S. Hoffmann, eds, *After the Cold War. International Institutions and State Strategies in Europe, 1989–1991*, Harvard, Harvard University Press, 1993, pp. 1–22 (p. 3). See also Peter van Ham, 'Can institutions hold Europe together?', in Hugh Miall, ed., *Redefining Europe. New Patterns of Conflict and Cooperation*, London, Pinter for the RIIA, 1994, pp. 186–205.

17 M. Doyle, 'Kant, liberal legacies, and foreign affairs', Parts 1 & 2, *Philosophy and Public Affairs*, 12, nos 3, 4, 1983, pp. 205–20 and 323–53 (Part 1, p. 213).

18   Raymond Cohen, 'Pacific unions: a reappraisal of theory that "democracies do not go to war with each other"', *Review of International Studies*, 20, no. 3, July 1994, pp. 207–24 (pp. 220–2). A similarly qualified view of the 'democracy-equals-peace' proposition is expounded by Chris Brown. See his article '"Really existing liberalism" and international order', *Millennium*, 21, no. 3, winter 1992, pp. 313–28. On the other hand, Strobe Talbot argues that this proposition 'is as close as we are likely to get in political science to an empirical truth'. See his article 'The new geopolitics: defending democracy in the Post-Cold War era', *The World Today*, January 1995, pp. 7–10 (p. 8).

19   Marianne Hanson, 'Democratisation and norm creation in Europe', in *European Security After the Cold War, Part 1*, Adelphi Paper 284, London, Brassey's for the IISS, 1994, pp. 28–41 (p. 40).

20   Lewis, *op. cit.*, pp. 274–5.

21   'A market economy as such, without any modifier, is a jungle where the strong eat the weak, where only the fittest survive. This can be no solution, neither from a social nor from a political point of view. A system in which the rich get richer and the poor get poorer is bound to fail.' Hannes Androsch, 'Transformation of Central and Eastern Europe', *The World Today*, October 1994, pp. 194–7 (p. 194).

22   Martin Palous, 'Weaving a security net. East Central Europe and the structures of international peace and security', in Jeffrey Laurenti, ed., *Searching for Moorings. East Central Europe in the International System*, New York, UN Association of the USA, 1994, pp. 39–60 (p. 42).

23   Daniel N. Nelson, 'The comparative politics of Eastern Europe', in Stephen White, Judy Batt and Paul Lewis, eds, *Developments in East European Politics*, London, Macmillan, 1993, pp. 242–61 (p. 259). See also Eric Herring, 'International security and democratisation in Eastern Europe', in Geoffrey Pridham, Eric Herring and George Sandford, eds, *Building Democracy? Democratisation in Eastern Europe*, London, Leicester University Press, 1994, pp. 87–118.

24   See for example Uri Ra'anan, 'Nation and state: order out of chaos', in Uri Ra'anan, Maria Mesner, Keith Armes and Kate Martin, eds, *State and Nation: The Breakup of Multinational States*, Manchester, Manchester University Press, 1991, pp. 3–32.

25   S. M. Lipset, quoted in John Oakley, 'The resolution of ethnic conflict: towards a typology', *International Political Science Review*, 13, no. 4, October 1992, pp. 343–58 (p. 367).

26   Ole Waever, Barry Buzan, Morten Kelstrup and Pierre Lemaitre, *Identity, Migration and the New Security Agenda in Europe*, London, Pinter, 1993, p. 22.

27   Michael Walzer, 'Notes on the new tribalism', in Chris Brown, ed., *Political Restructuring in Europe*, London, Routledge, 1994, pp. 187–200 (pp. 199–200).

28   K. J. Holsti, 'International relations at the end of the millenium', *Review of International Studies*, 19, no. 4, October 1993, pp. 401–8 (p. 407).

29   A. Giddens, *The Consequences of Modernity*, Cambridge, Polity, 1990, p. 520.

30   'Formal integration consists of deliberate actions by authoritative policy-makers to create and adjust rules, to establish common institutions and to

work with and through those institutions; to regulate, channel, redirect, encourage or inhibit social and economic flows, as well as to pursue common policies. Informal integration consists of those intense patterns of interaction which develop without the intervention of deliberate governmental decisions, following the dynamics of markets, technology, communications networks and social exchange, or the influence of religious, social or political movements. Informal integration is thus a matter of flows and exchanges, of the gradual growth of networks of interaction. By definition it is a continuous process in which sharp discontinuities are rare. Disintegration is of course represented by the decline of such flows and exchanges; integration is in no sense an inexorable or unidirectional process. Formal integration is by definition a discontinuous process, proceeding treaty by treaty, regulation by regulation, decision by decision.' William Wallace, *The Transformation of Western Europe*, London, Pinter, 1990, p. 54.

31 R. O'Brien, *The End of Geography*, London, Routledge for the RIIA, 1992.

32 Anthony McGrew, 'Conceptualizing global politics', in Anthony G. McGrew and Paul G. Lewis, eds, *Global Politics*, Cambridge, Polity, 1992, p. 3.

33 Hugh Miall, *Shaping the New Europe*, London, Pinter, 1993, p. 22.

34 Kolankiewicz, *op. cit.*, p. 479.

35 Anthony McGrew, 'Global politics in a transitional era', in Anthony G. McGrew and Paul G. Lewis, eds, *Global Politics*, Cambridge, Polity, 1992, pp. 312–30 (p. 320).

36 Joseph Frankel has argued that 'No state is any longer self-sufficient or safe within its boundaries, not even the superpowers, let alone the new mini-states; all are facing a diminution of their sovereignty. Nevertheless', he concludes, 'it is hard to see how the present division of mankind into states could lose its importance in the foreseeable future. This supposition readily leads to one possible future – an international system continuing much as it is now, but with states probably somewhat readier to coordinate their activities at the cost of further inroads into their sovereignty, and new non-state actors and transnational activities further supplementing their activities'. Quoted in Anthony G. McGrew and Paul G. Lewis, eds, *Global Politics*, Cambridge, Polity, 1992, p. 329.

37 Robert Cox, 'Structural issues of global governance: implications for Europe', in Stephen Gill, ed., *Gramsci, Historical Materialism and International Relations*, Cambridge, Cambridge University Press, 1993, pp. 259–89 (p. 263).

38 'The Treaty of Westphalia', Kalevi Holsti has written, 'organized Europe on the basis of particularism. It represented a new diplomatic arrangement – an order created by states, for states – and replaced most of the legal vestiges of hierarchy, at the pinnacle of which were the Pope and the Holy Roman Emperor'. Westphalia led to 'the creation of a pan-European diplomatic system based on the new principles of sovereignty and the legal equality', and 'paved the way for a system of states to replace a hierarchical system under the leadership of the Pope and the Hapsburg family complex that linked the Holy Roman and Spanish Empires'. K. J. Holsti, *Peace and War: Armed Conflicts and International Order 1648–1989*, Cambridge, Cambridge University Press, 1991, pp. 25–6.

39   Torbjörn Knutsen, *A History of International Relations Theory*, Manchester, Manchester University Press, 1992, p. 241.

40   Bull, *op. cit.*, pp. 254–5.

41   Pierre Hassner, for example, has pointed out that this 'new medievalism' would have no Pope and no Holy Roman Empire, unlike the medievalism of old, and that this might prove a recipe for conflict and disorder. P. Hassner, 'Beyond nationalism and internationalism', *Survival*, 35, no. 2, summer 1993, pp. 49–65.

42   Ken Booth, 'Dare not to know: international relations theory versus the future', in Ken Booth and Steve Smith, ed., *International Relations Theory Today*, Cambridge, Polity, 1995, pp. 328–50 (p. 343).

43   D. Held and A. McGrew, 'Globalisation and the liberal democratic state', *Government and Opposition*, 28, no. 2, spring 1993, pp. 261–88.

Select bibliography

Anderson, B., *Imagined Communities: Reflections on the Origin and Spread of Nationalism*, revised edn, London, Verso, 1991

Armstrong, J., *Nations before Nationalism*, Chapel Hill, University of North Carolina Press, 1982

Ascherson, N., *The Polish August. What Has Happened in Poland*, London, Penguin, 1981

August, F., and Rees, D., *Red Star Over Prague*, London, The Sherwood Press, 1984

Bartlett, C. J., *The Global Conflict. The International Rivalry of the Great Powers, 1880–1990*, 2nd edn, London, Longman, 1994

Batt, J., *East Central Europe from Reform to Transformation*, London, Pinter, 1991

Beddard, R., and Hill, D., eds, *Emerging Rights Within the New Europe*, Southampton, Mountbatten Centre for International Studies, 1992

Berglund, S., and Dellenbrant, J., eds, *The New Democracies in Eastern Europe. Party Systems and Political Cleavages*, 2nd edn, Aldershot, Edward Elgar, 1994

Bloomfield, J., *Passive Revolution: Politics and the Czechoslovak Working Class, 1945–48*, London, Allison and Busby, 1979

Booth, K., and Smith, S., eds, *International Relations Theory Today*, Cambridge, Polity, 1995

Bowker, M., and Brown, R., eds, *From Cold War to Collapse: Theory and World Politics in the 1980s*, Cambridge, Cambridge University Press, 1993

Brock, P., *The Slovak National Awakening*, Toronto, University of Toronto Press, 1976

Brown, C., ed., *Political Restructuring in Europe. Ethical Perspectives*, London, Routledge, 1994

Brown, J. F., *Eastern Europe and Communist Rule*, Durham, Duke University Press, 1988

Brown, J. F., *Hopes and Shadows: Eastern Europe After Communism*, London, Longman, 1994

Bull, H., *The Anarchical Society. A Study of Order in World Politics*, London, Macmillan, 1977

Buzan, B., Kelstrup, M., Lemaitre, P., Tromer, E., and Waever, O., *The European Security Order Recast*, London, Pinter, 1990

Clesse, A., and Ruhl, R., eds, *Beyond East–West Confrontation: Searching for a New Security Structure in Europe*, Baden-Baden, Nomos, 1990

Clesse, A., Cooper, R., and Sakamoto, Y., eds, *The International System After the Collapse of the East–West Order*, Dordrecht, Martinus Nijhoff, 1994

Crouch, C., and Marquand, D., eds, *Towards a Greater Europe: A Continent Without an Iron Curtain*, Oxford, Blackwell, 1992

Davies, N., *God's Playground: A History of Poland*, 2 vols, New York, Columbia University Press, 1982

Dawisha, K., and Hanson, P., eds, *Soviet–East European Dilemmas: Coercion, Competition and Consent*, London, Heinemann for the RIIA, 1981

Dawisha, K., *Eastern Europe, Gorbachev and Reform*, Cambridge, Cambridge University Press, 1988

Downing, B., *The Military Revolution and Political Change: Origins of Democracy and Autocracy in Early Modern Europe*, Princeton, Princeton University Press, 1992

Dunay, P., *Das Alte Ungarn im Neuen Europa? Ungarische Sicherheitspolitik nach dem Systemwandel*, HSFK Report 2/1993, Frankfurt am Main, Hessische Stiftung Friedens-und Konfliktforschung, 1993

Fedorowitz, J., ed., *A Republic of Nobles. Studies in Polish History to 1864*, Cambridge, Cambridge University Press, 1982

Feffer, J., *Shock Waves: Eastern Europe After the Revolutions*, Montreal, Black Rose Books, 1993

Galeotti, M., *The Age of Anxiety: Security and Politics in Soviet and Post-Soviet Russia*, London, Longman, 1995

Garcia, S., ed., *European Identity and the Search for Legitimacy*, London, Pinter, 1993

Garton Ash, T., *We the People: The Revolution of 1989*, Harmondsworth, Penguin, 1990

Garton Ash, T., *The Polish Revolution*, London, Granta, 1991

Garton Ash, T., *In Europe's Name. Germany and the Divided Continent*, London, Vintage, 1994

Gati, C., ed., *The International Politics of Eastern Europe*, New York, Praeger, 1976

Giddens, A., *The Nation-State and Violence*, Berkeley, University of California, 1987

Glenny, M., *The Rebirth of History. Eastern Europe in the Age of Democracy*, London, Penguin, 1990

Gordon, L., *Eroding Empire: Western Relations with Eastern Europe*, Washington, DC, Brookings Institution, 1987

Hammond, T., ed., *The Anatomy of Communist Takeovers*, New Haven, Yale University Press, 1975

Heinrich, H-G., *Hungary. Politics, Economics and Society*, London, Pinter, 1986

Holden, G., *The Warsaw Pact: Soviet Security and Bloc Politics*, Oxford, Blackwell, 1988

Holmes, L., *The End of Communist Power: Anti-Corruption Campaigns and Legitimation Crisis*, Cambridge, Polity, 1993

Hupchick, D., *Conflict and Chaos in Eastern Europe*, London, Macmillan, 1994

Hyde-Price, A., *European Security Beyond the Cold War: Four Scenarios for the Year 2010*, London, Sage, 1991

Kaldor, M., ed., *Europe From Below: An East–West Dialogue*, London, Verso, 1991

Kann, R., and David, Z., *The Peoples of the Eastern Habsburg Lands, 926–1918*, Seattle, University of Washington Press, 1984

Kedourie, E., *Nationalism*, 4th edn, Oxford, Blackwell, 1993

Keohane, K., Nye, J., and Hoffmann, S., eds, *After the Cold War. International Institutions and State Strategies in Europe, 1989–1991*, Cambridge, Harvard University Press, 1993

Kirby, D., *The Baltic World 1773–1993. Europe's Northern Periphery in an Age of Change*, London, Longman, 1995

Kohn, H., *The Idea of Nationalism: A Study in Its Origins and Background*, New York, Macmillan, 1944

Köves, A., *Central and East European Economies in Transition. The International Dimension*, Boulder, Westview, 1992

Kun, J., *Hungarian Foreign Policy. The Experience of a New Democracy*, Westport, Praeger, 1993

Lazar, I., *Hungary: A Brief History*, Budapest, Corvina, 1990

Lewis, P., *Central Europe Since 1945*, London, Longman, 1994

Longworth, P., *The Making of Eastern Europe*, London, Macmillan, 1992

Magris, C., *Danube: A Sentimental Journey From the Source to the Black Sea*, London, Collins Harvill, 1990

Mayall, J., *Nationalism and International Society*, Cambridge, Cambridge University Press, 1990

McCauley, M., ed., *Communist Power in Europe 1944–49*, London, Macmillan, 1977

Meiklejohn Terry, S., ed., *Soviet Policy in Eastern Europe*, New Haven, Yale University Press, 1984

Miall, H., *Shaping the New Europe*, London, Pinter for the RIIA, 1993

Miall, H., ed., *Redefining Europe. New Patterns of Conflict and Cooperation*, London, Pinter for the RIIA, 1994

Miall, H., ed., *Minority Rights in Europe. The Scope for a Transnational Regime*, London, Pinter for the RIIA, 1994

Morris, L. P., *Eastern Europe Since 1945*, London, Heinemann, 1984

Munuera, G., *Preventing Armed Conflict in Europe: Lessons From Recent Experience*, Chaillot Paper 15/16, Paris, WEU Insitute for Security Studies, June 1994

Myant, M., *Socialism and Democracy in Czechoslovakia, 1945–48*, Cambridge, Cambridge University Press, 1981

Pinder, J., *The European Community and Eastern Europe*, London, Pinter for the RIIA, 1991

Pravda, A., ed., *The End of the Outer Empire. Soviet–East European Relations in Transition, 1985–90*, London, Sage for the RIIA, 1992

Pridham, G., Herring, E., and Sandford, S., eds, *Building Democracy? Democratisation in Eastern Europe*, London, Leicester University Press, 1994

Pridham, G., and Vanhanen, T., eds, *Democratization in Eastern Europe: Domestic and International Perspectives*, London, Routledge, 1994

Prins, G., ed., *Spring in Winter. The 1989 Revolutions*, Manchester, Manchester University Press, 1990

Ra'anan, U., Mesner, M., Armes, A., and Martin, K., eds, *State and Nation in Multi-Ethnic Societies: The Break-Up of Multinational States*, Manchester, Manchester University Press, 1991

Rollo, J., ed., *The New Eastern Europe: Western Responses*, London, Pinter for the RIIA, 1990

Roskin, M., *The Rebirth of East Europe*, London, Prentice-Hall, 1991

Rotfeld, A., and Stützler, W., eds, *Germany and Europe in Transition*, Oxford, Oxford University Press for SIPRI, 1991

Rothschild, J., *Return to Diversity: A Political History of East Central Europe Since World War II*, Oxford, Oxford University Press, 1989

Schöpflin, G., and Woods, N., eds, *In Search of Central Europe*, Cambridge, Polity, 1989

Schöpflin, G., *Politics in Eastern Europe*, Oxford, Blackwell, 1993

Segal, G., *Openness and Foreign Policy Reform in Communist States*, London, Routledge for the RIIA, 1992

Seton-Watson, H., *Eastern Europe Between the Wars, 1918–1941*, New York, Harper and Row, 1967

Simecka, M., *The Restoration of Order. The Normalization of Czechoslovakia, 1969–76*, London, Verso, 1984

Simons, T., *Eastern Europe in the Postwar World*, 2nd edn, London, Macmillan, 1993

Smith, A., *The Ethnic Origins of Nations*, Oxford, Blackwell, 1986

Smith, A., *National Identity*, London, Penguin, 1991

Staar, R., ed., *East-Central Europe and the USSR*, London, Macmillan, 1991

Stokes, G., *The Walls Came Tumbling Down. The Collapse of Communism in Eastern Europe*, Oxford, Oxford University Press, 1993

Sugar, P., and Lederer, I., eds, *Nationalism in Eastern Europe*, Seattle, University of Washington, 1969

Swain, G., and Swain, N., *Eastern Europe Since 1945*, London, Macmillan, 1993

Szajkowski, B., *The Establishment of Marxist Regimes*, London, Butterworth, 1982

Teich, M., and Porter, R., eds, *The National Question in Europe in Historical Perspective*, Cambridge, Cambridge University Press, 1993

Turnock, D., *The Human Geography of Eastern Europe*, London, Routledge, 1989

Turnock, D., *Eastern Europe: An Economic and Political Geography*, London, Routledge, 1989

Van den Doel, T., *Central Europe: The New Allies? The Road from Visegrad to Brussels*, Oxford, Westview, 1994

Verheyen, D., and Soe, C., eds, *The Germans and Their Neighbours*, Boulder, Westview, 1993

Waever, O., Buzan, B., Kelstrup, M., and Lemaitre, P., *Identity, Migration and the New Security Agenda in Europe*, London, Pinter, 1993

Wallace, W., ed., *The Dynamics of European Integration*, London, Pinter for the RIIA, 1990

Wandycz, P., *The Price of Freedom: A History of East Central Europe From the Middle Ages to the Present*, London, Routledge, 1992

Watson, M., ed., *Contemporary Minority Nationalism*, London, Routledge, 1990

White, S., Batt, J., and Lewis, P., eds, *Developments in East European Politics*, London, Macmillan, 1993

Williams, A., ed., *Reorganising Eastern Europe: European Institutions and the Refashioning of Europe's Security Architecture*, Aldershot, Dartmouth, 1994

Zielonka, J., *Security in Central Europe*, Adelphi Paper 272, London, Brassey's for the IISS, autumn 1992

Index

Clinton, Bill, 247
CMEA, *see* Council of Mutual
Economic Assistance
Cohen, Raymond, 276
Cohen, Saul, 49
Cold War, 1–3, 6, 35, 78, 82–3,
88, 100, 108, 135, 140, 143,
151, 175, 177, 188–9, 223–
4, 230, 236, 241, 243, 248,
250, 274, 281
Commonwealth of Independent
States (CIS), 18, 28, 156–7,
163, 168–70, 177–8, 239,
246, 273
Conference on Security and
Cooperation in Europe
(CSCE), 3, 23, 32, 96, 112,
114, 175, 190, 192, 211,
233, 240–2, 249; *see also*
Organisation for Security and
Cooperation in Europe
(OSCE)
Constantine the Great, Emperor,
49
Coordinating Committee
(CoCom), 188
Corvinus, Mátyás, 20, 29
Council of Baltic Sea States,
109, 116–18, 132, 134, 151,
256
Council of Europe, 61, 84, 92,
112, 114, 119–20, 145, 149,
188–94, 211–13, 256, 274,
276, 288
Council of Mutual Economic
Assistance (CMEA), 125,
140, 144, 146–7, 149, 168,
173, 197, 207
crime, 117–18, 130–1, 176, 228
Croatia, 7, 33, 49, 67, 110,
113, 127, 171, 175, 229
CSCE, *see* Conference on
Security and Cooperation in
Europe

Csurka, Istvan, 218, 272
Czech lands,
German influence, 19–20, 22,
206
history of, 18–24
Czech Republic, relations with:
European Union, 86–7, 92,
199–205
Germany, 24, 91
Hungary, 99–100
NATO, 86–7, 92
Poland, 85–7
Russia, 168–9
Slovakia, 89–93, 227
Czechoslovakia, 4, 7, 21–23,
112
creation of, 26, 80
February coup (1948), 2, 22,
27
Prague Spring (1968), 23,
27, 143, 232–3
break-up of the Federation,
23, 86–7, 89–92, 118,
127–8, 132, 168–9, 191,
199
Czechoslovakia, relations with:
Council of Europe, 191
European Union/European
Community, 197, 199
Germany, 167–8, 208
Hungary, 31, 94, 99, 237
Poland, 15
Russia, 167–8
USSR, 22, 166–7, 232

Danube, 47–8, 93, 95–7, 101,
109, 131, 223, 225
Davies, Norman, 12
Delors, Jacques, 200
Denmark, 117, 121, 249–50
Dienstbier, Jirí, 23, 244
Downing, Brian, 13
Doyle, Michael, 275
Dubcek, Alexander, 23